NATURE CONSERVATION IN BRITAIN

The Formative Years

JOHN SHEAIL

NATURE CONSERVATION IN BRITAIN

The Formative Years

London: The Stationery Office

Applications for reproduction should be made in writing to The Stationery Office Limited,
St Crispins, Duke Street, Norwich NR3 1PD.

The information contained in this publication is believed to be correct at the time of manufacture. Whilst
care has been taken to ensure that the information is accurate, the publisher can accept no responsibility
for any errors or ommisions or for changes to the details given.

A CIP catalogue record for this book is available from the British Library
A Library of Congress CIP catalogue record has been applied for

First published 1998

ISBN 0 11 702308 6

Institute of Terrestrial Ecology

(Natural Environment Research Council)
Monks Wood,
Huntingdon,
Cambridgeshire PE 17 2LS

Illustration of hare by Sarah Young

Published by The Stationery Office and available from:

The Publications Centre
(mail, telephone and fax orders only) PO Box 276, London SW8 5DT
General enquiries 0171 873 0011   Telephone orders 0171 873 9090   Fax orders 0171 873 8200

The Stationery Office Bookshops
123 Kingsway, London WC2B 6PQ   0171 242 6393   Fax 0171 242 6394
68-69 Bull Street, Birmingham B4 6AD   0121 236 9696   Fax 0121 236 9699
33 Wine Street, Bristol BS1 2BQ 0117   9264306   Fax 0117 9294515
9-21 Princess Street, Manchester M60 8AS   0161 834 7201   Fax 0161 833 0634
16 Arthur Street, Belfast BT1 4GD   01232 238451   Fax 01232 235401
The Stationery Office Oriel Bookshop The Friary, Cardiff   CF1 4AA 01222 395548   Fax 01222 384347
71 Lothian Road, Edinburgh EH3 9AZ   0131 228 4181   Fax 0131 622 7017

The Stationery Office's Accredited Agents
(see Yellow Pages)

and through good booksellers

Printed in the United Kingdom for the Stationery Office by Anthony Rowe Ltd, Reading
J65962   C20   12/98

For Monks Wood

with gratitude for a career working with ecologists

CONTENTS

PREFACE

By any reckoning, the appointment of the Nature Conservancy in 1949 was a pioneering venture. The first official body of its kind anywhere in the world, it was charged with establishing and managing a series of National Nature Reserves, giving advice generally on nature conservation, and undertaking the relevant scientific research. As a research council, it was responsible to the Minister for Science. Its statutory powers came from the National Parks and Access to the Countryside Act, which otherwise dealt with planning issues. This book reconstructs the thinking of those behind the creation of the Nature Conservancy, and traces the way in which it came to exert an influence far beyond its terms of reference and size of resources. The successes and failures of those formative years provide considerable insight into the motives and preoccupations of the burgeoning environmental movement in Britain.

Every generation believes it is living through a turning point in history. The post-war generation was no exception. Whilst recording the expertise and experience in nature conservation gained since the 1940s, the book reveals the almost heroic attempts that were made to implement early aspirations in conservation management and research, and to cope with the dangers posed by pollution and habitat destruction.

This, the first book to examine the history of the Nature Conservancy in depth, makes extensive use of the Conservancy's archives and the memories of those who worked for it. Additional information is drawn from the publications and files of the Minister for Science, the Scottish Office, and departments such as the Ministry of Agriculture and, perhaps most important of all, the Treasury. Much of this material has not previously been published.

Britain has a distinguished record in the field of nature conservation. This book is intended to help both the British and overseas reader to understand how this came about. Some individual readers will seek insights into particular aspects of 'the inside story'. No single book, however, can entirely meet this need. The illustrative material drawn from the period of the Nature Conservancy must be necessarily selective; it can only give an impression of the extraordinary range of initiatives taken by its members and officers. At the time of writing, access to Government records was limited to the years up to 1968. The treatment of the period of the Nature Conservancy Council is accordingly much slighter. Until those wider and deeper insights are available, it is hoped that this book will afford some insight into the general ethos of those who had responsibility for directing the official bodies responsible for nature conservation in Britain.

I am grateful to Professor Mike Roberts, Director of the Institute of Terrestrial Ecology (Natural Environment Research Council) for the opportunity to write the book, and for the support of Derek Langslow, Chief Executive of English Nature. Acknowledgement is made to the remarkable collection of reflections and reminiscences brought together by James

Robertson, Dick Seamons and Suzanne Davies, as part of the NCC's Thin green line Project in the late 1980s. John Creedy and Dick Seamons have helped in many ways. Grateful thanks also to Iain Stevenson at TSO, and to Chris Madsen, for turning a manuscript into the present book.

Except where otherwise stated, the photographs are drawn from the collection held by English Nature; of these, those on pp 4, 5, 53, 107, 175, 201, 220, 229, 231, 241 and 245 were taken by Peter Wakely. Photographs on pp 15 (©*Times Newspapers*), 19, 23, 25, 68, 99 (©*Cambridge Evening News*), 102, 103, 104, 105, 117, 121, 124, 141, 144, 149 (©*Cambridge Evening News*), 161, 173, 183 and 193 were provided by the Institute of Terrestrial Ecology. Scottish Natural Heritage supplied photographs on pp 54 (©*The Scotsman*) and 221. I am grateful to Mr R.E. Boote for the photographs on pp 45, 169, 187 (©*Staffordshire Sentinel Newspapers*) and 212; to Dr N.W. Moore for pp 74 and 253; to Mr E.M. Nicholson for pp 27 (©*News of the World*), 90, 158, 190, and 260 (©Jane Bown); to Professor M.E.D Poore for p 189; to Mrs P. Quirke for p 163; and to University College London for p 7.

It is a pleasure to record the generosity of so many other people who provided insights and material for this book. Their identities will become abundantly apparent to the reader. As always, my wife, Gillian, has been a constant source of encouragement and support.

May Day 1998

John Sheail

Archival references in the Public Record Office are denoted by the abbreviation PRO; those in the Scottish Record Office by SRO, and Parliamentary Debates by PD. The help of staff in the Public Record Office, Scottish Record Office and Cambridge University Library is gratefully acknowledged.

Place names, units of measurement and other conventions are taken from the original documentation.

CHRONOLOGY

A chronology of selected events in the history of the nature conservation movement referred to in this book:

1958 National Trust founded

1904 Royal Charter conferred on Society for the Protection of Birds

1912 Society for the Promotion of Nature Reserves founded

1913 British Ecological Society founded

1914–18 First World War

1915 List of 'Areas worthy of Protection' in the British Isles submitted by Charles Rothschild to Board of Agriculture

1926 Council for the Preservation of Rural England founded; Norfolk Naturalists' Trust founded

1931 Report of National Park Committee

1939–45 Second World War

1941 Conference on Nature Preservation in Post-war Reconstruction

1942 Nature Reserves Investigation Committee appointed; Report of the Committee on Land Utilisation in Rural Areas (the Scott report)

1945 Report on National Parks in England and Wales (the Dower report); Labour Government elected

1947 Agriculture and Town and Country Planning Acts; Report on Conservation of Nature in England and Wales (the Huxley report); Report on National parks and the conservation of nature in Scotland (the first Ritchie report)

1949 Report on Nature Reserves in Scotland (the second Ritchie report); Royal Charter granted to the Nature Conservancy; National Parks and Access to the Countryside Act

1951 Conservative Government elected; Beinn Eighe declared first National Nature Reserve

1952 E.M. Nicholson appointed Director-General of Nature Conservancy

1953 East Coast Floods; Formal opening of Merlewood Research Station

1954 Formal opening of Furzebrook Research Station; Cairngorms NNR declared; Protection of Birds Act

1956 IUCN General Assembly and Technical Meeting, Edinburgh; The Playfair Committee

1957 Isle of Rhum NNR declared

1958 Dungeness nuclear power station Public Inquiry

1959 Deer (Scotland) Act

1960 Formal opening of Welsh headquarters and research station at Bangor

1961 World Wildlife Fund established

1962 One hundredth NNR declared; first showing of the film, *The Living Pattern*

1963 First British edition of *Silent Spring*; First National Nature Week; Formal opening of Monks Wood Experimental Station; First 'Countryside in 1970' Conference

1964 Labour Government elected; Snowdon (Y Wyddfa) NNR declared

1965 Ministry of Land and Natural Resources established; Science and Technology Act; Royal Charter conferred on Natural Environment Research Council; Second 'Countryside in 1970' conference; Report on Broadland published

1966 White Paper, *Leisure in the Countryside* published; M.E.D. Poore appointed Director of Nature Conservancy

1967 Tees Valley and Cleveland Water Board Act; Wreck of the *Torrey Canyon*; Countryside (Scotland) Act

1968 Countryside Act

1969 Silsoe Conference, Farming and Nature Conservation; Irish seabird 'wreck'

1970 European Conservation Year; Conservative Government elected; Third 'Countryside in 1970' conference

1972 White Paper, *The framework of government research and development* (the Rothschild report)

1973 Nature Conservancy Council Act; Sir David Serpell appointed Chairman and R.E. Boote Director of NCC

1974 Labour Government elected

1977 Publication of *Nature Conservation Review*

1978 Amberley Wild Brooks Public Inquiry; Acquisition of the Ribble NNR

1979 Conservative Government elected

1980 Parsonage Down NNR declared; World Conservation Strategy; Sir Ralph Verney appointed Chairman and R.C. Steele Director-General of NCC; *Theft of the Countryside* published

1981 Wildlife and Countryside Act

1983 William Wilkinson appointed Chairman of NCC

1986 Agriculture Act; *Nature Conservation and Afforestation* published

1987 European Year of the Environment; *Birds, Bogs and Forestry* published

1988 Timothy Hornsby appointed Director-General of NCC

1989 Dismemberment of NCC announced

1990 The first 'Environment' White Paper: *This Common Inheritance*

1991 Environmental Protection Act

1992 Natural Heritage (Scotland) Act; Rio Earth Summit

1994 White Papers on Biodiversity and Sustainability

1995 The White Paper, *Rural England*

CHAPTER ONE

BEGINNINGS

A new millennium is an obvious time to review the achievements of the conservation movement. The year, 1999, is in any case of considerable significance. It marks the fiftieth anniversary of the Nature Conservancy, which was the first official body to be established in the UK, and indeed in the world, for the specific purpose of conserving wildlife on a national basis. More than usually, the questions are posed: '*When* and *where* did nature conservation begin?' '*How* and *why* did it come about?', and '*What* was accomplished?' It is the purpose of this book to provide some of the answers.

The words 'nature conservation' first came to prominence in the decade of the 1940s. They were given substance in the founding of the Nature Conservancy, and it is on the Conservancy that this book focuses. More particularly, it tries to discover *who* took and tried to implement the decisions that determined whether Nature (or Biodiversity as it is now called) might flourish or become further impoverished. Where they survive, the working files of the Conservancy and relevant parts of Government can now be studied in the archives. Those for the later period remain (at the time of writing) confidential. The historian must continue to rely on the published record.

There was nothing inevitable about the decisions, nor indeed the circumstances, that caused the Nature Conservancy to be established in 1949. Rather, it is a story of hints, suggestions and possibilities that opened up opportunities for an official body for nature conservation to be formed. It had much to do with what Keith Thomas, in his book *Man and the Natural World*, would have characterised as an innate human curiosity. In what different ways might the natural world be exploited? Thomas traced how, in the early modern period, theologians began to discard long-established dogmas of man's place in the world. Moralists urged the kinder treatment of animals. Aesthetes saw the earth as a place of beauty and contemplation, rather than simply a resource to be plundered (Thomas 1983).

There were numerous beginnings to the study and protection of natural objects for their own intrinsic fascination. Cambridge, Oxford and other historic centres of learning might seem obvious places to start any exploration, but so too might more humble locations. Elizabeth Gaskell's nineteenth-century novel, *Mary Barton*, refers to the warm and devoted followers of botany among the common handloom weavers of Lancashire who know

> the name and habitat of every plant within a day's walk from their dwellings and who steal the holiday of a day or two when any particular plant should be in flower (Gaskell 1848).

For the most part, these were sociable people, eager to share and display their information, whether at meetings or in the published proceedings of their respective society (Harrison 1961).

Such beginnings might have as much to do with sentiment as study. The first Wild Bird Act arose from anger at the cruel and indiscriminate slaughter of seabirds on the Bempton cliffs of Yorkshire in the 1860s, as 'scores of excursionists poured from the neighbouring towns' to shoot the birds as they fed their young. Largely at the instigation of local clergymen, an East Riding Association for the Protection of Seabirds was formed. Circulars were printed and the support of the Archbishop of York was enlisted. The local Member of Parliament, Christopher Sykes, and the Duke of Northumberland promoted a Sea Birds Protection Bill, which they justified both on humanitarian grounds and as a means of protecting those bird species of value to farmers and fishermen. The Bill, which introduced a close season from 1 April until 1 August, received the Royal Assent in 1869. Precedents were provided for further Bills that gave protection to a much wider range of birdlife (Sheail 1976 22–36).

Both David Allen's pioneer study, *The Naturalist in Britain: a Social History*, and Ranlett's account of late Victorian preservationist bodies, illustrated how information and enthusiasm for such causes were communicated through extensive networks (Ranlett 1983). It might seem an obvious step to merge the various clubs and societies, but there were those who resisted. A large number of smaller groups, each representing something locally unique, might have far greater impact than a single, all-embracing body. Rather than amalgamating, loose hierarchies began to form. The British Association for the Advancement of Science became the pinnacle of one such hierarchy. Its annual meetings acted as a national forum for members of 'corresponding societies'. Naturalists' Unions were also formed at the county or regional level. The Yorkshire Naturalists' Union was the first and most successful. Six small societies had amalgamated in 1864 to form the West Riding Consolidated Naturalists' Society, with a combined membership of 300 and the motto 'Union is strength'. Its journal, *The Naturalist*, bound members ever closer together. The need for a large circulation to keep subscription costs down also meant there was a powerful force for enlargement. The 27 societies then in existence for the whole of Yorkshire decided in 1877 not to merge, but rather to become affiliated as component members of the Yorkshire Naturalists' Union (Allen 1976).

Such obvious skills and enthusiasm might be harnessed more systematically to gain better knowledge and understanding of the countryside. For W.G. Smith and his students at the Yorkshire College, Leeds, the only hope of extending their vegetation mapping to the whole county was to enrol and organise members of the Yorkshire Naturalists' Union. A guide drawn up by Smith (1903) gave not only 'floristic details', but descriptions of 'the social conditions and life of the plants'. Valuable experience had been gained by the time the Yorkshire botanists met the distinguished Cambridge botanist, A.G. Tansley, in Smith's house in December 1904. Together, they decided to form the British Vegetation Committee. In bringing together all those actively engaged in the mapping of British vegetation, the Committee marked an important stage in what McIntosh (1985) described as the emergence of 'self-conscious' ecology. Where the Yorkshire group sought more rigorous and effective ways of collecting and analysing their findings, Tansley saw such keenness and diligence as an opportunity to apply what he had begun to 'preach'. The two parties had probably first met at the British Association earlier in the year, when Tansley had presented the first major ecological paper to be written from a British perspective. Entitled 'The problems of ecology', it emphasised the need for discipline, whereby standards were sought and followed in describing, with precision, the manner and rates by which vegetation changed through space and time (Tansley 1904).

By the time the British Vegetation Committee was subsumed into the British Ecological Society, in 1913, as the first national ecological society in the world (Sheail 1987), ten memoirs had been published, with accompanying vegetation maps, for different parts of the British Isles. Tansley had always seen such maps as a necessary stage in ranging beyond intuition to a fuller and more precise understanding of how vegetation had attained its present, gross appearance (Schulte Fischedick 1995). In 1911, Tansley organised the first International Phytogeographical Congress, during which the world's leading ecologists spent a fortnight touring the United Kingdom, meeting local ecologists in their study areas. With Tansley as editor, seven members of the Vegetation Committee contributed sections to 'a book having the character of a guide to British plant associations'. Called *Types of British Vegetation*, it was the first attempt at 'a scientific description of British vegetation' (Tansley 1911).

Nature preservation appeared to have made encouraging progress by the First World War, in terms of assembling both an informed knowledge base and an organisational structure. Some naturalists were keen to do more than simply observe the loss of species and localities. Much depended on the type of threat. There was little to be done where the losses came about through the 'progress of civilisation', often in the form of building development or construction of railway lines. The greatest wrath was generally reserved for the obsessive collector. The principal reason why N. Charles Rothschild, a leading entomologist and the younger son of the first Lord Rothschild, joined others in acquiring parts of Wicken Fen and conveying them to the National Trust was because it seemed the only way to prevent over-collection of the distinctive insects and plants on those last undrained relics of the Cambridgeshire fenland. Sites such as this were managed as vigilantly as game preserves.

The overlapping membership of the various societies ensured that there was a considerable fund of expertise and experience to draw on. The Royal Society for the Prevention of Cruelty to Animals was an obvious model. The Selborne Society for the Preservation of Birds, Plants and Pleasant Places was the first national society to be explicitly concerned with the preservation of wildlife; there were 45 branches by 1893, and the membership by the turn of the century exceeded 1,500. Its nature-study journal, *Nature Notes*, was supplied to school libraries and sold through bookshops. The Society for the

Protection of Birds obtained its royal charter in 1904. Although continuing to campaign against the international traffic in bird plumage, it became increasingly active over the whole field of bird preservation. Whatever their individual purpose in trying to curb human thoughtlessness, greed or cruelty, each society was driven by the conviction that, in saving plant and animal life, it was also contributing to the quality of human life. As part of the considerably larger Victorian and Edwardian social movement, such preservationist bodies demonstrated what could be achieved through appealing to both sentiment and reason. They might also provide the expertise and experience required by Government and parliament when the further protection of wildlife was contemplated.

It is entirely appropriate that the names of Robert Hunter, Octavia Hill and Canon Rawnsley are principally remembered for their part in the founding of the National Trust for Places of Historic Interest or Natural Beauty in 1895. Through their individual and wide-ranging involvement in so many 'worthy' causes, they realised that power came not only from forming associations of almost hand-picked persons in capturing and directing political opinion, but from going one stage further in equipping such bodies with the legal powers required to hold and manage land. By a Memorandum of Association, drawn up under the Companies Acts, the founders of the National Trust sought

> to promote the permanent preservation, for the benefit of the Nation, of lands and tenements (including buildings) of beauty or historic interest; and as regards lands, to preserve (so far as practicable) their natural aspect, features, and animal and plant life.

Perhaps more significantly, parliament granted the Council of the National Trust, under a Private Act of 1907, unique powers to declare inalienable those of its properties deemed to be held 'for the benefit of the nation' (Cannadine 1995).

It was, however, one thing to have such powers, but another to use them effectively. Although the National Trust had acquired, by 1910, 13 sites of special interest for their wildlife, there was frustration at the lack of any considered policy in choosing sites to be protected. With the support of key figures in the British Museum (Natural History), Rothschild founded the Society for the Promotion of Nature Reserves (SPNR) in May 1912. All the posts were honorary, and Membership was by invitation only. Its objects were

1 to collect and collate information as to the areas of land in the United Kingdom which retain primitive conditions and contain rare and local species liable to extinction owing to building, drainage, disafforestation, or in consequence of the cupidity of collectors,

2 to prepare schemes, showing which areas should be secured as nature reserves,

3 to obtain such areas and, if thought desirable, to hand them over to the National Trust,

4 to preserve for posterity as a national possession some part at least of our native land for its faunal, floral and geographical features,

5 to encourage the love of Nature and to educate public opinion to a better knowledge of Nature Study.

Woodwalton Fen, Huntingdonshire.
Charles Rothschild bought this relic of 'primitive fenland' in 1910 and gave it to the SPNR in 1919, which in turn leased it to the Nature Conservancy in 1954. Naturalists attempting to reintroduce the large copper butterfly in the inter-war years found that the open fen pastures, isolated among arable cropland, rapidly became 'dense impenetrable thickets of sallow bushes' and woodland, as reed and sedge harvesting, peat-cutting, grazing and haymaking ceased (Rothschild and Marren 1997, 122–3).
(*left*) The bungalow built by Rothschild and (*right*) a ride and frozen dyke, February 1991.

The Executive Committee, at its first meeting, noted 'the desirability of preserving in perpetuity sites suitable for nature reserves' by means of the press, personal persuasion, and correspondence 'with local societies and individuals'. Above all, the SPNR was intended to be a 'ginger group' to the National Trust.

Rothschild was by now an active partner in the firm of Messrs N.M. Rothschild and Sons and the leading authority on the fleas of the world. It was also through his drive and resources that the SPNR compiled a list of 273 areas deemed 'worthy of permanent preservation' either as 'typical primeval country', breeding places for 'scarce creatures' and localities for rare plants, or for their rock sections and other features of geological interest. The survey had made good progress by the time the First World War broke out. Rothschild's solicitors provided details of the ownership of each area. An official of the Board of Agriculture and member of the executive committee of the SPNR, T.F. Husband, wrote to Rothschild, describing plans of the Development Commission to reclaim extensive areas of 'wasteland' for increased food production. Taking this as a 'straight tip' that very extensive works were contemplated, Rothschild decided that, far from abandoning the survey at 'the present sad time', the Society should accelerate its listing of areas that should be left in their 'primitive state'. A provisional set of lists for England, Wales, Scotland and Ireland was sent to the Board in June 1915, and a revised set a year later. Little, if any, use was made of them (Rothschild and Marren 1997).

THE INTER-WAR YEARS

Nature preservation failed to take off. Whether measured in terms of legislation, public awareness or nature reserves, the tangible achievements of the inter-war years were meagre (Sheail 1976). The Government refused to contemplate further wild-bird legislation until the relevant ornithological bodies could agree on an optimal approach. Despite early recognition of the power of the wireless, little attempt was made to secure popular support. Although more land was changing hands than at any time since the dissolution of the monasteries, the acquisition of reserves was minimal.

Beyond the immediate circumstances of individual societies, some explanation may be found in the appalling losses of the Great War: time and again, their proceedings report the loss of young men — members who had already begun to play a large role in their respective fields of natural history or ecology — falling to the sniper's bullet or dying of their wounds in hospital. Rothschild, already among the established leaders of the preservation movement, contracted the encephalitis associated with the Spanish influenza epidemic that swept Europe towards the end of the war (Rothschild and Marren 1997, 8). His long illness and death in 1923, at the early age of 46, dealt what an obituarist in *Nature* described as a formidable blow to 'nature' in a literal sense, as well as his own extraordinary array of scientific interests (Anon. 1923). The nature-preservation movement lost the patronage he would undoubtedly have secured.

Although local authorities had discretionary powers to acquire and manage land for amenity purposes, they rarely did so. As a founder member of the Middlesex County

The scientific career of **Frank Oliver** fell into three phases – physiology, palaeobotany and ecology. His detailed studies of the shingle spit at Blakeney in Norfolk made him a pioneer in the dynamic approach to the study of vegetation in Britain.

Council and chairman of the RSPB for many years, Sir Montagu Sharpe was one of the few figures in local government to exert any influence in that direction. Although politicians such as Ramsay MacDonald and Neville Chamberlain gave personal support to the preservation and recreational movements, central government consistently refused to set a precedent for the use of Exchequer monies, either for the purchase of land or for payment of compensation in situations where consent for development under the rudimentary forms of statutory town planning might be withheld on amenity grounds (Sheail 1987).

The most active ecologist in the nature-preservation movement was Frank W. Oliver, Professor of Botany at University College London. His book, *The Exploitation of Plants*, published in 1917, included a chapter called 'Exploitation without consumption'. Here he described how vegetation might be used as a substitute for civil engineering, say, in preventing landslips and coastal erosion. It should also be safeguarded for its contribution to 'the characteristic and unparalleled beauty of English scenery' (Oliver 1917). Oliver himself played a key role in raising funds for the acquisition of Blakeney Point and Scolt Head Island, off the north Norfolk coast. When the National Trust refused to accept custody of a further area – the Cley Marshes – in 1926, a Norfolk Naturalists' Trust was established, as a special non-profit paying company to hold and manage the property and other land acquired as nature reserves. In a discussion on nature reserves, at the British Association meeting in 1927, Oliver (1928) spoke of how 'one might look forward to the time when every county would have its County Trust'.

Oliver himself retired shortly afterwards to Egypt but, in an earlier paper on nature reserves given to the third meeting of the British Ecological Society in December 1913, he may have come closest to explaining why nature preservation excited so little interest among ecologists and the public generally. Whilst commending the efforts of the SPNR, he observed how small was the threat to the countryside. Oliver (1914) also recalled how the ecologists taking part in the International Phytogeographical Excursion of 1911 had found England (meaning the British Isles) an 'almost empty country'. He might have added that, whilst individual species might be lost, there seemed to be no possibility of plant communities (the focus of ecology) becoming extinct (Sheail 1981a). Even where sanctuaries were declared, the protection that could be given might still be limited. As Oliver recounted, it would have been extremely short-sighted of the National Trust to close Blakeney Point to public access. Local people had roamed the area since time immemorial, collecting samphire, shooting or picnicking. It was impossible to cancel rights summarily and live in peace with your neighbours.

Why then did ecologists involve themselves in nature preservation? As the Yorkshire ecologist, W.B. Crump, explained in an article published in *Country Life* in 1913, a nature reserve was the obvious location for survey and experimental work. In Crump's words, a reserve should be

> no mere refuge for vanishing or persecuted species. It is an outdoor workshop for the study of plants and animals in, and in relation to, their natural habitats, a twentieth-century instrument of research as indispensable for biological progress as a laboratory or an experimental station (Crump 1913).

7

Such long-term studies were however, severely compromised if the owner sold the land, changed its use or management, or simply denied access (Oliver 1914). Tansley complained, in his Presidential Address to the British Ecological Society in 1938, that his own studies on successional change had twice been brought to an abrupt end. There was accordingly an enthusiastic response to an invitation, made by the Chairman of the Forestry Commission, that 'ecological reserves' might be established on the Commission's properties (Tansley 1939a). In welcoming such an initiative, the botanist and agronomist Geoffrey E. Blackman predicted that ecologists would ultimately want the opportunity to carry out multifactorial experiments based on experimental planting laid out in randomised blocks, where individual environmental factors could be changed experimentally (Anon. 1944a). The level of control would have to be so complete and permanent that there was no alternative to actually owning such sites.

POST-WAR RECONSTRUCTION

Regardless of the rhetoric of post-war planning, the strengthening of the preservation movement should not be taken as evidence of a last desperate stand to save the country-side. Far from there being any sense of pending loss and catastrophe, the appointment of the National Parks Commission and Nature Conservancy, in 1949, were evidence of a growing confidence that such dangers could be warded off, provided there was sufficient foresight and planning.

A comparison of two pioneering books, one published after the Great War and the other after the Second World War, reveals a generally encouraging picture. A volume entitled *The Influence of Man on the Animal Life of Scotland*, written by the distinguished zoologist James Ritchie and published in 1920, traced the decline and, in some instances, extinction of species as a result of forest destruction, marsh drainage, and the killing of predators for game preservation. Through town expansion, intensive cultivation and, above all, the exertions of gamekeepers, mankind had been 'an impoverisher of the country's natural heritage'. Animal life was controlled by the owners of country estates, who might favour and even introduce desirable creatures of the Chase but invariably persecuted species that might feed on game. The only exception was the fox, which was itself an object of the Chase (Ritchie 1920).

By the time H.L. Edlin, the publications officer of the Forestry Commission, came to write his book *The Changing Wild Life of Britain* in 1952, during that most formative period in the national-parks and nature-conservation movements, much had changed. Many of the great estates had been broken up, and with the resurgence in both numbers and distribution of species such as the carrion crow and Scottish wild cat, which game-keepers had previously kept so rigorously in check, a richer, more natural, fauna was evolving. Together with the concurrent spread of interest in nature study, there was also a feeling that the country's wildlife was not so much the personal property of the owner of the land, but rather, in Edlin's words, 'a heritage of the people as a whole'. There was not only a more conscious attempt to preserve what remained, but an appreciation of 'the human share in enriching our flora and fauna'. As woodlands were replanted and forests extended, the number of tree-loving mammals, birds and lesser plants was expected to increase. Greater productivity in farming would provide more food for both the human population and wildlife (Edlin 1952).

There seemed to be every possibility that this generally encouraging picture would be reinforced in two ways. It was generally expected that town and country planning legislation would be strengthened to prevent the kind of urban sprawl that had led to some 2 per cent of the land surface of England and Wales being built over between the wars. More positively, the appearance, wildlife and recreational potential of the countryside were all expected to benefit from the greater prosperity accorded to the two principal industries – forestry and farming. If the ministers with oversight for those industries had seen fit, all this could have been accomplished with comparatively little adjustment to either the terms of reference of the Forestry Commission or the basis on which farming was given unprecedented financial and expert support after the Second World War. An all-encompassing approach to the rural estate would have made notions such as a National Parks Commission or a Nature Conservancy redundant.

This comprehensive vision of rural management had already begun to fragment, even before the war ended. The Forestry Commission, founded in 1919, designated its first National Forest Park in Argyllshire, followed by another in the Forest of Dean in 1939 and Snowdonia in 1940. A proposal for a national forest park of 80,000 acres (32,000 hectares) in the Keilder Forest was shelved in 1938 until the plantations were better established (Sheail 1987, 185–92). In its Post-war Forestry, published as a White Paper in 1943, the Forestry Commission pressed for both large-scale afforestation and more intensive management of existing woodlands. As an integral part of that programme, it anticipated the addition of one new National Forest Park each year, at a capital cost over a ten-year period of not more than £50,000 (Forestry Commission 1943). In October, the Commissioners decided to establish a National Forest Park of 40,000 acres (16,000 hectares) at Glentrool. The Scottish Secretary, Thomas Johnston, was unaware of this until he received a letter inviting him to nominate a representative to the Park's advisory committee. As the 'planning minister' for Scotland, he took strong exception to the lack of previous consultation. The Lord Privy Seal, Clement Attlee, upheld the complaint and, soon afterwards, Johnston and the Minister of Town and Country Planning (for England and Wales) met to discuss ways of presenting 'a common front against any proposals by the Forestry Commission to pursue an independent policy with regard to national parks'. They affirmed that the primary responsibility for national parks lay with the two planning ministers (Scottish Record Office (SRO), HH 1, 2587).

A fragmented approach had in effect been created. The Forestry Commission not only maintained but extended its investment in outdoor recreational facilities: National Forest Parks were established in Glenmore (1948), the Queen Elizabeth Forest (1953), and Border Forest (1955). Recreational facilities were provided on a more modest scale in other forests. Whilst a National Parks Commission was established in 1949, and ten National Parks were subsequently designated in England and Wales, Scotland was to have neither Parks nor a National Parks Commission. Even in England and Wales, the management of the national parks was hampered by shortage of funds and a lack of executive planning powers on the part of the National Parks Commission.

Turning to agriculture, the inter-war years are recalled for the way large areas of arable were grassed down – or simply abandoned – in a desperate attempt to survive the severely depressed market conditions. It was however another kind of development, namely mechanisation, that prompted Lord Astor and Seebohm Rowntree to write more positively of an Agricultural Revolution taking place. Tractors became more numerous, larger and more powerful. Combine harvesters and milking machines were introduced. Machinery permeated every branch of farming. An increasing number of 'off-farm' trucks and lorries collected produce for market and distributed the farmers' needs to their holdings (Astor and Rowntree 1935). There was also speculation outside the industry about the consequences of agriculture ceasing to be a major employer. Rural communities were seen as a stabilising influence on the political life of all nations. The distinguished historian, G.M. Trevelyan, and many others, considered those who worked on the land to be generally healthier than their counterparts in town and city (Trevelyan 1929). Astor and Rowntree (1938) believed that it was impossible to maintain, let alone increase, employment levels and, at the same time, pay the wages needed to raise standards of rural housing, health and education. It was believed that policies would be better directed towards capitalising on mechanisation and other advances in agriculture for the benefit of those remaining in the industry. Opportunities for inhabitants of towns and cities to come into closer contact with the countryside and food production should be expanded.

The way in which such aspirations impinged on wider land-use issues provides a further instance of the influence of individual personalities on the course of events. Lord Reith, the famous former managing-director of the BBC, was appointed Minister of Works and Building by Winston Churchill in October 1940, primarily to apply his considerable managerial talents to repairing blitz damage and constructing munitions and other public works. He had already developed an interest in post-war reconstruction during his five months as Minister of Transport and insisted that his new Ministry should be given the added responsibility for planning post-war reconstruction. Through the good offices of the Lord President of the Council, Sir John Anderson, he secured personal responsibility for planning the 'physical' reconstruction of post-war Britain (Stuart 1975). Within a month, he had drafted a Cabinet Paper warning that, without an effective national plan, the present disorder in land use would reach crisis point by the end of the war. Among the many objects of such a plan, there should be a limit to urban growth, preservation of fertile areas of farmland, and protection of areas of natural and historical interest. The powers of a central planning authority were required to lay down general principles and supervise schemes (PRO, CAB 67, 8-9).

The difficulties of securing a more holistic, yet substantive, approach to the use of town and countryside were demonstrated by reactions to Reith's Paper. Although Churchill wrote that he had read it 'with great interest', he stressed the need to concentrate on more immediate tasks. Other ministers were less generous in expressing their anger at Reith's apparent attempt to poach on their 'estates'. Such reactions demonstrated the fact that any ministerial initiative required the support of 'skilled administrators and professionals', if it was to survive the competing interests of departments (PRO,

CAB 118, 79 and PREM 4, 92/9). Reith (1949) himself wrote that 'no one could have shown greater assiduity and devotion' than H.G. Vincent who, as a Principal Assistant Secretary, took charge of his 'planning' responsibilities. Vincent believed that the only way the new Ministry might acquire legitimacy in the field of post-war reconstruction was to play a supportive role by undertaking the research, and therefore acquiring the insight, required by other Departments (Sheail 1981).

The outstanding initiative of the pre-war years in the field of land-use planning had been the appointment, in 1937, of a Royal Commission on the Distribution of the Industrial Population, under the chairmanship of Sir Montague Barlow. Its primary purpose was to identify ways of mitigating the imbalance that had developed during the inter-war years between the acutely depressed industrial areas of the North and West, and the relatively prosperous South and East of the UK, where both urban and industrial growth were comparatively rapid. Its report, published in January 1940, was not only highly relevant to any programme of post-war reconstruction but also raised fundamental questions as to the role of a central planning authority (Royal Commission 1940). Reith lacked the powers required for a comprehensive study of the Commission's recommendations regarding a more equitable distribution of new industries and their workforces and, therefore, 'decentralization from overgrown and congested cities'. The location of industry was a matter for the Board of Trade. The promotion of housing fell within the purview of the Ministry of Health. For Vincent, in Reith's Ministry, the only course was to identify those aspects of major public concern that did not fall primarily to another Minister. One of these topics was the impact of industry and housing development on rural land-use.

Reith appointed a Committee on Land Utilization in Rural Areas, under the chairmanship of Lord Justice Scott, to investigate the implications of the Barlow report, and more particularly the potential impact of new industry and the housing it would require, on the countryside. As Scott later wrote, his Committee recognised a fundamental difference between agriculture and other forms of industry, such as manufacturing.

The Councils for the Preservation of Rural England and Wales, and the Association for the Preservation of Rural Scotland, arose from concern about the impact of development on the countryside in the 1920s. The example of residential and holiday development along the cliff tops at **Peacehaven** in **Sussex**, led to fears that the entire length of scenic coastline might become yet another form of ribbon development.

Whereas, given the uncertainties of international trade, it was practically impossible for a manufacturer to adopt a long-term policy for the location of a factory, agriculture was forced to take a long-term view of the land. Not only was farming the only livelihood to be gained from the land without causing irreversible change but, once developed for other purposes, the land could never be used for farming again. There was accordingly an obligation to protect farmland. The Committee's report of August 1942 pressed for the universal adoption of a policy to protect farmland, unless it could be shown that there was some alternative use of permanent value to the Nation. Agricultural prosperity was the key to meeting the needs of both the rural population and those visiting the countryside for relaxation and enjoyment (Minister of Works and Planning 1942; Sheail 1997a).

Again, as with the forestry industry, the opportunity for the farming industry to capitalise upon, and provide leadership to, this wider interest in the countryside was allowed to slip. An exchange of views recorded in a Ministry of Agriculture file of 1942 is particularly revealing. An Assistant Secretary, Basil C. Engholm, had been a secretary of the Scott Committee. He wrote an internal minute, emphasising that the Ministry's position could be strengthened by concerning itself with all rural matters rather than the purely technical aspects of farming. Engholm believed that voluntary bodies pressing for the protection of natural beauty and, therefore, a large body of urban opinion would be more likely to support 'a strong and progressive agricultural policy'. His was a minority voice. In the margin of Engholm's memorandum, another Assistant Secretary insisted that nothing should be done to deflect the Ministry from its central task. It was already overstretched in producing the food required to sustain a country at war. The overriding priority after the war would be to establish 'a sound and progressive policy' for farming (PRO, MAF 48, 665).

In terms of priorities for the countryside, there seemed to be nothing incongruous or short-sighted in the dual approach adopted by ministers of both the Wartime Coalition and post-war Labour Governments towards the use of the post-war countryside. The overriding purpose of the Ministry of Town and Country Planning (as it became in March 1943) was to prevent the suburban sprawl of the inter-war years. The Town and Country Planning Acts considerably strengthened the role of central and local government in regulating the location, type and design of building development (Cullingworth 1975). The wartime files of the Ministry of Agriculture were equally insistent on the need to insure against disruption of overseas food-supplies, whether caused by war or the impoverished state of the nation. Following the example of inter-war Canada and the United States, where the soils of extensive areas had become exhausted, would be as short-sighted as copying the manufacturer who set his prices without considering depreciation or maintenance of the plant (PRO, MAF 53, 162). The purpose of the unprecedented support given to farming by the Agriculture Act of 1947 was to keep the land 'in a state of fertility and productivity'. Taken together, the effect of these major pieces of legislation was to provide both the security and prosperity required to achieve higher food output. If these goals were met, farmers would indeed become, in the words of the Scott Committee, 'unconsciously the nation's landscape gardeners'.

THE NATIONAL PARKS MOVEMENT

Long before the major pieces of post-war legislation were enacted, a wide range of voluntary and professional groups had sought to fill the 'niche' that the Forestry Commission had been prevented from taking over and the Ministry of Agriculture had declined to occupy. Within the range of bodies that emerged, two categories may be discerned: those concerned with the protection of visual amenity and opportunities for outdoor recreation and others more concerned with nature preservation.

Regardless of its particular preoccupation, each group sought to influence the debate and eventual plans for post-war reconstruction. As early as October 1941, the Commons, Open Spaces and Footpaths Preservation Society began lobbying Government ministers on the need to include greater facilities for outdoor recreation in plans for post-war reconstruction. This group asked for improvements in the preservation and upkeep of commons, footpaths and bridleways. In January 1942, the Association for the Preservation of Rural Scotland convened a conference of representatives from thirty organisations, which set up a new Scottish Council for National Parks in order to exert pressure on the Government. In England and Wales, a deputation from the Standing Committee on National Parks met with the Minister of Works and Buildings, Lord Reith, in the same month, and again emphasised the need for a series of national parks and a national parks authority (Cherry 1975).

Such advocacy, in the thick of war, can only be understood in the context of the longer pre-war situation. The outstanding initiative of the inter-war years, in terms of the amenity and outdoor-recreation movements, was the foundation of the Council for the Preservation of Rural England (CPRE) in 1926. The immediate stimulus came from a paper written by the architect and town planner, Patrick Abercrombie, calling for a strong central council made up of all the relevant bodies concerned with the preservation of the countryside. Whilst the constituent bodies would remain responsible for executive action, the purpose of the Council would be to coordinate such action and, more importantly, to raise public awareness through single, simple and more direct appeal. The new Council had 22 constituent members and a larger number of affiliated bodies. Its achievement was to secure the support of the 'old country squire', as well as those who had recently moved to the countryside and were horrified to find ribbon development and urban sprawl. The Association for the Preservation of Rural Scotland, and the Council for the Preservation of Rural Wales were formed along similar lines, in 1927 and 1928 respectively (Sheail 1981b).

The CPRE could claim two early successes. The general support gained by a Rural Amenities Bill, drafted by the CPRE as a Private Member's Bill, encouraged a Government measure that eventually became the Town and Country Planning Act of 1932. This empowered local authorities to devise and implement planning schemes wherever, in their judgement, building development appeared to warrant them (Sheail 1981b, 71–9). In September 1929 the CPRE also persuaded the Prime Minister, Ramsay MacDonald, to appoint a National Park Committee to investigate the need for one or more national parks for the 'preservation of the natural character, including flora and fauna' – subjects in which MacDonald had a keen personal interest. The Committee's report of April 1931 advocated a series of parks with three objectives: to safeguard areas of exceptional national interest against disorderly development and spoliation; to improve the means of access for pedestrians to areas of natural beauty; and to promote measures for the protection of flora and fauna. The report also suggested that the most effective way of selecting and managing the parks would be through the appointment of one national parks authority for England and Wales and another for Scotland (Financial Secretary 1931). Despite initial support, the economic crises of 1931 prevented the Labour Government from taking any initiatives. The voluntary bodies responded by forming local pressure groups, such as the Friends of the Lake District, and a Standing Committee on National Parks.

Although ostensibly acting under the aegis of the CPRE, the Standing Committee soon developed a more vigorous campaigning style and a radical agenda of its own. The driving force was its Drafting Secretary, John Dower, the architect, town planner, rambler and fell-walker (Sheail 1995a), who had already written a pamphlet entitled *National parks – an appeal*. In 1938, more than 40,000 copies of his pamphlet, *The case for national parks in Great Britain*, were distributed, accompanied by a vigorous press campaign and a series of national meetings. A draft 'Summary of proposed provisions for a National Parks Bill', drawn up in 1939, envisaged the creation of a national parks commission, appointed by a minister without departmental responsibilities. This commission would designate national parks and nature sanctuaries and then act as the planning authority within the areas designated. The Standing Committee succeeded in

Beinn Eighe, as photographed from Allt an Daraich, in July 1931. The National Park Committee recognised, in its report of 1931, that national parks of the kind found in North America and Africa could only be established, if at all, in the Highlands and Islands of Scotland.

Pleasure-boating, the motor-cycle and cars; the pressures of holiday-making were already apparent in this photograph published in *The Times* on 28 March 1933. It was captioned: 'A scene at Horning Ferry, one of the most beautiful parts of the Norfolk Broads. In common with many of the picturesque places in this neighbourhood, it can be reached by road'.

persuading officials of both the Treasury and Ministry of Health that there was a need for greater control over changes in land use and management in areas of outstanding natural scenery and recreational value – but the administrative problems remained. If an *ad hoc* national parks commission were to be set up, this would be taken as a precedent for transferring all the other problems that beset local government to some central Government department or statutory authority. This would not only detract from the traditional autonomy of local authorities, but would augment the already confused pattern of county councils, borough councils, and urban and rural district councils.

Dower joined the army as soon as war broke out, but contracted virulent tuberculosis. News that he had been invalided out and was looking for employment came to the attention of Vincent, who had already begun to assemble a nucleus of 'experts' within Reith's Ministry to advise on the physical planning of post-war reconstruction. In April 1942 Reith's successor, Lord Portal, referred in a speech to the need to include 'the preservation of extensive areas of great natural beauty and of the coastline' in any 'national planning of the use of land'. In August 1942 Vincent secured the appointment of Dower as a temporary civil servant, to carry out a factual enquiry. A report on the Lake District was to be completed in two months. The publication of the Scott report, and its support for the concept of national parks, made it even more likely that there would be consultations between Government departments. Dower was instructed to widen the scope of his enquiry (Sheail 1995a).

On his appointment, Dower officially picked up the reins he had laid aside for military service. Drafts of his report emphasised the need for a series of national parks and nature reserves, designated and administered under the aegis of a national parks commission. During the last days of the Wartime Coalition Government, in May 1945, the Minister of Town and Country Planning, W.S. Morrison, sought the consent of the Cabinet's Reconstruction Committee to the publication of Dower's report, as the work 'of a member of his Department acting as a consultant'. The Committee agreed and the report was published later that month, with a foreword to the effect that the

Government was not committed 'to acceptance of the recommendations and conclusions of the report' (Minister of Town and Country Planning 1945). The Reconstruction Committee was much more critical of the Minister's proposal to appoint a preparatory National Parks Commission. There were not only more pressing priorities but, as the Chancellor of the Exchequer and Minister of Agriculture pointed out, 'it was for Ministers [as opposed to an *ad hoc* Commission] to shape and control policy'. The Minister of Town and Country Planning was invited instead to appoint a National Parks Committee to explore the question further (PRO, CAB 87, 10). As Dower remarked, the change did not require 'any radical difference to the choice of members'. Although failing health precluded him from being chairman (he died in October 1947), Dower exerted considerable influence over the drafting of the Committee's report, published in July 1947 (Minister of Town and Country Planning 1947a).

In essence, the administrative dilemma of the 1930s remained: was it worth risking the disruption of the entire framework of town and country planning for the sake of the better preservation of the most outstanding parts of rural Britain? The national-parks movement had, if anything, become even more radical as many of its more 'moderate' figures took up wartime duties or became part of the dramatic expansion of post-war statutory planning. Whilst such radicalism was needed to secure any priority in the legislative programme, there was a risk of the movement's over-reaching itself, particularly after the loss of its principal 'patron', Hugh Dalton, a senior Labour politician and outdoor enthusiast. As Chancellor of the Exchequer, he had established a National Land Fund of £50 million, with the intention of using the greater part to acquire most of the land needed for national parks. He resigned following a Budget Leak. Not only did this mean the effective demise of the Fund, but the political initiative passed to prominent local-authority men, whose number included the Prime Minister, Clement Attlee, Herbert Morrison, Chuter Ede, and the Minister of Town and Country Planning, Lewis Silkin. As the County Councils' Association pointed out, it was hardly possible for the Government to take away from the park areas the greatly strengthened planning powers so recently granted to county councils under the Town and Country Planning Act. Although the National Parks and Access to the Countryside Bill received the Royal Assent in December 1949, the powers conferred on the National Parks Commission had been emasculated. It might designate national parks (subject to ministerial direction) but could do no more than advise the local authorities, in whose hands the planning powers effectively remained.

NATURE PRESERVATION

Advocates of nature preservation began, as the national-parks movement had begun, with an inter-war agenda. In 1940 an accord was reached, at long last, between the British Oological Association and the Association of Bird-watchers and Wardens. Oologists agreed that taking the eggs of rare birds could be made illegal, on condition that a licensing system permitted 'accredited' collectors to collect a limited number of eggs of specified species. The main architect of the agreement, Geoffrey Dent, urged the RSPB to undertake a survey of those species and parts of the country requiring such protection.

Dent may be identified as one of the two unsung heroes of the early movement. A successful businessman and all-round field naturalist and sportsman, he had joined the RSPB in 1923 and served on its Watchers' Committee and Council since 1938 (Axell 1978). He used these positions to urge the Society to convene a series of meetings of interested persons to work out a commonly-agreed nature preservation policy. As he warned in May 1940

> if the Societies interested do not get together, and form a common policy of their own, no government is likely to do much, or listen to them, and we shall lose several more breeding species in the next twenty years.

Experience in America, in the Dominions, and in 'most advanced European countries' had shown that the only effective way of preserving 'native wild life for the benefit of future generations' was by supplementing the preservation laws with the provision of national parks or reserves to act as breeding reservoirs for species that might otherwise be exterminated. A small committee under Dent's chairmanship soon produced a memorandum setting out the functions of such sanctuaries, together with lists of the rare bird-species and areas urgently in need of protection (Sheail 1995b).

The initiative passed to the Society for the Promotion of Nature Reserves (SPNR) – or, to be more accurate – to Herbert Smith, the other unsung hero, a crystallographer who, on becoming Secretary of the Natural History Museum in 1921, found he was also Secretary of the SPNR. Following a meeting with the Secretary of the RSPB, Smith persuaded his Council to convene a Conference on Nature Preservation in Post-war Reconstruction, in July 1941, to which two representatives from each of over thirty organisations were invited. Although several bodies ignored the invitation and two failed to find delegates, every interest except geology was represented. As well as the RSPB memorandum, the Conference considered others by E.J. Salisbury, and J.C.F. Fryer and H.M. Edelsten, written from botanical and entomological perspectives respectively. Contributions from such distinguished figures were critical in converting what was, for many participants, a token appearance, into more sustained support. E.J. Salisbury had succeeded Oliver as Quain Professor of Botany at University College London in 1929. He was elected to the Royal Society in 1933, and became Director of the Royal Botanic Garden at Kew in 1943 (Clapham 1980). His paper emphasised that, whatever the benefits of national parks, they could not in themselves secure the protection of wildlife. The survival of a large proportion of plants and animals depended upon 'active control', based on knowledge and 'informed imagination'. There should be 'a properly constituted body' for that purpose. The Conference resolved that the widest possible range of habitats should be included in any series of reserves (Sheail 1995b).

Through Smith's persistent effort, two further meetings of the Conference were held to consider drafts of a memorandum for submission to the Prime Minister. Publication of the memorandum in November 1941, and the distribution of some 500 copies, attracted considerable publicity despite the war situation. Enough had been done to ensure that representatives of the Conference joined a deputation on national parks that met Reith in January 1942. The proceedings of the Conference had, however, been marred by a bitter clash between representatives of the CPRE and the Standing Committee on National Parks on the one hand, and the local-authority associations on the other. The dispute concerned the respective powers of the proposed national parks authority. As chairman of the drafting committee, W.L. Platts (representing the County Councils' Association) introduced a section recommending that national parks should be placed in the hands of county councils. Julian Huxley and Herbert Smith had to intervene at a meeting of the Standing Committee on National Parks, in August 1941, when a resolution was proposed to withdraw from the Conference and 'torpedo' its efforts. Whilst the compromise they secured was enough to avert outright hostility, any sense of rapport between the national-park and local-authority interests within the Conference had been lost.

The clash led to an even greater concentration on 'the scientific aspects of nature preservation'. A yearning to break free from the amenity and recreational elements can be discerned, especially following the appointment of Cyril Diver as 'scientific' secretary to the drafting committee. Diver's work as Clerk to the Committees of the House of Commons provided long vacations with ample opportunity for a continuing study of the behaviour of web-spinning spiders, and the genetics of molluscs, and, after 1930, the ecology of the South Haven Peninsula of Dorset. Diver became a member of the British Ecological Society in 1932, and was its president between 1940 and 1942 (Merrett 1971).

Quite fortuitously, an opportunity to de-couple from the national-parks movement arose with the news that Lord Reith had left office but the Paymaster-General, Sir William Jowitt, had been appointed chairman of a Ministerial Committee on Post-war Reconstruction. A copy of the Conference memorandum was therefore sent to him and, in May 1942, a deputation of the entire drafting committee was hastily convened. Although Jowitt also accepted the need for nature reserves in any post-war planning scheme, he warned that the Government was unable to give any priority to the question. He suggested that the Conference itself should conduct the enquiry, and provide the Government with the necessary data. With some reluctance, the Conference accepted the challenge, and a Nature Reserves Investigation Committee (NRIC) was formally constituted in June 1942 (Sheail 1995b).

The leading role of biologists was no longer in doubt. Although the Chairman of the NRIC, Sir Lawrence Chubb, was a leading figure in the amenity and outdoor movement, there was no local-authority representation. The Committee otherwise consisted of biologists. Tansley had become Chairman of a Nature Reserves Committee, appointed by the Council of the British Ecological Society, in May 1942, specifically to assist the NRIC by putting forward lists of 'places suitable for preservation, with relevant information about them'. It was not long before the Society sought a more direct role. As Tansley pointed out, it included the great majority of those best qualified to advise on the location and scientific management of reserves. In April 1943, the Council of the British Ecological Society accordingly approved Tansley's proposal that the terms of his Committee should be widened 'to consider and report on the whole question of conservation of nature in Britain', with a view to the Society's publishing 'a definitive report' (Sheail 1987, 134–5). Whilst Tansley's initial correspondence with the NRIC met with a cool reply from

Cyril Diver, the first Director-General of the Nature Conservancy, described by Julian Huxley as 'a born naturalist'.

Having attained the rank of Captain in the First World War, he successfully applied for a Clerkship in the House of Commons since it would give him long vacations for fieldwork. His extensive researches on the South Haven Peninsula in Dorset led to his election as President of the British Ecological Society. His drafting skills were much used in the preparation of reports on nature conservation, successively by the British Ecological Society, the NRIC, and the Huxley Committee (Merrett 1971).

Smith, the two surveys complemented one another. A circular letter to the 360 members of the British Ecological Society, in June 1942, appealed for information and opinions regarding the types of habitat, plant and animal communities, and species or races of plant and animal which should be preserved, and the procedures for securing reservation. For its part, the NRIC was able to develop a regional sub-committee structure, largely through local natural-history societies and relevant university departments, (Sheail 1976).

Drawing on his 'big book', *The British Islands and their Vegetation* (Tansley 1939b), Tansley played a key role in devising a framework for selecting representative reserves and 'scheduled' areas, or (as the NRIC called them) 'conservation' areas. Based on an arbitrary limit of fifty reserves, the eventual lists comprised 49 national habitat reserves, 33 scheduled areas, and a further 8 sites where the wildlife was already preserved (Sheail 1987, 136–7). Under Diver's guidance, the NRIC drew heavily on the Society's lists in compiling its own, circulated in draft form in April 1945. Although Tansley described it as 'an able document', Dent complained that 'the ecological approach' had been overdone. Unless there were some good 'propaganda reserves', where particular birds or mammals could be seen in large numbers, there would be little public support. Nor could reserves be left to take their chances. With remarkable prescience, Dent wrote of the way modern agriculture would totally change even those areas under cultivation. Quite apart from the new weedkillers and still more deadly insecticides, too little account had been taken of the dangers posed by drainage boards and afforestation (Sheail 1995b). With modest amendment, the NRIC list of 55 proposed national nature reserves, covering 0.2 per cent of the land surface of England and Wales, was published in December 1945. The list included 15 of the habitat reserves identified in the earlier lists of the British Ecological Society (Sheail 1976).

The lists gave expression to what was being attempted, but the larger task of explaining why the reserves were necessary still remained. No-one was more highly qualified to do this than John C.F. Fryer. Appointed to the new post of Entomologist to the Board of Agriculture in 1913, he had become Director of the Plant Pathology Laboratory in 1919. With an inborn love of natural history, he had personally taken part in the re-introduction of the Large Copper butterfly to the SPNR reserve of Woodwalton Fen from 1927 onwards (Edelsten 1950–51). Such experience had given him first-hand insight into the opportunities for research on such reserves, as well as an understanding of the formidable challenges of managing water levels and plant succession in order to preserve the intrinsic wildlife interest. In a highly-influential memorandum of October 1942, Fryer wrote that the present generation had an obligation to posterity to ensure that neither individual species, nor characteristic communities, were lost.

Significantly, the word 'preservation', which conveyed a sense of looking backwards, was being used less frequently. Another ordinary word, 'conservation', was increasingly used to project the more positive and vigorous approach of meeting the challenges of post-war reconstruction. The NRIC memorandum of March 1943, entitled *Nature Conservation in Great Britain*, defined conservation as the pursuit of scientific and economic studies, the enjoyment of nature by the public, and promotion of education in natural history. Those aims could not be met by simply protecting wildlife from harmful forms of land use. There had to be expert management under some form of unified direction. Reserves where this could be achieved would have a twofold purpose: they would enable major strides to be made in botany and zoology, and they would act as reference points for tackling applied questions in agriculture and forestry such as soil deficiencies, disease and pest infestation. Such reserves would help to identify further plants and animals of value to mankind.

Perhaps the most cogent statement was made by Tansley's Special Committee, under the title, 'Nature conservation and nature reserves', and approved by the Council of the British Ecological Society for publication in October 1943. The ecological case was argued on the grounds of research, public enjoyment and education. Vegetation was an integral part of the beauty and interest of the countryside. In a section on 'the social background of nature conservation', the report conceded the possibility of conflict. There must be development of natural resources if Britain was to retain its position as a leading nation in the world. And yet, without a national scheme of conservation, the next generation would find a precious piece of its heritage hopelessly impoverished.

Turning to the implementation of such a concept, Tansley's Special Committee had earlier endorsed the NRIC's report in urging the Government to 'take formal responsibility for the conservation of native wild life, both plant and animal'. A Wild Life Service should be established to hold and manage nature reserves. It should, however, be more than a nature-reserves body employing ecologists. If ecologists could establish themselves as the primary body responsible for devising and implementing a national programme of nature conservation, they would have gone a long way towards transforming themselves into a new and powerful force. The Society's report, largely drafted by Tansley, envisaged a National Wild Life Service responsible not only for the supervision of a series of national nature reserves, but for 'continuous research on the problems of conservation and control, whether within or outside the reserves' (Anon. 1944b).

With the publication of its report, 'Nature conservation and nature reserves', in the Society's journals (Anon. 1944b), the British Ecological Society turned its attention more explicitly to the wider issue of 'wild life and ecological research'. Although reserves were still of fundamental importance, the Society now had a considerably larger objective in view. As the opening sentence indicated, the object of the further memorandum was to press the case for a Central Authority

> to organise and direct ecological research essential to the progress of scientific knowledge and the economic well-being of the country, and to secure a degree of wild life conservation which is the necessary material of such research.

Both a biological service and a new research council should be formed. The biological service would administer the national nature reserves, promote 'fact-finding research', and disseminate advice on the conservation, regulation, control and management of plant and animal populations. As well as having responsibility for the biological service, the ecological research council would also act as a funding body for ecology, in the same way as the Medical Research Council and the Agricultural Research Council supported their own respective disciplines (Sheail 1987).

CHAPTER TWO

THE NATURE CONSERVANCY

There was nothing inevitable about the founding of the Nature Conservancy. In no sense did it represent any kind of natural outpouring of a popular movement. It was essentially the by-product of a number of policy decisions taken by ministers, officials and other interest-groups for quite different reasons. Such modest opportunities would have passed unfulfilled had it not been for the vision, commitment and acumen of a very small number of persons alive to the possibilities of their particular kind of nature conservation. These ecologists came to wield an influence entirely out of proportion to their number in securing the gestation and birth, in 1949, of what proved to be a weakling child called the Nature Conservancy.

The outlook for nature protection, as designed and engineered by ecologists, hardly looked promising. The chances of establishing a fourth research council were bleak in the extreme. Officials insisted that there could be no place for a research body within the Ministry of Town and Country Planning. It was, however, their own Minister who brought about the circumstances that caused such an agency to be formed. As already recounted (page 15), W.S. Morrison applied to the Cabinet's Reconstruction Committee on 7 May 1945, the day before 'VE Day', for its consent to the appointment of a National Parks Commission. Although declining to give consent the Committee suggested, perhaps as a consolation, further study of how a series of national parks might be chosen, established and administered. None of the persons present would have realised, or indeed cared, that establishing a further enquiry would give ecologists a further two years to persuade ministers that nature conservation should not only be an explicit responsibility of government, but that it should be ascribed to the sector of ministerial activity concerned with science, rather than planning.

Whilst John Dower deplored any separation of nature reserves from national parks, his report (see page 15) provided the opportunity for such a division to be discussed. In his scheme of things, a wild life conservation council would be appointed by the national parks commission (Minister of Town and Country Planning 1945). Dower had come to know Charles S. Elton well in the 1930s. Following publication of his seminal work, *Animal Ecology*, in 1927, Elton had become founder-editor of the *Journal of Animal*

Ecology. He was a key figure on Tansley's Special Committee. In heeding the advice of the Cabinet's Reconstruction Committee to appoint a National Parks Committee, it was entirely logical that the Minister should also appoint a nature reserves sub-committee, both on its own merits and 'so as to keep on good terms' with the ' "Nature Reserves" and wild life interests'. Dower insisted that the Committee should have wider terms of reference and higher status. If it was to be 'a committee of first class scientists', taking 'a broad scientific approach', nothing less than a Wild Life Conservation Special Committee would suffice. The distinguished biologist, Julian Huxley, had already been appointed to the National Parks Committee, with a view to his becoming chairman of that Committee. Dower's arguments prevailed (PRO, HLG 93, 1 and 51–2).

Meeting separately, yet in parallel with the National Parks Committee, the Huxley Committee provided an obvious opportunity to demonstrate the essentially scientific context of nature conservation. Tansley and Elton became even more strongly placed to refine and disseminate the arguments developed within the British Ecological Society. They were ably supported by the other members of the Committee: the naturalist E.N. Buxton (who was also on the main Committee); Diver; Edmund B. Ford; J.S.L. Gilmour; and E.M. Nicholson. Individually and together, they brought an extraordinary array of expertise, experience and prejudice. Ford, an ecological geneticist and distinguished authority on the form and behaviour of invertebrate life, wrote in August 1946: 'I am very anxious that collecting should be interfered with as little as possible.' He insisted that, whatever constraints on collecting the Committee might recommend, none should apply to invertebrates. A.E. Trueman and J.A. Steers were appointed to cover the geological and physiographical aspects respectively. Plans to include a marine ecologist were dropped, 'to avoid offence to the Ministry of Agriculture and Fisheries' (PRO, HLG 93, 1).

Although Huxley signed the report which became universally known as 'the Huxley report', he attended only the first few meetings. He was appointed in May 1946, first as the Executive Secretary of the Preparatory Commission, and then as the Director-General of UNESCO. Almost all the Chairman's work therefore fell on Tansley, as Vice-Chairman. Not only were Diver's drafting skills again used to the full but, as the only member to have served on both the NRIC and Special Committee of the British Ecological Society, he was well placed to assure members that the task for which they had been ostensibly assembled had already been largely completed. The list of 73 reserves, published in the Committee's report of July 1947, included nearly all of those previously identified by the NRIC in its lists of proposed national nature reserves and geological monuments (Minister of Town and Country Planning 1947b). With the Committee's Secretary, Richard S. Fitter, organising the fieldwork required to check and update the earlier lists (Fitter 1990), the Committee could give its almost undivided attention to deciding what kind of Wild Life Service was required.

For Tansley, in his 74th year, the appointment of the Committee offered a remarkable opportunity to address – if not resolve – what he had so perceptively described as 'the problems of ecology' in his paper to the British Association, some 40 years earlier. How might ecology be established as a reputable science, using physical sciences as the role model? Throughout a long career, he had judged every concept and technique according

Julian Huxley wrote of his own ability to throw himself wholeheartedly into a multiplicity of activities.
Huxley's stature as a biologist, writer and broadcaster enabled John Dower to secure special status for his Wild Life Conservation Committee, appointed in 1945. He was soon afterwards appointed Director-General of the newly-formed UNESCO (Huxley 1973).

Sir Arthur Tansley on Knoll Hill, near Corfe Castle, in April 1954, during a field excursion from the Furzebrook Research Station. The Conservancy's Annual Report, in a tribute following his death in November 1955, described his seminal role in promoting the concept of nature conservation and service as the Nature Conservancy's founder-Chairman, saying that this marked 'the culmination of some forty years' activity in broadening and remoulding botany as a comprehensive and integrated modern science'.

to its utility in helping to define different types of vegetation and thereby advance understanding of the processes by which they had evolved. That search for rigour in both observation and expression can be found, for example, in his personal correspondence and in drafts of *Types of British Vegetation*, and its much later revision and expansion as *The British Islands and their Vegetation* (Sheail 1995c). The chief intention was not so much to create a special department in biology but rather to promote an ecological viewpoint that gave 'particular direction to the study of special departments'. The fundamental facts about plants and animals could then be 'naturally arranged and presented to the greatest educational advantage' (Tansley 1914). According to that perception, both farming and forestry came to be seen as essentially ecological problems of a particular kind. As Sherardian Professor of Botany at Oxford from 1927 to 1937, Tansley was closely involved in giving training courses to foresters; his objective was always to inculcate habits of relating species to habitat, and of perceiving vegetation as a stage in 'multiform succession' (Godwin 1977).

If ecologists appeared to make only halting progress in applying their distinctive perspective to farming and forestry, there were no bounds to their rapidly-developing leadership of nature conservation. As well as bringing a uniquely comprehensive viewpoint of what was required, ecology also gave a new definition of the word 'countryside'. The ecologists' holistic viewpoint would encompass both intensively-used land and areas of semi-natural and natural vegetation. It would take in the whole of *Britain's Green Mantle*, which is also the title of a summary volume of Tansley's earlier writings (Tansley 1949).

The report of the Huxley Committee proved to be 'a remarkable distillation of wisdom and foresight'. As Ratcliffe (1977a) observed, in a paper given some 30 years later at the Royal Society, it conveyed

> a holistic conception of nature conservation as a single great endeavour, with both objectives and methods resting on a firm foundation of science.

Even so, Tansley and his fellow members might appear to have sacrificed the larger goal of a unified rural policy encompassing landscape, wildlife and recreation for the more limited goal of 'scientific perception of wildlife protection'. A distinction must, however, be drawn between the strategy and the tactics required to realise that much larger goal. Although the references made by the Huxley Committee to scenic beauty may have the appearance of tokenism, it is important to recall that the overriding purpose was to capture the interest of the Science Minister in the Cabinet, the Lord President of the Council. The report has to be read together with a slim, illustrated book entitled *Our Heritage of Wild Nature. A plea for organized nature conservation*, published in 1945. It was there that Tansley revealed most clearly that other side to his 'heart'. As he wrote, no other country of comparable size had such variety of rural beauty. Far from a love of the countryside withering away, he expected it to grow even stronger as motor transport made it possible for town dwellers to explore further afield. When planning the large-scale changes in land-use that would inevitably take place, consideration had to be given not only to 'order, efficiency and material wellbeing', but also to 'beauty and dignity'. If spiritual refreshment was to be drawn from the countryside, there had to be 'national parks' in the widest sense, where the public had freer access and increased facilities to enjoy natural beauty. Just as the finest examples of ancient and medieval architecture were protected, so there had to be 'sufficient examples of natural vegetation' (Tansley 1945).

The point was not so much whether ecologists were aware of the wider significance of plant and animal life, but how they thought their particular insights and experience might be most effectively deployed in establishing that third force in the countryside, which otherwise encompassed amenity and recreational bodies. Compared with the already powerful voices speaking on behalf of amenity and recreation, Diver feared that the purely scientific side was in danger of being overlooked. If, tactically speaking, a closer focus on the scientific value of reserves helped to distance nature conservation from the contentious issue of national-park administration, it also brought greater assurance of Government patronage. In a leading article in the journal, *Nature*, Miriam Rothschild wrote anonymously that the word 'nature' had come to be associated in the public mind with 'a somewhat childish and eccentric form of botanizing, bird-loving and butterfly-hunting'. If the more fashionable word 'science' could replace it, there might be much greater respect and collaboration from other rural interests (Anon. 1946).

The substitution of the word 'conservation' for 'preservation' conveyed an implicit sense of a new beginning. Through an explicit commitment to the scientific management of land and natural resources, the Nature Conservancy could capitalise on the dramatic growth of interest in the science of ecology (Sheail 1993). The National Parks Commission never received that degree of tangible support from landscape planning and design.

THE HUXLEY AND RITCHIE COMMITTEES

Writing of the beginnings of the modern nature conservation movement in the 1940s, Nicholson (1977) recalled both the reckless boldness of Tansley and other members of the Huxley Committee in pronouncing on matters that are still far from resolution, and their immense wisdom and judgement in steering a course through 'the ecological minefields'. Nicholson found ironic commentary on the workings of the British system of Government in the fact that a survey which Charles Rothschild had identified as necessary before the First World War should have been begun at the time of the blitz and completed as V1 and V2 rockets fell around London. In Nicholson's view, the achievement stemmed from the wartime suspension of 'the normal mechanisms for ensuring inaction' (Nicholson 1970). Whatever the mechanisms might have been, they applied at least as much to the voluntary and academic bodies in the field of wildlife protection, as to ministers and their officials.

Whilst such advocacy and survey work might be represented as expressions of escapism from the preoccupations of war, the advancement of concepts and techniques in nature conservation can be perceived as a contribution, albeit modest, to raising wartime morale. It provided something to fight for, as well as against. In a sense,

John Fryer's participation in attempts to reintroduce the large copper butterfly to the SPNR's Woodwalton Fen nature reserve in Huntingdonshire from 1927 onwards gave him first-hand insight into the opportunity and constraints for reserve management. Such knowledge and experience was skilfully deployed in discussions of the Cabinet's Scientific Advisory Committee and his own Agricultural Research Council in the mid-1940s.

arrangements for nature conservation might be seen as a further expression of the shift towards collectivism. Academic and voluntary bodies, and their sponsoring ministers, wanted more centralised direction of the management of the countryside. But these aspirations could not have been achieved without technical and managerial competence. As Cullingworth wrote, in his study of planning for post-war reconstruction, 'the more that political issues can be made into technical issues, the greater is the chance of achieving political success' (Cullingworth 1975). Through the political initiative of Reith and later ministers, and the administrative underpinning of Vincent, and then Nicholson at the Lord President's Office and Fryer in the Agricultural Research Council, openings were created for the extremely modest pre-war expertise and experience in reserves selection, administration and management to be developed into the political reality, as realised by the Royal Charter and relevant sections of the 1949 Act.

If the decision of the Cabinet's Reconstruction Committee had entirely unexpected repercussions for nature conservation, the further involvement of two persons, Sir John Fryer and E. Max Nicholson, was both fortuitous and far-reaching. Had it not been for them, the establishment of the Wild Life Service might well have been shelved. Both had the personal motivation, expertise and experience, and position in Government, to provide clear direction and firmness of resolve. Fryer had become Secretary of the Agricultural Research Council in July 1944. In a tribute published not many years later, Edelsten (1950–51) wrote of Fryer's extraordinary tact, wisdom and clear-thinking. Imperturbable, quiet, never ruffled or upset, he had the confidence of administrators, the Ministry, agricultural members of his Council, and research workers.

Max Nicholson was the most senior official of the Office of the Lord President of the Council. Nicholson later recalled how, as a child around 1911, he had become fixated with watching and trying to understand birds. The post-war slump forced him to leave school early, but a talent for writing made it possible to earn a living from nature writing. He had also begun to write on current affairs when Geoffrey Dawson, the editor of *The Times*, persuaded and assisted Nicholson to fulfil his ambition of going up to Oxford to read history in 1926, the year his first book, *Birds in England*, was published. Another title, *How Birds Live*, followed in 1927. He founded the Oxford University Exploration Club. After Nicholson had organised the first national bird census (of heronries) in 1928 and founded the Oxford Bird Census, plans were laid for similar team enquiries on a national basis. They led to the establishment of the British Trust for Ornithology (BTO) in 1932, together with the first university centre of its kind, the Edward Grey Institute for Ornithology. It was with Fryer that Nicholson negotiated its first grant. Greatly influenced by Charles Elton, his interests came to encompass ecology as well as ornithology.

Meanwhile, Nicholson found a living as assistant editor and leader writer of the *Weekend Review*. When Walter Elliot, Harold Macmillan and other politicians challenged columnists to do more than criticise government policy, Nicholson responded by drafting 'A national plan for Britain', which excited so much interest that it led to the formation of a socio-economic research group, Political and Economic Planning (PEP), a pioneering think-tank with Israel Sieff as its Chairman and Nicholson as Director. Draft plans followed for a national health service, education and much else. PEP provided Nicholson with abundant opportunity to meet distinguished figures in higher education and public affairs, including John Reith of the BBC, the scientist Sir Henry Tizard and, in the amenity movement, John Dower and Clough Williams-Ellis. At the outbreak of war, Nicholson took up the post of Controller of Literature in the Ministry of Information. He returned to PEP after only seven weeks. Cyril Hurcomb, another member of PEP (and an ornithologist) persuaded Nicholson, at the fifth attempt, to become again a wartime civil servant. Hurcomb had been successively Permanent Secretary of the Ministry of Transport since 1927 and Chairman of the Electricity Commissioners after 1938. It was as Director-General of the Ministry of Shipping that Hurcomb invited Nicholson to join him in March 1940. Nicholson became Head of Allocation of Tonnage on the trans-Atlantic convoys in January 1941 (Smith 1996).

The wartime post further exploited Nicholson's formidable powers of advocacy and management; in his liaison with the American shipping administration and attendance at the strategic conferences at Cairo, Quebec, Yalta and Potsdam, he also became familiarised with high-level official and inter-governmental business. As recounted in his later books (Nicholson 1970 and 1987), the binoculars were always to hand. Among the surviving personal papers of a secretary in the Ministry of War Transport is a carbon copy of Nicholson's list of birds seen among the devastated remains of Berlin during the Potsdam conference. The top copy had been passed to another attendee at the conference, Chief of the General Staff, Sir Alan Brooke. Julian Huxley invited Nicholson, as a leading ornithologist and close colleague, to join his Wild Life Conservation Special Committee (PRO, HLG 93, 1). Nicholson was shortly afterwards appointed by Herbert Morrison, as head of the Lord President's Office following the election of the Labour Government.

For Nicholson personally, and for ecology and conservation generally, this was, in his words, 'an astonishing stroke of luck'. From being out in the cold, far from the corridors of power, there was now the possibility of giving effect to what had been discussed and advocated for so long. He had been a leading figure in the Post-War Aims Group, which held its first meeting a month before war broke out. The subject of post-war recovery and planning particularly interested Labour members of the Wartime Coalition Government. Especially with a post-war Labour Government, there would be a chance to apply concepts and methods of organisation and planning (pioneered in his case through the BTO, PEP, and the allocation of cargoes in trans-Atlantic convoys) to the larger issues of public policy.

Nicholson was exceptionally well placed to exert influence. The stature of the post of Lord President of the Council had risen considerably during the war. As well as being responsible for a wide range of 'home front' duties, Herbert Morrison was President of the Committees of the Privy Council covering scientific research. In his memoirs, Morrison wrote 'it was my belief that science and the scientist had a real contribution to make to the well-being of our country in peace and war' (Morrison 1954). According to his biographers, Morrison

> relied very much on his professional advisers, and especially the passionate enthusiasm of Nicholson. Morrison's contribution, and it was not a minor one, was to rationalize the scientific machinery and to give scientific development the full backing of his own substantial political muscle (Donoughue and Jones 1973).

Herbert Morrison working on his papers at the Office of the Lord President, May 1946.

As Morrison's principal adviser, Nicholson was outstandingly well placed to promote nature conservation as one of his minister's 'scientific' responsibilities. In the knowledge that the Minister of Town and Country Planning was under considerable political pressure to establish a national parks commission, and that application for the necessary legislation would have to come before the (Cabinet) Lord President's Committee, Nicholson was able to insist on equally rapid progress in drawing up recommendations for nature conservation. Morrison would expect to receive recommendations as to how the reports of both the National Parks Committee and Huxley's Committee should be implemented at one and the same time.

Nicholson was able to ensure progress not only on the 'coat-tails' of the national parks movement but by making full use of his position as a member of the Huxley Committee and secretary of the Morrison's Scientific Advisory Committee to turn what could have become a procedural difficulty to the advantage of nature conservation. The Huxley Committee was unanimous, from its first meeting, that nature conservation should fall within the scientific, rather than the planning, sector of Government. Although its report was intended for the Minister of Town and Country Planning, Nicholson was able to indicate that the Scientific Advisory Committee was also considering the question. As well as his own influence, there was pressure from the British Ecological Society and, more importantly, a submission from E.J. Salisbury, in his capacity as Biological Secretary of the Royal Society of London. Developing advice he had given to the Conference on Nature Preservation in the early years of the war, Salisbury emphasised both the importance of nature reserves for biological research, and the extent to which their management would depend upon 'highly technical considerations', declaring that their preservation required 'expert guidance' (PRO, HLG 93, 48–9).

The Cabinet's Scientific Advisory Committee responded by inviting John Fryer, who was one of its members, to compile a note on 'Nature conservation and research on the British terrestrial flora and fauna'. He too emphasised the close interdependence of nature conservation and 'the scientific study of biology' (PRO, HLG 93, 48). That note in turn formed the basis of a report to Herbert Morrison, in July 1946, highlighting the benefits of 'a comprehensive national policy on biological conservation and control', both for pure science and for a wide range of practical problems in forestry, agriculture, land drainage, water supply, and freshwater fisheries. To be effective, such a programme required a series of national nature reserves; the fostering of research through an ecological research institute; and the creation of a service of fully qualified scientific officers to manage the reserves, act as a clearing house for information, and provide a general advisory service. In the knowledge that such proposals were being put to the Lord President, the Huxley Committee recommended in its own report that a biological service should be established, to be responsible for selecting, acquiring and managing nature reserves, and to carry out the survey and research work required. It would serve as a central bureau of information, operate an advisory service, and encourage educational activities. A series of ecological research institutes should also be set up, with one in Scotland and four in England and Wales (Minister of Town and Country Planning 1947b).

The relationship between the biological service and the institutes was not clearly defined. Although a close working relationship was sought, the Huxley Committee thought it would be wrong for the biological service 'to dictate the research to be undertaken'. From his experience as Director of the Oxford University's Bureau of Animal Population, Elton believed the most productive research groups were those where individuals were given 'the utmost freedom to try unpromising looking ideas', to engage in 'fool experiments', and to break away from the 'hardening traditions' of their group (Sheail 1989). Tansley had been a long-standing critic of what he perceived to be a trend towards totalitarianism in science. In his Herbert Spencer Lecture to the University of Oxford in 1942, on 'the values of science to humanity', he had again emphasised that 'the highest type of research, that which has been productive of the most fundamental discoveries, is essentially the work of individual minds, freely dealing with their chosen material' (Tansley 1942; Godwin 1977).

Whilst the close accord between the recommendations of the two Committees had gone a long way to securing the support of the Lord President and Minister of Town and Country Planning, there was continued anxiety over the position of Scotland. One of the advantages of making nature conservation a responsibility of the Lord President was that his powers extended to Scotland. The proposed Wild Life Service would in effect be a body for Great Britain. This was important because much wildlife interest was to be found in Scotland, but its record of survey and protection had so far been disappointing. Despite early assurances given to the NRIC that comparable surveys would be undertaken in Scotland, little had been accomplished. Although the wartime Secretary of State, Tom Johnston, had discussed the possibility of inviting Dower to carry out a survey of national-park areas in Scotland, a planning officer from the Department of Health, Arthur Geddes, had been appointed, working under the supervision of a

Committee of four Scotsmen. The Chairman was Sir J. Douglas Ramsay, formerly His Majesty's Commissioner to the Balmoral Estate and a member of the Scottish Council for National Parks. Following the appointment of the National Parks Committee for England and Wales in 1945, Douglas Ramsay was made Chairman of a Scottish National Parks Committee, but it was not until January 1946 that it established a special Scottish Wild Life Committee. With James Ritchie, the Professor of Natural History in the University of Edinburgh, as Chairman, it comprised J. Douglas Ramsay and Frank Fraser Darling from the main Committee, together with J.R. Matthews, John Berry and Murray MacGregor. A report was published with that of the main Committee in 1947 (Secretary of State 1947). There was, however, so much detailed survey work to be undertaken that a detailed report, containing lists of proposed national nature reserves, did not appear until March 1949. It recommended 24 national nature reserves and 4 national park reserves (Secretary of State for Scotland 1949).

Not only was there delay but, right from the beginning, the Ritchie Committee displayed 'a disturbing tendency' to press for an independent Scottish Wild Life Service. The Permanent Secretary in the Scottish Office, Sir David Milne, obtained the Secretary of State's consent to make what Nicholson described as a 'helpful intervention'. He left Ritchie 'fully seized' of the need for ecological research to be coordinated on a Great Britain basis. Further pressure was applied when the two Committees met in April 1947. Members of the Huxley Committee warned of the number of potential nature reserves that might be destroyed by the time a separate Scottish body was formed. There was dissension within the Scottish Committees themselves. Where the Douglas Ramsay Committee assumed that nature conservation would be one of the responsibilities of a Scottish National Parks Commission, the Ritchie Committee insisted that nature conservation should be given independent status.

It may have been the dissenting voice of Frank Fraser Darling that decided the matter. A naturalist and author of distinction, his pre-war writings on the life and character of the Highlands and Islands had been followed in 1941 by *Island Years*, a further first-hand account. The wartime Secretary of State, Tom Johnston, saw in these works a new evangelism that was so badly needed in developing the natural resources of the region (Morton Boyd 1986). A meeting in June 1942 led to his eventually being commissioned to undertake a West Highland survey. His membership of the Ritchie Committee, and the chance to meet members of the Huxley Committee, led him to write, in a letter of July 1946,

> for once I feel that this kind of committee stuff is important. We are fashioning something new and which should have lasting effect, both for the wild life and civilisation … it is really grand to work with a bunch of men who, though in middle or later life, feel the enthusiasm and urgency which youth feels. The eagerness coupled with the intellectual capacity of middle age, should get something done (Morton Boyd 1986, 197–8).

In all these deliberations, Fraser Darling strongly opposed any separation from a Great Britain nature-conservation body. He felt that it was only by being part of a larger Wild Life Service that Scotland would be able to keep abreast of ecological research.

The Ritchie Committee conceded, on the condition that the Scottish part, based in Edinburgh, would have a greater degree of autonomy. Only by doing so would the Service have the whole-hearted support of the Scottish people (Secretary of State 1947). In a letter to Fraser Darling, in November 1947, Nicholson confirmed that 'much greater relative weight' would be given to Scotland.

THE CHARTER AND THE ACT

As the country strove to recover from one war and prepare for the possibility of another, the Government was beset with many critical issues. Although Herbert Morrison might have met and talked freely with Max Nicholson almost every weekday, what caused him to spare even a second thought for nature conservation?

A Londoner born and bred, Morrison claimed no knowledge of nature. He had, however, become Leader of the London County Council in 1934 and, for the remainder of the decade, applied his organising genius to a range of programmes that included the pioneering concept of a Green Belt and the acquisition of tracts of countryside for that purpose (Cherry 1982). A nature-conservation body, of the kind put forward by the Huxley Committee and his own Scientific Advisory Committee, offered outstanding opportunity for bringing peacetime science to bear on a critical realm of town and country planning and agricultural policy. As with the Green Belt, Morrison would emerge as a pioneer. It would be a political gesture that owed everything to his own ministerial domain.

In April 1948, Morrison submitted the proposals to his own Lord President's (Cabinet) Committee. In drafts prepared by Nicholson, he wrote that he was impressed by 'the broad unanimity reached by successive bodies of experts'. These proposals could be justified by the fact that

> the Government is constantly taking action liable permanently to affect the fauna, flora and even the geography of the country without having at its disposal any channel of authoritative scientific advice about the probable results, such as is available in all other fields of natural science (PRO, CAB 132, 9 and 10).

The Cabinet Committee approved the recommendations in principle. In a letter, Nicholson wrote of Tansley's 'wise and patient work' at last bearing fruit. Action could now begin (PRO, FT 3, 4; Sheail 1995c).

In February 1949 Morrison announced to parliament that the nature conservation board and biological service, as recommended by the Huxley Committee, would be subsumed into a single body, called by the 'more convenient title' of the Nature Conservancy (Parliamentary Debates, Commons, 461, 104–6). As Nicholson explained in a letter to the Scottish Office, the word 'board' had to be dropped to avoid giving the impression that another research council or 'government authority' was being formed (Scottish Record Office, DD12, 875). Nicholson later claimed Morrison came up with the name 'Nature Conservancy' in his presence. A letter written by Tansley, as the

Chairman-designate of the new body, conveys a different impression. As he told Diver in December 1948, he had always disliked the term 'Biological Service'. It was too wide in the sense of including biologists with no special interest in nature conservation. It was also too restrictive in excluding geology and physiography. The word 'Nature' had to be in the title, for that was what the new body was all about. And, as Tansley discovered, the Oxford Dictionary defined the word 'conservancy' as meaning 'official conservation', which again was 'exactly our object'. Given the sensitivities of 'board', 'council' or any other corporate word, Tansley wondered whether the new body should not be simply called the 'Nature Conservancy' (PRO, FT3, 4). Whether Morrison or Tansley first or together alighted on the title, what really mattered was Morrison's dislike of the word 'board' for its bureaucratic associations. He wanted to strike a fresh note.

Morrison's immense authority as Deputy Prime Minister, and manager of all parliamentary business, was of inestimable value in smoothing the way. Considerable demands were nevertheless placed on Fryer and Nicholson in turning the Cabinet Committee's approval in principle into a reality. Both men had to persuade those who could so easily have raised objection that appointing a scientific body of such modest status and material needs posed no conceivable threat to their respective fields of responsibility. Given Morrison's role as senior minister in domestic affairs (the Minister of Town and Country Planning was not in the Cabinet), Nicholson was well placed to ensure that nature conservation avoided becoming embroiled in the increasingly contentious issues concerning the balance of power between a national parks commission and local authorities, and between central and local government. Although determined to preserve and extend their responsibilities for planning, both the local authorities and the Ministry of Town and Country Planning were relieved to learn that the new and ill-defined responsibilities for nature conservation could be left to others (Sheail 1996a).

As the Secretary of the Agricultural Research Council, John Fryer was also ideally placed to remove the anxieties of his own Council and the Royal Society of London that there would be duplication of responsibility and even competition for highly skilled staff. To Fryer, the obvious course was to place the Nature Conservancy, if only temporarily, under the aegis of his Council. At a meeting in January 1948, concern was expressed lest the Conservancy's different perspective on land use might prejudice the 'absolutely vital' relationship which the Agricultural Research Council had developed with the Ministry of Agriculture. In dismissing such fears, Nicholson emphasised that the Huxley Committee had regarded the establishment of 'the best and closest relationships with the Agriculture Departments' as an absolute priority. As further 'protection against future embarrassments', Nicholson approached the Permanent Secretary of the Ministry, Sir Donald Vandepeer, and secured from him a letter formally encouraging the Council to accept sponsorship of nature conservation. Further assured that there would be extra resources to meet the additional responsibility, the Council somewhat grudgingly approved what its Secretary had played so large a part in bringing about (PRO, T 223, 258). Fryer died suddenly in November 1948.

The astuteness with which Nicholson and Fryer pressed their case for a 'scientific' Wild Life Service was further illustrated by discussion with Treasury officials. If they had expounded on the wider amenity, recreational, educational and cultural value of reserves which they both favoured, officials might have concluded that nature conservation should be left in the planning sector of Government, or indeed transferred to the Ministry of Education. It suited them, therefore, to keep attention firmly fixed on the scientific dimension. In doing so, they secured the best of both worlds. On the one hand, the Economics Section of the Treasury acknowledged the value (for the Government) of having better warning of the problems likely to arise from 'the degree and direction of man's interference with nature'. On the other hand, the Treasury section was unable to place any monetary value on the savings that might accrue from preventing wild species from becoming extinct, or the implications of such losses for crop and livestock production. As one official remarked, if 'the scientists say the job ought to be done, then we should not oppose it'. Although reluctant 'to see new things started' at a time when the economy was in such a parlous state, the Permanent Secretary, Sir Edward Bridges, conceded. The Chancellor of the Exchequer was advised that he might safely approve the appointment of the Nature Conservancy. It filled 'a real gap in the Government's scientific activities, which should not involve any excessive continuing financial burden' (PRO, T 223, 258–9).

Not only was there consensus as to its need, but a legal technicality meant that the Conservancy secured an independent status. Cyril Diver wrote later of being 'dragged very reluctantly out of my job in the House of Commons' to become, in November 1948, Director-General (designate) of the new body (PRO, HLG 102, 56). As things stood, he found that the Royal Charter to be given to the new body would in effect be a supplementary charter to that held by the Agricultural Research Council. It meant, for example, that all agreement, dedication and guardianship schemes for the nature reserves would have to be made in the name of the Agricultural Research Council. As he informed Nicholson, that 'would be unsatisfactory to them and to us' (PRO, FT 3, 1). But even if that difficulty could be resolved, the new body would have to be equipped with statutory powers to acquire and hold land by compulsion, if necessary. Such powers could only be granted to a wholly independent body.

Time was of the essence. The obvious way to confer such powers was to make them part of the National Parks and Access to the Countryside Bill. This opened up the possibility of making the Nature Conservancy a statutory body, like the National Parks Commission. But that would have destroyed any affinity and opportunity for a close working relationship with the Agricultural Research Council. As a Treasury official remarked, a 'less complicated vehicle' was needed. This was achieved by awarding the Conservancy the requisite statutory powers, together with a separate Royal Charter, that placed it at Ministerial level under an enlarged Committee of the Privy Council for the Agricultural Research Council and Nature Conservancy (PRO, T 223, 259). By May 1949, all pretence of the Conservancy being part of the Agricultural Research Council was dropped. As Morrison informed other ministers, it was 'on a similar footing to the Medical and Agricultural Research Councils, but of course on a smaller scale'. He sought their goodwill in assisting the Conservancy in its 'difficult and important task' (PRO, HLG 102, 56).

The Royal Charter summarised the purpose of the Conservancy as to provide scientific advice on the conservation and control of the natural flora and fauna of Great Britain; to establish maintain and manage nature reserves in Great Britain, including the maintenance of physical features of scientific interest; and to organise and develop the research and scientific services related thereto.

As Diver emphasised in August 1949, nature conservation was not intended to be a purely negative activity. Even where some prohibition was required, the overriding intention was positive management on scientific lines either by the Conservancy's officers or by landowners acting on their advice (PRO, FT 3, 1).

Throughout this period, close rapport had been maintained among those who had served on the Huxley Committee through their being made into a Panel of Scientific Advisers. As its Chairman, Tansley sought to ensure that the lists of proposed national nature reserves were widely circulated within the Ministry of Town and Country Planning, and that the Panel received due warning of any threat to them. Tansley himself was anxious, in November 1947, about Tregaron Bog: 'literally the *only* unspoiled bog left in England and Wales', it should be 'fought for to the last ditch'. In August 1948, Diver brought to the Panel's attention the risks to Wicken Fen posed by a sewerage scheme being planned by the Newmarket Rural District Council. In April 1949, Miriam Rothschild pressed for assistance to prevent further drainage of farmland surrounding the nature reserve acquired by her father at Woodwalton Fen in Huntingdonshire.

'Nature Conservancy' was the name given to both the organisation and its governing body. The term 'Nature Conservancy members' will be adopted in this book, to distinguish the latter. As founder-Chairman, Tansley was joined by four botanists (J.R. Matthews, R.C. McLean, H. Godwin and W.H. Pearsall), two zoologists (Elton and Ford), two ornithologists (N.B. Kinnear and Nicholson), a geologist (Trueman), coastal physiographer (Steers), and Sir William Taylor. As well as including most members of the expert Panel, the choice also included, in a personal capacity, persons associated with the Natural History Museum (Kinnear), University Grants Committee (Trueman was its Chairman), the Forestry Commission (Taylor was a Commissioner) and the Lord President's Office (Nicholson). Two members were nominated by the Scottish Secretary. A further personal intervention by Morrison meant that three Members of Parliament were appointed. They would 'watch the public interest and keep an eye on the experts' (PRO, FT 3, 4). As Nicholson later emphasised, this was a decision of crucial importance. Chosen as a representative of the three main parties, each quickly developed a sense of belonging to the Conservancy. Their presence did much to deter 'irresponsible' interference on the part of other Members. Morrison himself handed over the Royal Charter at a brief ceremony at 11 Downing Street, on 19 May 1949.

Nicholson had taken 'a preliminary look' at how powers might be devolved to Scotland in June 1948. Morrison wanted the Conservancy to be an example of how a Great Britain Service could be administered partly from Scotland. The person appointed as Chairman of the Conservancy's Scottish Committee had to look after the Scottish angle and help to build up the organisation as a whole. Poor health ruled out Ritchie. The obvious choice was James R. Matthews, the Vice-Chairman of Ritchie's official committee and

Professor of Botany at Aberdeen. Of the candidates for the post of Director for Scotland at the Scottish headquarters in Edinburgh, John Berry was easily the best. He held a senior post in the North of Scotland Hydro-Electric Board and, as well as having considerable experience of fisheries and water-pollution research, was also Chairman of the Scottish Ornithologists' Club. A landowner himself, familiar with the problems and outlook of the Scottish laird and sportsman, very vigorous and resourceful, he was a good mixer and team-worker. As Nicholson observed, he seemed to have abnormally few critics as 'figures in Scottish public life go' (PRO, CAB 124, 2626).

Again, through Morrison's chairmanship of the relevant Cabinet Committee, Nicholson was in a position both to monitor and give instruction to the parliamentary draughtsman on the National Parks and Access to the Countryside Bill. The clauses conferring powers on the Conservancy to designate National Nature Reserves and Local Nature Reserves, to enact powers of compulsory acquisition, and to schedule Sites of Special Scientific Interest, formed the most minor of the three components of the Bill. In a measure that 'bristled with contentious points' affecting public rights of way and access to open countryside, the apparently modest wildlife clauses required by a scientific body aroused very little comment during the Bill's passage through parliament. Whereas more than one-tenth of England and Wales was expected to be designated as national parks, the proposed series of National Nature Reserves was intended to cover only about 70,000 acres (28,000 hectares), most of which was either of little economic value or already owned by the State or preservationist bodies. The cost of acquiring the land was estimated to be only £500,000.

In a sense, the low profile given to nature conservation in the Bill conveyed a false sense of consensus among those with an interest in the countryside. Buried within the documentation were already signs of the friction that might arise. As early as May 1945, Sir William Taylor (writing from a forestry perspective) warned that the scheduling of areas of wildlife importance would either be so weak as to be ineffective, or it would prevent afforestation and land reclamation, and thereby promote a tremendous clash between naturalists and other land-users (Sheail 1976, 160).

THE TREASURY VIEW

The years following 1949 might be seen as the point when the almost heroic struggles of a very small handful of persons gave way to the largely impersonal, corporate endeavour represented by the Nature Conservancy and Government more generally. Beyond applying directly to the Treasury for grant aid, and scientific briefings given to the Lord President of the Council, it might be thought that the Conservancy enjoyed considerable autonomy. The archives convey a very different story; they show how the Conservancy was required to operate in an essentially hostile environment. This Section focuses on the Treasury's attitude towards the Conservancy; the next Section focuses on the Lord President of the Council. Particular attention is drawn to the continued importance of individual personalities, whether exerting influence as politicians, civil servants, members or officers of the Conservancy.

The report of the Comptroller and Auditor General for 1952 on Grants for science and the arts described how the growth of the Conservancy had been limited to 'the bare essentials' of a 'nucleus' staff of ecologists, with modest provision for the training of young scientists, two institutes for fundamental research, and 'salvage operations' whenever proposed nature reserves were threatened. The enactment of the National Parks and Access to the Countryside Bill called for a revision of the estimate for the first year's grant-in-aid. It was increased from £40,000 to a round figure of £100,000 for 1949–50. An even larger sum of £152,000 was approved for the year 1950–51, the Treasury concluding that, having agreed with some misgiving to the establishment of the Conservancy, some growth had to be allowed or it would never get into its stride (PRO, T 223, 353).

Whilst the impression gained from the published record is of a somewhat impersonal decision-making institution called the Treasury, the most worrying feature for the Conservancy was not so much the straitened economic circumstances but the evident hostility expressed, albeit in confidential discussion, by senior personnel within the Treasury. Diver protested not simply at the removal of the £7,000 identified in the revised estimate for purchasing reserves, but the assertion that the Treasury did 'not view land purchase with favour'. Although the Conservancy was keen to acquire as much land as possible by gift, lease or a Nature Reserve Agreement, Diver argued that it must be able to buy, where necessary, the freehold of the property; it would otherwise be powerless to prevent 'first class places going down the drain'. Not only had ministers accepted that need, but a scrutiny of the Rothschild lists prepared during the First World War was instructive, if depressing, in revealing how many 'areas worthy of protection' had already been lost.

The Conservancy's proposals for long-term research fared no better. Far from congratulating the Conservancy's Scientific Policy Committee for contemplated studies of water-resource management and the impacts of deforestation and hill and downland grazing, Sir Edward Bridges wondered whether the greater part could be 'conserved in the frigidarium'. Although 'all very entertaining', and containing 'some priceless utterances', the Conservancy should concentrate on 'the more urgent things of less remote benefit'. There was an obvious danger of the Conservancy over-extending itself. As one of the more obvious bodies to be covered by the Government's 'go-slow' policy, it would have little scope for growth. As well as the time needed to build up a trained staff, the Conservancy had to avoid 'treading on the toes of established experts' (PRO, T 223, 353).

The gravest threat to the Conservancy's continued existence probably occurred under the Labour Government that had created it. Although its annual grant-in-aid was very small in Treasury terms, a Third Secretary, Sir Edward Playfair, wrote, in February 1951, that the Conservancy was constantly cited in discussions with ministers as an example of the kind of thing which should be cut. He accordingly referred its estimate of £234,336 for 1951–52 to 'higher authority'. The immediate response was a demand that the Conservancy should follow the example of the Agricultural Research Council in stabilising expenditure. But, as Playfair pointed out, the Conservancy was 'a new show'. Its name, 'the Nature Conservancy', gave the impression of its being far 'more trivial and useless' than in fact it was. Its purpose was not so much to protect nature for its own sake, but to develop an institute of biological and ecological research. Although placed on 'a care and maintenance' basis, cuts in capital expenditure would be short-sighted. Once the 'bits of land' required as nature reserves were used for other purposes, that 'particular balance of nature' would be lost forever. Conservancy representatives were told they would have to wait still longer for their first research institutes. Playfair recounted however that, after the meeting, 'our hearts burst'. They recommended approval of the modest sum of £20,000 required to purchase the two houses sought, one in the Lake District at Merlewood, and the other on the South Coast at Furzebrook, in the Isle of Purbeck (PRO, T 223, 353).

The approval of the Chancellor of the Exchequer, Hugh Gaitskell, was still needed. Not only did he regard the Conservancy as 'an obvious head to strike', but the 'Budget situation' was so bad that even a 'standstill' in its estimate should only be allowed if it proved impossible to 'suspend' its activities altogether. Having talked to Nicholson, Playfair successfully argued that so drastic a cut would not only fail to make significant savings, but it would mean the permanent demise of the Conservancy. It would waste the valuable scientific equipment already bought. Compensation would have to be paid for the dismissal of everyone. The 'moral effect' would be so 'disheartening' as to make it extremely difficult, if not impossible, to recruit new and suitable staff at a later date (PRO, T 223, 353).

The respite was likely to be brief. There were obvious uncertainties following the election of a Conservative Government in October 1951. It was bound to scrutinise the bodies appointed under the 'corporatist' philosophy of Labour Ministers. Not only did the Conservancy represent- in some quarters- a further intrusion of the State into the ownership and management of land, but the potential of its powers, largely overlooked during the promotion of the National Parks and Access to the Countryside Bill, was now becoming clear. Not only did 'the gravity of the times' provide abundant pretext for curbing, if not removing, these powers but, in some Treasury eyes, the Conservancy had

The *Annual Report* covering the period 1950-51 records how a sub-committee of the Conservancy's Scientific Policy Committee concluded that, of the properties available in the southern part of the Lake District, **Merlewood** should be the Conservancy's first research station. Equipment of the main laboratories was completed by January 1954.

Adaptation of the building for the Conservancy's second research station, at **Furzebrook** in Dorset, was completed in April 1954.
The staff in September of that year comprised Mike Brian (Acting Director), Norman Moore (Senior Scientific Officer) and Olive Balme and Derek Ranwell (Scientific Officers), together with a laboratory steward and secretary.

hardly helped itself. It appeared to have learnt nothing. In the words of one official:

> I admire the spirit that goes marching on regardless of what is happening about one, but when times are hard there are limits to what one can afford to spend even on the younger members of the family.

Regardless of the wisdom of seeking to hold the Government to the commitments made at the time of the Conservancy's inception, the credibility of making such 'formidable demands' was undermined by the Conservancy's failure to spend what it received (PRO, T 223, 353). Whilst it was admittedly difficult to forecast precisely when land might be acquired or highly-specialised staff appointed, an underspend of £15,000 on current expenditure and £75,000 on land and buildings in 1950–51 did little to attract the praise that Diver had expected from the Treasury. Frederick Bath, the Treasury official on secondment to the Conservancy as its Administrative Officer, complained to the Conservancy's Deputy Chairman, William Pearsall, in January 1950 of a lack of 'agreed aims of a practical nature on policy, priority and pace of actions'. The staff could not see the wood for the trees (Sheail 1987, 188–9). The Conservancy's failure even to publish a statutory Annual Report appeared symptomatic of deeper problems.

Only one person seemed to have the calibre required to give the Conservancy both the credibility and assertiveness needed to win the respect and, therefore, resources required of Government. Nicholson was still only 48 and had already reached the level of a Deputy Secretary. Tansley and Pearsall pressed him to succeed Diver as Director-General. As Nicholson remarked later, it seemed far more exciting than remaining at the core of 'a do-nothing government', with all its attendant constraints. Before taking up his new appointment, Nicholson was seconded to the United Nations to lead a study of resource development in Baluchistan. There he contracted polio and was extremely ill for three months. Only through sheer will-power was he able again to walk and take up his new post in December 1952. Tansley retired a month later as the Conservancy's first

Arthur B. Duncan in February 1953, immediately after his appointment as Chairman of the Conservancy. Recording his retirement in 1961, the *Annual Report* of that year paid tribute to his wise guidance, close personal interest in the staff, and mastery of so many aspects of their work.

Chairman. He was replaced by Arthur B. Duncan, a founder-member of the Scottish Committee, a sheep farmer and forester, President of the Galloway Cattle Society, and an acknowledged expert in ornithology and certain invertebrate groups.

At officer level in the Treasury, three possibilities for the future of the Conservancy were discussed during the early part of 1952. The best option was to retain the Conservancy on 'a modest care and maintenance basis', with no substantial expansion for some years. Nicholson would be expected to support such a policy. As Playfair remarked, Nicholson was not only 'a zealot for birds, but also for economy once he has it in mind'. Alternatively, the Conservancy might be put on 'a caretaker basis', in which case there would be scarcely a role for him. Only the reserves would be kept going; the scientific staff would be sacked. Having again itemised the Conservancy's responsibilities for research and for training ecologists, for employment most obviously in the Commonwealth, there appeared to be no halfway house between the present 'care and maintenance' model and what would be, in effect, abolition. Apart from the mortal effect in terms of the Conservancy's standing in scientific circles, less than £50,000 per annum would be saved by a 'caretaker' regime. Although officials set their minds against abolition, Playfair warned that ministers might nevertheless be forced to suspend its operations for the three years required to meet the costs of the Defence Programme. Nicholson also recognised the danger of 'more violent economies', but emphasised that the value of a body like the Conservancy far exceeded the amount of money Government spent on it. A lot was achieved through the support of local authorities and other bodies, given free of charge (PRO, T 223, 353).

In his autobiography, John Boyd-Carpenter described how, on being appointed to his first ministerial post, as Financial Secretary to the Treasury, his 'riding orders were to cut'. The only way the new Conservative Government could make the kind of cuts that would lead to lower taxation was by eliminating as many activities as possible and, therefore, the need for the organisations that performed them. Even where the aim was admirable, the test of any activity was whether its value exceeded that of leaving the money 'to fructify in the pockets of the people'. A good example was the Crown Film Unit, whose films were of such high artistic quality that no commercial producer could afford to make them. As Boyd-Carpenter (1980) remarked, those with a high regard for film-making attacked his decision to close the Unit as vandalism. Given his boast that there were many other instances of that kind, the Conservancy was perhaps lucky to escape so lightly. To the Treasury recommendation that its grant-in-aid should be set at £158,000 for the year 1952–53, Sir Edward Bridges appended his own proviso, that

> we maintain a really tough attitude about new acquisitions and only sanction purchases if this is really essential to prevent the loss to science of some area of great value.

Boyd-Carpenter went a step further and required the provision for 'new acquisitions' of £12,500 to be struck out. In the unlikely event of the Treasury's being convinced that 'the universe would come to an end if they didn't acquire some new Elysium', a supplementary Estimate could be made. The Conservancy was informed that any new acquisition would require the personal approval of the Financial Secretary. That would only be given where 'the land is unique, is up for sale, and will be lost for good if it is not bought now' (PRO, T 223, 353).

There was even greater political prejudice by the time the Conservancy's estimate of 1953–54 was considered. Major Niall Macpherson had forwarded, with evident enthusiasm, a letter received from Professor Frank Balfour Browne, highly critical of the Conservancy's activities. Nicholson had briefly considered Balfour Browne as founder-Chairman of the Scottish Committee. He had, however, been retired for some years, his research was very specialised, and he lacked both the contacts and background required (PRO, CAB 124, 2626). Balfour Browne wrote that the Conservancy, as a 'Socialist creation', continued to waste public funds by employing a rather large staff to control the activities of specimen-collectors, and protested if any area containing rarities appeared threatened. Boyd-Carpenter asked for the letter to be placed 'at the top of the Estimates' for the forthcoming year. It did nothing to change his view of the Conservancy as 'a sort of advanced form of nature study'. Although Treasury officials believed Nicholson had achieved considerable economy in slimming the Conservancy's estimate to £170,000, Boyd-Carpenter insisted on having it cut to £159,000 (PRO, T 223 353).

Playfair's successor at the Treasury, Sir James Crombie, asked Nicholson for a concise statement setting out the practical, as opposed to the purely scientific, aspects of the Conservancy's work. The document of December 1953 described how its programmes to advance scientific knowledge were already providing 'substantial economic results as a by-product'. At the Moor House field station in the Westmorland Pennines the Conservancy was working with: the Tees Valley Water Board in studying the role of peat as a sponge for conserving water supplies; the Forestry Commission and agricultural interests in seeking ways of re-establishing woodland at such an altitude; the Electrical Research Association in assessing the scope for installing windmills; and Durham university in the training of post-graduate students. At the Anancaun field station of the Beinn Eighe National Nature Reserve, attempts were being made to rehabilitate the native Caledonian Forest, with experimental fences being erected for the first time to assess the impact of grazing and browsing by deer and sheep. Long-term experiments had been established with the Forestry Commission close to the new Merlewood research station.

Following the Chancellor's letter of November 1953, seeking 'all possible "major economies" in departmental expenditure' the intervention of the Lord President of the Council himself was required for the Conservancy to stand any chance of its estimate being accepted. Known to his friends as 'Bobbety', Lord Salisbury was a High Tory, Lord President of the Council and Leader of the House of Lords and, at times, acting Foreign Secretary (Colville 1981, 176–8). In a letter, he assured the Chancellor that a substantially-larger estimate of £250,000 was needed for 1953–54 if the Conservancy was to fulfil obligations placed upon it. Even that sum was a good deal lower than what was spent by various European countries and North America. Such was the 'disheartening' rate of loss of 'scientific sites' to airfields and housing estates, there would be few left within a decade or so.

In recommending that the Conservancy should be given the same Vote as the previous year, Boyd-Carpenter wrote that 'it must be very amusing to operate' but contributed nothing to the national economy. He rejected out-of-hand the provision made, and consent sought, for the removal of the London headquarters to Belgrave Square. However unsuitable the present premises, there was bound to be criticism of moving to such an expensive part of London. The Ministry of Works supported the Conservancy's view that nothing cheaper could be found in central London. When Boyd-Carpenter pressed for a place in the countryside, or a New Town, officials warned that the Lord President was certain to object to such a precedent being established for a research council. Nicholson wrote that the Conservancy had to keep in constant touch with the learned societies and other organisations, on whose assistance and goodwill it so heavily depended. Although officials accepted the need for the Conservancy to be accommodated in London, Boyd-Carpenter continued to insist, in a minute to the Chancellor of the Exchequer, R.A. Butler, that there was 'no real reason for providing them with accommodation of so sumptuous a nature in so expensive a district' (PRO, T 223, 355).

Turning to the estimate as a whole, Boyd-Carpenter warned that any increase would set a bad example to others. Butler's response was to minute that the Financial Secretary was 'right to snarl'. He was, however, 'keen on this Service'. Citing the introductory chapter of G.M. Trevelyan's *History of England*, Butler wrote, 'everyone is destroying Nature ... a reasonable defence was to be tolerated'. The move to Belgrave Square was a good idea. The limits of Butler's tolerance were, however, made clear in a letter to Lord Salisbury, of December 1953, in which he wrote, 'I very much sympathise with the work of the Conservancy'. It was impossible, however, in the present financial climate, to exceed an estimate of £168,000, with the balance of £30,000 from the current financial year being used to purchase and adapt the Belgrave Square premises. As Butler pointed out, very few services had obtained even the 25 per cent increase allowed to the Conservancy. Salisbury wrote of his disappointment that all but insignificant works would have to be further postponed on the reserves and research stations. The Conservancy moved into Belgrave Square in April 1954 (PRO, T 223, 355).

The financial outlook appeared even graver after the Chancellor's warning in April 1954 of a substantial budgetary deficit for 1955–56, and the appointment of a Cabinet Committee under Viscount Swinton to secure a reduction of £100 million in civil expenditure. Lord Salisbury supported Nicholson in warning that proposed cuts of 5 per cent and even 10 per cent would simply postpone the anticipated return on investment already made in advancing ecological knowledge. The Conservancy had already reduced the number of post-graduate studentships from 12 to 8 (PRO, CAB 124, 2594). It was clear, however, that Salisbury would either have to accept a cut of £50,000 from the Conservancy's estimate or go before the Committee to defend the full estimate of £250,000. Although very unhappy, Salisbury wrote that there was no alternative but to concede. At a time when so much productive research was being severely cut, the expenditure of large sums on the preservation of rare birds and butterflies could hardly be described as essential. The Conservancy should cut out altogether some branch of its activities. However painful, this would leave adequate funds, even on a reduced budget, for running the rest adequately. Nicholson's response was to protest that Government departments were constantly wanting the Conservancy to take on more tasks (PRO, CAB 124, 2594).

THE LORD PRESIDENT OF THE COUNCIL

The powers of ministers over the Conservancy were ill-defined. The only statutory requirement was that the Conservancy should present an annual report to the Lord President of the Council. The relationship was otherwise determined by the Lord President acting as Chairman to the Privy Council Committee which, in practice, never met. The Secretary of State for Scotland was simply required to approve the appointment of the Conservancy's Scottish Committee (PRO, CAB 124, 1600). Whereas the Conservancy's Chairman and Director-General met the Lord President at regular intervals, even that degree of contact was denied the Scottish Secretary.

Far from implying little responsibility for the Conservancy on the part of ministers, such a loosely-defined relationship caused the Lord President to be even more anxious as to his vulnerability to parliamentary and public criticism. Such anxieties became especially pressing during the enquiry into, and repercussions of, the Crichel Down case. The Minister of Agriculture resigned following the public outcry over the high-handedness of his officials in dealing with the landowner (Nicolson 1986). This long-drawn out, but highly significant, episode further illustrated how nature reserves were something of a mixed blessing in the political climate of the 1950s. On the one hand, they were a key element in attracting public support for nature conservation: in terms of public understanding, they crystallised and gave tangible expression to all that the Conservancy strove to achieve. As Ratcliffe (1977a) wrote later, they were to many people 'the cornerstone of the whole movement'. On the other hand, it was precisely because they were such an obvious manifestation of the conservationists' increasing stake in the countryside that they gave rise to the most fundamental appraisal of the Conservancy. Paradoxically, it was Nicholson's success in putting the Conservancy onto a more rigorous administrative footing that caused Lord Salisbury to voice such misgivings.

Not only was it a priority for the Conservancy to make up the backlog of statutory reporting to parliament but, as an historian by training, Nicholson saw the *Annual Report* not so much as a chore, but as a chance to put on record both the Conservancy's achievement and aspirations. A combined report for the period up to 30 September 1952 was published in December 1953, together with another covering the following reporting year. From reading a draft of the report for the year ending 30 September 1955, Lord Salisbury learned that the number of reserves in that year had almost doubled to 35, covering an aggregate area of 79,035 acres (31,900 hectares), and that it was the Conservancy's intention to publish, as an appendix, a list of 99 Proposed National Nature Reserves. Salisbury described how, when looking through the list, he realised for the first time the extent to which much of the land was sought for its ecological character and value for scientific research rather than because it contained rare species. Whilst the acquisition of representative examples of plant and animal life was fully satisfactory from the scientific point of view, the programme also had to be considered from a wider angle, such as the impact on forestry. Unless some rarity was at stake, would it be wise to freeze the present pattern of use by imposing permanent restrictions over large areas (PRO, T 223, 292)?

Salisbury wrote that it was 'desirable' for Ministers to be aware of the size of the programme and, less explicitly, to consider whether it was too ambitious. Did the Conservancy really need all the land identified? As he remarked, there was already the discernible 'beginnings of an agitation' among Conservative backbenchers. The draft appendix was not only of such 'enormous and quite tactless length' but it might easily reduce the market value of such sites. There would be justifiable alarm at the prospect of the Conservancy 'spattering' the whole of the UK with 'living museums'.

Once again, a crucial role in the Conservancy's defence was played by officials with whom Nicholson had worked closely whilst at the Lord President's Office. Playfair wrote of his high regard for the quality of the Conservancy's work; he believed the Lord President's anxieties amounted to 'a storm in a teacup' caused by its lack of tact in dealing with a small number of landowners. A Conservancy officer had made a clumsy attempt to schedule part of the property of a backbench Conservative member, Major John Morrison, as a Site of Special Scientific Interest. As well as writing an angry letter to Lord Salisbury, Morrison threatened to send another to the Prime Minister, protesting that it was 'high time the rights of the ordinary citizen were respected'.

According to Playfair, Salisbury's initial intention was to summon a meeting where, like Cronos, he would 'devour his own child'. Somewhat 'mollified' by a 'useful talk' with Nicholson, which had been arranged by his officials, Salisbury acceded to what Playfair described as a more leisured and sensible course. The 'enormous appendix' was to be 'suppressed', and a meeting of Ministers would be convened to consider the Conservancy's policy on nature reserves. A memorandum was drawn up, the first 22 paragraphs of which were extracted from an even longer paper previously prepared by Nicholson. The last three paragraphs were written by Salisbury.

Although the memorandum called for 'no particular course of action', it provided Playfair with a pretext for further special pleading. The Conservancy had been forced to carry out its 'rather difficult nation-wide survey' work on a shoe-string. The Government's various economy drives had frustrated every attempt to build up staff, laboratories or holdings of land. The name 'Nature Conservancy' had not only given rise to infinite misconceptions as to its purpose but also had the capacity to irritate people, and none more so than John Boyd-Carpenter who, as First Secretary to the Treasury for the first three years of the Conservative Government, had become the Conservancy's 'fervent' enemy. As Playfair minuted, with unusual frankness for a Departmental file, he had caused the rate of growth to be held well below the level that a new organisation would find tolerable. From the visits Playfair had made with another Treasury official, Geoffrey M. Wilson, to the various laboratories and reserves, he believed the Conservancy should now be given 'a hearty vote of confidence', as 'a cheap and well-run part of the national machinery of scientific research'. The work would greatly extend basic knowledge of 'marginal' land and resources, and might ultimately have an economic application. In Playfair's opinion there were bound to be difficulties in dealing with landowners, who naturally resented any restriction imposed on their activities. On the evidence of Major Morrison, the Conservancy had compounded its problems through tactlessness and a tendency to bite off more than it could chew. It simply lacked staff of sufficient standing to handle the delicate negotiations required.

Startopsend reservoir, 1955.
The variety of NNRs is exemplified by the Tring Reservoirs, Hertfordshire and Buckinghamshire, nominated by the Huxley Committee and leased in 1955. Built in the early nineteenth century to serve the Grand Junction Canal on former marshland, they were important sites for breeding and migratory birds and for their relict marshland plants and animals.

There were signs too that Lord Salisbury realised he had acted precipitately in convening an *ad hoc* Ministerial meeting before the issues were 'clearly marked out'. Most exceptionally as chairman, he ruled against formal minutes being taken. Beyond Morrison's letter, he agreed that there had only been 'murmurings' at a recent meeting of backbenchers. Even there, the Conservancy was simply characterised as 'a bunch of starry-eyed idealists', whose actions conflicted with those of landowners and such bodies as the Forestry Commission. No minister had challenged the need for the Conservancy or the content of its programme. Officials had long concluded that there was little in the reserve-acquisition programme to concern the Ministry of Housing and Local Government (HLG 82, 180). Nor had the Conservancy been idle. The Administrative Officer, P. Hilary Cooper, had long conversations with officials in the Ministry of Agriculture and Scottish Office, who promised to do what they could to give the Conservancy a 'fair wind' (PRO, FT 3, 1).

It was, however, Boyd-Carpenter's successor as First Secretary of the Treasury, Henry Brooke, who dug the Lord President out of the hole of his own making. As Brooke recalled in a minute to Treasury officials, the meeting was obviously going nowhere. Since the Conservancy was obviously doing 'a good job', he suggested that the obvious course was for it to be given guidance as to how further conflict might be avoided. Ministers readily approved the appointment of an informal inter-departmental committee of officials for that purpose. Playfair was appointed chairman, with Wilson as the Treasury representative. On Playfair's advice, the Committee's terms of reference were drawn widely in order to give the Conservancy the chance, once and for all, to 'clear the whole field of complaint'.

Great importance was placed on keeping even the existence of the Committee confidential to those in the Government service. There was a risk that members of the Nature Conservancy, being 'a body of responsible persons', would protest, or even resign, if they came to hear of an enquiry appointed simply on the basis of complaints of 'a private nature'. Any canvassing of opinion had to be confined to those in the public service. The Chairman of the Advisory Council on Scientific Policy, Sir Alexander Todd, and the Chairman of the Cabinet's Natural Resources (Technical) Committee, Professor Solly Zuckerman, found the Conservancy's research programme both appropriate and satisfactory; although more fundamental than might have been expected of a Government agency, it reflected the need to forge 'fresh cross-links between different disciplines'. Whilst agreeing that the breadth and variety of its research was unusual, the Chief Scientific Adviser to the Ministry of Agriculture, Professor H.G. Sanders, similarly confirmed that the Conservancy was performing a valuable function. The Director of the Royal Botanic Gardens, Sir Edward Salisbury, believed there had been a tendency to acquire land before 'they knew how to look after it'. There had also been 'very strained relations with the Forestry Commission'. Such problems had, however, been largely overcome since the appointment of Nicholson as Director-General. The Secretary of the Agricultural Research Council, Sir William Slater, thought it inevitable that, with so little money and staff, there should be 'some raw edges'. Either the Conservancy's budget should be doubled, or its activities severely curtailed.

The two key witnesses to the Committee were the Deputy-Director of the Forestry Commission, Sir Henry Beresford-Peirse, and Nicholson himself. Although he could point to no general disagreement, Beresford-Peirse said there was certain to be some overlap between their land requirements. Although the Conservancy might require only samples of moorland or forest land on various types of soil, its claims were thought on occasions to be inflated. However small its reserves might be, their designation might provide a pretext for landowners to resist the much larger requirements of the Commission. The Committee found Nicholson's evidence considerably more convincing. He outlined the need for a representative range of reserves, and for each to be of sufficient size to provide 'an adequately undisturbed foraging area' for the larger birds of prey and rare mammals. The Conservancy endeavoured to preserve existing public rights of way. Whilst acknowledging that any published list of proposed National Nature Reserves might cause undue alarm amongst landowners, Nicholson asserted that it could equally well be argued that such a list was essential proof that the Conservancy was fulfilling its statutory task. In his view, the principal obstacles were those of securing adequate scientific assessment and the resources required to put the reserves into 'good shape', whether they were purchased, leased or acquired under a management agreement. Although it might be argued that the Conservancy had pressed ahead too fast, it had to take account of the other competing demands for the land.

In its report of April 1956, Playfair's Committee affirmed that there had been very little criticism of the scale of the Conservancy's acquisition programme. It was the choice and size of the individual reserves that had aroused most concern. The Committee emphasised the importance of resolving any conflict of interests with other land users prior to designation. Sites should not be acquired before the Conservancy had adequate resources to manage them. Equally, once the Conservancy was committed to creating a reserve, those resources had to be provided. Lord Salisbury found the report of April 1956 sufficiently 'reassuring' to require no further meetings of Ministers.

A Nature Conservancy party in December 1972 brought together **Max Nicholson** *(right)*, Director-General of the Conservancy, 1952–66, **Bob Boote** *(left)*, Deputy-Director Conservation and Management, and **P. Hilary Cooper**, who joined the Conservancy in April 1953 as Administrative Secretary. Cooper transferred to the headquarters staff of NERC in 1965.

As Playfair minuted, his Committee had 'looked very carefully at the teacup and emptied it to the last drop'. It had hardly been able to find 'a significant pattern of tea-leaves in the bottom'. Although both the Conservancy Chairman, Arthur Duncan, and Nicholson saw the outcome of the enquiry as 'entirely satisfactory' (PRO, FT 3, 195), the Appendix of Proposed National Nature Reserves was never published. Much more significantly, the report emphasised the importance for the Conservancy of demonstrating the more positive aspects of its work. If the reserves were to be perceived as something more than a means of sterilising farm and forest land, they had to be used more actively as outdoor laboratories and classrooms. They had to be places where practical experience could be gained in managing the wider countryside for the benefit of residents and visitors alike.

CHAPTER THREE

NATIONAL NATURE RESERVES

In celebrating its tenth anniversary, the Nature Conservancy wanted to range beyond the generally small number of persons who read annual reports. It accordingly did what no public body had previously done: it bypassed official channels and independently published and marketed a highly illustrated booklet. Some 6,000 copies were sold for one shilling and sixpence and 17,000 more were distributed free of charge in the first three years.

The booklet opened with the words

> Our country, as we used to know it, is vanishing before our eyes. We see its coasts and fields chosen as sites for houses and power stations. Its green hills sprout steel masts and pylons. Its old oakwoods are clear-felled. Its grasslands, once bright with wild flowers, are now ploughed up and reseeded. Its waters and its air are polluted. We seek peace and no longer find it (Nature Conservancy 1959).

The same foreword noted how, after the war, parliament had taken a number of steps to safeguard 'the national heritage in the countryside'. The Nature Conservancy was one of the instruments created for that 'new public purpose'. Its success would determine in no small way 'the sort of country that our children and their children will call their homeland'. The foreword concluded: 'Will wild nature be once more a partner understood and valued by all, or become a mere doormat worn down by shabbiness?'

As the booklet explained, the word 'nature' was used to cover all living things except man, domesticated animals and cultivated plants. Through their membership of the Nature Conservancy and its territorial committees for England, Scotland and Wales, and a Scientific Policy Committee, '49 men and women of outstanding experience and knowledge' guided the Conservancy in its work. Not only did they constitute the largest supervisory body of any Government office, but those persons were drawn from every part of Britain and 'many walks of life'. Of a staff of almost 200, rather more than one-third were scientists. A regional structure was established for England and Wales in November 1953 that came to consist of seven regions. In addition to the reserves, each regional officer was responsible for close liaison with local planning authorities, local

Tom Huxley (*left*) with the Minister of State in the Scottish Office, **Lord Forbes**, looking at an exhibition board at the Tenth Anniversary party of the Nature Conservancy on 24 March 1959. Following a Nature Conservancy research studentship at the Bureau of Animal Population, Oxford, Huxley was appointed an Assistant Conservation Officer in Edinburgh in 1956; he become Regional Officer for South Scotland three years later.

naturalists and their societies, and land owners and occupiers generally. More specialist assistance might be obtained from headquarters where, for example, the Land Agent's Section was based, and from the research and field stations.

The Conservancy's grant-in-aid had risen to £350,000 in 1958–59, of which half was spent on scientific work and one-fifth on the National Nature Reserves. Half of the number of reserves proposed by the post-war Committees had been acquired. Over half of that area was held on the basis of a Nature Reserve Agreement – a sort of dedication agreement – 8 of which ran in perpetuity, 26 for 100 years or more, 6 for 50 years, 6 for 25 years and a few for the minimum period of 21 years. The annual average cost was as little as £7 per acre but, even where purchase was unavoidable, the average investment was under £2 per acre. For the most part, the reserve areas represented land that nobody wanted, or had wanted, for hundreds of years.

As the anniversary booklet observed, the coal, electricity, and timber-growing industries could take public understanding for granted. The Conservancy could make no such assumption. The general public had little interest in nature conservation except where it directly impinged on their particular properties. Worse still, 'the old traditions and prejudices' might cause 'a small number of persistent critics in a few localities' to misunderstand the Conservancy's aims, methods and programmes. It was therefore a considerable achievement that there had been controversy over only seven of the 72 National Nature Reserves so far declared. There was unrestricted public access to 75,046 acres (30,300 hectares) of the total area of 133,081 acres (53,800 hectares) of reserve declared up to the end of 1958. Most of the remainder was accessible by permit.

Encouraged by the popularity of 'nature' programmes on radio and television, the Conservancy believed increasing numbers of people would come, in time, to seek more

active involvement in nature conservation. As the booklet emphasised, this was important because the establishment of nature reserves with Crown Land status, and the appointment of teams of scientists, did not in any way diminish the need for voluntary effort. The Conservancy had, for example, welcomed the creation in 1959 of a Conservation Corps, through which young people might undertake practical work on reserves and other sites of similar character.

Drawing principally on the archives of the Nature Conservancy and Government departments, this Chapter illustrates the opportunities and constraints that arose through assembling and managing the series of National Nature Reserves (NNRs). In doing so, it explores the first rudimentary steps in transforming what had previously been a 'private hobby of a minority of enthusiasts' into 'a soundly-based and generally accepted element in national policy and practical trusteeship towards the land'.

RESERVE ACQUISITION

It said much for the authors of the Huxley and Ritchie reports that their message was clear and simple. Despite the greater opportunity for larger reserves in Scotland and the uplands generally, they shared the same broad objectives. In the words of the Ritchie Committee, the intention was to safeguard and perpetuate

> the natural assemblages of plants and animals which they now contain, plant and
> animal assemblages which might settle there under more favourable conditions, and
> special features of geological interest. Such reserves would offer invaluable oppor-
> tunities for scientific study (Secretary of State 1947)

(left) The view from **Whin Hill**, looking over the lagoons and reedswamp of the Minsmere Level on the Suffolk coast, 1955.
The marsh and heath had been recommended by the Huxley Committee for both its ornithological and ecological interest. Its acquisition by the RSPB provided early insight into the practical aspects of drawing up agreements with landowners for the tenure and management of reserves.

If that still sounded academic, Max Nicholson somehow found the time to convey the essence and variety of those nature reserves already established by the Conservancy and voluntary bodies, in his illustrated guide, *Britain's Nature Reserves*, published in 1957. Some reserves might be smaller than a hundred acres (40 hectares) whereas the largest, the Cairngorms, was just under 40,000 acres (16,200 hectares) (Nicholson 1957). Nicholson had obtained first-hand insight into the practical issues arising from acquiring and holding reserves even before there was a Conservancy. He had first gone bird-watching in the Suffolk marshes in 1934, at about the same time as he met Geoffrey Dent, who had a holiday dwelling at Thorpeness. It was Dent who first drew his attention to the way birdlife had colonised the grazing lands of the former Minsmere Haven, which had been deliberately flooded during the war to impede an enemy invasion. News that the owner intended to reclaim the marshes led to a hurried meeting attended by Nicholson and others in 1946, at which the owner agreed to lease some 1,600 acres (650 hectares) to the RSPB. As Nicholson recalled in April 1949 whilst preparing instructions for the parliamentary draughtsman, the episode had provided him with valuable insight into how the Conservancy might acquire and hold land with minimum disturbance to landowners.

Far from regarding the lists of proposed nature reserves, drawn up by the Huxley and

Ritchie Committees, as some remote and idealised goal, the Conservancy was impatient to acquire even more extensive tracts of countryside and coast as rapidly as possible. The Ritchie Committee had chosen Coille na Glas Leitire (the 'Wood of the Green Slopes') as its national park reserve in the Northern Highlands. This area of 723 acres (290 hectares) was a remnant of the native western Scots pine forest – the Caledonian Forest – in Wester Ross but constituted only a small part of the first National Nature Reserve (NNR) declared, namely that of Beinn Eighe (some 10,500 acres, or 4,250 hectares) in November 1951. The owner, who lived in a small cottage below the mountain, had received an offer for the timber on the estate. John Berry, the Conservancy's Director for Scotland, knew the area well from his time with the Hydro-electric Board. On a visit to the owner, he explained that, if the Conservancy were to acquire the entire estate, the present owner would not only retain the magnificent view but be able to continue walking on the mountain. Berry recalled later how both the owner and his brother said 'Snap'. It was considerably harder to explain to the Director-General, Cyril Diver, that a deal had not only been negotiated but struck. Treasury rules had been broken, but none could deny it was an astonishing bargain at £3,300, or 8 shillings and threepence per acre. The published objectives of the Reserve were to re-create the natural climax forest from existing woodland and to encourage the montane climax communities. A field station was established at Anancaun for the continuous study of the ecology of the forest, moorland and montane habitats (SRO, DD 12 895).

The mountain slopes of **Beinn Eighe** are of great biological, geological and physiographical interest. This NNR was the first to be established in Great Britain, primarily in order to study and conserve the large remnant of Caledonian pine woods.

The priority for the Scottish Office departments was to assess how far such designations might affect other user-interests. The Conservancy's ambitions for the Cairngorms provided the clearest warning of the conflict that might lie ahead. The Ritchie Committee had proposed an area of 38,336 acres (15,495 hectares), encompassing the central area above 2,500 feet (760 metres), as one of three national park reserves in the Southern Highlands. Although conceding that its original intention of acquiring some 65,000 acres (26,250 hectares) was unrealistic, the Conservancy remained adamant that it should take immediate advantage of the opportunity to negotiate Nature Reserve Agreements on 40,000 acres (16,160 hectares). The reaction of the Inverness County Council was to urge the Department of Health for Scotland, in October 1952, to hasten the legislation that would enable establishment of a national park of the kind recommended by the Douglas Ramsay Committee. As the Department's assessor told the Conservancy's Scottish Committee, in November, the Council was anxious to avoid anything that might prejudice the establishment of a national park. Having been informed that such legislation was a long way off, the County Council passed a unanimous resolution in January 1953, calling upon the Conservancy to designate a National Nature Reserve, without prejudice to the climbing public or the ultimate formation of a national park (SRO, DD 12 876 and 892).

That was the easier part. Although the Conservancy pledged that there would be no interference with public rights of access, suspicion and animosity remained (SRO, DD 12 892). The *Dundee Courier and Advertiser* warned, in September 1953, that the imposition of bye-laws could have the effect of making 'all our youngsters trespassers in the land of their birth', and threaten visitors with fines and penalties. *The Scotsman* was more supportive, but there was 'a sting in the tail' of its editorial of 11 December 1953. Whilst welcoming the protection that would be afforded to wildlife, the Cairngorms also contained the finest scenery. The question of public access should be properly addressed through the designation of the area, not as a nature reserve, but as a national park (SRO, HH 43, 81 and DD 12, 891).

An official of the Department of Health for Scotland summed up its attitude as one of regret that the Conservancy should take so large a view of its responsibilities. The Scottish Secretary's agreement to see a deputation from the local councils made the Conservancy suspect even more strongly that the Department was encouraging them to be obstructive. Nicholson wrote, in April 1954

> we cannot accept in any shape or form that St Andrew's House Departments should
> either discuss with county councils or any other outside bodies the discharge of our
> administrative responsibilities for the selection, boundaries and management of
> Nature Reserves.

Although denying a charge of interference, officials of the Scottish Office insisted that the Secretary of State had every right to concern himself, as the planning minister for Scotland, with the manner in which nature conservation impinged on other forms of land use and management (SRO, DD 12, 891).

The deputation met the Minister of State, the Earl of Home, in May 1954. The Clerk to the Inverness-shire County Council expressed concern lest the Conservancy might try to exclude the area of the NNR from the provisions of a future national park. The Conservancy's Administrative Principal in Scotland, R. Aylmer Haldane, emphasised that there could be no question of the Conservancy interfering with any national-park development, or more generally with the rights of public access. Lord Home confirmed, from experience in England and Wales, that there need be no incompatibility between the designation of national parks and nature reserves. Public access would in any case be protected since the Secretary of State had to approve any draft bye-laws (SRO, DD 12, 891). The reserve of 39,689 acres (16,000 hectares) was declared in July 1954, making it one of the largest in western Europe. One-eighth of the area had been purchased and the remainder acquired through a series of Nature Reserve Agreements (Nature Conservancy 1954, 20–1).

The third area in the Conservancy's larger strategy of establishing three reserves of an aggregate 100,000 acres (40,450 hectares) in the Highlands was the Inverpolly Forest of Wester Ross. It included the last comparatively undisturbed remnant of the other Highland forest type, the primitive birch-hazel woodland. An estate of 16,500 acres (6,670 hectares) of wild, remote and rugged countryside had suddenly come on the market. The ungrazed and unburnt areas of primitive woodland offered outstanding opportunities for the long-term research required to bring about the rehabilitation of forestry and agriculture. As Nicholson wrote, in July 1955, there were large dividends to be obtained from the scientific evidence obtained from such a huge area of North-west Scotland, from which the country presently derived almost no return (PRO, T 223, 352).

In his support for a supplementary estimate to cover the cost of purchase, Lord Salisbury wrote that, despite initial doubts, he felt it was an exceptional opportunity that could not be missed. The District Valuer had given a figure of £12,900 for the land, plus an additional £1,800 for the coastal salmon-fishing. Whilst Nicholson conceded it was a large sum, it had to be seen in the context of the 50,000 acres (20,000 hectares) that had already been acquired in Scotland for just over £10,000, largely through Nature Reserve Agreements. The proposed reserve might be extended at a later date through similar Agreements, negotiated with sympathetic neighbours. If, however, the Conservancy failed to negotiate for the publicly-advertised property, which had been recommended by the Ritchie Committee, Nicholson warned of the grave blow it would deal to all future negotiations. There would be considerable doubt as to whether the Conservancy was to be taken seriously.

Although the Chancellor of the Exchequer, R.A. Butler, approved a supplementary estimate of up to £15,000, negotiations were broken off. The vendor rejected the District Valuer's price, and Lord Salisbury urged the substitution of another property. Fortunately, an adjacent owner was so afraid that the Inverpolly estate might fall into the hands of a syndicate that would interfere with local stalking and fishing that he bought the property himself and presented the freehold to the Conservancy subject to the retention of the stalking right (PRO, T 223, 352).

As for the other property, Nicholson had just learned through 'private' channels, that Lady Bullough was considering how to dispose of her property of the island of Rhum in the Inner Hebrides. Nicholson recognised that the monies saved at Inverpolly and elsewhere in the Conservancy's estimate through, for example, abandonment of plans to buy

(*right*) **Inverpolly NNR**. This wild and almost uninhabited area includes the whole of **Loch Sionascaig** and the Torridonian sandstone peaks of **Stac Polly**, **Cul Mor** and **Cul Beag**. As well as a rich assortment of lime-loving plants, pine martens, red deer and roe deer, wild cats and golden eagles were also found there.

an island in Loch Lochmond, might be enough to buy Rhum, an island of 27,000 acres (10,900 hectares) with a population of 43 inhabitants and a castle. The Chairman of the Conservancy's Scientific Policy Committee, William Pearsall, believed it would be outstanding for both research and training purposes. In addition to the inherent variety of its geology, flora and fauna, the island would make an ideal location for the programmes already planned for red deer and golden eagles, as well as moor burning, windbreaks and other problems affecting nature conservation in the West Highlands. Lady Bullough's concern was to find a trustworthy new owner to care permanently for the island. Although now living in England, it was her wish to be buried beside her late husband in a temple on the island. Whilst personally handling negotiations, in which Lady Bullough agreed to sell at the District Valuer's price of £23,000, Nicholson discovered Lord Salisbury's grandfather had spent his honeymoon on the island. Officials were in no doubt that this was an important factor in causing Lord Salisbury to indicate he was prepared to do battle with the Chancellor for its purchase (PRO, CAB 124, 1602).

Whereas other Treasury officials regarded the cost as reasonable, Sir Edward Bridges warned that islands were often very cheap to buy but enormously expensive to run. A great deal could be spent on 'this kind of thing with no obvious return'. The Financial Secretary, Henry Brooke, however, was not averse to purchase. With notice of Lord Salisbury's formal support, Harold Macmillan minuted his consent as Chancellor of the Exchequer, in August 1956, stipulating that there was no commitment to running what promised to be highly expensive advanced training and research facilities in ecology and conservation on the island (PRO, T 223, 352).

The Scotsman published this photograph of the **Isle of Rhum** at the time of its acquisition in 1957. The Nature Conservancy's Handbook 1968 describes how, as the main centre in Britain for studying and managing red deer, Conservancy scientists were restoring the vegetation that had previously been impoverished by too much burning and grazing (Nature Conservancy 1968b).

THE PARALLEL ROADS OF GLEN ROY

The Royal Charter and legislative powers of the Conservancy made it explicitly clear that nature conservation was to include the maintenance of 'physical features of scientific interest'. Nature protection in Britain had always set considerable store on preserving geological and physiographic features, both for their own intrinsic value and as an essential part of the plant and animal life of the countryside. They were included among the areas 'worthy of preservation' on the Rothschild lists. A series of 'geological monuments' and 'geological conservation areas' was recommended by a geological sub-committee appointed by the Nature Reserves Investigation Committee (NRIC). It was neither possible nor necessary to include a representative locality of every rock type: different zones of chalk were so widespread; sections of a clay pit would be lost naturally through erosion and flooding. The proposed 41 geological monuments were, for the most part, inland artificial sections found in resistant rocks such as Carboniferous Limestone. The Huxley Committee endorsed the choice, adding the Blackhall Rocks of Durham (Sheail 1976, 160 – 3).

Although the Ritchie Committee had not inherited such a list and lacked the resources to compile one, it was not long before the Conservancy became acutely aware of the importance of Scotland for research and training in the geological and physiographical sciences. Indeed, the Parallel Roads of Glen Roy provided one of the first instances of ministers consciously debating amongst themselves the merits of preserving an individual area. The Conservancy's *Annual Report* for 1956 described the Parallel Roads as 'one of the most important natural monuments of Ice Age phenomena in the United Kingdom' (Nature Conservancy 1956, 27 – 8). The 'roads' or terraces ran for many miles along the steep hillsides. Between 20 and 50 yards (18 –45 metres) wide, the highest followed the contour at 1,150 feet (350 metres), the two others being at 1,070 and 857 feet (325 and 260 metres). Each was a 'fossil' strand-line of a glacier lake, and the different levels corresponded with 'overflows' at different 'cols' in the surrounding ridges of hills as the ice in the lower valleys melted some 15,000 years ago. Regarded as a 'Wonder of the World' since the eighteenth century, photographs of them were found in even the most elementary of textbooks (PRO, CAB 124 2638).

The designation of some 30,000 acres (12,000 hectares) of Glen Roy and neighbouring glens as a Proposed National Nature Reserve in 1955 appeared to be a somewhat academic exercise. It seemed inconceivable that their geological interest could be impaired. News that the Forestry Commission had purchased the lower part of Glen Roy therefore came as a 'bombshell'. The most that could be achieved from discussion was a joint submission by the Conservancy and Forestry Commission, setting out for ministers their respective positions. Having visited Glen Roy, the Joint Parliamentary Under-Secretary at the Scottish Office, Niall Macpherson, put forward a compromise, whereby the Forestry Commission might plant the area below the lowest 'road' in Glen Roy, and the whole of the plantable land in the side valley of Gleann Glas Dhoire. None of the 'roads' in any part were to be planted or otherwise damaged.

At a further meeting, in June 1956, the Permanent Secretary at the Scottish Office, Sir David Milne, conceded that only 600 acres (240 hectares) of forest were at stake in

George P. Black, geologist, at the Yellow Craig SSSI in East Lothian, August 1961.
The Conservancy's last Annual Report relates how the Geological Section, based in London, continued its programme of conserving the 950 geological sites and 48 caves of special scientific interest. As with canal and railway cuttings in previous centuries, it was anticipated that the expanding motorway programme would produce further geological exposures worthy of being scheduled as SSSIs.

Glen Roy was world-famous for its narrow terraces that marked successive shore-lines and beaches of a glacier-dammed Pleistocene lake. The NNR was eventually designated in 1970.

Glen Roy. That area was, however, critically important, in terms of ensuring that the afforestation of some 900 acres (360 hectares) of nearby common grazing-land would be an economic proposition. The Crofters' Commission, appointed as recently as 1955 to reorganise, develop and regulate crofting, attached considerable importance to the grazing area being afforested as a much-needed source of local employment. As Milne emphasised to the meeting, the Secretary of State was bound to have regard to the social consequences for the crofting community, as well the arguments for preserving the scientific importance of the area.

The Conservancy's expert adviser, Sir William Pugh (the Director of the Geological Survey), remained implacable in his opposition to anything but a complete embargo on any afforestation within the 10,000 acres (4,000 hectares) that contained the most striking remains of the 'Parallel Roads'. Even the most modest planting would 'impair the impressiveness of this most classical of all glacial lakes'. When Macpherson objected that afforestation up to the lowest 'road' could not possibly impair the view from the opposite side of the valley, Pugh emphasised the importance of preserving intact the laminated clays, known by the Scandinavian word 'varves', on the lower slopes and valley bottom. A kind of 'geological clock', where the bands represented the deposits of successive years, the varves helped to date events both during and immediately after the last Ice Age.

Officials of the Lord President's Office confessed, in January 1957, to the extreme difficulty of advising Lord Salisbury as to where the balance of advantage lay. Difficulties in securing sufficient land had already forced the Forestry Commission to reduce its national planting programme. The Lord President himself was about to publish a report of the Cabinet's Natural Resources (Technical) Committee on *Forestry, Agriculture and Marginal Land*, which strongly emphasised the social value of forestry in the more remote uplands. The Crofters' Commission described how the local communities had already suffered grievously from depopulation. One man might be employed for every

100 acres (40 hectares) planted. The Conservancy claimed that, whereas afforestation could be undertaken in many places without damage to the scientific interest, there could be no substitute for 'the glacial lake relics'. Whilst admitting to bias (he was a geologist by training), Roger Quirk, the Under-Secretary in the Lord President's Office, believed geologists were fully justified in claiming the 'geological monument' to be 'uniquely famous and impressive', for both education and research. The Royal Society of Edinburgh was one of five learned bodies to protest to the Secretary of State that even restricted planting would cause immense damage, as well as creating precedent for the proposal of further afforestation. A deputation met a further Joint Parliamentary Under-Secretary, Lord John Hope, in February 1957. Having listened to their argument, he remained sceptical as to the scale and significance of any losses to science.

The Scottish Secretary, John S. Maclay, wrote in February 1957, to ask for Lord Salisbury's support in adopting Macpherson's proposed compromise. Only 578 acres (233 hectares) would be planted, leaving the greater part of the Glen, some 9,000 acres (3,600 hectares), for scientific study. Quirk pressed Salisbury to consult Sir William Pugh, who was not only 'a very sensible person' but, as the Director of the Geological Survey, he was in effect the Lord President's 'principal geological adviser'. Whilst agreeing to do so, Salisbury wrote 'the arguments are all against destroying this unique geological site for an extra square mile of planting'. He accordingly suggested that a compensatory woodland area might be established on the Rhum National Nature Reserve.

Lord Home succeeded Lord Salisbury as Lord President of the Council in March 1957. It accordingly fell to him to receive a further letter from Maclay, rejecting the compromise and stressing that the purpose was not so much to meet the planting targets of the Forestry Commission, but to find a means of rehabilitating the crofting communities. As Quirk was quick to point out, Lord Salisbury had long ago rejected the fallacy of making such a sacrifice in scientific terms for the mere six jobs that would arise from planting in Glen Roy. Lord Home urged further investigation of a proposal by the Conservancy that the Glen be left unplanted and road access improved, to develop its tourist potential. Not only was this likely to generate at least as much employment, but the United States national parks service offered an obvious model of how coach parties from Fort William might be encouraged.

The decisive turning-point came in August 1957, with a further letter from Maclay, in which he insisted that the only way to assure full employment for at least a dozen families living in the three crofting townships was to carry out the proposed afforestation in the three Glens. Lord Home minuted, 'I am prepared to agree to the 600 acres and I have always thought I should do so.' Maclay gave an assurance that, if further land came onto the market or was offered to the Forestry Commission, no decision would be taken without the approval of the Scottish Office, following consultation with the Conservancy. With that decision taken and guarantee given, the priority for the Lord President's Office was now to minimise opposition to the Government announcement, when it came. The International Zoological Congress planned to celebrate the centenary of Charles Darwin, in 1958, with a visit to Glen Roy. Wide publicity was being given to his letter to Charles Lyell, in 1838, in which Darwin described the Parallel Roads of Glen Roy as the most astonishing of all the phenomena he had seen around the world.

Officials were particularly concerned, however, by rumours that the Conservancy was continuing to encourage moves to whip up public concern. Ministers would be incensed, since its case had been fully 'championed by a Minister in private' (PRO, CAB 124, 2638).

Whilst Nicholson warned that the Conservancy's *Annual Report* could hardly avoid expressing regret at the Government decision, the customary scrutiny of the draft text by Departments ensured that such feelings were expressed in the most moderate terms. It acknowledged that the discussions that had led to the eventual settlement between the Conservancy and the Forestry Commission had taken account of social factors. It observed that

> while this compromise solution calls for considerable sacrifice by the geologists, and indeed on the other hand for the Forestry Commission, it offers a prospect of safe-guarding a very large part of Glen Roy and its parallel roads (Nature Conservancy 1958, 41–2).

With the details regarding the exact location of the new plantings settled, the Conservancy acquired extensive parts of the upper Glen as a National Nature Reserve (PRO, CAB 124, 1614).

PERCEPTIONS OF RESERVE MANAGEMENT

The Conservancy's problems did not end once a reserve had been acquired. Apart from the acute lack of resources to carry out even basic management work, it was impossible to please every neighbour and self-appointed critic. If nothing was done, the Conservancy was accused of acting like an absentee landlord, leaving its reserves unkempt and neglected. Equally, if the woodlands and other forms of vegetation were closely managed, the Conservancy was accused of duplicating the work of the Forestry Commission and agricultural scientist.

The challenge of explaining the Conservancy's approach to reserve management was perhaps most graphically demonstrated by the furor over the island of Rhum NNR. Conscious of the need to keep the Department of Agriculture for Scotland fully informed of what was happening, Nicholson wrote, in September 1957, that the over-riding purpose of management was to secure 'the balanced long-term development of the natural resources of the island' for scientific research and training, afforestation, nature conservation and venison production. However favourably the Department of Agriculture looked upon such a strategy, considerably greater political weight was given to other perceptions. Balfour Browne published a further letter in the *Glasgow Herald* of 22 November 1957, claiming that the mistaken policies of the Conservancy, and partic-ularly the purchase of Rhum, had further antagonised agriculturalists and many others in Scotland. On 7 December, there followed a letter in the *New Statesman*, jointly writ-ten by the author Sir Compton Mackenzie and the Laird of Canna, J.L. Campbell, which used the criticisms voiced against the removal of livestock from Rhum as pretext for a general attack on the Conservancy.

It was hardly the most auspicious introduction for Lord Hailsham, who had succeeded Lord Home as Lord President of the Council (as well as Chairman of the Conservative Party) in the September 1957. The backbench Conservative member, Major John Morrison, forwarded copies of the letters to both Hailsham and the Chancellor of the Exchequer, Peter Thorneycroft. His purpose was to remind the Chancellor of an earlier conversation in which both men had touched on the 'futilities' of the Conservancy. It wasted money and annoyed 'a lot of ordinary decent citizens' (PRO, T223, 355). Taken together, the letters confirmed what Hailsham described as his suspicions that the Conservancy had made 'a whole lot of enemies, largely through sheer inexperience in dealing with people'. The obvious course was for the Conservancy to be given guidance in improving its public relations.

Lord Hailsham was accordingly in no mood to accept Nicholson's dismissive comments that Balfour Browne had never recovered from his disappointment at not being made Chairman of the Conservancy's Scottish Committee. As for the other letter, Campbell had been carrying on a 'one-man pin-pricking campaign' for some weeks. In Hailsham's words, there should be no more 'derogatory stuff about senility and backgrounds, and personal vendettas'. They might be true, but it was no way for the Conservancy to make friends. From a political perspective, there was much to be said for appointing Major Morrison as a member of the Conservancy. Although 'something of a hair shirt', he held opinions which should be represented. He was duly appointed (PRO, CAB 124, 1577).

Nicholson's further rebuttal of the charges laid against the Conservancy's management of Rhum was as forthright, but couched in more general terms. He complained of the irritation of having to suffer attacks from 'quite uninformed people' who imagined themselves to be expert. Ecology and conservation shared the misfortune of other extremely complex subjects that impinged on daily life, such as road traffic and broadcasting. Although an understanding of them required immense study, that did not stop a small minority from authoritatively talking such nonsense. This time round, it was Nicholson's more substantive explanation of the Conservancy's responsibilities for reserve management that caused difficulty. In Hailsham's mind, it raised the question of who was ultimately responsible for the Conservancy's activities in Scotland.

Nicholson sought to quell such doubts by referring to the Conservancy's Royal Charter and statutory powers. He referred in particular to the general assumption that the Lord President was primarily responsible for scientific research and advice, even in Scotland, where they related to Great Britain as a whole. As Nicholson asserted, and officials of the Lord President's Office affirmed, the dual system worked 'pretty satisfactorily'. As Hailsham minuted, it was like the gearbox: 'fort brutal mais ça marche'. The only misgiving to be voiced in the correspondence was that of an official in the Scottish Office, who complained that, even where it was 'a strictly Conservancy matter', parliament still expected the Scottish Secretary to answer any questions relating to Scotland. He should therefore be consulted when political or public controversy might be expected. As Nicholson remarked, it was not always easy to foretell where it might arise (PRO, CAB 124, 1579).

To Hailsham's legal mind (he had been made Queen's Counsel in 1953), explanation might only generate further anxieties. He acknowledged that the exchanges had helped enormously to clear his mind, but Nicholson was surely in error in placing so much emphasis on the Conservancy's responsibility for undertaking research. Hailsham sought assurance that such studies did not extend beyond the limits set by the Royal Charter. Nicholson's response was to emphasise the futility and wastefulness of undertaking the more applied kind of research without addressing the fundamental principles behind it. As Roger Quirk of the Lord President's Office pointed out, the Charter simply required the Conservancy 'to organise and develop the research and scientific services related thereto', in respect of acquiring and managing reserves and generally giving conservation advice (see page 33). In his view, critics of the Conservancy had failed to realise how conservation had progressed from the old-fashioned 'static' concept of reserves as places where rare species were merely preserved, to a much broader, dynamic concept that focused on the interaction of whole wildlife communities, one species with another, and with its soil and climate. Such a dynamic concept of reserve management required an active programme of research (PRO, CAB 124, 1577).

Still Hailsham was troubled. He wrote that, without legal advice to the contrary, nothing would induce him to regard the Conservancy primarily as a research body. Its Royal Charter suggested precisely the opposite. As with all legal questions, the Conservancy turned to the Treasury Solicitor for guidance as to the limitative effect of the words 'related thereto' in its Charter. As Nicholson reported, in January 1958, the Treasury Solicitor had drawn a distinction between a body created by Royal Charter and one established by statute. The effect of the Charter was to clothe the Conservancy in all the powers of a natural person. *Prima facie*, it could do anything an ordinary person might do, subject to such behaviour not being prohibited by law. Although it might be criticised in parliament or in public for acting unreasonably, it could never be accused, on a point of principle, of acting *ultra vires*. In so far as the Treasury Solicitor had been able to find any judicial pronouncements, the expression 'relating thereto' had always been interpreted in an expansive, rather than limitative, sense. Nothing more was heard of this particular 'point of principle'.

For both Lord Hailsham and the Conservancy, a meeting with members of the House of Commons, in February 1958, provided an opportunity to put a balanced picture of the Conservancy's activities. As Nicholson observed, any new organisation was likely to incur misunderstanding. An analogy could be drawn with the Agricultural Research Council. When it was founded in 1930, some of the most vocal farmers thought that they knew all the answers, and that it was a waste of public money to employ long-haired scientists. Despite the war, it had taken agricultural research roughly a quarter of a century to win general acceptance. It would take at least as long for the modern approach to nature conservation to become widely known and understood. Present misconceptions as to the purpose and methods of the Conservancy were compounded by its requirement to operate in 'often remote and unsophisticated areas', where local opinion **had** already been prejudiced by drastic interventions by Government bodies such as the Defence Services. Considering the number of reserves acquired and managed throughout the length of Britain, Nicholson found it remarkable that the number of persons voicing loud and direct criticism could still be counted on the fingers of two hands (PRO, FT 3, 143).

Even the Conservancy's relationship with the Wildfowlers' Association of Great Britain and Ireland (WAGBI) had improved. Before the Conservancy had even begun to give much thought to wildfowl refuges, members of the Association had strenuously attacked any move to restrict shooting. Major Morrison had given considerable prominence to such fears during the debates on the Protection of Birds Bill of 1954. As Nicholson pointed out in his briefing for Lord Hailsham, a series of informal discussions, organised by the Conservancy, had not only effected a 'complete reconciliation' but WAGBI was now actively involved in the management of important experimental wildfowl refuges. Some 20 square miles (50 square kilometres) on the Humber were supervised by a committee whose chairman and secretary were both wildfowlers, and had a warden provided by the Conservancy. Shooting on the important nature reserve of Caerlaverock on the Solway, which had been created on the initiative of the Duke of

Murdo McRury, Warden of **Loch Druidibeg NNR. South Uist.**

This reserve was the most important surviving breeding-place in Britain of the native grey lag goose. The loch shore was broken into innumerable bays and islets by small peninsulas covered with peat or boulders.

Norfolk, was supervised by a panel that consisted of the Conservancy's representative as chairman sitting with a representative of WAGBI and the Duke's factor. The *Shooting Times* had recently commented that 'the welfare of wildfowl is in good hands, due chiefly to the co-operation which now exists between the various bodies interested in wildfowl conservation'.

The survival of the Conservancy had owed much to the 'good offices' of Sir Edward Playfair at the Treasury, and Roger N. Quirk now came to play a crucial role in the Lord President's Office. After taking a first in the Cambridge Natural Sciences Tripos in 1931, he entered the civil service and moved with the rank of Under-Secretary from the Gas Division of the Ministry of Fuel and Power to Nicholson's vacated post in 1952. In a private capacity, he published widely on historical and archaeological subjects, and instigated the major excavations in the city of Winchester. Described as 'a careful but enthusiastic scholar, and a friend of charm and kindness', his deep love of the Lake District made him 'a strong and effective champion of the preservation of its beauty'. He had a holiday home there. The official files refer to visits he made to the Merlewood Research Station and reserves in the area.

Such personal detail may go some way at least towards explaining how such an official, concerned with all the sciences covered by the Lord President's Office, invested so much effort in explaining the purpose and character of nature conservation, and the Conservancy's predicament, to a succession of Lord Presidents and the officials of both his own and other Departments. From this knowledge and insight, he described the criticisms made of the Conservancy's activities as 'much ado about very little'. Due to the very vigorous representations made by a small, but powerful, group of Conservative members of parliament, one might have thought there was 'a really large volume of complaint simmering up and down the country'. There was no such evidence. Given 'the ticklish nature' of acquiring and managing land, Quirk was impressed at how little trouble there had been. The minor instances of irritation and modest cost to the Exchequer were a very small price to pay for the protection of scientifically valuable sites and the advancement of research which, one day, might even pay the nation dividends (PRO, CAB 124, 1577). That was certainly the view of the *Farmer and Stockbreeder* of 31 March 1959, following publication of the Conservancy's booklet, *The First Ten Years*. Most of its work was unsung and certainly unlauded, and yet, according to the leader writer, it had achieved far more than most comparable concerns in twice the time – and on a grant that most Government departments would laugh at.

Politically, however, the most valuable support came from the most unlikely of sources. Especially in view of what had gone before, the Conservancy had every reason to fear an investigation into its affairs by the House of Commons' Select Committee on Estimates. As Quirk later reported to Lord Hailsham, the Committee's Chairman, Sir Spencer Summers, opened his cross-examination of Arthur Duncan and Nicholson in a rather hostile manner but, by the time members had visited the Roudsea Wood NNR, the Merlewood research station and Moor House, they were clearly sympathetic to the Conservancy's work. The Select Committee's report was published in July 1958. The first page of the Conservancy's *Annual Report* of that year highlighted both its appreciation of the importance of the work undertaken, and a congratulatory editorial published by

The Times (Nature Conservancy 1958). The Committee was supportive of both the purpose and direction of the Conservancy. It even condemned some of the excessive economies that had been imposed on the facilities at the Moor House field station (Parliamentary Papers, 1957–58). Lord Hailsham acknowledged that the report had greatly strengthened both his own position and that of the Conservancy. It was remarkably uncritical.

Ironically, the Committee's sharpest criticisms were directed at the Lord President himself. With hindsight, the rebuttal made by Lord Hailsham and his officials gives some insight into the striking changes of attitude towards the organisation of research and development over the following decades. The Select Committee's principal misgiving arose from the fact that the Committee of the Privy Council never met and that, by implication, its chairman, the Lord President, failed to exercise proper control over the Conservancy or indeed the other research councils for which he was responsible. Lord Hailsham insisted that such criticism arose from a misunderstanding of the authority vested in the Lord President. It was in any case a basic tenet of research councils that they could not be rigidly controlled or directed. The very nature of their work precluded such a thing. It was enough to use a light rein, which could be tightened if the need arose. As an official in Hailsham's Office remarked, it was a typically English system, deriving its strength from its flexibility. The results were its justification (PRO, CAB 124, 1572).

CHAPTER FOUR

CONSERVATION ADVICE
AND RESEARCH

Whereas the National Parks Commission was regarded in some political circles as supernumerary (Cherry 1975, 153–61), the Nature Conservancy was seen as positively alien to the good government of the countryside. It came close to abolition on more than one occasion. To stand any chance of survival it needed to retain the confidence of the Treasury and Lord President, which in turn depended on rapidly developing a reputation not only for managing its own reserves but more generally for the conservation advice given and ecological research undertaken. Beyond those most directly affected by its land-holding responsibilities, the Conservancy had to exert its authority among a formidable array of administrative and scientific bodies, each with a vested interest in a particular aspect of resource management.

Leading figures among the 300 delegates who attended the General Assembly and Technical Meeting of the International Union for the Conservation of Nature and Natural Resources (IUCN) in Edinburgh, June 1956.
The Nature Conservancy's Director Scotland, **John Berry**, is seated in the centre, with **Hester Lloyd** (Assistant Conservation Officer) on his left and, on his far right, **Max Nicholson**, with **Derek Ovington** behind him.

A sense of the rapidly-developing authority of the Nature Conservancy under Max Nicholson was given by that body's prominence at the Technical Meeting of the International Union for the Conservation of Nature, held in Edinburgh in June 1956 (see page 246). In addition to the rapidly gathering expertise and experience being gained by the Conservancy through its own activities, Nicholson had made an extensive visit to the United States, in May 1955, through the invitation and generosity of Fairfield Osborn and his Conservation Foundation. Osborn was the author of *Our Plundered Planet*, one of a cluster of volumes – also including William Vogt's *Road to Survival* and Aldo Leopold's *Sand County Almanac* – which were published around 1948–49. For Nicholson, the chance to tour the wildfowl refuges, national parks, forests and other sites of scientific interest east of the Mississippi, was of seminal importance. Most immediately, it was an outstanding opportunity to gather material for the keynote paper he gave to the Edinburgh Assembly on 'Nature conservation and the management of natural areas', which included a long American annex. The paper emphasised that the object should be not only to protect, but to 'reinforce' and even manage nature; nature conservation must not only safeguard but, where necessary, assist in restoring 'the effective and balanced workings of the processes of nature'; it recognised the need for human beings to work with, rather than against, nature. As Nicholson emphasised, this did not mean simply leaving it all to nature. Only scientific investigations could show whether *laissez faire* would suffice in a particular situation, or whether some limited intervention was required for a period of time. The key to nature conservation was therefore research, both on the needs of particular sites and more generally to learn how the physical elements of the earth were processed by nature in varying situations to support not only plant and animal life, but mankind itself (Nicholson 1956).

If much of this summarised what had been said and written before, the paper was noteworthy for its insistence that the time had come 'to leave behind the missionary period when informed opinion still had to be convinced that nature conservation was a good thing'. It was time for practical example. With a confidence that came from recognition of the scale and permanence of what was being achieved, conservation bodies should now direct their energies to developing a more 'concrete' approach that analysed problems, assessed what was feasible, measured the efficacy of particular techniques and treatments, knew where to look for the relevant data, and identified where the gaps in expertise remained.

Tansley himself had initiated the kind of dialogue required to turn promise into achievement. Whereas he had once seemed complacent as to the effect of modern farming, his memorandum to members of the Nature Conservancy, in July 1952, told a very different story. 'The great post-war extensions' meant that urgent action was required if anything like an adequate area of semi-natural chalk vegetation was to survive. John Hope-Simpson, one of his former research students and now a lecturer in Bristol university, warned Nicholson, at a meeting of January 1954, that grassland 'improvement' might be as disastrous to the wildlife of many sites as being ploughed up or afforested (PRO, FT 3, 192).

In Tansley's view, the time had come to grapple with practical issues such as reconciling the protection of a representative sample of habitats and communities with the fact

The Nature Conservancy's field station at **Moor House**. Pioneer research on high-altitude climate, bog growth, peat erosion and the effects of grazing and burning was undertaken here, following the purchase of the NNR in Westmorland in 1952. The building was reputed to be the highest occupied house in Britain.

that it was considerably easier to manage a few really large reserves than many smaller ones. With particular reference to the spread of myxomatosis, Hope-Simpson stressed the need to sustain grazing by livestock. Close study would, however, be necessary to assess the intensity of such management. Heather and other characteristic plants would, for example, be eliminated if grazing pressures were too high on grass-heaths. Whilst full use should be made of the standard techniques and statistical methods developed by the Grassland Research Station, for example, Hope-Simpson emphasised that they should never be taken up uncritically. There were often good reasons why an ecologist should do things differently (PRO, FT 3, 192).

The overriding purpose of the two research stations, at Merlewood and Furzebrook, was to develop the distinctiveness and relevance of the ecological approach. William Pearsall had strongly advocated a research station in the southern Lake District. Cyril Diver pressed for Furzebrook, similarly close to his research areas on the Dorset coast. Although conceived as a unified project, the work on woodlands at Merlewood fell into three sections: the Plant Soil Section was concerned primarily with the botanical aspects; the Fauna Section studied the invertebrate animals of woodlands, with special emphasis on the fauna of soils and litter; and the Microflora Section dealt with the fungi and bacteria involved in litter-breakdown, together with microbiological aspects of soil fertility. Merlewood also had laboratories to support the moorland studies being carried out at the Moor House Field Station and, from 1958, a central Chemical Service for the routine chemical analyses required throughout the Conservancy (Nature Conservancy 1960, 59).

The Conservancy's first scientific advertisement of August 1949 sought applications from men and women with degrees in botany or zoology, and an interest or knowledge

Three photographs taken from a fixed point established by A.S. Thomas among the calcareous grasslands and yew woods of the **Kingley Vale NNR,** in Sussex, acquired from 1952 onwards. The photographs, taken in 1956, 1965 and 1969, illustrate (*top to bottom*) the extent of succession to coarse grassland and scrub following myxomatosis and the near-extermination of rabbits in 1953-54.

of the British flora and fauna and their habitats. Women in the Conservancy reached a senior position. Nellie Bower as a Principal, Irene Fairey as financial officer, Julia Laptain and Olive Balme as regional officers, and Verona Conway as one of only two Senior Principal Scientific Officers. As anticipated, some of the first and more senior appointments brought considerable overseas experience. E. Barton Worthington was appointed Deputy-Director (Scientific) in 1956. His early career as scientist to Lord Hailey's inter-war African Survey and founder-Director of the Freshwater Biological Association between 1937 and 1946 had been followed by survey work in Middle Eastern countries. He had most recently been Secretary-General of the International Scientific Council for Africa South of the Sahara (Worthington 1983). W. Joe Eggeling had joined the Colonial Forestry Service in 1931. His inventory and management plan of the Bodongo Forest of Uganda became models of their kind. Appointed chief conservator in 1945, he moved to a similar position in Tanganyika five years later. Back in Scotland in 1955, he saw an advertisement for a Conservation Officer for Scotland. He applied, and found himself one of three candidates interviewed by all the members of the Nature Conservancy, who happened to be meeting in Edinburgh. Eggeling's expertise and experience were put to good use in establishing reserves and drafting their management plans (Morton Boyd 1994). He produced the first check list of plants for Rhum and an authoritative study of the Isle of May, acquired as a NNR in 1956 (Eggeling 1960).

Arthur S. Thomas had been a botanist in the Agricultural Department of the Gold Coast and Uganda. His papers on the impact of human influence on tropical ecology, published in the *Journal of Ecology* in 1945–46, emphasised that it was only by considering 'the whole community – the climate, the soil, the plants and the animals, including man', that a 'true picture' might emerge. Drawing on his African experience, Thomas sought to bring the same breadth and rigour of analysis to the survey of vegetation change on the Conservancy's lowland Reserves, undertaken with a succession of students each summer. His 'permanent' transects soon highlighted the value of 'dull routine recording' in providing 'an accurate account' of events of 'major ecological importance', such as the virtual disappearance of rabbits following the virus epidemic, myxomatosis, in 1953. Although there was a striking increase in the height of the turf and a spectacular display of flowers, without Thomas's transects it would have been easy to overlook the decline of those species that had previously enjoyed a competitive advantage in intensively grazed rabbit pasture (Thomas 1960; 1963).

Cyril Diver's most enduring legacy as Director-General was perhaps his inspired choice of early research staff and students. It was an obvious priority for members of the various Committees of the Conservancy to identify those few persons (often their former research students) with appropriate expertise and experience. Perhaps more importantly, such candidates needed the commitment to forego the apparent security of a career in a university or agricultural research station. One such scientist was Verona M. Conway. Her deep concern for conservation dated from the mid-1930s when, as the Yarrow Research Student at Girton College, Cambridge, she had studied plant succession at Wicken Fen. Her supervisor, Harry Godwin, had found that mowing converted the sedge-dominated grassland into one dominated by the moor-grass *Molinia*; her task was to discover the mechanism of change. Conway's series of three papers in *New Phytologist* were a model of clarity and logical development of a problem and its solution, describing the anatomical structure and development of the species, the environmental influences to which the plant was exposed, and the physiological impact of a management treatment. The work for which she was awarded a PhD in 1937 successfully combined observation, analysis and experiment (Pigott 1988). It was William Pearsall, the head of the Botany Department at Sheffield, who encouraged her to investigate the ecology and origins of the blanket bogs of the south Pennines. There followed further papers, and an international fellowship from the American Association of University Women which enabled her to spend a year at the University of Minnesota. To influential figures such as Godwin and Pearsall, Verona Conway had all the qualities sought for appointment to the Conservancy in 1949; six years later she was the first woman to become head of a Government research station. As Director of Merlewood, she was Officer-in-charge of the research being undertaken at the old shooting-lodge at Moor House, acquired as a Conservancy field station due to Pearsall's persuasion.

The head of a research station carried a twofold responsibility: research supervision and career guidance, and projecting the station's worth within the academic and wider communities. Verona Conway was 'a very kind, deeply committed and very intelligent person with her own special sense of humour' (Pigott 1988), but she was also shy and reserved in manner. There were, however, few better qualified to describe to a non-specialist audience the principal 'Lines of development in ecology'. This paper was published in the *Proceedings of the Chemical Society* in 1957. It began by explaining the concept of the 'ecosystem', whereby the living organisms of any tract of land or water must affect one another to a greater or smaller extent. They in turn influenced, and were influenced by, their physical environment. Ecologists usually studied ecosystems in terms of the total range of species in an area, the number of each of those species, and the way these numbers fluctuated. Another approach was to trace the flow of energy through the different parts of the ecosystem and, more particularly, the circulation of nutrient substances, including water, nitrogen, carbon, phosphorus and metals. A large branch of ecology, called 'limnology', concentrated on the dynamics of lakes and small bodies of water, which were thought to be simpler and more sharply delineated than terrestrial systems. The challenge for the Merlewood research station was to extend the same approach to British woodlands. Although woodlands were obviously affected by human exploitation, Conway (1957) explained that there were grounds for thinking that some at least came close to the type of equilibrium expected of virgin vegetation. Very intensive studies were made of the biological and chemical processes at work in the litter of fallen twigs and leaves, and in the upper soil layers, of the National Nature Reserve of Roudsea Wood, within a short distance of the research station. Beyond the intrinsic scientific importance of this work, it had obvious relevance to applied ecology or conservation, in the sense of planning for the higher production rates that came with maintaining soil fertility at what Conway called its proper level.

J. Derek Ovington was of a younger generation. After gaining a doctorate from Sheffield University in 1947, he worked for two years as a forest ecologist at the Macaulay Institute of Soil Research. Following his appointment to the Conservancy in 1950, research on the impact of new forests on soils and flora continued, with Ovington working from University College London, where Pearsall was now head of the Department of Botany. Later, at Merlewood, Ovington's assertive and impatient manner came well to the fore, as he made the fullest use of an ever-increasing number of assistants in collecting, sorting, weighing and otherwise assembling large volumes of material. Much of the work was carried out at Roudsea Wood. A wide range of nutrient mixtures was applied to the trial sites, simulating the effects of leaf falls on soil and ground fauna. Ovington's earlier collaborative work with the Forestry Commission also helped to establish long-term experimental plots of different hardwood and coniferous mixtures in the Gisburn Forest, to the west of Skipton in Yorkshire (Bocking 1997).

Ovington was an obvious choice of speaker for the Edinburgh meeting of 1956. His paper emphasised the need for reserve management to be tailored to the needs of the plant and animal communities present. There had to be a scientific understanding of existing conditions, based on knowledge of past events and informed speculation of future developments, both within and outside the reserve area. Even where management was essentially *laissez faire* it should be regarded as an experiment, with detailed observation of every aspect. Although some research might be attempted elsewhere, the reserves were the key areas for experimentation, where the precise limits of trial plots reflected both the nature of the habitat and its inherent variability. Close attention had to be paid to the extraordinary complexity of what was being studied. Any change in the basic features of the reserve was likely to have considerable consequences. The selective felling of trees, for example, would not only change the stocking density and species composition of the woodland, but also modify light intensity, water supply, temperature and other microclimatic factors at ground level. Soil-forming processes would also be altered due to the reduction of root composition, litter fall and nutrient turnover. If the effects of tree felling were excessive, the ground flora might become so luxuriant as to inhibit tree regeneration (Ovington 1956).

An obvious way to assuage fears in the Agricultural Research Council and Royal Society that the Conservancy would create even greater competition for the extremely few professional ecologists available, was for the Conservancy to train its own ecologists. Cyril Diver attached considerable emphasis to the award and support of post-graduate research studentships. After an interview by Pearsall, Elton and Diver, Owen Gilbert obtained one of the earliest awards to study zoology under Tom Reynoldson in the University of Wales at Bangor. He joined two other Conservancy research students, Derek Ranwell and Derek Ratcliffe, both in the botany department under Paul Richards. They were working on the coastal dunes of Anglesey and vegetation of Snowdonia respectively. All three later joined the Conservancy, and Gilbert moved to Merlewood soon after it opened in the summer of 1953.

Another early award was made to M.E. Duncan Poore, a research student of Harry Godwin at Cambridge. His PhD subject fell into two parts: the ecology of the Woodwalton Fen nature reserve in Huntingdonshire, and the application of continental phytosociological methods to British vegetation, with fieldwork mainly carried out in the Breadalbane area of Perthshire. His documentation of the impact of large-scale turf removal from the raised bog in the late nineteenth century, and the cessation of livestock grazing, helped to explain the rapid spread of 'dense impenetrable thickets of sallow

Donald N. McVean directed the Conservancy's research on the generation and extension of native woodland in Scotland. The aim was to devise ways of re-establishing forest by natural means as opposed to planting, with far less ploughing.

bushes' that had caused the Society for the Promotion of Nature Reserves to come close to selling the Woodwalton Fen reserve in the late 1940s (Sheail and Wells 1983). The reserve was leased to the Conservancy in 1953. As well as publishing his findings in the *Journal of Ecology* (Poore 1956), Poore drafted the first management plan for the reserve (Nature Conservancy 1958, 5–9). Appointed to the Conservancy's Scottish head-quarters in 1954, Poore and Donald N. McVean proposed, as supplements to their region-al work, two possible schemes for research: a vegetation survey of the Scottish mountains and a comparison of the effects of sheep and cattle (and combination of both) on hill-grazing land. Both were taken up.

Whilst a considerable priority was given to establishing the research stations at Merlewood and Furzebrook and the field stations at Moor House and Anancaun, it was never intended that the Conservancy's scientists should do everything themselves. As Nicholson emphasised to the Commons' Select Committee on Estimates, it might be far more effective to make grants to universities or other centres of research. Over one-third of the grant money was given to bodies such as the Wildfowl Trust, the Edward Grey Institute of Field Ornithology, and the British Trust for Ornithology. Nicholson insisted that it was far more cost-effective to assist their work than for the Conservancy to appoint its own ornithologists.

Another major recipient of grant-aid was the Botanical Society of the British Isles (BSBI) for compiling its *Atlas of Plant Distribution*. The venture had begun with a paper given by A. Roy Clapham at the BSBI conference of 1950, in which he put forward the idea of publishing an accurate, up-to-date and detailed atlas of British vascular plants, available for purchase in convenient form at a reasonable price. A resolution encourag-ing the Council of the BSBI 'to discuss the possibility of preparing and producing a series of maps of the British flora' was carried with acclamation, and work began in the Botany School, Cambridge, in April 1954, directed by S. Max Walters and, from March 1959, by Franklyn H. Perring, another Conservancy research student. Over 1.5 million records

Staff of the Nature Conservancy assembled at the **Merlewood Research Station** in 1954. Back row, left to right: unknown man, **W.A. Macfadyen, M.E.D. Poore, Verona Conway, E.M. Nicholson** (Director-General), **J.D. Ovington, J.G. Skellam, W.H. Pearsall** (Deputy Chairman of the Nature Conservancy), **G.N. Sale, J.D. Lockie, Mrs E.M Clarke, A.S. Thomas, D.S. Ranwell, N.W. Moore, J. Heath, Hester Lloyd**; Middle row: **R.E. Hughes, A. Miller, J.E. Satchell, F.H.W. Green, R.J. Elliot, D.N. McVean** (seated), **M.D. Mountford, Olive Balme, Helga Frankland, J. Grant Roger**; Front row seated: **J. Berry, E.A.G. Duffey, K.R.S. Morris.**

were contributed by about 1,500 professional, amateur and voluntary workers. Records were received from all but seven of the 3,651 10-kilometre squares of the Ordnance Survey National Grid, covering the whole of the British Isles. In a sense, the project was the victim of its own success. To the consternation of the Conservancy, which met 70 per cent of the eventual cost of £36,000, two extensions of grant-aid were required. More time was needed to edit such a large number of records. As well as providing for the first time such comprehensive, yet detailed, information, the project pioneered the use of data-processing machinery from the receipt of records to the insertion of symbols on a map. Duncan Poore later recalled taking Frank Perring to see a demonstration of Hollerith sorting equipment in, having already seen its potential in cryptographic work at Bletchley and in Colombo, Ceylon, during the war. The Atlas, showing the distribution of about 1,700 species, was eventually published for the BSBI in 1962 at a cost of five guineas (Perring and Walters 1962; Harding and Sheail 1992).

ADVICE TO MINISTERS

The Conservancy may have been a pioneer body, but each of its three main responsibilities impinged on a range of existing interests. Its relationship with the Agricultural Research Council had to be handled with extreme sensitivity – even to the point of the Conservancy not being called a research council. There were suspicions and, at times, hostility concerning its land-holding responsibilities. The resentment shown towards its third Charter-responsibility – that of giving expert advice – also called for considerable diplomacy. The position was well summarised by John Morton Boyd, who was appointed as Regional Officer for the Western Highlands and Islands in 1957. Although the field seemed wide open for the most energetic missionary work he soon found that Scotland was packed full of agencies covering agriculture, forestry and water resources, tourism and recreational development. It was a matter of jostling for elbow room. The Conservancy had to find 'its living space by a quite enormous effort of displacement' (Macklin 1991).

The challenges at local, regional or national level had to be met full on. The Conservancy's advisory work was not only intrinsically important, but it was also an obvious way of making the Conservancy better known. Over time, expert guidance was given on an extraordinary array of subjects, including grouse, reindeer, and the predation of golden eagles on lambs, as well as matters such as legislation for the registration of common land, and afforestation in national parks. The Conservancy was also involved in issues of coastal defence, following the East Coast Floods Disaster of the 31 January 1953, when 307 lives were lost along a thousand-mile length of coastline. At the instigation of Alfred Steers, the coastal physiographer who had been on the Huxley Committee, Nicholson suggested to Lord Salisbury that a proposed enquiry into the engineering aspects might be extended to include 'the fundamental long-term factors' affecting the extent and frequency of such tidal inundations. Not only did this suggestion provide Lord Salisbury with a pretext for associating himself with the committee's appointment under Lord Waverley, but further lobbying secured the inclusion of Steers as one of its members (PRO, FT 3, 469). In addition to the official report making reference to the Conservancy, evidence submitted to a further Sea Defence Advisory Committee led to the recommendation, in August 1959, that the Conservancy should establish a coastal research station to investigate the role of vegetation in maintaining saltmarsh and sand-dune systems. Whilst this did not imply any additional funding for the Conservancy, it indicated an increasing awareness among civil engineers regarding the relevance of the expertise and experience available from the Conservancy (PRO, FT 3, 470).

Although the Conservancy benefited from being so proactive in obtaining opportunities to tender expert advice, this brought even greater likelihood of upsetting other agencies who claimed to have the requisite authority to provide whatever advice was required. Some animal and plant groups and species already received a measure of statutory protection. In short, there was abundant opportunity for the Conservancy's role to be overlooked or misconstrued – or even manipulated. Such instances, particularly those regarding bird protection, the management of the grey seal, and the conservation and control of the red deer, will be explored in this Chapter through the files of the Lord President's Office.

Among the unfinished business of the inter-war years was the enactment of further Wild Bird Protection legislation. A draft Bill, drawn up by the Home Office in October 1953, attempted to codify and modernise the voluminous and largely obsolete legislation

The Saltfleetby-Theddlethorpe Dunes NNR on the Lincolnshire coast was designated in 1968. The Lindsey County Council secured exceptional powers to regulate holiday-shack development and more permanent housing development in the dunes between the wars. The more northerly dunes, marshes and creeks became a bombing range in 1932 (Sheail 1977).

dating from 1880, if not earlier. Nicholson described the Bill to the Lord President as 'the somewhat belated fruit of more than thirty years' discussion by various official and unofficial committees'. Although generally agreed in principle it contained a number of unsatisfactory compromises, including proposals to establish Wild Bird Advisory Committees (PRO, CAB 124, 2627).

Since the First World War, the Home Secretary and Secretary of State for Scotland had looked to their respective Advisory Committees for expert advice on administration of wild-bird legislation. The Advisory Committees were largely made up of amateur naturalists, wildfowlers and representatives of local authorities, and the acute dissensions that marked their proceedings had been a major factor in deterring ministers from earlier legislative initiatives. As Nicholson told the Lord President, it had always been assumed that such 'an historical anachronism' would be abolished once the Conservancy was established. Ministers would look to the Conservancy for advice. Both the Conservancy and Lord President's Office were accordingly appalled to learn that the Home Office had not only 'clung strongly to the view' that ministers should retain their advisory committees, but that they should be put on a statutory footing. As a further complication, lack of parliamentary time for Government legislation had caused the Home Office to press Lord Templewood to adopt the measure as a Private Member's Bill. Lord Salisbury supported the suggestion that one of the more prominent members of the Nature Conservancy, Lord Hurcomb, might move an amendment at the Committee Stage, whereby the Advisory Wild Bird Committee for England and Wales would be appointed by the Conservancy and its equivalent for Scotland also be appointed by the Conservancy with the approval of the Scottish Secretary. A meeting of the Cabinet's Legislation Committee, in November 1953, refused to do more than invite further discussion on the topic.

Whilst Roger Quirk of the Lord President's Office pressed to give the Conservancy 'a big part', Home Office officials insisted that only the Home Secretary and Scottish Secretary were sufficiently competent to appoint representatives of both 'the scientific, bird preservation interests' and wildfowling interests. Nicholson vigorously rejected such a narrow interpretation of the Conservancy's terms of reference. It alone had the expertise to make suitable appointments and provide an adequate secretariat to the Advisory Committees. With the question still unresolved, Lord Hurcomb could do no more, on the second reading of the Bill, than express concern at the absence of any reference to the Conservancy (PD, Lords, 184, 345).

Quirk adjudged that it was time to compromise, most obviously by suggesting that the Lord President (on behalf of the Conservancy), and Home Secretary or Scottish Secretary should jointly appoint members and establish a secretariat. The Permanent Secretary at the Home Office, Sir Frank Newsam, claimed that this would be anomalous, since responsibility for the rest of the Bill had been placed squarely on the latter two ministers. He would go no further than to assure the Conservancy that it would be consulted as to the composition of the Committees, and that it might make representations when it disagreed with the advice tendered by the Committees. The fact that the response came too late to preclude any amendment at the Lords' Committee Stage of the Bill caused Nicholson to become even more convinced the Conservancy had been 'tricked and misled' by the Home Office throughout 'this long business'. Quirk agreed that the Conservancy had been treated unreasonably. Lord Salisbury was advised to 'bring heavy pressure' on the Home Secretary to override his officials and accept compromise. There were, however, acute fears that any controversy might further delay the passage of the Bill and thereby endanger its enactment. Concern as to whether there would be sufficient time for the Commons to debate the Bill had already caused Lady Tweedsmuir to promote an almost identical Bill in the Commons with the intention of having it complete its passage much earlier in the Session. There was less pressure on the Lords' timetable.

At a meeting with Lord Salisbury and the Scottish Secretary, Sir David Maxwell Fyfe (the Home Secretary) refused to countenance any amendment but agreed that an undertaking should be given during the second reading of Lady Tweedsmuir's Bill. The Joint Under-Secretary of State, Sir Hugh Lucas-Tooth, accordingly had two objectives in that part of his speech. Firstly, he emphasised that the Bill was necessarily 'a careful balancing of the scientific point of view against the legitimate interests of agriculture and of field sports'. It was important that these other interests, and local authorities, should be given effective opportunity to make their views known. Secondly, he stressed the uniqueness of the Conservancy. The two ministers undertook to consult the Lord President, as the minister responsible, and agree with him the membership of the Committees. The Conservancy would be invited to appoint one of the two joint secretaries to the Committees. Since it was always open for a Government body to make representations to ministers when it disagreed with another Government body, neither minister would act on the advice of his Committee without affording opportunity to the Conservancy to comment (PD, Commons, 521, 1526–7).

Although disappointed that not even the Home Secretary's 'vague invitation' had been embodied in the wording of the Bill, the Conservancy had no alternative but to concede. Only time would tell whether the setback had more than symbolic significance. Lord Salisbury congratulated Quirk on the settlement negotiated. The Bill, with the unamended clause, received the Royal Assent in June 1954 (PRO, CAB 124, 2627).

GREY SEALS

As one of the few native animals to be given statutory protection, the grey seal was bound to excite interest. Although locally abundant in the British Isles, the estimated world population was only about 46,000, distributed between the North Atlantic and Canadian maritime provinces, and the Baltic Sea. Of an estimated 36,000 in Britain, over 80 per cent inhabited the northern and eastern coasts of Scotland.

The first Grey Seals (Protection) Act of 1914 had imposed a statutory close season that coincided with the breeding season. It was prompted by fears that the British population had been reduced to as few as 500. There were other concerns too. Lord Charnwood, who introduced the measure in the House of Lords, described the raids made on the rookeries as an 'unquestionably dirty business'. Motoring jackets made of sealskin had become so

James MacGeoch, the Honorary Warden of the **North Rona and Sula Sgeir NNR**, wearing a Nature Conservancy armband, as he inspects a quern stone by the door of the ruined chapel on North Rona, in October 1959.
Situated about 44 miles north-west of Cape Wrath, this reserve – acquired by a Nature Reserve Agreement in 1956 – is notable for its large breeding colony of grey seals and gannets.

popular that there was risk of raids becoming more frequent. The Government decided not to oppose the Bill since no livelihood was immediately threatened. In order to guard against the possibility of the seals becoming so abundant as to cause damage to salmon fisheries, the Bill was introduced for a trial period of five years only. In the event, it remained in force on an annual basis throughout the 1920s, under the Expiring Laws Continuance Act (Sheail 1976, 37–9).

Claims of damage to salmon-fishing gear and to the fish themselves caused the Irish Free State to drop the Act from its own Expiring Laws Continuance Act in 1923, and the Scottish Secretary ordered a review in 1926. Surveys undertaken by W.L. Calderwood and James Ritchie in 1927 and 1928 suggested that the population had risen to at least 4,300. Although this was high enough to remove any threat of extinction, there were fears that any attempt to repeal the Act would incur fierce opposition from naturalists. Calderwood and Ritchie warned that it might also encourage Norwegian whalers to raid the rookeries. A further Bill was therefore enacted in 1932, putting the close season – which would now cover the entire breeding season – onto a permanent footing, but with powers for ministers to withdraw or modify its length where there was evidence of damage to salmon fisheries.

Allegations by the River Tweed Commissioners that grey seals from the Farne Islands caused mounting damage to nets and losses of fish from this world-famous salmon river, led the Ministry of Agriculture and Fisheries to seek the Conservancy's advice in July 1955. The Farne Islands were owned by the National Trust and managed as a nature reserve. The request provided an outstanding opportunity for the Conservancy to prove its value as an adviser to Government departments in assessing claims and counter-claims. A survey made by John D. Lockie of the Conservancy's Scottish staff that autumn confirmed that both an increase in seal population and damage to fisheries had occurred. His interim report of January 1956 emphasised, however, that far too little was known of the seal's life-cycle and habits for any scientific advice to be given as to how the population might be better regulated or losses to the fisheries reduced. A meeting with representatives of the Ministry and Scottish Home Department, in March 1956, invited the Conservancy to draw up a short-term research programme. A further meeting, a month later, also attended by representatives of the Tweed Commissioners, the National Trust, and the Northumberland, Durham and Newcastle-upon-Tyne Natural History Society, agreed on a programme designed to assess the amount of damage caused and the efficacy of possible control measures. Fishermen made standardised observations at six stations, and reported seals drowned through entanglement in the nets. A Conservancy grant was made to the Natural History Society for marking the calves, counting the population at different times of the year, and investigating the causes and extent of death among juveniles. More generally, grants were made by the Conservancy for tagging young seals in order to ascertain their range of movement, both from the Farne Islands and in Scottish and Welsh waters (Nature Conservancy 1956, 19–20).

Members of the Nature Conservancy were informed, at their meeting of January 1957, that their Scottish Committee saw no alternative to regulating the seal population. The evidence collected indicated that damage would occur whenever the Farnes' population exceeded 1,000, and it was then estimated at over 2,500. As Chairman, William Pearsall reported that the Scientific Policy Committee saw no alternative but to halve the population. There was simply no other way of discovering what size of reduction would reduce net damage. Cyril Diver and Lord Hurcomb doubted that the scientific case had been made, or whether fishermen would even then be satisfied. Since the seals would continue to 'raid' the nets, Fraser Darling thought that the cull would still be regarded as insufficient. However incomplete the evidence and distasteful the task, Nicholson insisted that the Conservancy could not back away. It was its duty to identify the limit beyond which, on biological grounds, the growth of the seal population required regulation (PRO, CAB 124, 1573).

Members of the Conservancy recommended a three-part approach. Most importantly, survey and research work on the seal colonies alleged to be causing the damage should continue. The Scottish Home Department should also sponsor studies of better ways to protect the fishing nets. And thirdly, as an exceptional and interim measure, the Minister of Agriculture should draft an Order under the 1932 Act for an annual cull of 300 calves. The recommendations were endorsed by interested parties at further meetings in April and June 1957. The National Trust and its Farne Islands Committee pledged to cooperate so far as was practicable in implementing the control measures found essential by the Minister to prevent further increase in the seal population. The Tweed Commissioners also increased the bounty paid for whole seal-carcases found drowned in the nets (Nature Conservancy 1957, 28–9, and 1958, 54–5).

A draft Order was laid before parliament in July 1957. The veteran campaigner for national parks and greater access to the countryside, Arthur Blenkinsop, moved a motion to have it annulled. In seconding the motion, another Newcastle member, Edward Short,

Members of the Nature Conservancy and Scottish Committee in 1959. Front row, left to right: **Professor P.W. Richards, Col. H. Morrey Salmon, A.B. Duncan** (Chairman), **Sir Basil H.H. Neven-Spence, E.M. Nicholson** (Director-General); Second row: **J. Berry** (Director Scotland), **Col. J.C. Wynne Finch, Professor W.H. Pearsall, A. Blenkinsop MP, Lord Hurcomb**; Third row: **Professor J.A. Steers, J. E. Richey, Professor J.R. Matthews**; fourth row: **Lt-Col C.M. Floyd, Major D.C. Bowser, F. Fraser Darling, Col. J.P. Grant**; Back row: **Michael Noble, MP, J.W. Campbell, Cmdr Sir Geoffrey Hughes-Onslow, Professor V.C. Wynne-Edwards, G.V. Jacks, E.B. Worthington** (Deputy Director-General, Scientific), **P.H. Cooper** (Administrative Secretary)

described the grey seal colony as 'an object of considerable local pride throughout the north of England'. Although a member of the Nature Conservancy, Blenkinsop emphasised that he was acting in a personal capacity. His motion was nevertheless valuable to the Conservancy in making it clear that the initiative had come from the Ministry. The Joint Parliamentary Secretary, Joseph Godber, explained how, in deciding to proceed with 'a small exceptional cull', the Ministry had sought to balance the damage suffered by the valuable salmon fisheries of the Tweed with 'our natural repugnance to interfere with the seals'. The Ministry had taken the best advice in minimising the scale of the slaughter and ensuring it was undertaken in a humane way (Parliamentary Debates (PD), Commons, 592, 1082–107).

As if there were not problems enough in securing research funds, grey seals on land might be studied by the Nature Conservancy but, once at sea, they moved into the ambit of fisheries research. At the Conservancy's instigation, the Treasury approved a formula whereby it received a three-year grant from the Development Commission, whose terms of reference included the supervision and grant-aid of fisheries research. The grant was conditional on the appointment of a Consultative Committee to provide overall guidance and report on the research findings. It comprised representatives of the Government departments and three independent members, under the chairmanship of the Deputy-Director of the Conservancy, Barton Worthingon. At its first meeting, in August 1959, E.A. (Ted) Smith was appointed as a special research officer, based at the Conservancy's Scottish headquarters.

The potential sensitivity of these studies, quite apart from their findings, was highlighted by a series of highly critical letters in *The Scotsman*. Lord Hailsham expressed concern. As Nicholson explained, they arose from an article by Smith, on 30 December 1961, which had simply reviewed the research being carried out on the habits and life history of the grey seal, for the most part in the Orkneys where the largest colonies were to be found. A letter from Balfour Browne had protested that the Conservancy should be concentrating its research on population dynamics – which was exactly what the Orkney seal research was all about. As Nicholson's note pointed out, it was another instance of the same individuals attacking the Conservancy, whatever the pretext. A letter published on 24 January 1962 by John Berry, the Conservancy's Director for Scotland, sought to put the record straight. It described how, as a research organisation, the Conservancy had an obligation to give scientific advice on the conservation of wild fauna. In the present instance, that purpose could only be met by investigating the efficacy of the range of controls that the fishing industry might implement. Field-scale experiments were essential.

Worthington's Consultative Committee included Fraser Darling, Professor Humphrey Hewer who had studied grey-seal breeding biology and worked out their life table, and Leo Harrison-Matthews, Director of the London Zoo and an authority on marine mammals. Each recognised that, whilst artificial fibres would strengthen the nets and loud noise might be used to scare the seals away, much more was required to protect the fisheries. The population in the British Isles had doubled during the previous 12 years, and was likely to do so again unless management was applied. There was no alternative to controlling numbers at the colonies (Worthington 1983, 146–9). The Committee's report (accompanied by appendices on the population, reproduction, life table and food of the grey seal, written for the most part by Smith) recommended that trial culls should be undertaken on the Orkneys and Farnes, with the aim of reducing numbers by one quarter over a period of five years (Nature Conservancy 1963a). Although impossible to quantify, the report confirmed that the seals caused much damage to the fishery, and recommended a programme of control.

A Ministry spokesman announced in December 1962, in answer to a Parliamentary Question, that the Conservancy would soon publish the Consultative Committee's report. It would be for ministers to consider whether further orders were required under the 1932 Act (PD, Commons, 669, 50). The Conservancy took this to imply that the Fisheries ministers had publicly accepted responsibility for any cull that might be carried out. However, a letter from the Fisheries Secretary, Hugh Gardner, indicated that the Ministry saw things very differently. As he argued, the aim was not to bring about drastic improvement in the fisheries (which would have required much greater slaughter), but to continue the previous experiments to discover how a longer-term solution might be achieved. The responsibility for the further cull should therefore rest with the Conservancy. Although the Ministry would need to collaborate by making a further Order and issuing licences to those authorised to kill the seals, it would be the Conservancy's task to identify the people and methods. On the assumption that there was bound to be an outcry from the humanitarian interests, Gardner wrote that it would be for the Lord President to answer criticism in parliament.

Such an interpretation of the Conservancy's responsibilities made it all the more necessary that Lord Hailsham, as Lord President, should be informed of what was proposed. The most contentious area, the Farne Islands, was only just outside the North-east of England, where the Prime Minister had just given him special responsibility for easing unemployment. His officials were sure that publication, let alone implementation, of the recommendations of the Consultative Committee would cause a public outcry. Even if the fishing grounds required protection and the methods of killing pregnant seals or their young were considered humane, a lot of people would still find 'the proceedings unpleasant and unsporting'.

Nicholson was no less forthright. Whilst stressing his support for the recommendations and the Conservancy's duty to heed ministerial requests for expert advice, Nicholson emphasised that this research had not been initiated by the Conservancy, and nor was such control needed on general conservation grounds. The work had been undertaken entirely as a requirement by ministers for scientific information relevant to meeting their responsibilities for commercial fishing. It would be 'constitutionally incorrect' for the Lord President or the Conservancy to assume such responsibility as Gardner sought. In backing Nicholson's line of argument, officials of the Lord President's Office pointed to the 20 instances where ministers had accepted responsibility for answering questions on seal culls. There was no reason for transferring responsibility, other than the transparent one of trying to distance themselves from an increasingly embarrassing subject. Lord Hailsham summed up his attitude in a minute which made it apparent that

> I am afraid I am on the side of this innocent and beautiful creature. But clearly the report must be published and the beastly work of butchery will, I suppose, be pursued.

Any culling must, however, be 'done for and defended by' the Ministry.

Christopher Soames, the Minister of Agriculture, wrote to Lord Hailsham on the day the Consultative Committee's report was published, in early March 1963. He emphasised the need for immediate agreement as to which of them should answer questions and deal with any criticism in parliament. Although the time might come when the executive departments should take responsibility for the culls, the fact that there was need for a further five-year experiment indicated that this point was still some way off. By ensuring that responsibility rested with a scientific body like the Conservancy, which had established good working relations with the National Trust, it would be easier to minimise the inevitable public criticism and opposition from local interests. In a further letter of May 1963, Soames appeared to go a significant stage further, by implying that it was the responsibility of the Conservancy to decide whether a cull was needed and how it might be carried out (PRO, CAB 124 1574).

As Lord Hailsham remarked, it was difficult to see how the Conservancy could assume such a responsibility without becoming an executive department. Worthington insisted that the situation on the Farne Islands was closely parallel to that in Orkney, where the cull was regarded as an executive operation being carried out by the Fisheries Department on the basis of the scientific and technical advice tendered by the Consultative Committee. Lord Hailsham strongly supported the Permanent Secretary of his Office, Frank F. Turnbull, in insisting that the nub of the question was the purpose of the cull. He accordingly wrote to Soames, in late May 1963, asserting that it would be wrong for the Conservancy to accept responsibility for deciding what action should be taken on the recommendations of the Consultative Committee's report. A cull would bring no benefit to the seal colonies themselves. A cull could only go ahead if the two fisheries ministers believed it was a necessary stage in preparing for the larger measures of control that might eventually be required to protect fisheries. As for who should take responsibility, Lord Hailsham insisted it would be quite inappropriate for the Conservancy to be held responsible for such executive work beyond its own nature reserves.

On this occasion, pressures on the parliamentary timetable worked in favour of the Conservancy. It was the Scottish Secretary, Michael Noble, who forced matters to a conclusion. As he pointed out to Soames, if the fisheries of south Scotland were to benefit from the much-needed cull on the Farne Islands during the autumn, a draft Order was urgently required. Soames wrote in early July that he was not altogether convinced by Hailsham's arguments, but that the time for making an Order was getting very short. He would have to accept responsibility. The fact that the cull would be undertaken by the Fisheries Departments, as opposed to 'the nature conservators', would plainly lead 'to squawks from nature lovers'. He enclosed a draft of a letter that the Chairman of the Conservancy might send, indicating the Conservancy's support. A Ministry press notice announced a few days later that, following widespread complaints of damage to fisheries caused by the estimated population of 3,500 grey seals, the Minister had made an Order with the approval of the Nature Conservancy for a limited cull on the Farne Islands by Government officers, with a representative of the RSPCA present (PRO, CAB 124, 1574).

RED DEER IN SCOTLAND

Red deer were the largest land animals in Britain, and one of Scotland's most valuable natural resources, both for the sport of deer stalking in mountain areas and for their potential contribution to meat supplies and tourism. Scotland was probably the only European country where these impressive animals could be seen so easily by the casual visitor (Nature Conservancy 1957, 35–9). And yet many claimed that lack of adequate management of the population had led to large-scale degradation of the 3 million acres (1.2 million hectares) of deer forest, together with widespread damage to neighbouring farm- and woodlands. The lack of a close season and chronic, indiscriminate poaching had given rise to cruelty and destruction described as 'a blot on the British reputation for sportsmanship and good treatment of animals' (PRO, CAB 124, 2637).

The immediate stimulus to post-war attempts at legislation was the report of the (Scott Henderson) Committee on Cruelty to Wild Animals, whose report of June 1951 drew particular attention to the cruelty involved in deer poaching in Scotland and the absence of any effective powers for suppression (Home Secretary 1951). Early in 1952 a Poaching of Deer (Scotland) Bill was introduced to the House of Lords, where 16 peers spoke in its favour and none against, except in pressing the Scott Henderson Committee's recommendation for a close season. Although the Bill successfully completed its passage through the Lords, the Secretary of State decided to suspend its introduction to the Commons pending further study of how a close season might be achieved at the same

Red deer taken in snow, November 1965.
The Nature Conservancy played a pivotal role in securing greater protection and regulation of numbers under the Deer (Scotland) Act 1959.

time as safeguarding agriculture and other interests. It was an issue on which the Conservancy was expected – and indeed keen – to advise. And yet, as the Secretary of State himself indicated in reply to a Parliamentary Question in April 1952, there had been no census of the deer population since 1931. Whilst the total population was thought to exceed 100,000, there was simply no reliable information available. The Conservancy placed a research contract in October with F. Fraser Darling, as 'a world authority on deer problems'. Later extended, it provided census data on roughly a third of the grounds in Scotland (Nature Conservancy 1958, 51–3).

The Secretary of State had appointed a Committee on Close Seasons for Deer in Scotland, in July 1951, under the chairmanship of Robert H. Maconochie. When data from Fraser Darling's annual census were provided, the Committee found a marked change taking place in the management of the deer forests and neighbouring grounds. Where once the deer and agricultural interests had been in the same hands, the straitened circumstances of many owners had forced them to let the stalking to tenants. This had played a large part in the breakdown of tolerance between the deer-forest owner and sheep farmer. Government pressures to intensify the use of forest and hill lands had aggravated the situation. But although there was agreement as to the causes of the problems, there was continuing deadlock as to how they might be resolved. A majority report recommended that a statutory close-season for red deer should be introduced as soon as possible and that regional deer control boards, with responsibility for both conservation and control, should be appointed. Three members of the Committee, in a minority report, insisted that deer numbers should be reduced before any close season was enacted (Secretary of State 1954).

The Secretary of State, James Stuart, announced in October 1954 that the differences revealed by the Committee were so large that he had regretfully decided that the introduction of further legislation would be premature. This announcement, and a leader and ensuing correspondence in *The Times*, caused Lord Salisbury to enquire about the Conservancy's position. Nicholson replied that the Conservancy was vitally concerned. The Scottish Committee deplored the hasty decision, taken without consultation. The issue was too important to the grazing economy of the Highlands to be simply left. There had been instances of cruel and indiscriminate slaughter even on the Beinn Eighe NNR, where a butcher from Inverness and another in the hotel business had been caught poaching. More specifically, Nicholson interpreted Lord Salisbury's enquiry as encouragement for the Conservancy to attempt to break the impasse. A Sub-committee was appointed, comprising Arthur Duncan (the Conservancy's Chairman), Col. J.P. Grant of Rothiemurcus, Professor V.C. Wynne-Edwards of the Scottish Committee, and C.S. Elton, with Fraser Darling as Chairman. From discussions with the Scottish Landowners' Federation, the Committee quickly concluded that 'prospects of a sound and generally acceptable scheme' were good. The Scottish Office assessor on the Conservancy's Scottish Committee was pressed into trying to 'get things back on the rails' by suggesting that the Conservancy be formally invited by the Secretary of State to tender advice. Lord Salisbury supported such a move, a note was passed in the Cabinet Room and Stuart's reply, scribbled on 10 Downing Street stationery, elicited an agreement that Lord Home (at that time Minister of State at the Scottish Office) should meet the Sub-committee. The Conservancy's strategy was not to press for immediate legislation, but rather to secure the Secretary of State's blessing to establish a standing committee to exploit the apparent keenness of the interested parties to break the deadlock. As well as developing a comprehensive scheme to keep the deer and their grazing effect under close surveillance, such a committee might advise on a close season, on more effective control of poaching and, where necessary, on 'organised reduction of superfluous numbers' of deer. Both Nicholson and Roger Quirk were afraid of the Scottish Office reaction. Salisbury minuted

> I will weigh in if you think it absolutely necessary. But I suspect it will infuriate the
> Scots, if we chivvy them on this.

At the meeting with Lord Home, the Sub-committee considerably extended its proposal for an impartial scientific inquiry by emphasising the advantages of 'remitting responsibility for deer control to a standing committee of the Conservancy'. From discussions with each of the parties to the impasse, it was clear that they respected the Conservancy for its impartiality and scientific authority. Lord Home rejected any notion of his formally inviting the Conservancy to hold discussions. He was, however, prepared to write to the relevant organisations, drawing their attention to the initiative being taken by the Conservancy on an informal basis. Although the Government would 'sympathetically consider any proposals that had general backing', Lord Home personally doubted whether the time was ripe.

If the Scottish Office was confident that further inquiry would 'run into the sands', both ministers and officials had reckoned without Nicholson. As he wrote to the Lord

President, in August 1956, the meetings held with the four main interests – the Scottish Landowners' Federation, the British Field Sports Society (Scotland), National Farmers' Union of Scotland, and the Blackface Sheep Breeders' Association – were cordial and constructive. Agreement had been quickly reached. Their joint report was certainly a signal achievement for the Conservancy: all four parties recognised that 'deer have their proper niche in the pattern of pastoral and sporting life' and yet there was urgent need to control their population in the interests of economical land husbandry. Despite the voluntary efforts of many landowners, some form of executive body was required to prevent the depredations of marauding deer, which could only increase as the amount of wintering ground was reduced by afforestation and other developments. There was also unanimity that the Conservancy should undertake the executive tasks required, under the supervision of the Secretary of State. Not only was the problem essentially one of conservation and the control of wildlife, but the Conservancy had already carried out much pioneer work through the Scottish Deer Survey. It was 'the appropriate neutral body'.

The challenge was now to secure the support of ministers. As Nicholson remarked in a letter to Sir David Milne, the Permanent Secretary at the Scottish Office, the enthusiasm of some of the signatories for a full-blooded scheme was 'a trifle embarrassing', but their unanimity was so encouraging that it would be a pity to disappoint them or 'let the thing go cold'. Although he expected the proposals to be 'watered down', Nicholson warned of a risk of the Blackface Sheep Breeders' Association withdrawing; its agreement had been conditional on an assurance of immediate and radical action.

An even more finely balanced argument had to be presented to Lord Salisbury. Whilst acknowledging 'the natural doubts' of ministers as to the propriety of conferring executive powers on the Conservancy, Nicholson wrote that it was an 'essentially sentimental view' to believe that nature conservation extended no further than keeping nearly extinct species alive. As corresponding organisations in North America had shown, there was essentially no difference between discharging that responsibility and regulating over-abundant species. It was a biological problem which the Conservancy was pre-eminently well equipped to tackle. Although far from keen to assume executive powers beyond its reserves, members of the Conservancy and the Scottish Committee felt that it would be intolerable to allow such cruelty, ill-feeling, soil degradation and damage to agriculture to continue. Since the present proposals were the only ones shown to command any degree of acceptance and support, the Conservancy would be failing in its duty if it did not declare a readiness to undertake the task, if required by Government and local interests.

Lord Salisbury was not impressed. Irritated by the way the Conservancy had maintained interest in such 'a tiresome situation', he perceived the 'seeds of considerable possible trouble'. Whilst there could be no objection to its having responsibility for the deer census and research, the Conservancy's assumption of executive powers was quite another matter. However much it may be desired by others, he was not at all attracted to the idea of the Conservancy, and therefore himself, becoming the vehicle by which any proposals were implemented. As Lord Salisbury minuted, he had always insisted the deer problem should be handled in Edinburgh. If that were the case, the obvious course was for the Secretary of State to appoint an *ad hoc* body, on which the Conservancy would be well represented. A private conversation with Lord Home confirmed that he too had serious misgivings as to whether the Conservancy should be allowed to pursue the proposals further.

The Conservancy's *Annual Report* for 1957 recounted that discussion revolved around two main problems: the extent of compulsory powers, and who should exercise them. In its own words, 'The Conservancy had always regarded with distaste the use of compulsory powers in relation to land.' It had never sought to use the powers for compulsory purchase conferred by the 1949 Act. The Conservancy was, however, sympathetic to the worries of farmers and sheep breeders lest the imposition of a close season should lead to over-stocking, for which there was no legal remedy. Throughout discussions it had therefore supported such compulsory powers as might be mutually acceptable to landowners and agricultural interests. It did so in the belief that, where both interests cooperated with a scientific (and therefore neutral) body, such powers would never, in practice, be needed. Such an opinion was based on the goodwill shown towards the Conservancy, as a scientific body, during the course of the Red Deer Survey. Turning to the second problem, the *Annual Report* saw an equally prominent role for the Conservancy. Deer management and control could not be based on some rule of thumb. It had to reflect close knowledge and understanding of the specific herd and feeding grounds. Experience in other countries with much greater deer problems had provided ample evidence of the penalties of leaving such management to administrators and executive staffs, working with only intermittent biological advice. The field officers and ancillary staff should always work directly to biologists (Nature Conservancy 1957, 35–9).

Whilst there was no expression of gratitude towards the Conservancy, there was no denying that progress had been made. Although still highly sceptical as to whether the proposals contained in the joint report really commanded universal support, the Scottish Office recognised that the four main parties now supported the recommendation of the majority report of the Maconochie Committee that there should be some form of deer control, with powers to enter land and kill deer in default of the owner taking the necessary action. A meeting held between representatives of the Scottish Office and the Conservancy, in November 1956, was also described by Quirk as being very friendly. Three main powers were seen as crucial: to follow up and destroy marauding deer; to exterminate colonies of deer that had settled on farmland; and, finally and most contentiously, to instruct owners to thin out their herds where numbers in deer-forests were deemed to be too high. From the chair, the Permanent Under-Secretary at the Scottish Office warned that parliament would insist on adequate safeguards against the arbitrary use of such drastic powers. The Conservancy representatives agreed, but warned of the impracticability of a right of appeal where immediate action was required. There had to be a measure of delegation to local bodies and to the individual stalker.

Nothing was likely to be resolved until a decision was taken as to whether the Conservancy should 'father and foster' both scientific and executive functions through a Deer Committee representative of the major interests. Not only was Lord Salisbury 'very loth for the Nature Conservancy' to be given such a role, but his officials were sure that Scottish national opinion would demand that this responsibility resided with Scottish ministers. Whilst continuing to insist that the Conservancy did not seek both functions, Nicholson claimed that, as it was the only independent body with the necessary scientific knowledge, there was no alternative to its being given the further responsibilities of wardening and field control, with its officers armed where necessary with a compulsory order or warrant from the Secretary of State's Office.

The turning point was a letter from the new Secretary of State, John Maclay, in March 1957, asserting that parliament was likely to demand that such power should only be exercised under direct ministerial control. The Secretary of State therefore had no alternative but to appoint a Deer Committee representative of all interests, charged as an executive body for the regulation of stock in the deer forests, for extermination of colonised deer, and for eradication of marauding animals. There should be a right of appeal against all decisions taken by the Deer Committee, except where action had to be taken quickly in relation to marauding deer. The letter anticipated that the Conservancy would be represented on the Deer Committee as well as providing the scientific advice required in formulating its general policy. Not only did Lord Salisbury find Maclay's outline of a future Bill 'thoroughly sensible', but he rejected out-of-hand the Conservancy's assumption that 'only trained biologists can safely kill deer'. The work of the Deer Committee could 'surely be entrusted to men who had probably spent their own lives and their fathers before them, in learning about deer'. With the decision taken, the priority for the Conservancy was to assist the Scottish Office in drafting a Bill.

Still there was little sign of gratitude towards the Conservancy. Not only might resentment at the Conservancy's persistence be discerned on the part of the Scottish Office, but there remained considerable scepticism. As an official in the Department of Agriculture for Scotland noted, in May 1957, translating the substance of the report into the precise terms required for a Bill was likely to revive old controversies. Such doubts were fully shared by Lord Home, in his new capacity as Lord President. Recalling his time as Minister of State, he wrote in May 1957

> I was once bitten by this, and don't intend that it should happen again. I very much
> doubt whether forest owners will accept compulsory entry on to their land.

He was sure any agreement would be repudiated, once it became public property. In the event, it was the Conservancy that read the situation most accurately.

The Secretary of State announced to the Commons, in July 1958, that the Government had approved in principle the proposals of the joint report, and a Deer (Scotland) Bill was introduced to parliament in the autumn of 1958. Although 70 amendments were put down, it left the House of Lords little altered. The Scottish Standing Committee of the Commons considered some 45 amendments in the course of no fewer than 17 sittings but, as the Conservancy's *Annual Report* of 1959 affirmed, there was no departure from the principles agreed in the joint report (Nature Conservancy 1959, 70–1). Using the precedent of the Crofters' Commission, the Bill empowered the Secretary of State to appoint a Red Deer Commission. Made up of representatives of the Conservancy and other interested organisations, it was required after consultation with the Conservancy to determine the appropriate level of red-deer stock for any area carrying a population; to seek agreement with the owners and occupiers as to how that might be achieved; and, under the supervision of the Secretary of State, to enforce such compliance where necessary. The Bill received the Royal Assent in May 1959.

The Red Deer Commission, made up of members from the farming, crofting, hill-sheep farming, sporting, landowning and forestry interests, included two persons from the Conservancy's Scottish Committee as founder members. Vero Wynne-Edwards was made Vice-Chairman. An officer with over 5 years' experience of the Conservancy's Red Deer Survey resigned to take up the senior post on the Field Staff of the Commission. The Conservancy's Deer Unit was strengthened by the appointment of three additional stalkers (Nature Conservancy 1960, 54).

CONSERVATION RESEARCH

Although the Conservancy appeared to be thwarted in so many directions, the Monks Wood Experimental Station was an outstanding instance of an initiative that sprang wholly from within the Conservancy, and which was unmistakeably the Conservancy's to promote and publicise. The achievement was all the more significant for its origins, namely an increasing awareness that all was not well in the management of the reserves. There was need for much greater competence. The vision for such an experimental station affirmed what the founding figures of the Conservancy had always believed: the value of close rapport between the practitioner and researcher. If regional officers could claim to have identified the need for applied research, the scientist was a principal beneficiary at a time of growing concern regarding the organisation of Government research and development.

Max Nicholson made clear his own views on a wholly-integrated approach to management and research in the paper given at Edinburgh in 1956. Particularly at such an early stage in the developing science and art of nature conservation, they were one and the same thing. Any adequate management of natural areas had to come near to applied research. Close and systematic observations, and field trials, were needed to appraise the response of natural habitats to various forms of management in different conditions. Similarly, any adequate research project must be so involved with the actual processes of nature that it became almost a trial in the treatment of the area. From this standpoint, it was hardly an exaggeration to say that no management was worth serious attention unless it embodied some element of research or experiment, and that no research need be considered which did not represent a prototype or test capable of contributing to some possible management-treatment (Nicholson 1956).

None questioned such sentiments but there was nonetheless confusion and, at times, tension regarding individual responsibilities. As Joe Eggeling recalled, he was never given a job description of his duties as Conservation Officer for Scotland. It was left to him to decide whether to write scientific papers or to ensure the protection of individual sites. He reasoned that if his staff were to be highly motivated, they too had to be allowed a measure of specialisation. Such differences of emphasis and ambition could, however, quickly turn into competition and resentment over personal promotion or

E.F. Warburg (*left*) and **J. Grant Roger** (later Regional Officer, North-east Scotland) looking at a whitebeam, *Sorbus arranensis*, at the southern end of Glen Diomhan NNR, North-west Arran, in September 1958. This small woodland contained two rare whitebeams, both of which were confined to Arran.

access to resources. Staff were soon identified as belonging to one of two camps: research or conservation. Even where they shared the same buildings, close rapport and collaboration could not be taken for granted.

Helga Frankland was later to recall how, on her appointment as Deputy Regional Officer for the North of England, based at Merlewood, there was definitely a 'them and us' feeling between research and regional staff. The research staff, knowing full well that their standing depended on a good record of academic publications, continued to pursue their separate specialisms. Without this, neither the individual scientist nor the Conservancy (as a research council) would have any credibility within the scientific community. The wardens responsible for the reserves rarely read research publications and were, in any case, often resentful of the expert, who was full of ideas but who patently had no day-to-day experience of actually looking after land.

An administrative adjustment with far-reaching implications was instituted in 1956, when a report by the Treasury Organisation and Methods Division recommended that the conservation work be made 'a primary executive function' of the Conservancy. The *Annual Report* of that year described the establishment of a Conservation Branch as giving formal recognition to the two main streams of work within the organisation. Although Barton Worthington had been appointed to take charge of the Branch, the title of his post, Deputy-Director (Scientific), indicated a reluctance to draw hard-and-fast divisions. He was also required to assist with the Conservancy's research and scientific work (Nature Conservancy 1956, 5–6).

The regional officer was likely to play a key part in determining the relationship between the management and research parts of the Conservancy. According to an Establishment Notice, regional officers might continue their personal research, particularly where it related to 'the evolution of the habitat' within their respective regions. Some needed no encouragement. Eric A.G. Duffey had held a Conservancy research

Norman Moore (Regional Officer for the South-west Region), with **Derek Ranwell**, speaking of the Management Plan for the Yarner Wood NNR, during a visit made by the British Ecological Society to the reserve in July 1957.
This sessile oak wood was acquired from 1952 onwards, some parts being allowed to develop naturally.

studentship before being appointed to the Conservancy, first for 'regional work in East Anglia' and then as Regional Officer in April 1953. His region extended from the Norfolk Broads to Huntingdonshire. An invertebrate ecologist, his specialism was spiders. Fridays were 'spider days' in the Norwich office, when the door was firmly shut against all interruption. It was Martin George's responsibility to deal with any crises that day, but he recalled how he too had been advised to pick a day each week to pursue a topic of his own. Springtails were suggested as a good group to study.

Norman W. Moore was appointed in August 1953 as the Regional Officer for South-west England, based at the Furzebrook research station. As an assistant lecturer at Bristol, his part-time study of dragonflies so impressed his professor that it was submitted successfully for a PhD. Moore's region extended from the Scilly Isles to Dorset and Herefordshire. Ian Prestt, his early assistant, recalled that local natural history societies expected a Government scientist in a suit. Moore's appearance with a butterfly net, collecting jars and vacuum flask quickly won their respect and cooperation. On his appointment, Diver had told Moore 'to get to know South West England better than anyone else' (Moore 1987, 31). By the time he left Dorset in 1960, having visited practically every heathland, Moore was able to publish a paper in the *Journal of Ecology*, illustrating how the original heath of 16 areas, largely in three blocks separated by river valleys, had become over 100 fragments. The consequences for a range of plant and animal species were illustrated (Moore 1962).

Duffey and Moore were accordingly well qualified to warn of changes taking place both on the reserves and in the countryside at large. As Duffey commented, in his Management Plan for the Woodwalton Fen NNR, the most urgent tasks on acquisition were those of fencing, dyking and other kinds of estate management. As these were completed or became routine operations, attention turned to equally urgent tasks that required an ecological solution. In April 1958 he estimated that more than half of the reserve area was undergoing rapid successional change. If the biological interest which had caused the reserve to be designated in the first place was to be preserved, some sort of balance had to be rapidly imposed (PRO, FT 3, 553).

When the Scientific Policy Committee had addressed the need for biological recording in 1955, discussion had been largely academic but there had been two exceptions. Drawing on his work at Woodwalton Fen, Duncan Poore had illustrated the need to enumerate the types of community present on each reserve, and to establish baselines from which to measure future change. The other paper had been largely written by the Conservancy's statistician, J.G. Skellam. It warned that

> it is not enough to declare nature reserves, to make tentative plans for their management and then for ecologists as a whole to settle down in their laboratories to long-term research, blinded by the phenomenon of plant dominance, or enthused with an exaggerated belief in the balance of nature and a misplaced confidence that the inertia and stability that extensive climax systems may have enjoyed in the past will apply equally well when they are reduced to mere fragments.

Skellam warned that the remnants might already be degenerating, not so much in appearance or the more obvious and less mobile species, but in overall diversity. There was simply no way of knowing whether this was happening or not.

Not only had the Conservancy, under Nicholson, acquired many more reserves, but Duffey and Moore, as regional officers, were acquiring the evidence to demonstrate that

> we are already losing habitats and species in our declared reserves, simply because we do not know enough about the requirements of the species which it is our duty to conserve.

Despite careful searches, Moore had failed to find two of the rarities of the Morden Bog NNR in Dorset. There was little that could be done to protect such species until more was known of their special requirements. Encouraged by Elton and Skellam to combine their independent observations, a joint paper was drawn up in May 1958. It observed that, despite the requirements of almost every reserve Management Plan approved by the Conservancy's various committees, there remained a serious paucity of knowledge and understanding of the individual reserves. Moore recounted how the research on shingle movement and the growth of cord grass (*Spartina townsendii*) being carried out at Furzebrook had helped him in drawing up the Management Plan for the Bridgwater Bay NNR, but such studies had not been intended for that purpose. In 1957, Moore had himself set up pilot schemes focused on the most immediate priorities for reserve management in his region, which were the effects of heather burning and autecological studies of threatened species such as the Dartford warbler. Whilst enough had been done to confirm the usefulness of such work for conservation purposes, progress was painfully slow. With their increasing management commitments, regional officers had even less time to carry out the research themselves, or even deploy their few assistants. Meanwhile, the situation deteriorated, both through seral succession and the increasing number of reserves to be managed.

The joint paper met with a forthright response from both the research stations and

Nicholson himself. The coastal physiographer, Clarence Kidson, wrote in July 1958 that it preached 'a dangerous heresy'. However much interest the paper might have aroused at a recent meeting of the Conservation Group of regional officers, it was important to stress that conservation needs could only be met in a scientific sense by fundamental research, free of the subjectivity associated with *ad hoc* investigations of a more applied kind. Given the Conservancy's straitened circumstances, any investment in research at the regional level was bound to be detrimental to the research stations. It would attract the very serious charge of changing horses in mid-stream. The lack of adequate supervision and contact with experts in the relevant fields of research would inevitably lead to a lowering of standards. There would be a severe risk of the Conservancy becoming merely an agency for managing nature reserves.

The head of the Furzebrook research station, Michael Brian, was equally critical of the 'very vulnerable paper' but sought a more calculated response. Rather than outright condemnation of 'applied' research, Brian wrote that it was both unwise and unnecessary to regard research that had an immediate and obvious application as being necessarily separate from more fundamental studies. Not only might existing projects on his own Station encompass more applied work, but such work was better supervised by his own full-time and highly experienced scientists. He had wanted for some time to enlarge his own studies of ant biology to cover the whole heathland system. But if such a line of argument seemed prudent in defending his Station's income and status, Brian confessed to having little enthusiasm for applied studies. As he told Nicholson, 'I do not want you to think because I am so volunteering that I do not appreciate the peaceful conditions for fundamental research that have been established here.'

At a time when the Conservancy desperately needed to demonstrate the vital contribution that a series of National Nature Reserves might make to the wellbeing of the countryside, Nicholson could hardly be expected to welcome news from his own regional officers that such designation might do little to halt the losses in wildlife. Copies of the joint paper were tabled, their contents discussed in confidence, and then collected up after the meeting of the Conservation Group of officers. Worthington's suggestion that

Access to parts of some Scottish nature reserves was difficult, if not impossible, by conventional means. This illustration from the Conservancy's *Annual Report* for 1959 shows a helicopter transporting fencing and bridging materials at the **Inchnadamph NNR.**

they might be circulated to the Scientific Policy Committee was firmly rejected. Although admiring the initiative shown, Nicholson wrote that the paper had clearly been written under pressure. Everyone knew that there was a great deficiency in knowledge and understanding as to how reserves should be managed. He was particularly dismayed by claims that the Conservancy's research was 'unlikely to help us solve the urgent management problems'. It would be wrong to give regional officers responsibility for carrying out research. Such posts would hardly attract and hold those with the best research minds.

Duffey and Moore remained adamant as to the seriousness of the situation. A further version of their joint paper was given to the Scientific Staff conference of October 1958, under the title, 'Does the Conservancy's research provide an adequate basis for conservation?' The answer was an emphatic, 'No.' Whilst ordinary estate management might suffice — in the sense that periodic burning would maintain some sort of heath, and grazing a type of grassland — it could not guarantee the survival of rare or local species or habitats of a particular type. Something much more discriminating was required. And yet, in ignorance of the particular needs of those habitats or species, the Conservancy had persisted with what were regarded as traditional methods. Since so few records were kept of even these rudimentary forms of management, comparatively little was learned. Duffey and Moore saw no alternative to giving the Conservation Branch the resources to help itself. Whilst the fullest use should be made of the universities and amateur naturalists, their help could only be sporadic. Although the research carried out by the Conservancy's own stations would extend general understanding of ecological processes, and thereby help to improve the basis of reserve management in years to come, it could not be relied upon to tackle the more immediate problems.

In a pre-circulated paper, Verona Conway was at pains to emphasise how, whilst having great sympathy with the joint paper, her priority was rather to help foster greater collaboration in addressing what was the central question for everyone, namely how ecosystems worked. A gradation of research could be discerned that extended from *ad hoc* studies, survey and management trials at one end to deeper comprehension of underlying processes and population dynamics at the other. Although the general balance of the Conservancy's research was nearly right, Conway thought some greater weight might be given, in future recruitment, to the short-term end of the range. But in making such an adjustment, none should feel precluded from contributing to any part of the spectrum that constituted 'conservation research'.

In summing up discussion at the conference, Nicholson claimed that any differences of opinion were largely those of semantics. Essentially, there was a gap between the research-station scientists and conservation staff in the field. There was an obvious need for closer contact, most obviously through regional officers asking for more help on specific problems, but this could not be the whole answer as the number of reserves increased. In discussion, the Conservation Officer for Scotland, Joe Eggeling, suggested that the solution lay in establishing a pool of scientists that could be drawn upon to undertake *ad hoc* problems. Nicholson agreed, citing as an example the research that was needed on the use of herbicides and insecticides. There were, however, dangers. During his recent visit to the United States, he recalled visiting a very good research centre, which had been 'debased' through being 'overloaded' with such *ad hoc* problems. The answer might perhaps be found in another direction, namely in the establishment of a separate station to deal with problems such as management experiments and public relations, to which enquiries and visitors might be referred. As well as planning a research station for Wales in 1959, 'we might have to start something which would be a connecting link between long-term fundamental research and the work of the regional officer.'

THE MONKS WOOD EXPERIMENTAL STATION

To have ignored the warnings of staff with the most intimate knowledge of the reserves, or to have postponed a response, might only have led to even greater embarrassment. There were obvious limits to how far the truth – that legal designation of reserves by an institution that also undertook research did not necessarily bring assurance of preservation, let alone enhancement, of their value – could be concealed. Once convinced of the impending crisis, there was no holding Nicholson back in pressing for what he called 'a centre of applied research and demonstration'. One of the most positive achievements of the Nature Conservancy, it was perhaps Nicholson's most personal achievement of any tangible kind.

In a wide-ranging memorandum addressed to the Scientific Policy Committee in January 1959, Nicholson wrote that the time was ripe to build a bridge between fundamental research workers and those who used or managed land. There were several 'applied' fields where the absence of 'any facilities for testing, experimenting, exchanging specialist experience and giving advice' was a source of intense embarrassment. There was need for

> a new and adequately staffed centre for the effective experimental study, testing, demonstration and dissemination of applied knowledge in animal and plant ecology, and the factors underlying successful management of the fauna and flora.

Far from such a proposal appearing to be a desperate device to save the Conservancy from disaster on its reserves, it became in Nicholson's hands the obvious next step in establishing the Conservancy as a major entity in rural management. Indeed, it appeared to Lord Hailsham and his officials as yet another example of the Conservancy overreaching itself. At a meeting with Hailsham in July 1959, the Chairman of the Conservancy, Arthur Duncan, sought consent for a new purpose-built station, where 'users would come and see practical demonstration within the scope of the Conservancy's work'. Hailsham agreed to further study of the proposal, but warned that the Conservancy was likely 'to face a stiff battle on costs' (PRO, CAB 124, 1606; Sheail 1985, 37–40).

The revised joint paper by Duffey and Moore continued to receive powerful support from members of the Scientific Policy Committee. Cyril Diver recalled that the Conservancy's original intention had been to recruit both laboratory- and field-based scientists. Priority had necessarily been given to building up the research stations. It was now time to develop a strong regional organisation, in which regional officers were free to spend a fair proportion of their time on field research and training. Charles Elton saw no alternative to 'management research' being undertaken, or directed, by those charged with drawing up the reserve Management Plans, namely the regional officers. As an amalgam of scientist, estate manager and public-relations officer, the regional officer was ideally placed to provide such necessary training for new and younger staff. As Worthington wrote, the preparation of Management Plans was an ideal form of training in reserve management (PRO, FT 3, 553).

Once again, the Conservancy was able to capitalise on the extraordinarily varied career of Max Nicholson. His wartime responsibility for maintaining liaison between London and Washington on the Combined Shipping Adjustment Board had necessitated several trips a year to America. Whenever possible, he 'escaped' to spend some time in the field with American naturalists. His early involvement in the affairs of IUCN (page 260) helped him to maintain and develop contacts with such leading American conservationists as Hal Coolidge and Ira Gabrielson. Further links were established during his visit to America in 1955 (page 66). He was aware of the anxieties of American agencies and academics about what they perceived as the inadequacies of higher education, but also knew that considerable strides were being made by leading universities in developing advanced courses. Nicholson drew heavily on such insights in drafting a paper in May 1959 on 'Education for conservation', as it affected adult and higher education, as well as schools. Far from advocating 'a blinkered and piecemeal approach' for any one of those sectors, the paper emphasised that conservation could never fulfil its purpose unless it was dovetailed into everyday activities and the essential interests of people everywhere. Any sound policy for education and information relied as much upon understanding those activities and interests, as it did upon comprehension of the scientific and practical aspects of conservation itself.

Nicholson was well placed to spot the analogous situations arising on both sides of the Atlantic, and an opportunity emerged by which his American experience might be drawn upon. As Chairman of the Conservancy's Scientific Policy Committee, William Pearsall was not only well versed in the debate on the state of the reserves but, prior to his retirement as Professor of the Department of Botany at University College London, he had begun to explore with Nicholson the mutual benefits of establishing a postgraduate diploma course in conservation and ecology. In a joint paper of November 1959, Nicholson wrote that British universities had neglected many of the more important problems arising from the use, planning and managing of land and natural resources. There was a need for broad and deep fundamental training in the physical — and particularly the biological — sciences, together with some insight into the social sciences. Practical experience should also be provided in field survey and experimentation.

Pearsall's contribution was to outline how the deficiency might be met through a one-year course, starting each July. It would include techniques for recognising and assessing the importance of animal numbers, plant communities, soil capability and other major factors in ecology, as well as predicting the outcome of ecological changes and 'the risks inherent in various types of intervention' such as land reclamation, burning, grazing, clearance of vegetation and interference with water levels. In 1960, through what

Nicholson later described as the helpfulness of the Chairman of the University Grants Committee, Lord Murray of Newhaven, and the Provost of University College London, twelve students were accepted for the first formal inter-disciplinary course of its kind (Nicholson 1974).

By the time of his meeting with Lord Hailsham in May 1960, Nicholson's concept of the Huntingdon station had come to include five major elements: studying the side-effects of toxic chemicals; becoming the field station for the one-year Diploma Course at University College London; and conducting research on woodlands, vertebrates and general land-management respectively. Taking them in turn, officials of the Lord President's Officer agreed that research on the effects of toxic chemicals on wildlife should be the really 'big' part of the proposal, in both a scientific and political sense. In providing facilities for the University College course in ecology and conservation, the Conservancy could claim it was responding both to the recommendations of the Select Committee on Estimates and, more generally, to Lord Hailsham's keenness to improve collaboration between the research councils and the universities. In agreeing to these two elements, Lord Hailsham regarded the others and, indeed, the proposal for a third station, as having 'all the marks of an empire-building scheme by enthusiasts'. Whilst not 'wishing to be in any way destructive', Quirk wondered whether there was not risk of spreading 'the Conservancy's already rather slender energies over too thin a field'. The Lord President had to be mindful of the 'revolutionary view' taken by a recent committee that the principal failing of Government research was that there were too many research stations, distributed in too small 'packets'. By bringing them together, it would be easier to concentrate effort, move staff around, cross-fertilise disciplines, and make common use of apparatus and facilities (PRO, CAB 124, 1606).

Nicholson's response to such misgivings was twofold. The Conservancy's two existing research stations were in the wrong part of the country for such purposes. More positively, a new station within the Huntingdon area of the East Midlands would not only be within easy access of University College London, but it would also be close to the largest, and perhaps most neglected, group of National Nature Reserves, namely Woodwalton Fen, Holme Fen, Monks Wood and Castor Hanglands. Between them, they covered fenland peat, Oxford Clay and boulder clay deposits, and oolitic limestone. In October 1959 a paper was prepared by Eric Duffey, outlining the potential of such extensive and varied conditions for developing techniques in conservation ecology; this included the biological and habitat requirements of rare species, the concept of 'indicator species' of different associations of plants and animals, the role of 'key species' in modifying successional change, and the application of phytosociological methods as a valuable new ecological tool.

Still Lord Hailsham hesitated, minuting 'I am suspicious of this scheme without exactly knowing why.' An obvious source of advice was Sir William Slater, the Secretary of the Agricultural Research Council. It was, however, 'a delicate operation asking one research council to comment on the proposal of another'. The most questionable aspects were in any case outside his Council's particular sphere of expertise. Officials accordingly turned to Sir Alexander Todd, the Chairman of the Advisory Council on Scientific Policy (which had replaced the wartime Cabinet Scientific Advisory

Committee). Like others, Todd saw merit in the proposals, but was less convinced as to the need for a new station rather than enlargement of an existing one. Nicholson protested that, whilst Lord Hailsham was entitled to seek advice from wherever he chose, it was rather a new principle for the Advisory Council to be given a supervisory role over the research councils. When advised by the Permanent Secretary to the Office 'not to rush the Minister' in coming to a decision, Nicholson replied that a number of scientists had already been recruited; they would not tolerate unsatisfactory working conditions for long.

As Nicholson insisted, the most pertinent advice was likely to come from the Ministry of Agriculture. He had been invited, in the autumn of 1958, to give evidence to an external Visiting Group to the Ministry's Pest Infestation Control Laboratory. As he told the Conservancy's Scientific Policy Committee, there had been, at the scientific level, a 'complete identity between the views of the Ministry's scientific advisers, both on their staff and on the Visiting Group, and the Nature Conservancy'. The Ministry was clearly keen to transfer all the underpinning research on rabbit, wood pigeon and other rural pests to the Conservancy, once the necessary accommodation had been built. The Ministry had accordingly endorsed the Conservancy's concept of building an applied experimental station. In a letter to the Ministry in September 1959, Nicholson proposed the appointment of a Working Party 'to work out exactly what research should be set in hand at Huntingdon'. The Head of the Laboratory, Ieuan Thomas, with the Head of the Land Pests and Birds Research, H.V. Thompson, were invited to join the Working Party, which otherwise consisted of Pearsall and Elton of the Conservancy's Scientific Policy Committee, Duffey and Moore, and Derek Ovington. The Ministry readily agreed. As the Permanent Secretary wrote later, 'I am sure that the closest co-operation between us will be of the greatest advantage to all concerned, and the more we can strengthen this co-operation the better I shall be pleased' (Sheail 1985, 39–42).

Under the chairmanship of Thomas, the Huntingdon Working Party reported in March 1960, outlining the research programmes and estimating the needs of the four units that would make up the proposed Experimental Station: the Conservation Research Unit; the Toxic Chemicals and Wild Life Unit; a Vertebrate Ecology Unit; and a Woodlands Research Unit. The greatest bone of contention and the main reason for the delay in the Working Party's report was the question of where the new station would be best located. In a progress report of January 1960, Thomas recommended that an alternative site should be found in the Cambridge area. Nicholson stressed that a balance had to be drawn between the ideal and the practical. When the members of the Nature Conservancy voiced objections to the Huntingdon site, Arthur Duncan refused to 'contemplate asking Ministers and the Treasury to approve an alternative site, and therefore leave the Reserves of the East Midlands under-used'. It would probably mean 'rejection of any new Research Station at all'. The Working Party nevertheless insisted that a separate note should accompany its report. It not only repeated its objection to the choice of a Huntingdon site but, this time, stated a preference for a station near Oxford (PRO, FT 7, 5; Sheail 1985, 40–4).

Encouragement for the station came from an unexpected quarter. Following the General Election of September 1959, Lord Hailsham was offered a new post of Minister for Science, coupled with the office of Lord Privy Seal. It meant he became even more receptive to initiatives where science demonstrably met a pressing public need (Hailsham 1975; Lewis 1997,178–89). At a meeting a month later, Hailsham was particularly supportive of research on toxic sprays and plans for the post-graduate training courses. Members of the Nature Conservancy formally resolved in November that Treasury approval should be sought for negotiations to purchase a site. Nicholson described to the Treasury how 'we are all lined up to kill several birds with one stone by this very carefully thought out project'. The Ministry of Agriculture had not only approved the project, but one of 'their key men' was involved in the 'detailed elaboration of our plans'. Nicholson wrote that he confidently expected Lord Hailsham's approval of the scheme, in as much as 'we have anticipated in an almost uncanny way some of the points on which he is asking the Research Councils to take the initiative', particularly in providing support for the universities. Many experts and interested parties had been consulted. In Nicholson's words, 'I have rarely had experience of anything affecting so many interests where all concerned were so keen and so convinced that it will give them important help in meeting their problems' (PRO, FT 7, 5–6).

The omens were good. Although the Treasury refused to make any commitment preceding the final report of the Working Party, it agreed to estimates for 1960–61 to include six posts, subject to plans for the station being agreed in principle within a year. As Nicholson warned, there was clearly a risk of those posts, earmarked for research on toxic chemicals and woodland management, being lost if the Huntingdon site was rejected. In April 1960, the Scientific Policy Committee approved the report of the Working Party and, in the words of the minutes, recommended that the 'Director

A meeting of the Nature Conservancy at 19 Belgrave Square in 1959.
Left to right:
Colonel H. Morrey Salmon,
Lord Hurcomb (Chairman of Committee for England),
Arthur Blenkinsop MP,
Professor W.H. Pearsall (Chairman of Scientific Policy Committee),
Professor L. Dudley Stamp,
P.H. Cooper (Administrative Secretary), **E.M. Nicholson** (Director-General), **A.B. Duncan** (Chairman), **E.B. Worthington** (Deputy Director-General, Scientific),
Professor A.R. Clapham,
Lord Strang, Professor
P.W. Richards (Chairman Committee for Wales), **Colonel J.C. Wynne Finch, Major John Morrison MP.**

The founder-Director of the Monks Wood Experimental Station, **Kenneth Mellanby**, beside the meteorological station during the 1960s.

The tower rising above the single-storeyed, purpose-built laboratories comprised 14 study bedrooms, designed to accommodate students from the University College London Conservation Course and other visiting groups.

General should be authorized to proceed with negotiations for setting up the Station as proposed'. Members of the Nature Conservancy endorsed the somewhat vaguely phrased recommendation. A day before the meeting of the Scientific Policy Committee, Nicholson had written to Lord Hailsham, asking him to approve a formal submission to the Treasury on the 'proposed experimental station near Huntingdon' (Sheail 1985, 44).

After a long discussion in May 1960, Lord Hailsham agreed to the Treasury's consent being sought for the new station, particularly in respect of research on toxic chemicals and provision of the post-graduate conservation course. He accepted the Conservancy's arguments that, if approved for other purposes, the station would also be the best place for vertebrate and reserve-management research. A strong line had to be kept, however, between research on agricultural problems and research on nature conservation. Ever mindful of adverse comment, he stressed 'the unwisdom in keeping protected populations of pest species, such as wood pigeons' (PRO, CAB 124, 1606 and FT 7, 6).

The Treasury's consent for the purchase of 66 acres (26 hectares) of farmland to the south of the Monks Wood NNR for £3,500 was obtained within a few days. The imposition of a ceiling of £100,000 meant, however, that only the first phase of the building programme could proceed. In Nicholson's words, the 'only postponable part of the project' was the Vertebrate Ecology Section. It was a decision taken with considerable reluctance. There were still hopes of personnel of the Infestation Control Laboratory being attracted to the Station. All that remained was to find a name for the station. After some considerable debate, the name 'Monks Wood Experimental Station' was chosen. By adopting the name of the National Nature Reserve, there would be no need to insert two names into one small part of the map!

CHAPTER FIVE

HABITAT PROTECTION AND POLLUTION CONTROL

The British Ecological Society celebrated its golden jubilee in March 1963 with a symposium, during which William Pearsall and Sir Edward Salisbury gave accounts of 'the history of ecology in Britain'. Pearsall described the creation of the Nature Conservancy as the most important post-war development, not only for the opportunities afforded for ecological study on its nature reserves, but also for its research stations and the employment of staff who must of necessity have an ecological background. It was development of a quite different order from the occasional nucleus for ecological research that had begun to appear in the 1930s. The effect on the science of ecology was likely to be profound. The growing number of reserves had already resulted in a rapid development in experimental studies. Conceptually, significant progress had been made in understanding the natural ecosystem as a productive unit (Pearsall 1964).

If ecologists had begun to reap the rewards of their early advocacy for what had come to be known as the Nature Conservancy, that strengthening in the status and resource base of ecology had come not a moment too soon for them to exert influence on the wider use of land and natural resources. Where it had taken the Conservancy some ten years to recognise the need for closer management of wildlife on reserves if their distinctiveness was to be preserved, there was increasing evidence that a similar input was required for the whole countryside. It could no longer be taken for granted that farmers and foresters, and land owners and occupiers generally, would act as 'guardians of the countryside'. Those self-same forces now had the capacity to transform the countryside in ways that were both unprecedented and irreversible.

It would be misleading to suggest that the Conservancy, or even ecologists generally, actively sought the role of policing the introduction and extent of modern farming and forestry practices. Not only did they lack the requisite powers, but any thoughts of a more authoritarian stance were quickly dissipated in the political climate of the 1950s and the fall-out from Crichel Down. Since the only powers generally available to the Conservancy were those of dialogue, sound argument and persuasion, the obvious course was for ecologists to be seen working with, rather than against, land owners and occupiers. That broader and more constructive approach was not only much more in tune

The Lord President of the Council and Minister for Science, **Lord Hailsham**, arriving for the formal opening of the Monks Wood Experimental Station, in October 1963.
In acknowledging the range of research and educational roles that the Station was intended to fulfil, Lord Hailsham's speech focused for the most part on the impact of toxic chemicals on the environment.

with what ecologists were trying to achieve, but it was anticipated that, through such expert guidance, owners and occupiers would see the wisdom of taking greater account of wildlife and the countryside generally.

An outstanding example of such collaborative dialogue and investigation between conservation scientists and rural-interest groups was the research undertaken on the red grouse. A 'Grouse Enquiry' financed by the Scottish Landowners' Association had been initiated in 1956, with the aim of finding a way to reverse the species' widespread decline since the 1930s. The Conservancy took over financial responsibility in 1960, forming a Unit on Grouse and Moorland Ecology in Aberdeen university, located at Banchory on Deeside. Led by David Jenkins and Adam Watson, it became an integral part of the Conservancy in 1968. A census was made at different times of the year on selected moorland areas of north-east Scotland, and a close record was kept of changes in environmental factors that were most likely to have a bearing on the birds' wellbeing. The results strongly suggested that the carrying capacity of the moorlands was ultimately determined by the state of the ling heather. The most economical way of bringing long-term improvement to the bird population was to introduce a burning regime, using small fires on a 10- to 12-year rotation. Beyond the goodwill that the Conservancy hoped to generate by being so closely associated with such relevant research, the studies provided supportive evidence for the long-held contention of conservationists, namely that the natural predators of the grouse fed largely on the 'doomed surplus' of birds, which would have died anyway during the ensuing winter (Nature Conservancy 1970a).

The Monks Wood Experimental Station was formally opened by Lord Hailsham in October 1963. As the brief prepared for the ceremony explained, the word 'Experimental' had been chosen to emphasise that it would be a centre for applied ecological research and demonstration, and for the Conservancy's educational role, particularly for the training of post-graduate students for whom accommodation was provided in the form of 14 study-bedrooms and a canteen (shared with station staff) on the site. The Director, Kenneth Mellanby, was described in *Nature* as 'one of the few senior entomologists with experience in both medical and agricultural entomology'. He was the first Principal of the University College at Ibadan, in Nigeria, and had, since 1955, been head of the Department of Entomology at the Rothamsted Experimental Station (Anon. 1961a). The anticipated staff complement of 38 in its first year would be distributed between three Sections. Norman Moore took charge of the Toxic Chemicals and Wild Life Section, Derek Ovington of the new Woodland Section, and Eric Duffey of the Conservation Research Section. The fullest use of the four local National Nature Reserves was envisaged. The Nature Conservancy took over the BSBI mapping scheme in July 1963, which had led to the publication of the *Atlas of the British Flora* (see page 72). A national Biological Records Centre under Franklyn Perring was established at Monks Wood in April 1964 (Harding and Sheail 1992).

Not only had the timing for establishing the station been impeccable, in terms of taking the Conservancy over a further threshold of political and indeed public perception, but the decision to include both habitat protection and pollution control within its terms of reference proved to be inspired. Although there had been scarcely any reference to pollution in the Huxley or Ritchie reports, there was increasing concern for its impact

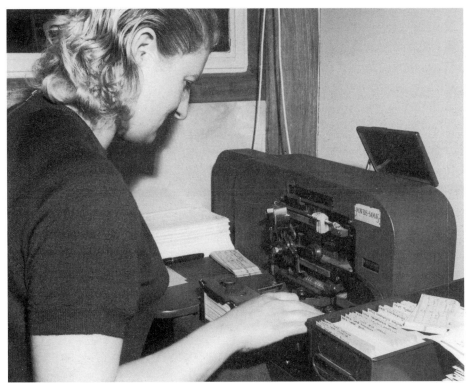

Maggie Horrill and Henry Arnold compiling species maps in the Biological Records Centre at Monks Wood.

(*top right*) Each record of an occurrence was punched on to 40-column computer cards, using a standard Powers Samas/ICL card punch. Information included species code number and Ordnance Survey 10km reference.

(*top left*) The cards were sorted and then loaded, species by species, into a tabulator specifically modified to print the necessary mapping symbols at the correct pitch onto pre-printed base maps of Britain and Ireland.
(*bottom*) By the early 1970s, the database was held on an Atlas 2 computer at the Computer Aided Design Centre in Cambridge. Communication was via teletype and telephone modem link.

on wildlife. The Conservancy had not only foreseen this, but set about tackling the issue within the wider context of conservation research. If those studying habitat requirements required knowledge of the effects of toxic chemicals, scientists unravelling such impacts needed to make comparisons between organisms both under and free from such stress.

The sciences of habitat protection and pollution control were at a stage where a few enthusiastic and highly committed individuals could make a contribution far out of proportion to their number. Barry Pendlebury recalled how, having previously worked with the Atomic Energy Authority (AEA) and the Ministry of Agriculture, he was appointed to the post of Lecturer-Demonstrator at Monks Wood, which was an amalgam of giving talks, organising the visits of students from University College and elsewhere, and acting as warden-naturalist for the Monks Wood and Woodwalton Fen NNRs. For him, 'it was like a dream come true'. The Conservancy appeared at the forefront, fighting many bitter battles with the chemical companies. Each time, its evidence was dismissed as circumstantial; more proof was required. Another recruit from the AEA, Don Jefferies, was finally forced down the road of actually feeding captive stocks of birds with the insecticides to show that they caused infertility and eggshell thinning. Suspecting that herons might be particularly affected by the new agricultural pesticides, Ian Prestt sought a means of studying the great heronry of Troy in Lincolnshire at close quarter. Pendlebury suggested using the Dexion towers no longer needed for monitoring temperature and humidity. At considerable personal risk of injury, many hours were spent in the hides at the top of the high towers, looking down on the herons' nests.

By late 1962, Eric Duffey had recruited to his Conservation Research Section an invertebrate ecologist, Michael G. Morris, and a plant ecologist and agricultural botanist,

Terry C.E. Wells. It was not long before the Section's all-embracing title required revision. Its new name, the 'Lowland Grassland and Grass-heath Section' described more closely the habitats on which it had already begun to specialise. In 1967 a further plant ecologist and an invertebrate ecologist were appointed, together with an historical geographer. A summary of the Section's findings was published as *Nature Reserves and Wildlife* (Duffey 1974), and a single integrated account of the historical, botanical and zoological studies of semi-natural grasslands in lowland areas of England in *Grassland Ecology and Wildlife Management* (Duffey et al. 1974).

The desperate problems of preserving the wildlife interest of the nearby Woodwalton Fen NNR were turned to advantage. Its value in establishing and demonstrating the principles of conservation management helped to justify the heavy investment required to stop the drying-out of the peat soils and the invasion of scrub (which now covered 90 per cent of the reserve). For the first time, cattle were used specifically as a management tool for conservation (Duffey 1971; Williams et al. 1974). A series of Monks Wood symposia provided opportunities to disseminate the Section's findings, and to learn of the highly relevant studies being made elsewhere (Duffey and Morris 1965; Wells 1965a). From his participation as a student in the surveys conducted by A.S. Thomas, and his own pioneering studies from 1963 onwards, of the effects of cutting and sheep-grazing on the chalk grasslands of the Barton Hills NNR in Bedfordshire, Terry Wells could at last offer first-hand and relevant advice to reserve managers. In a review article for the *Handbook of the Society for the Promotion of Nature Reserves*, he emphasised the variety of conditions likely to be encountered both within, and between, sites. Where grazing ceased, coarse grasses increased rapidly. Unless checked, hawthorn scrub might

One of the fenmen cutting the reed on **Woodwalton Fen NNR** in May 1960. Close management such as this was essential to recreate the mosaic of fenland communities and provide opportunity for further trials to re-establish the large copper butterfly. Directed from the nearby Monks Wood Experimental Station, such trials were managed by the Reserve Warden, **Gordon Mason**, shown below with the butterfly's food plant, the great water dock.

quickly establish a closed community. Singly or perhaps in combination, the techniques of grazing and browsing, cutting and burning might be used. If these failed to improve the diversity of the sward, the more radical alternatives of rotovating or ploughing might be adopted (Wells 1965b).

Most reserves had been selected on the assumption that, if the flora was conserved, the invertebrates could look after themselves. Writing of chalk grasslands, Michael Morris identified three components of animal habitats. Vegetation might have relatively little importance where animals exploited other fauna, their carrion, dung or discarded fur and wool. Secondly, a large number of herbivorous invertebrate animals might be restricted to one or more plant species, and the timing and intensity of vegetation management would accordingly have a considerable impact on their access to roots, leaves, stems, buds and flowers, fruit and seed. Thirdly, there were animals that depended on the gross structure of the vegetation; whereas invertebrates that were adapted to the variable and extreme microclimate of bare ground were likely to disappear if grazing pressure was removed, grazing might eliminate species which over-wintered where the ground zone was insulated by field-type vegetation. It followed that no single method of managing chalk grassland was likely to maintain the habitats of all, or even many, of the characteristic populations of invertebrate animals. The optimal approach was found, by experimentation, to be a double rotation — one of three years and the other of about ten years. This would maintain the fauna characteristic of grazed, recently-grazed, and long-ungrazed grasslands, as well as those dependent on different structural types of grassland at different stages of their life histories (Morris 1969).

With its focus on grassland and scrub habitats in lowland areas, the greater part of the Section's work was undertaken in the Conservancy's South and East Anglian regions. Indeed, the collaboration achieved with the regional staff of the South Region became a model of its kind. Personalities helped. Where some former researchers, increasingly immersed in the administrative and managerial details of running a region, might believe they had little to learn from colleagues at Monks Wood, there were no such inhibitions within the South Region. The new Regional Officer, Michael J. Woodman, took up his post at the time the Monks Wood Section was being formed. After spending some years in industry, Woodman had joined Merlewood as a scientific assistant in 1956. Although warned that it was a post without prospects, he was transferred to Furzebrook a year later to join Jim H. Hemsley who, as the first Regional Officer for the South Region, had previously had the office to himself. The out-posted staff were Noel King, who had obtained the post of warden of the Old Winchester Hill NNR after a career as a merchant-navy chief officer, and Colin Tubbs, previously a short-story writer and journalist and now warden for the whole of the New Forest. Richard Jennings, an ex-farmer, was warden-naturalist at the Aston Rowant NNR. George Barker had worked as a schoolboy on Old Winchester Hill; on leaving university he returned there as warden-naturalist. John Blackwood was appointed Assistant Regional Officer in 1963. Their region comprised six counties and contained, at that time, six National Nature Reserves.

There was an obvious synergy between the Monks Wood Section, which sought a test-bed for developing the concept and practice of conservation management, and the region's urgent need to prevent succession to coarse grass and scrub on its grassland

Paul Harding collecting invertebrates from pitfall traps at **Foxhole Heath, Suffolk**, as part of studies by the Conservation Research Section (Lowland Grassland and Grass Heath Section) at the Monks Wood Experimental Station, November 1963. Comparisons of the fauna of nearby heathlands helped to assess the importance of different types of grass heath, and their management, for the conservation of distinctive ranges of Breckland invertebrate life.

A visitor reading the sign to the **Old Winchester Hill NNR** in 1967.
Recommended by the Huxley Committee as 'an experimental reserve', these rough chalk grasslands were acquired in 1954. Together with patches of well-grown yew and other chalk-loving trees, juniper scrub had colonised the southern slopes.

reserves. The farming skills of Jennings proved invaluable in looking after the sheep that were required both for experimental plots and for more immediate management of the Aston Rowant NNR. A mobile 'estate-work team' was assembled, with its own stock, tools and equipment, to help on other reserves. The sheep of a neighbouring farmer grazed the paddocks at Old Winchester Hill. He invariably found the 'old' grassland of the reserve more drought-resistant than his own 'improved' pastures in a dry summer. He was one of the first voluntary wardens to be appointed for a NNR.

By the 1960s, the South Region had 200 Sites of Special Scientific Interest (SSSIs), as notified to the local planning authorities for their flora, fauna, or geological or physiographical interest, under the 1949 Act. As Woodman recalled, many of the files were blank, or simply contained such comments as 'Good for birds'. Information often had to be gathered at very short notice for a planning inquiry that might affect a Site. To prepare for such frenzied occasions, or for the tedious requests of headquarters for statistics (such as the number of SSSIs owned by the National Trust), a more rapid means of information retrieval had to be found. Blackwood and Woodman devised a punched-card system with a map for each Site. A needle was poked through, say, 'the National Trust hole', and out fell the relevant cards within seconds.

How might a detailed, yet comprehensive, knowledge of the semi-natural vegetation of a region be acquired, with such meagre resources? The approach of the seven staff of the South Region was to sit round a table and agree a dozen or so broad vegetation categories. Sheets of the Ordnance Survey 1:25,000 series were allocated, with instructions to colour such areas appropriately. With a good pair of binoculars, the close network of roads, bridleways and paths made it possible to see most of the countryside without trespass. As the coloured sheets came together over the ensuing 18 months, the New Forest emerged as top grade as anticipated. Other areas, such as the Chilterns, proved more 'patchy' in their wildlife value. Blackwood and Tubbs (1970) went on to demonstrate the practicality of rapid habitat-survey through publication of a quantitative survey of chalklands for the whole of England in an early issue of the journal, *Biological Conservation*. Of the 107,605 acres (45,546 hectares) that were found to survive, about 70 per cent were in Wiltshire. At a more local scale, such mapping made it easier to decide priorities for more detailed investigation and also proved invaluable in helping planning officers to appreciate the difference between the 'green' of farmland and that of semi-natural habitat. They were able to see at a glance where the wildlife interest principally resided. As Woodman recalled, they caused one County Planning Officer to have a 'Road to Damascus' type of conversion.

So strong were the pressures for building development, intensive farming, and greater opportunities for outdoor recreation, that the Conservancy staff might have been expected to devote all their energies to defending the existing and proposed reserves and SSSIs. Whilst none doubted the need to defend them, a 'fortress mentality' would have been short-sighted. To use Woodman's analogy, if the countryside was represented by a Christmas tree, and the reserves were the 'fairy on the top', you could not possibly expect her to survive if the tree went up in flames.

Public contact was, in any case, essential. The individual officers of the regional staff were the 'face' of the Conservancy within their ascribed county. Noel King moved to

North Meadow NNR, Cricklade,
in April 1976.
This reserve carried Britain's largest wild population of the snake's head fritillary.

Wiltshire and became Chief Warden in 1967. He later recalled how one felt like an explorer and missionary, in terms of both the natural and social history of the communities visited. An outstanding 'discovery' was the extensive mosaic of chalk grasslands that comprised the grounds of the Porton Down Chemical Defence Establishment. With the active support of the Head of the Range Section at Porton, the Region was able to draw up a Conservation report, and a major research paper on the distinctive grassland communities was written at Monks Wood for publication in the *Journal of Ecology* (Wells et al. 1976). It was one of the first examples of recognition being given to the nature-conservation value of Ministry of Defence lands.

There was intense interest too in the possibility of the Conservancy acquiring its first alluvial-grassland NNR. Such 'unimproved' habitats were becoming increasingly rare. The flood meadow of North Meadow, Cricklade, was particularly outstanding. The local Natural History Society had, however, never recommended it for preservation, on the premise that nothing would ever prevent the gypsies picking the fritillaries. Nor was the

Conservancy's Land Agent over-keen to engage in the complexities of purchasing common rights in the meadow. But, as recalled later by Assistant Land Agent Brian Bradley, Noel King displayed a remarkable ability in winning the confidence of the many people involved. Even so, he failed with one man, who owned much of the meadow – and slept out-of-doors in a wheelbarrow. It was only when he died that the daughter could sell.

In pursuit of the Region's 'Beyond the Reserves' policy, much time was spent participating in such exercises as the *East Hampshire Area of Outstanding Natural Beauty Study of 1967*. It began when the County Planning Officer was asked to draw up a policy for the Area of Outstanding Natural Beauty (AONB). Woodman obtained a role for the Conservancy, and soon every relevant agency was involved. A set of policies was drawn up for each part of the AONB, taking into account the needs of recreation, conservation, farming and forestry. The report attracted much attention when it was launched by the Minister of Housing and Local Government in London (Hampshire County Council et al. 1968). In Buckinghamshire, Richard Jennings was closely involved in the early planning of the New City of Milton Keynes, playing a key role in encouraging the Development Corporation to appoint a full-time ecologist to guide and watch over the development as it took shape. In the New Forest, the fact that Colin Tubbs' office was next door to that of the Forestry Commission's Deputy Surveyor helped in developing a close working relationship. This was of great assistance in determining how to respond to the enormous pressures for recreation and building development. Some two-thirds of the 90,000 acres (36,400 hectares) of the New Forest were open to public access.

THE CHEMICAL REVOLUTION

For many years, chemists had sought a synthetic contact insecticide capable of being made in the laboratory and manufactured on a large scale. The 'discovery' of DDT in the early 1940s gave a tremendous fillip to the search for a compound that could kill every insect with which it came into contact, but left unharmed the crops on which it was spread (Mellanby 1992). In addition to the strides made in developing organochlorine and organophosphate compounds, the war years saw the development in America and Britain of the synthetic plant regulators, MCPA and 2,4-D. An infrastructure was already in existence to promote these pesticides in farming and forestry (Dunlap 1981). A new era of chemical control had begun.

Not all scientists were mesmerised by what had been discovered. In a paper, published in *Atlantic Monthly*, Wigglesworth (1945) warned that DDT might act 'like a blunderbuss discharging shot in a manner so haphazard that friend and foe alike were killed'. In the discussion of a paper on 'The use of the new insecticide DDT in relation to the problems of tropical medicine', given to the Royal Society of Tropical Medicine in February 1945, Kenneth Mellanby (on a short visit to London from Burma) warned that 'DDT was clearly no panacea which could be broadcast indiscriminately to kill off all noxious pests'. There was need for much research on its effects on 'apparently unimportant insects and other forms of life'. It was the only way to ensure that it had no serious effect on the 'balance of nature'. Much to his annoyance, Mellanby forgot the interjection until coming across it in the *Transactions* of the Society, some forty years later. It would undoubtedly have figured large in his New Naturalist volume, *Pesticides and Pollution*, published in 1967 (Mellanby 1967 and 1992, 61–2).

It was a Committee on Health, Welfare and Safety in Non-Industrial Employment (the Gower Committee) that first brought the potential side-effects of the new pesticides to public notice, following the death of operatives both in Britain and, more particularly, North America. By the middle of 1950, officials of the Ministry of Agriculture realised that their Minister had to be seen taking some action to protect people handling such compounds. A conference of representatives of farmers, workers, manufacturers and contractors was convened, with a Deputy Secretary in the chair,

> to ventilate the question of how best to ensure the safety of the workers without depriving the agricultural industry of the advantages which the new substances could bring by the way of greater production and increased efficiency.

The conference welcomed the appointment of a Working Party of leading scientists, with Professor Solly Zuckerman as its chairman (PRO, MAF 132, 1). This too recommended statutory backing for safety measures which many employers had already implemented on a voluntary basis. The Government agreed, and an Agriculture (Poisonous Substances) Bill was passed without opposition in 1952 (Sheail 1991a).

By the time the Working Party had reported, there was mounting concern about the possibility of people being harmed by pesticide residues in their food. The Working Party was reconstituted to assess the risk. The issues were much less clear cut. Under pressure from the Ministry of Agriculture, the Zuckerman Working Party agreed that, rather than extending statutory control, an Inter-departmental Advisory Committee should be appointed 'to keep under constant review all risks that may arise from the use of toxic substances in food production and storage'. Manufacturers would voluntarily submit new compounds, or new uses for existing compounds, to the scrutiny of the Committee and its Scientific Sub-committee, prior to the products being marketed (PRO, MAF 130, 61; Working Party 1953).

The deliberations of the two Working Parties, and the decision to appoint an Inter-departmental Advisory Committee, provided the vital context for considering the threat of pesticides to wildlife. In a report of 1955, a third Zuckerman Working Party found evidence of changes to wildlife occurring on an unprecedented scale. As expected, the Working Party recommended that membership of the Advisory Committee should be expanded to include representatives of nature-conservation interests. Whilst the adjustments were made, none doubted the scale and complexity of the task ahead (Working Party 1955; Sheail 1985, 19–29). In a paper submitted to the Working Party, on behalf of the Association of British Insecticide Manufacturers, E.F. Edson described how difficult it was to imagine a problem with more facets and imponderables than that of the accidental killing of field animals by chemicals. It was not simply that so few facts were available, or that advances in selective toxicity were one of the most difficult tasks humankind could set itself. So many conflicting interests were also involved (SRO, AF 60, 89).

Nature-conservation interests were in danger of having little to show for their representation at meetings of the Inter-departmental Advisory Committee on Poisonous Substances. It was assumed that the wildlife aspects were 'on ice'. It was thought impossible to test the potential effects of pesticides on wild species. Such assumptions were strongly contested by the Conservancy's two representatives. Robert E. Boote had been appointed as a Principal to the Conservancy's headquarters in 1954. A native of Stoke-on-Trent, he had obtained a degree in economics at London University, and returned from military service in 1946 to a post with the Stoke-on-Trent City Council, becoming Chief Administrative Officer for the Staffordshire County Planning and Development Department. Soon taking charge of the operational side of the Conservancy's work, his immediate priorities were: reorganising procedures for selecting, acquiring and managing the reserves, devising ways of implementing the Protection of Birds Act of that year, and – as his third major assignment – surveillance of pesticide use. Boote's scientific briefing came from the Conservancy's representative on the Scientific Sub-committee, Olive Balme, the Regional Officer for South-east England, who had been conducting trials on the impacts of the new herbicides on roadside verges (Sheail 1985, 6–15).

Olive Balme's research provided the first instance of a curb being imposed in order to protect the wildlife interest. Cyril Diver had expressed his misgivings over the use of such new compounds as 2,4-D and MCPA for verge management, in a letter to the Ministry of Agriculture in July 1950. He warned that the 'simplification of the roadside verge' could be harmful for both nature conservation and agricultural interests. The removal of plant species would deprive the fauna dependent on them for food and shelter. Such disruption to 'the balance of nature' might have important repercussions for the control of pests and diseases in nearby farm crops. Similar concerns had been expressed by the Advisory Entomologists of the National Agricultural Advisory Service. Professor J.W. Munro drafted a paper setting out the benefits of a joint Agricultural Research Council/Nature Conservancy study. The upshot was the appointment, in June 1951, of a small team under Munro. A Conservancy scholarship and a special grant from the Agricultural Research Council made possible the appointment of two entomologists. Olive Balme, just appointed as a plant ecologist by the Conservancy, was seconded to the team in August 1951. Whilst the entomological findings were somewhat inconclusive, the botanical trials suggested that, whereas the wildlife interest would be eliminated, the most conspicuous weeds would quickly recolonise the ground. Any lasting control would require repetitive spraying.

It was against this background of trials and observations that the Conservancy and the Ministry of Transport reached agreement in 1955 on how spraying might be regulated in future. The Conservancy would have no objection to selective sprays of the phenoxy-acetic-acid type if four conditions were met: spraying should be confined to trunk and class 1 roads at the earliest possible stage of growth; only a width of 10 feet (3 metres) from the roadside edge should be treated; there should be no spraying of verges known to have a wildlife interest; finally, it was emphasised that the guidance was only tentative and that further limitations might be recommended in the light of experience. The substance of the agreement was conveyed in a circular to highway authorities, issued by the Ministry of Transport in August 1955 (Sheail 1985, 6–15).

It was with such experience that the Conservancy approached the negotiations leading up to the Wildlife Panel, under the aegis of the Inter-departmental Advisory Committee on Poisonous Substances. As Bob Boote emphasised, it was in the interests of the industry itself to demonstrate that its products were harmless to both bees and those forms of wildlife beneficial to farming and forestry. For their part, the manufacturers agreed in principle to submit information as to the effects of chemicals on wildlife, if they could be advised 'on ways and means of obtaining adequate and reliable data'. The feeling that the Conservancy should take the lead in providing such information was strongly expressed by members at a meeting of the Nature Conservancy, in November 1958. The Chairman spoke of abundant evidence of toxic chemicals having a dangerous effect throughout the country, and a member, Colonel Charles Floyd, wrote that the problem was becoming more urgent every day. In one day, his farm manager had been pursued by no less than three salesmen from three different firms all trying to sell him new sprays for use in the following spring. The meeting called upon the Conservancy's Scientific Policy Committee to 'investigate as a matter of urgency the possibility of the Conservancy undertaking large-scale research into the effect on wild life of the use of toxic chemicals in agriculture'. Nicholson was hesitant, warning of the 'very complicated, fast-moving nature of the problems involved, and the need for additional finance, if research work were to be undertaken' (PRO, FT 3, 197).

Matters came to a head in early 1958, when a manufacturer accused the Advisory Committee of being unduly harsh in its attitude towards one of the firm's products. In correspondence, the firm asked whether 'the Nature Conservancy people would like to join us in looking for untoward effects on game and wildlife' during spraying trials. This was just the kind of practical collaboration Boote had been striving to achieve on the Committee. It would open the door for further discussions and illustrate the value of the Committee's having a specialist Wildlife Panel. Barton Worthington warned, however, of the considerable responsibility this would place on the Conservancy, if it gave its blessing to a pesticide under trial. Any observations or investigations would have to be made in an extremely thorough manner (PRO, FT 3, 213).

Further discussion was cut short by a series of economies imposed by the Government because of the general economic situation. Whereas Boote had written a memorandum, emphasising that the closer surveillance of the increased use of pesticides was 'of front rank importance in our conservation work and is a vital public relations issue' (PRO, FT 3, 207), Nicholson identified it as one of the activities that ministers had definitely decided to postpone. Instruction was given that the voluntary conservation bodies should be told of the decision. It was 'no use pretending we can just add more commitments without resources to cover them' (PRO, FT 3, 213). Since, without the scientists, there would be no scientific data to support those representing wildlife interests, Boote concluded there would be no point in seeking the appointment of a Wildlife Panel to the Inter-departmental Advisory Committee. In reply to a Parliamentary Question in July 1958, a Government spokesman confirmed that a shortage of funds and manpower had precluded any official initiative being taken on the question of toxic chemicals (PD, Commons, 590, 1574–5).

For the Conservancy, the reversal in expectations not only involved some loss of face, but would severely handicap its representatives in their deliberations on the Advisory Committee and the Scientific Sub-committee during what was clearly going to be a crucial period in the development and deployment of toxic chemicals. Refusing to 'take no for an answer', Boote prepared a paper for the Conservancy's Scientific Policy Committee, setting out the 'effects on wildlife of the use of toxic chemicals in agriculture'. Drawing heavily on the advice given him by members of the Ministry's Infestation Control Laboratory and other bodies, he explained both the current situation and the need for further initiatives to regulate pesticide use. The paper asked members of the Nature Conservancy to approve the appointment of a scientific officer to the Wildlife Panel, and to allocate scientific staff to work on toxic chemicals as the need arose and resources allowed (PRO, FT 3, 216). Boote's 'long and detailed paper' was ready in the autumn of 1958, but was placed so low on the agenda that it was not considered until January 1959. By then, popular concern was more evident, and its recommendations were approved.

At its meeting in March 1959, Boote informed the Inter-departmental Advisory Committee that the Conservancy now wished to proceed with the appointment of a Wildlife Panel. The Advisory Committee agreed, and asked the Minister to make the necessary arrangements. It first met in December 1959, by which time the need to develop a capability in toxic-chemical research as rapidly as possible had provided Nicholson with his most powerful reason for establishing what became the Monks Wood Experimental Station (Sheail 1985, 32–6).

'SILENT SPRING'

Whatever the long-term significance of the decisions taken by the Conservancy, they were but a side-play in the evolving debate within the agricultural industry itself. It was, for example, the possible threat to the bee-keeping industry that first caused the Department of Agriculture for Scotland to become involved. The Fifeshire Beekeepers Association warned, in March 1957, of the effects of indiscriminate spraying. Although the losses caused by the spraying of charlock in corn crops were probably exaggerated, officials conceded that the problem was a real one. There were, however, no powers by which the Secretary of State could prescribe when crops might be sprayed. It was noted, however, that the Ministry of Agriculture had asked the National Farmers' Union (NFU) and National Association of Agricultural Contractors to remind members that they should avoid spraying crops in flower. If absolutely necessary, they should first inform local officers of the Ministry, so that steps could be taken to warn bee-keepers in the area. Officials of the Department of Agriculture thought it 'politically prudent' to follow a similar procedure, using the three Scottish Agricultural Colleges to pass on such warnings as were necessary to the bee-keeping associations (SRO, AF 74, 168).

Such tokenism might suffice for bee-keeping, but there was a need for something much more substantive to counter the increasing hostility caused by damage inflicted by farmers' sprays drifting onto horticulturalists' crops. As the NFU reported to the

Ministry, its membership could not agree on the terms of an inquiry, let alone how to raise a levy on farmers to compensate horticulturalists. The only point of agreement among the membership was that the cost should be met by the Government. Both Agriculture Departments refused, insisting that the industry itself should resolve the issue. In July 1959, however, the Minister appointed a small Departmental Committee, under the Parliamentary Secretary, Earl Waldegrave, ostensibly to brief him on how a solution might be found. The President of the NFU was shown in confidence a copy of the report, completed in April 1961. Although there had been little effect on the horticultural industry as a whole, the report described how individual growers had been badly affected. It was often so difficult to prove the precise source of the damage as to preclude any possibility of obtaining even partial compensation. Although insurance of the crop would enable a claim to be made without the need to prove the source of the drift, the Committee acknowledged that growers should not be expected to finance the protection of their crops from the damage caused by others. Whilst steps could be taken to minimise drift, the Committee believed there would always be risk of human error: some drift was always possible. There was, in short, no practical solution. The Government refused to finance a levy, and the farming industry rejected a self-imposed levy. It was thought to be impracticable for a levy to be imposed on the pesticide products. Following consultations with the Agricultural Research Council and National Agricultural Advisory Service, a research panel of six members was appointed, and a Code of Conduct was drafted.

It was during these highly secretive discussions as to how the damaging side-effects of pesticide use (and the cost to individual members of the industry) might be mitigated, that the first reports were received of large-scale losses of birdlife. The first bird deaths that could conceivably be linked with new dual-purpose seed dressings to protect crops — the organochlorines dieldrin, aldrin and heptachlor — were reported in 1956. The Scientific Sub-committee of the Minister's Inter-departmental Advisory Committee appointed a Panel to investigate and make recommendations. It found that only grain-eating birds were affected, and that almost every incident occurred during the planting and germinating period. Since the losses were small in relation to the areas sown, the Panel rejected any notion of a major threat to birdlife. Such an assertion was largely contradicted by a Joint Committee of the BTO and RSPB, working through a network of observers (and supported by post-mortem analyses), in the sowing seasons of 1960 and 1961 (Cramp and Conder 1961; Cramp, Conder and Ash 1962). Editorials appeared in major newspapers, a minor debate was held in the House of Commons in March 1961, and a Parliamentary Question was put down for later that month (Sheail 1985).

It was not only the naturalist who was appalled by what was happening. The unexplained deaths of unprecedented numbers of foxes and game birds aroused serious concern. The Land Agent for the Sandringham estate in Norfolk was one of several to write to the Conservancy, seeking assurances that someone was investigating the reports of 'dopey' foxes. His main fear was that the mortality among pigeons and foxes would spread to his game coverts. The Royal Veterinary College had a team of three carrying out pathological studies, and the Conservancy decided to appoint J.C. Taylor, who had just become warden-naturalist in the Breckland, to collect and collate all relevant field evidence. By April 1960, he had confirmed that fox-death was largely confined to arable areas where large numbers of pigeons and other birds had died. Its incidence corresponded with sowing time, with two distinct waves in some parts coinciding with winter and spring drilling. In Taylor's view, the fact that the Royal Veterinary College and others had been unable to isolate a virus or provide evidence of a disease being transmitted from one animal to another seemed to confirm the evidence that the foxes had died from scavenging pigeons contaminated by chemicals such as dieldrin. By May 1960, the Laboratory of the Government Chemist had succeeded in devising the relevant methods for detecting dieldrin. Post-mortem analyses soon revealed large amounts in some carcases. Shortly before the publication of its *Annual Report* in December, which summarised Taylor's findings, the Conservancy learnt that the Ministry's Pest Infestation Control Laboratory had now accepted that fox-death was the direct result of using seed dressings (Sheail 1985, 68–74).

In correspondence with the Scottish Department, Ministry officials wrote, in March 1961

> Our Minister is very concerned about the problem and, at his special request, we are making every effort to obtain publicity warning farmers to handle seed dressings containing dieldrin, aldrin and heptachlor carefully.

As well as three press notices, arrangements had been made for the subject to be mentioned on television and radio, including the radio serial, *The Archers*. In preparing a Progress Report for the Minister in early April, officials described how, as the farmer's most trusted advisers, members of the National Association of Corn and Agricultural Merchants had an important part to play. The Ministry's Regional Controllers had been particularly active in making farmers aware of the dangers of seed dressings. Even so, field surveys suggested that many farmers, and especially those without game interests, remained ignorant or apathetic. A Ministry official, R.J.E. Taylor, was nevertheless hopeful that, within another season or two, the propaganda would have made its mark.

> Our experience with safety legislation and propaganda leads me to think that any publicity, whatever the merits of the subject, takes a considerable time to sink in and be assimilated on a really large scale. But in the end, results are obtained (SRO, AF 74, 168).

Such confidence in letting matters take their course was shaken by pressures in both the press and parliament. Under the banner headline, 'Poison in the air', the *Sunday Post* of 9 April 1961 published an article by an Angus gamekeeper, which declared that 'a silence is falling over the hills'. In phrases that anticipated Rachel Carson's book, *Silent Spring*, the correspondent wrote 'Many of the songbirds are singing no more.' They had first appeared, lying dead, some three or four years ago. The writer continued, 'I am told committees have been formed to "investigate the matter" '...Government Departments are 'conducting research into the problem', but in the meantime, 'the song birds are dying in their hundreds'. Something had to be done very quickly. A few days later, a Member of Parliament, Sir James Duncan, pressed the Secretary of State for a more centralised and thorough investigation of pigeon carcases found in Angus and neighbouring counties. As officials discovered, delays were caused not simply by the large number of carcases being sent to the Ministry's Infestation Control Laboratory. The methods of analysis had been developed only recently and the hydrocarbons were difficult to detect without long examination. However, the reply sent to Sir James placed most of the emphasis on the fact that such abnormal deaths had been reported from only a few estates. It was hard to make a statistical appraisal of the scale of pigeon deaths from one year to the next. Even where residues of the compounds were found, it was by no means certain that they were the cause of death (SRO, AF 74, 168).

By now, those with game interests and even some in the farming industry itself were becoming outspoken. Staff of the Edinburgh and East of Scotland Agricultural College were convinced that there was a definite connection between the sowing of dressed seed and death of the pigeons. The College Principal warned of how the localised nature of the reports of 'abnormal' death-rates simply reflected the fact that such losses were only reported from game estates; farmers would not bother to record the destruction of such pests as the wood pigeon. The Edinburgh College of Agriculture found deaths to be highest in those parts of Angus where wheat was grown over a fairly large area, especially along the coast and in the Forfar–Glamis area of Strathmore. The highest death rate coincided with the peak of sowing time.

The unexplained deaths of unprecedented numbers of game birds and foxes south of the Border meant that a working alliance of the utmost significance for nature conservation began to evolve between naturalists and sporting interests. In April 1961, Lord Shackleton, who had first come to know Nicholson well as Parliamentary Private Secretary to Herbert Morrison, initiated a debate in the House of Lords. Using information supplied by Bob Boote, Shackleton claimed he had never been so well briefed for a debate. In his speech, he emphasised that it was no longer enough to say that man had always interfered with nature, and that most farmers and manufacturers were responsible people. The use of chemicals had brought about a very dangerous situation: for the second year running, heavy casualties among bird and mammal life were being reported during the spring sowing season. In causing such a catastrophic situation, the agricultural chemist had achieved a record that would have been the envy of the Borgias (PD, Lords, 226, 405–76; Lords, 229, 509–16; Lords, 230, 807–38).

A few days after this debate an Under-Secretary in the Ministry of Agriculture, C.H.M. Wilcox, wrote to officials of the Department of Agriculture for Scotland, emphasising that 'our Ministers have been under heavy pressure' in both Houses of Parliament. It was a matter on which

> our Minister personally feels considerable concern, and he tells us that he had been much impressed by the strength of feelings on this subject among ordinary backbench members... [He has accordingly decided that] ...if no other means are available of preventing casualties for the future on the sort of scale that have been reported in recent months, he for his part would have no hesitation in introducing legislation for the control of the use of agricultural chemicals that are a menace to wild life and that he anticipates that Parliament would be very willing to pass such legislation.

Although there was no doubt that any ban would have to be imposed throughout Great Britain, officials of the Scottish Department had considerable misgivings as to the wisdom of threatening compulsory powers. Whilst they recognised that the Minister was under 'quite a bit of political pressure', officials warned that manufacturers might be far less responsive than when the Minister had sought the withdrawal of alkali arsenite as a potato-haulm and weed killer. In that instance, there had been a threat to human health. 'A hasty decision' in respect of wildlife might cause manufacturers to challenge the value of the Inter-departmental Advisory Committee and the voluntary notification scheme, devised primarily to assess risk to human food. Such ministerial intervention was likely to sap the confidence of industry in developing new pesticides (SRO, AF 74, 168).

The Ministry's Infestation Control Laboratory confirmed both the gravity of the situation and the scope for compromise. If dieldrin and heptachlor continued to be used at their present scale, there would be considerable bird casualties in many years, even if the agreed precautions were observed under field conditions. Further discussions with the Laboratory and the Plant Pathology Laboratory confirmed that the other widely used insecticidal dressing, benzene hexachloride (BHC), might be just as effective for protecting cereal seed against insect pests other than the wheat bulb fly. Officials accordingly recommended that, before the meeting scheduled with relevant interests in late June 1961, an agreement should be sought with manufacturers, merchants and the NFU for a voluntary ban on the use of dieldrin, aldrin and heptachlor as cereal seed dressings, save for autumn-sown wheat in areas where control of wheat bulb fly was necessary. The discussions should make it clear that, if 'the whole hearted cooperation of the industry' was not forthcoming, the Minister would probably find it necessary to ask Parliament for statutory powers to control the sale and use of agricultural chemicals that presented a hazard to human and animal life.

At that meeting, attended by representatives of industry and the conservation bodies, held in late June under the Ministry's chairmanship, it was again agreed that there was no certain proof that the chemicals actually caused the deaths. The circumstantial evidence, however, left little room for doubt, especially as some of the birds were found to have consumed the dressed seed shortly before they died. This was particularly striking in birds analysed in the springtime. Representatives of the Nature Conservancy accordingly pressed for a complete ban on the use of dressings containing aldrin, dieldrin and heptachlor. At the very least, such dressings should only be used under specific instruction given by an officer of the Ministry. The alternative suggestion made by the Ministry was eventually accepted by all parties, namely to restrict the use of these seed dressings to autumn and winter sowings where considerable damage from wheat bulb fly was expected. Formally negotiated under the Pesticides Safety Precautions Scheme (as it was now called), the voluntary ban took effect in January 1962. The surveys conducted by a Joint Committee of the BTO and RSPB reported only 41 incidents attributable to seed dressings in the spring of 1962 (compared with 292 during the comparable period of 1961). The Joint Committee attributed this to the ban and the excellent sowing conditions, both in the autumn of 1961 and the following spring.

These anxieties about the use of pesticides had been voiced some two years before

Frank Moriarty, one of a dozen or so scientists appointed to the Toxic Chemicals and Wild Life Section at Monks Wood, just before publication in Britain of Rachel Carson's *Silent Spring*.

Rachel Carson's polemic, *Silent Spring*, caught the public imagination, first in America where it was first published in the *New Yorker* in June 1962, and then in the UK, with the appearance of the British imprint in February 1963 (Carson 1963). Lord Hailsham had already borrowed a copy of the American edition from the Conservancy, when another arrived from Prince Philip, the Duke of Edinburgh. He 'absolutely agreed' that the book was thought-provoking, and that everyone should be goaded into ensuring that there were sufficient safeguards, particularly in the field of testing and research. Lord Hailsham was not so much concerned with the alleged inaccuracies of the book, but rather with whether Rachel Carson had got 'the real essence of the matter and drawn the right inferences from her premises'. She had obviously drawn attention to one of the most important side-issues of scientific development. Many of the substances used today were extremely powerful. They had unpredictable and horrible side-effects. By far the most dramatic example had been that of thalidomide. In Hailsham's words, 'we do owe it to our own species and others to avoid things like this if we can'. As he informed Prince Philip, the scare over seed dressings 'enabled us to tighten up our organisation and, on paper at least, it looks pretty watertight'. Although Rachel Carson had made a case for further examining the possible effect of DDT and 2,4-D, Hailsham expected the results of the enquiries he had instigated to be fairly reassuring (PRO, CAB 124, 1920).

Hailsham's principal concern was that publication of *Silent Spring* might let loose a campaign of hate against the use of 'chemicals'. There were always those in the 'muck and magic' school of agriculturalists keen 'to seize on events of that kind to promulgate their own pseudoscientific stuff'. Not only did Rachel Carson seem unaware of the danger, but she herself might have overestimated the extent to which insects and other pests could be controlled by their natural predators and parasites. Whilst there were possibilities in that direction, Hailsham doubted whether British scientists had missed many tricks on that point. On balance, the spraying of crops and the introduction of new substances had done immense good. In his acknowledgement of Lord Hailsham's letter, Prince Philip identified four groups of dangerous persons. Besides the cranks, there were semi-scientists and experts who refused to admit they might be wrong. Thirdly, there were farmers who could not bear to see anything living or breathing on their land unless it was directly profitable and, fourthly, a large group of commentators who neither wished, nor were able, to understand the real situation. Although chemicals should be used to raise agricultural production, Prince Philip believed the least amount possible should be used (PRO, CAB 124, 1920).

At a meeting with the Chairman and Nicholson, in December 1962, Lord Hailsham had indicated 'the political importance' of additional research on toxic chemicals, in the sense of the Government being 'well armed to deal with the allegations in Miss Carson's book' (PRO, CAB 124, 1609). There was an obvious opening for the Conservancy to press for additional resources. Nicholson applied for an extra 17 posts to meet 'the emergency situation'. The Treasury agreed, in January 1963, to 12 of the posts, in addition to the two posts already included in the estimates. Nicholson paid generous tribute to Lord Hailsham for his part in securing them (PRO, CAB 124, 1592).

The respective positions of the research councils and Lord Hailsham himself were set out in the drafts of the speech that Hailsham was to give at the formal opening of the Monks Wood Experimental Station in October 1963. The Secretary of the Agricultural Research Council, D. Rudd Jones, suggested a paragraph that stressed the importance of keeping

> the use of pesticides in agriculture in proper perspective. No one would suggest that we should abandon the use of the motor car in this country, and yet the atmosphere is polluted to the extent of 2,850 tons of lead every year from the combustion of anti-knock compounds in petrol. Similarly, no one would suggest that we should stop using coal, although 10,000 tons of lead are discharged into the atmosphere each year from the burning of coal. The risks of contaminating our environment with pesticides must be very small when compared with the enormous benefits we derive from their use (PRO, CAB 124, 1609).

Neither this draft, nor a fuller briefing, was used.

Lord Hailsham wrote most of the speech himself, in his highly distinctive handwriting. He began by remarking that most people had the rather woolly impression of the Conservancy as being concerned with national parks. They believed that the primary purpose of nature reserves was for outdoor recreation. The Conservancy was in fact 'a scientific organisation concerned with the scientific study of our environment – ecology to use a more technical term'. The speech focused on toxic chemicals, a subject that not only impinged on the responsibilities of several ministers but aroused strong emotion. There was need for what Hailsham called the practical judgement that went with balance and caution. In his words

> I am prepared to favour preservation of wild life absolutely against scientific farming. I am not prepared to back scientific farming absolutely if it results in the widespread destruction of wild life, particularly if it threatened whole species (PRO, CAB 124, 1609).

The recent episode, by which controls had been taken to prevent the indiscriminate use of a particular group of chemicals, had shown the effectiveness of the defences mounted by the Government, of which the Conservancy was an important part. In helping to mount these defences, it was not so much a question of whether enough research was being done, but whether it kept pace with the continuous and changing nature of the problem. In 'protecting the public advantage' the Minister for Science and each of the research councils had to keep

> a watching brief to see that scientific opinion is continuously directed to the relevant questions, and that public opinion is constantly advised about the biological consequences of a technological age (PRO, CAB 124, 1609).

In that sense, Lord Hailsham's presence as Minister for Science at the official opening of the Station symbolised the importance the Government attached to nature conservation.

THE FURTHER DIVIDE

Alongside the so-called 'Great Divide' that came to exist, in an institutional sense, between the interests represented by the Nature Conservancy and the National Parks Commission, there was another divide of perhaps more immediate significance. On the one side, there was the scientific and managerial expertise required for wildlife conservation and the protection of landscape amenity and, on the other side, similar expertise applied to commercial farming and forestry. The 'institutionalising' of the sciences — encapsulated by agronomy in the Agricultural Departments, sylviculture in the Forestry Commission, and ecology in the Nature Conservancy — developed during the decade of the 1960s to the point where ecologists came to be regarded as the spokesmen for nature conservation and inevitably, therefore, the leading critics of modern farming and forestry.

With the dramatic decline in bird deaths following the ban on the more toxic seed dressings in springtime, some observers thought that the pesticides problem had come to an end, and many more hoped that this would be the case. In the Conservancy's view, the much more serious long-term side-effects of the new generation of pesticides had still to be tackled. The residues were widespread and their toxicity was cumulative. They were being released at a rate faster than the environment could destroy them. The side-effects could no longer be regarded as a local problem. As the work of the Toxic Chemicals and Wild Life Section moved from preliminary reconnaissance towards a long-term programme of field and laboratory experiments, it was decided to concentrate on studying the effects of repeated applications of persistent chemicals on different forms of wildlife. Particular attention was directed towards the effects of organochlorines on animals at the ends of food chains, with special emphasis on avian predators and their eggs (PRO, FT 3, 144).

In order to understand the rate at which information flowed from the incipient programmes of the Toxic Chemicals and Wild Life Section, reference must be made to the remarkable head start provided by the close working relationships that had evolved over the years between Conservancy personnel, acting in both official and private capacities, and the voluntary bodies. Although appointed to work on other aspects of natural history and nature conservation, the staff of the Conservancy played, for example, a key role in ornithological research and bird protection by pursuing those activities out of working hours. With Donald N. McVean, Derek Ratcliffe had been engaged to survey and classify the vegetation of the Highlands. Although a huge and daunting task in itself, it also provided outstanding opportunity to develop, as a spare-time activity, close know-ledge of upland birds and, in particular, the peregrine falcon.

The opportunity for further survey of the breeding population arose in September 1959, when the Home Office sought the advice of the Conservancy as to whether the special protection given the species under the Protection of Birds Act of 1954 should be removed because of complaints that the peregrine was inflicting heavy losses on racing pigeons. The Conservancy insisted that there should be no change in protection until an up-to-date survey and objective assessment was made (PRO, FT 3, 144–5). It awarded the BTO a contract to establish the number and distribution of the breeding population of peregrines. The BTO appointed Ratcliffe to act as the main organiser in a personal capacity. It soon became clear that he would require some official time during the breeding season if results were to be obtained with the urgency that circumstances increasingly demanded. Because of the concurrent need for Ratcliffe to complete the monumental tome, *Plant Communities of the Scottish Highlands* (McVean and Ratcliffe 1962), Nicholson refused a dispensation until the 1961 season (Sheail 1985, 107–19).

Although the census of 1961 was not as complete as had been hoped, enough was learnt to indicate that, far from becoming more abundant, the peregrine had experienced a dramatic and abnormal decline in population since the previous survey of 1948–49. Many territories in southern England and Wales were deserted, and few pairs had tried to nest. In northern England and southern Scotland, most territories were still occupied but many pairs had failed to nest and few young were reared (Ratcliffe 1980). In July 1961, Ratcliffe flushed a peregrine from an eyrie on a sheepwalk and grouse moor in Perthshire, where she was incubating two obviously addled eggs (Moore and Ratcliffe 1962). An egg was sent to the Laboratory of the Government Chemist, which reported, in September 1962, that it contained (uncorrected for recovery) 115 micrograms of pp'-DDE, 50 micrograms of dieldrin, and 28 micrograms of heptachlor-epoxide. In acknowledging the report, Moore wrote that it gave 'very firm support to our hypothesis that the decline of the Peregrine Falcon is due to toxic chemicals; until recently this hypothesis had been considered very far fetched by many interested in the problem' (Sheail 1985, 113).

Following further debate in the House of Lords, instigated by Lord Shackleton in March 1963 (PD, Lords, 247, 1118–220), and more general anxiety expressed on television and in the press, the Inter-departmental Advisory Committee undertook a fresh review of organochlorine pesticides. Its report, completed in February 1964, rejected calls for a total ban on their use. There was no evidence of their constituting an immediate, or serious, threat to human health. Turning to wildlife, the Committee noted that the voluntary restrictions imposed on seed dressings in 1961 had succeeded in greatly reducing the number of casualties among seed-eating and predatory species. The task was now to see whether further restrictions were needed to counter any long-term effects. The chief impediment to reaching a decision was lack of information on the significance of different residue levels, and the amounts of different pesticides needed to kill different species. Hardly anything was known about the effects of non-lethal doses taken, perhaps, over a long period of time (Advisory Committee 1964).

In a statement to parliament, in March 1964, the Minister announced that the Government had accepted the Committee's recommendations. Assurances of cooperation had been received from all interested parties under the Pesticides Safety Precautions Scheme. A ban on most uses of aldrin, dieldrin and heptachlor would take effect in 1965, and of aldrin and dieldrin in sheep-dips at the end of 1965. A total ban on these substances, and an extension to cover some of the less toxic substances, would be considered further in 1967 (PD, Commons, 692, 244–52; Lords, 256, 1151–9).

Many of the changes taking place in the environment were so subtle that they could only be discovered, and their significance assessed, by scientists with the most intimate knowledge of the biological requirements and behaviour of the species. Even then, the

Ian Prestt (*left*) and **Tony Bell** of the Toxic Chemicals and Wild Life Section, examining birds of prey (mostly owls), found dead and sent (often by members of the public) to Monks Wood for examination and analysis for pesticide residues.

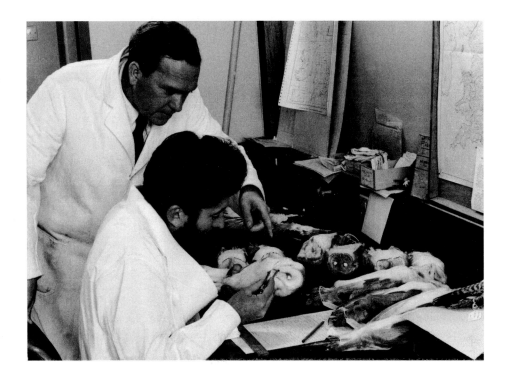

ecologist might be caught unawares. The study of the peregrine falcon highlighted the number and range of relationships that might exist between a species and other species, and its habitat. Some changes might be so complex and unobtrusive in character that they could only be perceived when they were well under way.

Ratcliffe (1958) and others had drawn attention to the largely unprecedented phenomenon of eggs of the peregrine falcon, sparrowhawk and golden eagle being broken or ejected from the nests of the parent birds. Could egg-breaking be another sub-lethal effect of pesticides, and could it have been a contributory factor in the 'crash' in population numbers? It had started well before the introduction of the dieldrin group of pesticides, but after the introduction of DDT and gamma-BHC. The possibility of a causal link was put forward in a paper circulated among colleagues by Ratcliffe in mid-1966. An index of eggshell thickness was devised, based upon the total eggshell weight, divided by the egg-length and multiplied by the egg-breadth. Whereas the pre-war values (retrospectively obtained by measuring specimens in egg-collections) had been very stable, there had been marked changes around 1946–47. Although DDT did not come into common agricultural use in Britain until 1948–49, military stockpiles of the insecticide were used, often on a locally-lavish scale, from 1945 onwards for domestic, horticultural and veterinary purposes. It became common, for example, to dust homing pigeons with DDT in order to control ectoparasites (Sheail 1985, 107–14). The degree of exposure of the peregrine to this type of contamination became clearer when the solvent rinsings of a series of peregrine egg clutches were analysed. As Ratcliffe (1980) noted, the detection of pesticide residues in shell membranes and egg contents, after an interval of nearly 30 years, was further proof of the persistence of the compounds.

The Conservancy obtained much-needed encouragement from two quarters. Not only might industry believe it had to be seen having dialogue with the Conservancy and voluntary bodies, but some intimation of the value of those discussions was provided by an invitation from the Association of British Manufactures of Agricultural Chemicals (ABMAC) in 1963 to form a liaison committee. One outcome was a symposium held in March 1964 on the theme: 'Agricultural chemicals – progress in safer use'. Organised by ABMAC and chaired by Lord Howick, the opening address was given by Sir Solly Zuckerman. Secondly, the Conservancy won both scientific and international recognition through a NATO-sponsored workshop held at Monks Wood in July 1965, which brought together for the first time scientists from many parts of the world working on 'different but complementary aspects of pesticides research'. It lasted for the comparatively long period of 12 working days. As instigator and director of the meeting, Norman Moore wrote how, in gaining a better perspective of the problem, the 71 participants became convinced 'of the paramount importance of the role of persistent organochlorine insecticides in the environment'. Many of the papers were published as a special supplement to the *Journal of Applied Ecology* (Moore 1966).

Such growing recognition from both business and its scientific peers did not protect the Conservancy's scientists from a barrage of criticism. As expected, agricultural and medical experts argued that the value of the insecticides in food production and preventative medicine more than outweighed any risks to the environment and wildlife. Not surprisingly, scientists employed by the pesticides industry subjected the findings of the Toxic Chemicals and Wild Life Section to the closest scrutiny. Using data from its own laboratories, Shell Research Ltd mounted a vigorous campaign to defend the use of dieldrin. Such assertions, where supported by data, deserved respect and consideration. What the Conservancy found so disconcerting was the bitterness and niggling opposition that emanated from scientists and administrators who had previously denied any possibility of pesticides having harmful side-effects. They now seemed so resentful at being proved wrong that they would stop at nothing in fighting a rear-guard action. Much of the criticism was made 'in confidence' or off-the-record, but Ratcliffe (1980) recalled how

> some of us had our first experience of scientists playing politics, and we learned how vicious a vested interest under pressure can be. It was clearly in many people's interests, one way or another, to believe that the wildlife conservationists were talking nonsense, and they left no stone unturned in trying to establish this... Tactics at times resembled those of the courtroom rather than the scientific debating chamber. There were tedious arguments about the nature of proof and the validity of circumstantial evidence. The attempts to deny effects of pesticides on wild raptors descended now and then to obscurantism.

The wide divergences in the interpretation of scientific data meant the *Further Review* was two years late by the time it appeared in December 1969. For many, it was the apotheosis of moderation and circumspection – a masterpiece of draughtsmanship rather than a programme for action. Critics claimed that it represented, not so much the collective wisdom of the Advisory Committee, but the deep divisions that had emerged among members. So wide was the gulf in views that, according to Jon Tinker in the *New Scientist*, 'this committee was hard put to agree on anything other than platitudes'. The report was so skilfully worded that if the chapter headings and recommendations were removed, the remainder could equally well serve as a demand for the total and immediate ban on all organochlorine pesticides, or for government-aid in promoting that part of the pesticide industry (Anon. 1969; Tinker 1970a).

For the Conservancy, the drafting of the *Further Review* was an unhappy affair. If the Conservancy held out against compromise on every detailed point that arose in the contentious paragraphs, it would have been accused by fellow-members of the Advisory Committee of obduracy. By conceding those points, it ran the serious risk of insidiously weakening the whole report in the eyes of the conservation movement. Although the report and its component parts were designed to represent the collective view of the Advisory Committee, the conservation movement was bound, both consciously and unconsciously, to attribute those passages dealing with wildlife to the Conservancy (PRO, FT 3, 111).

As the *Further Review* made its way through five drafts, the Conservancy's concern increased. In a minute of August 1969, Moore recalled the two overriding objectives of the report. One was to reassure the public that there were no acute dangers to man resulting from present organochlorine use. The second was to warn the public that the theoretical reasons against the use of organochlorine insecticides had now been reinforced by recent discoveries in the laboratory and field. Whilst the latest draft succeeded in meeting the first objective, the second had become scarcely discernible. All reference to specific studies of the sub-lethal effects of organochlorine insecticides, and particularly those on eggshells, had been either omitted or played down. These omissions would have a demoralising effect on those in the Toxic Chemicals and Wild Life Section, who had done so much to secure the evidence.

Officers of the Conservancy considered producing a minority report, or insisting on the insertion of a statement making it clear that the Conservancy was considerably more concerned about the sub-lethal effects of dieldrin and DDT than was otherwise suggested by the report. Both options were rejected on the grounds that such a form of dissent would cut across the concept of the Advisory Committee. It would be received badly by ministers. As a further alternative, a statement might be issued to coincide with the publication of the *Further Review*, welcoming the Committee's proposals but amplifying recent scientific evidence on the sub-lethal effects of pesticides. The statement was drafted but, again, never issued. There was a real danger of its publication associating the Conservancy with the highly emotive campaigning style that had recently led to restrictions being imposed on the use of cyclamates in human foodstuffs, and which was now being directed towards DDT (PRO FT 3, 112–3).

In its report, the Advisory Committee noted the growing concern over the general rise in environmental pollution resulting from new technologies and the disposal of waste products. Particular attention had been paid to pesticides because their effects could be identified far more easily than those of many other forms of pollution. Although organochlorines had been singled out for particular criticism, the Advisory Committee believed it would be wrong to attach any greater priority to their withdrawal. There were far more dangerous forms of pollution to be tackled first.

The Committee found no evidence to suggest that contamination of the environment

The visit of the Prime Minister, **Harold Wilson**, to the Monks Wood Experimental Station, January 1970. **Don Jefferies** (with **Arnold Cooke** looking on) describes the work of the Toxic Chemicals and Wild Life Section to the Prime Minister, with **Anthony Crosland** holding the peregrine falcon, and **Sir Solly Zuckerman** beside him.

Sir Solly Zuckerman (*left*) with **Martin Holdgate** at Monks Wood during the Prime Minister's visit of January 1970. **Duncan Poore** stands between them.

from organochlorines was getting worse. The discovery of residues almost anywhere in the world reflected the fact that scientists now had the skills and knowledge to make world-wide studies possible. Over the previous few years, the amounts present in the human body and food, and in wildlife, might have actually declined, whilst populations of peregrine falcons, sparrow-hawks and golden eagles had increased in some areas following the restrictions on the use of organochlorine pesticides in 1962 and 1964. The paragraph of the report dealing with eggshell thickness had been re-drafted so many times that it allegedly delayed the completion of the report by six weeks (Anon. 1969). It recounted that there was evidence of a reduced thickness of eggshells, increased incidence of egg-breaking by parent birds, and a reduction in breeding success (though not necessarily sufficient to affect population size) among predatory birds. There was a moderately close correspondence in time between these phenomena and the increased use of DDT, but this evidence was not precise enough to establish a causal relationship with certainty. Other factors which had not been investigated so fully might be relevant or even significant (Advisory Committee 1969; Sheail 1985, 167–74).

In a statement to parliament in December 1969, the Minister endorsed the Committee's findings and expressed the Government's hope that within a year the sale of DDT in small packs to home gardeners would have ceased, and that the use of aldrin, dieldrin and DDT on certain crops, and of dieldrin and DDT for certain purposes in food storage and in the household, would also have ended. The Minister affirmed the need to keep all the remaining uses of pesticides under close scrutiny, with a view to adopting less persistent forms as soon as they became available (PD, Commons, 793, 1351–5).

CHAPTER SIX

THE ENVIRONMENTAL REVOLUTION

For a research council with little by way of executive authority beyond its reserves, everything hinged on persuasion. That might be achieved through conferences, working parties, and less formal gatherings. Their proceedings seldom made the headlines. They were not intended to resolve issues. But they had a longer-term importance in establishing precedent for looking at issues in a more holistic fashion. They enabled the representatives of the different interest groups to get to know one another better. Roles could be identified, and working relationships forged. Previous Chapters have provided abundant evidence to show not only how the Conservancy exploited such opportunities, but itself brought together the various parties, in order to share knowledge, improve understanding, and define policy options more closely. In that sense, the 'Countryside in 1970' conferences and European Conservation Year represented a considerable achievement and, perhaps, a fitting climax to the career of the Nature Conservancy.

The Conservancy's dilemma as an advisory and educational body was given prominence in July 1961, when an Adjournment Debate on its research role was initiated in the House of Commons. In a largely hostile speech, Marcus Kimball attacked the Conservancy for failing to give adequate guidance on the effects of toxic chemicals on wildlife. Far from the Conservancy taking its place as a third advisory service on the countryside, together with the National Agricultural Advisory Service and the Forestry Commission, Kimball found 'a sad lack of contact between those responsible for the conservation of nature and those who are likely to damage or destroy it'. In responding to the debate, the Parliamentary Secretary for Science, Denzil Freeth, stressed that the Conservancy was a research council and, therefore, had neither the organisation nor resources to conduct a publicity or educational campaign (PD, Commons, 644, 1695–724).

Yet lack of money and manpower could not absolve the Conservancy from entering the field of public relations. This was not only seen to be a key element in protecting wildlife but, as a national body receiving grant-in-aid from the Exchequer, the Conservancy had a duty to explain its viewpoint and purpose to the general public. Of the latent public interest, there could be no doubt. The obvious success of the *New Naturalist Library* had given further notice of ecology's coming of age. Advances in colour photography made it possible to bring accurate wildlife images to the public. The publisher, W.A.R. Collins, had found naturalists and ecologists to be expert in conveying their own enthusiasm in a way that held the reader's attention (Marren 1995). Norman Moore recalled that nature had also provided marvellous material for television. The conservationist, Peter Scott, had skilfully used the series, *Birds in Britain*, and the *Look* programmes to put across the conservation message. David Attenborough and Jack Lester's *Zoo Quest*, and later wildlife series, were watched by millions. Newspapers and periodicals, as well as television, found good copy in the clashes between conservationists and developers (Moore 1987, 222).

And yet, as Bob Boote stressed in a series of papers that urged the significance of the public-relationship aspect, only 'a minute fraction of the public' had a clear idea of what conservation and ecology meant. In its evidence to the official Committee on Broadcasting, in February 1961, the Conservancy sought to raise awareness within the industry itself as to the educational role of the media in spreading scientific literacy and, more specifically, an understanding of conservation. That vast, but still passive, natural-history audience of over 10 million viewers and listeners, built up by the BBC over the previous fifteen years, had to be stimulated into taking a more active part in the practical aspects of conservation.

As well as providing field and laboratory facilities for college and university courses, the Monks Wood Experimental Station saw itself as a contributor to that wider educational function. Moore wrote in March 1962 of having given 15 lectures in the previous winter, both to put across an ecological perspective and to gain some insight of what his audiences thought of nature conservation. He wrote that, at one extreme, there were naturalists who sincerely believed that the pattern of nineteenth-century farming should be perpetuated and, at the other, there were some industrial chemists who thought, equally sincerely, that it was pointless to try and safeguard wildlife on farmland, as it was doomed anyway. Few naturalists had any experience of thinking ecologically – in terms of populations, limiting factors, food chains, indirect impacts, and so forth. Industry and government officials commonly regarded the Conservancy as a body opposed to what was, in effect, their idea of change. Moore believed that little could be achieved until the more dynamic aspects of the Conservancy's work and, therefore, the basic concepts of ecology were better understood. There would be little chance of reducing the misuse of the countryside, which came through ignorance of the impact of habitat destruction and pollution, until, say, the Agriculture Departments, the NFU, and other representative bodies recognised that they too had a part to play in supporting the desirability of conserving wildlife (PRO, FT 3, 542).

An obvious way for industry to support nature conservation was by sponsoring such ventures as film making. A meeting chaired by Boote in June 1960 responded positively to a proposal from the oil and petrol company, National Benzole, to sponsor a film on the Conservancy. A film about the National Trust in the series, *Our National Heritage*, had just been completed. The new film about the Conservancy would be shown in cinemas. The only opposition to the venture came from Major John Morrison. Although he did not doubt the ability of National Benzole to make 'very nice nature pictures', he believed it was quite wrong for the Conservancy to associate itself with such companies, one of whose sidelines was to produce and sell poisonous sprays. The Conservancy must not 'get behoven to commercial concerns such as this'. Nicholson sought to assure both Morrison and other members of the Nature Conservancy that the company had undertaken not to interfere in the making of the film, nor attempt to place any obligation on the Conservancy. Morrison was unmoved (PRO, FT 3, 542).

The 30-minute documentary, made by the independent producer, Ralph Keene, was to be different from previous nature films in focusing on those who worked with wildlife, namely the reserve wardens – a treatment which, in discussion, was widened to include regional officers and research scientists. The eventual press release described how it fell into two parts. The first part showed how some of the wonders of Britain's animal life fitted into the complex pattern of nature. There were sequences showing the kittens of the wildcat and the mock battle between black grouse at mating time, and – never before seen in a cinema – the 'dance' of the adders; the beautiful swallowtail butterfly was shown preparing for its first flight of summer. The second part of the film looked at Britain's nature reserves and the work of conservation. Conservancy scientists were shown studying the habits of the worm; finding the best way to raise oak seedlings so that woodlands remained in good health; inspecting the cliff-face nest of the peregrine falcon, which had 'mysteriously dwindled in the last ten years'. A sequence on the island of Rhum explained that the aim was to manage the island as 'a balanced whole', so as to enable its animals and plants to flourish again. Although the film showed that Britain was leading the way, there was still much to be done.

The film, *Living Pattern*, achieved immediate success in August 1962, securing a five-week run as a support film at the Odeon cinema in Leicester Square, London. Dilys Powell wrote in the *Sunday Times* that it contained 'affectionate and entrancing views of the wild life of the British Isles, an experience altogether enjoyable'. Commercial distribution in the provinces began with Manchester, Liverpool and Birmingham, where its coupling with Peter Ustinov's film, *Billy Budd*, guaranteed large audiences.

Whatever role industry and the media might play in the educative effort, the greater part of the initiative had to come from the conservation movement itself. It was hardly an encouraging picture. Where the amenity and outdoor-recreation bodies had once boasted the liveliest and most gifted leaders, by the post-war years they had almost all gone. Many, such as Patrick Abercrombie, who had played so notable a part in the CPRE, became heavily engaged in urban reconstruction and the furtherance of the planning profession itself. Despite 'a noble fight' by its Secretary, Herbert Griffin, the CPRE had become by the 1950s a 'geriatric affair'. It had largely failed to recruit young members.

Nor was there room for complacency in respect of the voluntary nature-conservation bodies. Nicholson was horrified to discover that Diver had suggested that some might disband now that the Government had taken responsibility for nature conservation. To Nicholson, this was crazy. The Conservancy needed their help in order to meet its Charter responsibilities. Even more importantly, nature conservation would never become 'a politically viable thing unless there was a very powerful voluntary movement behind the official body'. A priority for Nicholson was therefore to encourage the development of voluntary bodies and, above all, to concentrate their energies in a way that had enabled the CPRE to wield such influence in its heyday.

There was much to be done. The SPNR had hardly capitalised on its wartime role. Only three of the original 24 regional sub-committees of the NRIC were still active when the Society's Executive Committee recommended, in 1954, that all should be 'suppressed' and 'resurrected under a different name'. Three counties offered a model. The Norfolk Naturalists' Trust, founded in 1926, was joined 20 years later by one for Yorkshire whose immediate purpose was to save Askham Bog. The Lincolnshire Naturalists' Union formed a nature-conservation committee which became, in December 1948, the third Naturalists' Trust. There were 360 members by 1954, each paying an annual subscription of ten shillings. As the Secretary, A.E. (Ted) Smith, noted, members joined 'for what the Trust is doing rather than for what it provides them'. The immediate priority was to press the Lindsey County Council, which owned the site, to declare Gibraltar Point a Local Nature Reserve. It was the first to be declared in England under the National Parks and Access to the Countryside Act. The Skegness Urban District Council added an adjacent area of sand dunes. The Trust managed the entire area, constructing both a field station and bird observatory.

At a national scale, progress was hardly impressive. An offer from the SPNR to provide financial support for the founding of further local trusts fell on deaf ears. As its President, Lord Hurcomb, remarked in May 1955, something more specific than a general circular was needed to break down the extreme specialisation and parochialism of local-naturalists' bodies (PRO, FT 22, 13). It was not until 1957 that further Trusts were formed in Leicestershire and Cambridgeshire, both directly influenced by the Lincolnshire example. A West Midlands Trust, founded in 1957, later divided into three County Trusts. There followed Kent in 1958, Surrey, and the Berkshire, Buckinghamshire and Oxfordshire Trust (BBONT) in 1959, and the Essex, the Bedfordshire and Huntingdonshire, and the Hampshire and the Isle of Wight Trusts in 1960. The West Wales Field Society became the West Wales Naturalists' Trust in 1956, and a Scottish Wildlife Trust, covering the whole of Scotland, was established in 1964.

But what of the SPNR? Its charter imposed considerable constraints on what could be achieved by way of a wider membership or elected executive. Rousing public interest and providing expert advice and financial support were, however, entirely consonant with its purpose. Hurcomb found sympathy for a federation of regional naturalists' trusts among its officers, but none wanted to take on the organisational challenge. Appalled by how little the SPNR had spent, and the poor return on its investments, Nicholson circulated a memorandum in November 1955, emphasising that 'the days of an effective amateur-guided, spare-time operation in such matters on a national scale' were now over. If the SPNR would not provide the effective and adequate measures required for nature conservation, it should at least stand to one side (PRO, FT 22, 13).

In close liaison with Hurcomb and Nicholson, a meeting of representatives from the Lincolnshire, Cambridgeshire and Leicestershire Trusts was held in Cambridge in June 1957. Each recognised that greater cooperation would raise the efficiency of existing trusts, encourage more to be formed and generally lead to the more effective promotion of nature conservation. The view was endorsed and amplified at a larger meeting at

Hickling Broad in September, attended by representatives of all the trusts. The Council of the SPNR accepted the recommendations of a sub-committee that the Society should act as an expert adviser but, much to the fury of Nicholson and many in the movement, it concluded that the task of publicising and winning support for the nature-conservation movement would overwhelm both its legal powers and financial resources. Rather than undertaking the task itself, the SPNR should help to establish a new body to coordinate and publicise the activities of the growing number of bodies concerned with wildlife protection (Sheail 1976 233–7)

In practice, the task of forming the Council for Nature, as it was called, fell to Nicholson and the few active persons of the trust movement. It was consciously modelled on the National Audubon Society in America. Nicholson laid particular stress on the need to do things that were beyond the scope of an official body like the Conservancy. It could more easily mobilise public opinion, lobby members of parliament, and participate in press controversy. It would be far better placed to capitalise on the enthusiasm and energy of volunteers. At a meeting of early 1958, it was decided to widen the Council's objectives still further, by encompassing the whole field of natural history. Membership was to be open to both natural-history and nature-conservation bodies (Smith 1987).

Within its first five years the Council for Nature obtained the support of 390 national and local organisations, with an aggregate membership of something in the order of 100,000. The inclusion of natural history societies, however, meant that the Council for Nature was even less well placed to act as a 'federal centre' for the County Naturalists' Trusts. Led by Ted Smith, a further attempt was made to persuade the SPNR to accept that responsibility. This time it did. The first meeting of the County Naturalists' Trust Committee of the SPNR was held in November 1958, with all trusts represented. It soon began providing expert guidance on the formation of new trusts, recruitment of new members, and a wide range of financial and land-agency problems. It became a clearing house for the trusts, initiating such new ventures as a joint newsletter. With the appointment of a permanent secretariat in 1965, almost all of the SPNR's activities came to be focused on the county trusts.

Whilst there was nothing like the tidiness of organisation Nicholson and others had sought, the Council for Nature was evidence of both a growing assertiveness and a unity of purpose in the voluntary conservation movement. With considerable support from the Conservancy, the Council for Nature organised a National Nature Week in May 1963, to publicise not only the increasing threat to wildlife but the part that the natural-history movement and 'active conservation' might play, if supported by an informed public opinion. The Post Office marked the event by issuing two attractive commemorative postage stamps. The hundredth edition of the *Look* television programme was timed to coincide with the week. Over 46,000 people visited the main national event, a Wild Life Exhibition sponsored by *The Observer* newspaper and largely put together by Brian H. Grimes, the Technical Officer, and other staff at the Conservancy's headquarters. It was opened by Sir Keith Joseph, the Minister of Housing and Local Government. Although done on a shoe-string, the exhibits nevertheless helped to illustrate the scale of mankind's impact on the environment. The diorama with accompanying birdsong recorded by the BBC attracted widespread and favourable comment. The piles of tin cans and plastic, arranged to show how such rubbish was being produced and allowed to litter the countryside, made a considerable impression on both the Minister and Prince Philip, who made a visit later that week. A further innovation was the opening of nature trails. More than 1,725 school children from 81 schools walked the nature trail at Mousehold Heath, near Norwich. A thousand visitors, of whom nearly 700 were school children, attended an exhibition and trail at Alvecote Pools, Warwickshire. There were many requests for the trails on the Studland Heath National Nature Reserve, in Dorset, to be made permanent.

The achievement, most obviously in boosting the morale of the natural-history and conservation bodies, made all the more frustrating Nicholson's failure to form a triple alliance between the nature-conservation, amenity, and outdoor-recreational bodies. Where the Council for Nature had begun to channel and promote support for wildlife conservation, neither the CPRE nor any other voluntary body displayed interest, let alone an ability, to provide such complementary support for the National Parks Commission. Although Nicholson was grateful to the Chairman of the Commission, Lord Strang, and his Vice-Chairman, Pauline Dower, their considerable efforts to bring about such an alliance met with little response. But, with hindsight, there was perhaps a silver lining. The apathy shown by the amenity and recreational bodies in the early 1960s gave the nature-conservation bodies more freedom to engage in collaborative ventures with other types of organisation.

It was in this context that remarks made by Prince Philip, during his visit to *The Observer* Exhibition, quickly became so significant. What he found most remarkable was the way the event had brought together exhibitors who otherwise never met. National Nature Week had emphasised the merits of some larger discourse between the various

The Observer Wild Life Exhibition, the principal event of National Nature Week, May 1963. **Lord Hurcomb** is introducing **Sir Keith Joseph**, the Minister of Housing and Local Government, who deputised for Lord Hailsham in formally opening the Exhibition. **Aubrey Buxton, Dudley Stamp** and **Max Nicholson** are among the figures beside him.

interests. As Prince Philip remarked later, there were 'a lot of pious aspirations and a rather emotional attitude to change of any kind'. The greatest need was for criteria, against which the pros and cons of any development affecting conservation could be measured. Once these had been identified, developers and planners would have something by which to adjust their requirements. Some kind of general conservation policy was required to ensure that the best features of the countryside might survive for future enjoyment (Anon. 1963).

Using the publications and archives of the relevant bodies, this Chapter seeks to reconstruct the challenges and solutions as they appeared in the decade leading up to the 'Countryside in 1970' conferences and European Conservation Year in 1970.

INDUSTRY AND THE COUNTRYSIDE

Of the many bodies that perceived their role as one of reconciling conflict through greater understanding, none was more prestigious than the Royal Society of Arts or, to use its full title, the Royal Society for the Encouragement of Arts, Manufactures and Commerce, founded in 1754 and incorporated in 1847. Among its wide-ranging activities, the Society conducted enquiries into a wide range of commercial subjects, providing links between the various practical sciences. It was entirely in accord with the Society's purpose that Lord Strang should take the chair at a meeting in November 1959, at which papers were given by Sir Christopher Hinton, the Chairman of the Central Electricity Generating Board (CEGB), and by Sir William Holford, a Part-time Member of the Board and Professor of Town Planning at University College London. The timing was hardly fortuitous. The Government had approved in the previous July the construction of a nuclear power station at Dungeness. The Nature Conservancy had taken the unprecedented step of opposing the application at a public inquiry. Positions could not have been more polarised.

As Hinton remarked in his paper, although the word 'amenity' was usually taken to imply 'the conditions in landscape which the public wishes to see and enjoy', experience indicated that the roots of opposition to the Board's activities went deeper. The lives of those living in towns were dominated by the works of man. Visits to the countryside and coast offered the only chance of escape, and it was here, in Hinton's words, that the difficulties arose. No matter how magnificent a power station might be in itself, nothing could compensate for its intrusion, say, on the South Coast at Dungeness. However well designed and sited, pylons represented the 'tentacles of industrialization'. They were regarded with hostility, even in the dullest of landscapes. In as much as the nation required electricity, Holford posed the question as to what advice industry might be given. Besides scenic values, there were others, such as archaeological and scientific interest. Each appeared to strengthen the case for trusteeship, namely the obligation of the present generation to hand down to its successors as much of an unspoiled estate as possible. Time and again, the CEGB was confronted at Public Inquiries with the assertion that some feature was unique for its history, geography, beauty, ecology or some other interest (Hinton and Holford 1959).

Following the meeting, the Special Activities Committee of the Royal Society of Arts (which included Strang, Hinton and Holford) recommended that a study should be made of the impact of industry on the countryside, beginning with a pilot study of the Hampshire Basin. With a grant of £4,000 from the Nuffield Foundation, an independent social-research body, the Acton Society Trust, was given responsibility for conducting the survey. Two of its officers were seconded to assist Harold E. Bracey of the Department of Economics at Bristol University, who was in charge of the field work (Anon. 1961b). Their findings were published as a volume, *Industry and the Countryside*, in 1963 (Bracey 1963).

In his Introduction, Bracey emphasised that change no longer came slowly and sedately to the countryside. As witnessed at the Fawley oil refinery, Bradwell nuclear power station, and Severnside ICI site, it might come suddenly and on an unprecedented scale. And yet there was still little awareness of how Britain was entering a new Industrial Revolution, which might have even more resounding consequences than earlier ones. As Bracey warned, industry that had caused so much harm to amenity in the past was entirely capable of doing so again. Neither remoteness nor existing statutory safeguards might be enough. The President of the Ipswich and District Natural History Society had made the same point, in a letter of March 1959, protesting at the proposal to build a nuclear power station at Sizewell, on the Suffolk coast. As he wrote, where 'we considered that such areas as Sizewell would be safe from any future development of an objectionable kind', it now appeared that planning restrictions were of no consequence (PRO, POWE 14, 1127).

But although Bracey's study was remarkable for its breadth of investigation and analysis, it could offer little insight into what really perplexed ministers when taking such far-reaching decisions. That can only come, albeit still to a very limited extent, from reading the files they actually handled in the course of making up their minds. The Dungeness nuclear power station may be cited as an example. Formal application was made to the Ministry of Power, in June 1958, for consent to build a 500/550 MW nuclear power station. Nicholson gave immediate notice of the Conservancy's opposition. Whereas it had accommodated all previous proposals for nuclear power stations, the scientific interests at Dungeness were simply too high for such concession and compromise to be possible. Dungeness was unique as the 'sensitive tip of the biggest finger of shingle in Europe'. Besides 'its large areas of loose shingle arranged in ridges or "fulls" ', the Huxley Committee had described it as the best area in South-east England for migratory birds. As well as a very rich insect fauna, both resident and migratory, there were rare and uncommon plants, including mosses. The site chosen for the power station was the least-damaged part of the shingle promontory (PRO, POWE 14, 1125; Sheail 1991b, 148–52).

The Conservancy's decision to press its opposition raised procedural questions. Could such a body enter into public controversy on matters to be decided by a Government minister? Officials of the Ministry of Power realised, right from the start, that it would be difficult to insist on the Conservancy settling the issue behind closed doors. If prevented from airing the matter publicly, at least some of the distinguished figures of the Nature Conservancy would resign their membership in order to give evidence to a public inquiry in a private capacity. Some might choose to do both. The preservation of wildlife was in any case only one of the factors that had a bearing on the Minister's decision. It was probably better covered in a balanced report to the Minister, written by an experienced inspector who had heard the Conservancy's evidence together with much else. The last word was with the Ministry of Housing and Local Government, which raised no objection to the Conservancy's public stand. The Conservancy could not, however, have it both ways. In giving evidence to the Public Inquiry, the Conservancy must be precluded from the inter-departmental consultation that would occur during and following the Inquiry (PRO, POWE 14, 1125 and T 223, 351).

The Nature Conservancy was the only major objector at the three-day Public Inquiry of December 1958. *The Times* report of the first day's proceedings relates how Legal Counsel for the CEGB, in his opening address, described the criticisms of the Conservancy as 'intellectual opportunism, full of exaggerated language and false suggestions', a lamentable performance by a public authority. At best, the Conservancy's case was obscure and at worst equivocal, evasive and disingenuous, and the arguments irresponsible. Counsel continued

> The Nature Conservancy is a public body supplied by public funds. How it justifies this ill-advised and ill-informed incursion into matters which are quite outside its function is difficult to understand, but it is disturbing to see it. Perhaps we shall have some explanation at this inquiry or perhaps an explanation will be called for elsewhere hereafter (PRO, POWE 14, 1125).

As the minister responsible for the Conservancy, some kind of response was required of Lord Hailsham. Although sure the 'frolic' was entirely that of Legal Counsel, Hailsham minuted that convention pompously required him to assume that the CEGB were the authors until informed otherwise. As he wrote to the Minister of Power, Lord Mills, the Conservancy had a perfect right to oppose changes in the present character of Dungeness. Sir Christopher Hinton refused to disown the remarks, claiming it was not for a client to tell Legal Counsel how to present a case (PRO, CAB 124, 1605). The Inspector, H.W. Grimmitt, was equally critical, writing privately that the artificial rudeness of a court of law had no place at a technical hearing. The remarks might easily have led to a slanging match. The situation had been saved by the professionalism of the CEGB's Chief Planning Engineer and the sober words and good humour of Nicholson. Of the many hearings he had attended, Grimmitt had never heard a case presented so well as that made by Nicholson on the Conservancy's behalf (PRO, POWE 14, 1125).

As Dungeness was claimed to be the only suitable location for a nuclear power station (PRO, POWE 14, 1191 and 1208), the question was whether the objections were strong enough to preclude any nuclear power station being built in South-east England. The Inspector's report reasoned that the station would occupy only 10 per cent of the proposed National Nature Reserve at Dungeness. The key area for research on the shingle ridges would, however, be permanently destroyed. It would be the Minister's invidious task to decide between two entirely dissimilar sets of values: the country's need for more electricity and the demands for pure scientific research. Grimmitt recommended that the station should be built (PRO, POWE 14, 1125 and 1191).

Lord Hailsham pressed for a reconsideration of the alternative site of Redham Meads, in the Cliffe Marshes of the Thames estuary. This would not only remove the threat to Dungeness, but also provide much-needed employment in the Sheerness area of Kent. Lord Mills protested that it was too close to large centres of population. There was too little cooling water for any further expansion of the station to be possible (PRO, CAB 124, 1605). At Hailsham's instigation, Henry Brooke, the Minister of Housing and Local Government, took the chair at a meeting of himself and Lord Mills, to discuss the political difficulties of building a nuclear power station when there was so much public disquiet over the large stockpiles of coal and closure of uneconomic mines. Hailsham pressed for the Redham Meads site being adopted as an interim measure at least, until Government policy became clearer and the case for Dungeness more firmly established. Lord Mills asserted that, even if the nuclear power programme was reduced, there would still be a need for a nuclear power station at Dungeness. Brooke supported reference to the Cabinet. The Inspector's recommendations had been made with reluctance on a fine balance of arguments, directed mainly at the planning aspects. It was not the Inspector's responsibility to consider the political implications (PRO, POWE 14, 1190).

At a Cabinet meeting in June 1959, Lord Mills again emphasised that, even with Dungeness, less than half the nuclear capacity envisaged for 1965 would have been approved. Lord Hailsham described Dungeness as 'a unique geological feature' and a favourite area for bird watchers. He nevertheless supported the construction of the station 'on general grounds'. Brooke similarly gave his support, subject to the CEGB being warned that the Government might not give consent so readily in future. The Cabinet's main concern was the opposition likely to come from those demanding a halt to the nuclear programme on the grounds that such stations were three times as expensive to build as coal-fired stations, at a time when there was a large surplus of coal. Ministers agreed that there would be advantages in postponing construction until a more advanced and economical design could be produced. This would, however, result in the dispersal of the scientific and industrial staffs, with grave economic consequences, including damage to exports. The Prime Minister, Harold Macmillan, spoke of the long-term benefits to the economy and national prestige of allowing the nuclear power programme to proceed steadily (PRO, CAB 128, 33 and 129, 98).

The Minister's consent was announced in July 1959, and shortly afterwards the Nature Conservancy abandoned negotiations, which had almost been completed, for the acquisition of Dungeness as a National Nature Reserve. It claimed that the damage would be so considerable as to disqualify the site from further consideration. If that was interpreted in some quarters of the Ministry of Power as a fit of pique (PRO, POWE 14, 1191), Roger Quirk in the Lord President's Office was unusually forthright in commenting on a Government decision. The decision to build the station was

> an almost text-book example of the kind of way in which the 'official Establishment' are able to demonstrate to their satisfaction, that one more portion of what are, politely, termed our 'amenities' must be wrecked (PRO, CAB 124, 1605).

LEISURE IN THE COUNTRYSIDE

In a paper entitled *The Fourth Wave. The challenge of leisure*, Michael Dower described how 'three great waves have broken across the face of Great Britain since 1800'. The first was the sudden growth of dark industrial towns, the second the thrusting movement along far-flung railways, and the third the sprawl of car-based suburbs. The fourth wave had broken in the decade, 1955–1965. Drawing on American experience, Dower warned that this would bring both immense pleasure and threat of damage and destruction. Already, in Great Britain

> the weekend multitudes are congesting our roads, fouling our downs and commons with litter and soiling our lay-bys; their chalets and caravans threaten all parts of our coast, their cars and motorboats echo in quiet valleys and lakes (Dower 1965).

As Dower explained, leisure was a compound of six decisive factors: population, income, mobility, education, retirement and the free time of adults. Each had grown dramatically. The population of Britain was then expected to rise from 52 million to 70 million in the year 2000. The caption of a photograph showing a beach full of holiday-makers warned that, if everyone went to the seaside at the same time, there would be only three-and-a-half inches for each person. Pressures were similarly building up inland. The 'closed and congested countryside' was simply not designed to accommodate such a weekend invasion. A way had to be found to combine the 'freedom, informality and choice' that formed the basic ingredients of leisure and holiday-making, with the least damage to 'the character of this island' (Dower 1965).

How might the wildlife, amenity, and outdoor-recreation bodies respond? The Conservancy was most obviously affected through its reserves. Twelve National Nature Reserves had already been declared in the Snowdonia National Park when the possibility arose, in the early 1960s, of securing a Nature Reserve Agreement for the summit of Snowdon itself. This was indisputably outstanding both as a laboratory for the geological and biological sciences, and for its amenity and recreation. Whilst there had been no problems from walkers and climbers on the other reserves, the Conservancy was particularly concerned about the effect of intensive rock-climbing on cliffs bearing rich assemblages of arctic and alpine plants. It indicated that it would not tolerate 'the disturbing growth of uncontrolled and ill-informed public usage'. Sufficient progress regarding the provision of an effective wardening system was made with the National Parks Commission and Caernarvonshire County Council for Nicholson to inform Lord Hailsham, in June 1962, of the Conservancy's intention to declare 'the vital central nucleus' of Snowdonia, of some 6,500 acres (2,600 hectares) as a National Nature Reserve (PRO, CAB 124, 1608).

Lord Hailsham was furious that discussions had proceeded even that far. Himself an enthusiastic rambler, he regarded such designation as both unnecessary and certain to provoke public opposition. Nicholson had ensured that Lord Strang, as Chairman of the National Parks Commission and a member of the Nature Conservancy, was kept fully informed. At a joint meeting of the Conservancy and Committee for Wales, Lord Strang emphasised the need for diplomacy. Besides close consultation with his Commission and

Snowdon: Y Wyddfa, August 1963. Acquired through Nature Reserve Agreements in 1964 and 1966, this was the largest reserve in Wales. Its wide variety of habitats ranged from the oak woods near **Llyn Dinas**, through intermediate sheepwalk grasslands to the main arctic–alpine plant communities on the calcareous cliffs and the windswept sub-arctic heath of the exposed summits.

the County Council, the Conservancy should take other bodies concerned with 'the visiting public' into its confidence. Once this was done, and the terms of the Nature Reserve Agreement decided with landowners, the most tactful approach would be to notify the County Council of its wish to declare a reserve, rather than announcing a definitive decision.

Whilst the Conservancy canvassed positive support, Hailsham sought assurance that the Minister of Housing and Local Government shared his misgivings. The Ministry's Welsh Office would go no further than to say it awaited evidence of public reaction, especially as the purpose and management of the proposed reserve were 'regrettably vague'. The Permanent Secretary of Lord Hailsham's Office, Frank Turnbull, was anxious lest such vagueness might cause public feeling to be considerably more muted than if the Conservancy's intentions had been spelt out more fully. But if the Conservancy was deliberately vague in its public pronouncements, the Conservation Officer for Wales, R. Elfyn Hughes, recalled later that most of his time was taken up with detailed, yet confidential, discussions with some 200 local and recreational organisations. The only instance of strong and prolonged objection came from the Snowdonia National Park Committee. It was only ended when Lord Howick, who became Chairman of the Conservancy in March 1962, visited the small terraced house of the Chairman of the Committee in Llanberis. As Elfyn Hughes later remarked, they got on very well indeed.

The consensus of support for the proposed reserve effectively removed Lord Hailsham's grounds for opposition. The Central Council for Physical Recreation assured the County Planning Officer, in August 1962, that there had never been complaint, nor was any expected, about the effects of designating reserves within the Snowdonia National Park. A letter from the British Mountaineering Club to the Conservancy indicated that, 'so far as we are concerned, you are at liberty to get on with your negotiations with landowners'. A columnist in *The Times* of 4 August 1962 supported the proposal on the grounds that wardens were needed for the increasing flood of townspeople. The leader in the *Guardian* of the same day was more to Lord Hailsham's liking, in as much as it doubted whether designation would make any difference. Bye-laws and wardens were no more likely to prevent the 'black sheep' from trampling down 'scientific fences' and dropping litter than 'the contagious self-discipline of the mountain walkers'.

A dual arrangement was devised at a meeting in October 1962, attended by representatives of the Conservancy, National Parks Commission, County Council, and Welsh Office of the Ministry of Housing and Local Government. The greater part of the proposed reserve, including the summit itself, would be made subject to a National Park Access Agreement. The Park Committee undertook to provide adequate wardening to safeguard the scientific interest and experimental exclosures. By a Memorandum of Understanding, the Conservancy undertook to allow the general public freedom of access over the remainder of the reserve, subject to good behaviour. With the formal

Gwilym H. Owen and **Alan Stubbs** manning the Conservancy's stand at the Wild Life Exhibition at Alexandra Palace, London, during National Nature Week 1966.

Archie MacDonald, Warden of the Cairngorms NNR, beside the sign to the largest reserve in Britain, which was acquired from 1954 onwards. The vegetation here ranges from Scots pine, juniper and birch to the arctic–alpine plants of the corries, screes and exposed summits.

approval of the National Park Committee, and negotiation of the Nature Reserve Agreements completed, Nicholson sought formal approval from the Lord President and Minister of Housing and Local Government for the declaration of the Y Wyddfa (Snowdon) NNR of 4,735 acres (1,900 hectares). Lord Hailsham was thwarted in his 'inclination' to refer the whole matter to the Cabinet's Home Affairs Committee. Since the Minister, Sir Keith Joseph, pronounced himself entirely satisfied, and no other Department had a strong interest, any discussion would have been 'pretty flat' (PRO, CAB 124, 1608).

Contemporary files show that the Scottish Development Department took a considerably less relaxed view than its opposite number in Wales of the relationship between nature reserves and recreational use of the countryside. Whereas restrictions on public access might not matter too much where the nature reserves were small, an official of the Department warned, in February 1961, that the proposed Glenfeshie extension to the Cairngorms NNR would result in over half the area recommended by the post-war Scottish National Parks Committee being included in the nature reserve. The fact that no such parks had yet been created there made the County Planning Officer even more emphatic in demanding that nothing should be done to prejudice the provision of suitable tourist facilities and the area's future declaration as a national park (SRO, DD 12, 892).

As the Chief Technical Officer of the Department, Robert Grieve, reported after a meeting in June 1962 with the Conservancy's Director for Scotland, John Berry, and Land Agent, the Master of Arbuthnott, it took time – particularly for Arbuthnott – to appreciate why such extensive reserves were incompatible with the kind of development thought to be essential to a Scottish national park. Whereas in England and Wales the main aim was to preserve an otherwise highly urbanised landscape, the Scottish National Parks Committee had seen the challenge as one of rehabilitation. National parks were perceived as a means of coordinating the development required to exploit attractive scenery as a primary resource. In other words, development was regarded as essential. Grieve wrote how, with that distinction being grasped, the Conservancy's representatives were able to understand the Department's principal difficulty as to the 'apparent sterilisation of such a magnitude'.

Grieve warned that the Conservancy would find itself in the position of King Canute if it opposed tourist development. Its reserves would simply be overrun. Only by positively accommodating such pressures would sanctuaries be preserved. As Grieve minuted, this was the line of argument that had prevailed with the Scottish Landowners' Federation. Berry insisted that the only development the Conservancy really feared was a chair-lift. Although there would be little damage in winter, its cost would require the operators to keep it working in summer. That would allow thousands of tourists to wander over a fairly wide area of the plateau above Glenfeshie in summer, spoiling the rare flora (SRO, DD 12, 885).

The Conservancy's Scottish Committee forced the pace by confirming the Nature Reserve Agreement for the Glenfeshie estate in July 1962. The Cairngorm NNR would increase in size by 19,133 acres (7,700 hectares), making it, in the words of that year's *Annual Report*, one of the most important reserves in Europe (Nature Conservancy

1963b, 42–3). A Conservancy document circulated in that month described how most reserves in Scotland were held on such a basis, where the landowner might simply grant a right of access to carry out surveys and experiments. Although some might go further, public access was rarely affected. Officials of the Scottish Development Department conceded that, if the only question had been the assurances given to open-air interests at the time of the original designation in 1954, there would have been no difficulty. The Conservancy had met these assurances in full. It was the economic potential of the tourist industry that required careful consideration. The Department and County Council continued to be concerned over the 'damping effect' on tourism and winter sports of any Agreement.

Whilst the Scottish Committee had been fully entitled to take such a decision, an official of the Scottish Development Department, A.C. Sheldrake, wrote that the Conservancy was one of the most difficult 'neighbours' in terms of securing general cooperation over planning. Although it appeared to have seen the red light, there was still a tendency to delimit sanctuaries and assume that other interests, including tourism, should accept what was left over (SRO, DD 12, 885). Officials were, however, encouraged by the offer of the Principal in the Conservancy's Edinburgh headquarters, Aylmer Haldane, to postpone formal designation, if delay meant the Conservancy would have the full support of local interests. He was as good as his word. In a letter to the County Council in August, Haldane described at length the experience of England and Wales in demonstrating that, even in much-visited parts of the national parks, access was hardly affected. The Council's Planning Committee indicated, in October 1962, that it was satisfied with the further assurances and the Conservancy's attitude towards 'the provision of suitable facilities for tourists such as ski-ing'. The Scottish Development Department was left with no alternative but to give its formal support (SRO, DD 12 892).

THE MULTIPLE USE OF LAND

Throughout the negotiations over the Glenfeshie extension, Haldane insisted that, far from taking a narrow, sectional view, the Conservancy had always recognised the merits, as well as the difficulties, of developing a more integrated land-management policy. If not the first, the Conservancy had been among the earliest bodies 'to propagate the gospel of multi-use' (SRO, DD 12, 892). But before illustrating the Conservancy's attempts to give practical effect to such use of the countryside, some context is needed.

The historian's account of post-war research on the use and management of town and countryside is unbalanced. It has focused on the regulatory planning authorities, both in central and local government, and relevant professional and voluntary bodies. Much less attention has been given to the initiatives taken on the 'developmental' side. Here, too, central government played a part. One such instance began with the announcement by Herbert Morrison, as Lord President of the Council, in December 1947, of the appointment of a Committee on Industrial Productivity. Nicholson drafted the answer to a Parliamentary Question, which defined its terms of reference as recommending ways of reducing demands for goods and raw materials that might become scarce or cause balance-of-payments difficulties (PRO, CAB 124, 1094, and CAB 312, 39; PD, Commons, 445, 1863–6). As world shortages of basic commodities such as sulphur began to ease, the Committee focused increasingly on the best use of the nation's natural resources, particularly in farming and forestry. It was reconstituted in 1950 as the Natural Resources (Technical) Committee, with Solly Zuckerman continuing as its Chairman. The Agricultural Sub-committee, made up largely of independent scientists, was the most active of its specialised sub-committees.

The Agricultural Sub-committee was highly sceptical as to whether the amalgamation of holdings and other structural changes to farming would be enough to reverse the trends reported, for example, by the Commission on Crofting Conditions in Scotland (Cameron 1997) and the Welsh Agricultural Land Subcommission (Sheail 1996b). Both had highlighted how the outlying parts of the United Kingdom were becoming completely depopulated, with a consequent loss of agricultural output. The Agricultural Sub-committee therefore developed the concept of a 'multiple' use of rural land, whereby farming would be integrated with forestry in those districts where it would be more rewarding economically, and have 'better social consequences', than if one activity or the other were pursued independently. As well as representing one of the first serious attempts to make economic comparisons between two uses of land, the Committee's report of early 1957 drew attention to the growing importance of recreation and tourism, and the need generally for more advice and general knowledge among local communities regarding the options for land-use change (Lord President of the Council 1957).

A further review, published in 1966 under the title, *Forestry, agriculture and the multiple use of rural land*, set out a broad methodology of study. Land-use integration meant 'the co-ordination of multiple uses of land and associated activities within a given area'. The initial assessment should be based on economic criteria. In those instances where the values were not quantifiable, one should use 'the opportunity cost under the most productive quantifiable use'. The report stressed that, as well as providing a more precise measure of the national requirements for home-grown food and timber, there was need for information on 'important environmental influences and the intrinsic and technical production potential of land in general'. Besides questions of farm structure, ownership and tenure, close account had to be taken of the wider issue of amenity and recreation (Department of Education and Science 1966).

Nicholson had been intimately involved in the deliberations of the Natural Resources (Technical) Committee. Not only was he anxious that the Committee should take full cognisance of the ecological, as well as the economic, dimensions of the concept of multiple land-use, but he perceived the Conservancy itself providing a large part of the research and guidance so clearly needed. Rather than being one of a number of parties contending for the resources of the countryside, the Conservancy should rise above such conflict in using its advisory responsibilities under the Royal Charter, not only to inform but to bring together the contending parties in close and constructive dialogue. In doing so, the Conservancy would not only acquire unprecedented prominence, but the potential contribution of conservation ecology would at last be recognised in terms of

Colin Welch, an invertebrate ecologist of the Woodland Research Section at Monks Wood.

providing direction to major programmes for the greater wellbeing of the wider countryside. The scale of Nicholson's ambitions was revealed in a paper considered by members of the Nature Conservancy, in October 1961, on 'Conservation in the Scottish Highlands' (SRO, AF 45, 624).

Misgivings were expressed in two quarters. Some officials of the Scottish Office Departments protested that this was the first they had heard of the Highlands being a degraded environment. For W.H. Senior of the Department of Agriculture, there were 'lots of sweeping generalisations'. Another official objected to the assumption that ecologists were 'the best authority to advise'. But, for everyone, the nub of the question was how the Conservancy believed it might exert its authority, as a coordinative body, over the use of natural resources of the Scottish Highlands. Members of the Conservancy's Scottish Committee were equally troubled, warning of the resource implications and the likelihood that landowners would protest that they were already addressing many of the issues. Nicholson persisted. At a further meeting of April 1962, he spoke of how some 20 Sites might be selected, where the costs and dividends of Highland improvement might be evaluated. Such quantitative surveys could be supervised by a representative committee and serviced by Conservancy staff. The Scottish Office assessor, A.B. Hume, reported how the Chairman, Sir Charles Connell, skilfully guided discussion on the Conservancy's Scottish Committee, so as to secure a decision whereby, as a first step, the proposals should be discussed at a fairly high level in the Scottish Office departments, the Forestry Commission and possibly the Agricultural Research Council (SRO, DD 12, 885).

Although Senior claimed he was used to 'these higher flights of imagination', he readily conceded this was the highest yet. The patience of the Scottish Development Department became even more sorely tried, when a draft of a revised version of Nicholson's memorandum was circulated in July. A covering letter indicated that the Conservancy saw, as the next step, an invitation to the Secretary of State to approve its proposals. Hume expressed astonishment. The Conservancy's Scottish Committee had regarded the proposals as simply a basis for discussion. The memorandum was yet another example of the tendency to assume the broad responsibilities for land-use that properly belonged to the Secretary of State. More specifically, there was 'nothing to go to Ministers about'. Senior wrote that the Conservancy had done nothing more than try to justify its elaborate proposals by painting a dramatic picture of failure in the Highlands. No account had been taken of the Forestry Commission's contribution to productivity, employment and soil fertility, nor of the many successful farming practices and the long history of agricultural research (SRO, AF 45, 624).

Not all officials were quite so dismissive. W.W. Gauld of the Department of Agriculture had some sympathy with Nicholson's general objectives. He was, however, always suspicious when sectional interests such as the Conservancy made recommendations. They did not shoulder the financial responsibility, nor have to make a case to the Treasury. A small, informal group should first be convened to discuss the individual proposals, 'as between Government Departments'. In doing so, there was need to identify and work with the more 'reasonable' elements in the Conservancy. Another official had a useful 'private' conversation with the Conservancy's Scottish Director, John Berry. In drawing a distinction between the concepts of protection, conservation and development,

James Polson, Warden of Beinn Eighe NNR.
This photograph was published in the *Annual Report* for 1958, which recorded his award of the British Empire Medal in The Queen's Birthday Honours List.

Berry insisted that the responsibilities of the Conservancy extended beyond the preservation of the osprey or the unique natural flora of Ben Lawers. Conservation implied both preservation and the search for the 'best' use of resources, as defined scientifically. Berry cited the culling of deer on Rhum as an example where conservation ecologists might assist in keeping the population at a 'proper' level, and yet allow venison to be produced on commercial lines. It was only a short step from such management programmes to determining an overall strategy for the economic development of the Highlands. Berry pressed for the Conservancy to be drawn more explicitly into a closer relationship with the Scottish Office departments, in the sense of its becoming one of the principal advisers on the development of the Highlands and Islands. Such liaison might be accomplished more easily through the Conservancy's Scottish headquarters than through London.

Thus prepared, the Scottish Office agreed to Nicholson's suggestion of a meeting of representative bodies to discuss his ideas for some kind of coordinative research body. The Forestry Commission rejected any notion of pooling the research effort. Senior emphasised that such a coordinative body should not been seen as the first step to imposing a land-use policy on the Highlands. However upsetting it might be to find one's advice ignored, it was for the owner and occupier to decide how land should be used, or misused. As Senior wrote later, there was sufficient support at the meeting for some kind of fresh initiative that he had taken the prudent course of offering to establish a small liaison committee

> to keep under review scientific research on the use and conservation of hill land in Scotland, to encourage the closest liaison between the research workers concerned, and to bring to light directions in which it would be useful to encourage further research.

According to the minutes of the meeting, Nicholson thought the terms fitted the bill admirably. The purpose would essentially be to encourage closer contacts where the interests of agricultural production and nature conservation overlapped. In correspondence, the Secretary of the Agricultural Research Council welcomed the idea that Senior should become chairman. This would increase the chances of the liaison committee being quickly absorbed into the Scottish Agricultural Improvement Council, of which Berry had just been appointed a member (SRO, DD 12, 885).

The episode seemed to suggest that, if an initiative was to succeed, there had to be a clear motive, sufficient resources to fulfil its purpose, and consensus among the potential users as to its utility. Although the Highland initiative met the first criterion, the lack of the third meant it was doomed. There were more positive lessons to be learned from the Conservancy's most successful 'synoptic' survey, namely the *Report on Broadland*, published in 1965. It was neither pretentious nor self-assertive in origin. Much of its success could be attributed to the fact that it appeared to arise out of the needs of the user community, rather than being imposed upon it. In this instance, the shortcomings stemmed not so much from external hostility, but from misgivings as to whether there would be sufficient resources for 'synoptic' work on so ambitious a scale.

John Dower's report, and that of the National Parks Committee in 1947, had assumed that the Broadlands which straddled the Norfolk and Suffolk border would become a national park. However, the more the National Parks Commission investigated the area, the less happy it became. The area had no outstanding beauty. Even its value as a sailing ground was in decline, as natural and man-induced siltation caused the broads and watercourses to become too shallow for navigation. Not all, however, might be lost. The (Bowes) Committee of Inquiry into Inland Waterways recommended, in a report of 1958, that the terms of reference and membership of the Great Yarmouth Port and Haven Commission should be widened, as a first step to seeing whether, through more effective management, some of the water bodies might be preserved in a navigable state (Minister of Transport 1958). On the advice of the National Parks Commission, the Minister of Housing and Local Government therefore announced in August 1961 that, rather than declaring a national park, there should be further consultations with the relevant Government departments, the East Suffolk and Norfolk River Board, and other local bodies (PD, Commons, 645, 140–1).

There was no doubt about the importance of the Broads for nature conservation. It already included two NNRs and numerous SSSIs. The Conservancy's Regional Office at Norwich therefore welcomed a request from the Ministry of Transport for guidance as to how the waterways might be kept open. It was both a pretext for further research on the wildlife of the region and a chance to influence the future use of the waterways. Brian Ducker recalled spending many happy days exploring the waterways by launch, trying to produce a kind of mini-Domesday Survey. The report, drawn up over a period of 15 months, was subtitled: *A regional study of multipurpose use in an area of scientific interest and with a growing holiday interest.* It demonstrated how the inherent instability of the land–water system had contributed to the uniqueness of the area for recreation and wildlife, and how human pressures might soon destroy that distinctiveness. The Bure valley had an especially large share of boat traffic, pollution, and demand for building development. As well as putting forward a research programme, the report proposed the appointment of a Broads Scientific Advisory Committee and, more controversially, the establishment of an executive authority to act as a Broads Management Authority.

As Eric Duffey, the Conservancy's Regional Officer, commented in December 1962, the exercise had highlighted how the Conservancy could take initiatives that were not open to the 'more directly committed authorities'. Even so, there was concern lest the report's recommendations might be criticised for straying beyond the Conservancy's terms of reference. With the recommendation for an executive body removed, the more 'descriptive' parts were widely circulated in March 1963.

The time was ripe for the Conservancy to initiate what became its finest 'catalyst' operation. After separate meetings with the key interests in 1963, Bob Boote set up and chaired a group representative of all of them. The group met four times in 1964 and published, in July 1965, its *Report on Broadland*. This took account of the earlier material and an appraisal of trends in land and water use, together with a new set of

A range of **Nature Conservancy publications**, including the *Report on Broadland*, the Monks Wood triennial reports, and symposia volumes.

recommendations that included curbs on pollution and the better provision and management of boating and other holiday facilities. It called for discussions as to how public access might be extended. A strategic plan was needed for Broadland as a whole, which might consider the practicability of creating new broads and waterways in order to spread pressures more evenly and utilise redundant agricultural land for holiday and recreational purposes.

As the Planning Correspondent of the *Guardian* commented on 3 July 1965, the most impressive aspect of the whole exercise was the way it had induced a spirit of cooperation where previously there had been bitter antagonism. The report itself described how each proposal had been subject to 'full and critical examination by a large team', consisting of representatives of the Conservancy, local government, the river, harbour and water bodies, the holiday industry, the Country Landowners' Association and the NFU. They had agreed that the basic policy should be 'to conserve and enhance the Broadland environment for holidays and outdoor recreation, and research and education', taking full account of the interests of water undertakers, farmers and other land users. Thirteen of the 18 representatives of the Working Party also signed a supplement to the report, which outlined how the desired goals could be achieved through the designation of national recreation areas and an agency to administer them. As a matter of urgency, a consortium of planning, river and navigation authorities should be appointed to prepare the way, under an independent chairman. Although he had drafted the supplement with Reginald J.S. Hookway, the Deputy County Planning Officer for Norfolk (and shortly afterward Principal Planning Officer for the National Parks Commission), Boote joined some local authorities in not signing it. In his judgement, there was a risk that the Conservancy might be accused of making political comment.

A Broads Consortium was established in 1966. It consisted of the navigation, river, and local planning authorities. A Study and Plan was commissioned from the Planning Department of the Norfolk County Council, along the lines suggested in the earlier report. Among its main recommendations, considerable stress was laid on protecting the scientific interest. It was particularly important to divert recreational pressure from the north rivers which, it affirmed, could take no more (George 1992).

'THE COUNTRYSIDE IN 1970' CONFERENCES

As Lord Holford remarked later, the commissioning of, and reception given to, Bracey's book, *Industry and the Countryside*, provided clear evidence of a developing conscience in the 1960s towards the environment and waste of natural resources that was similar to that of the 1930s with regard to unemployment and the waste of human resources. There was a timeliness in Bracey's message that much closer consultation between industry and government was needed if existing amenities were to be safeguarded and new ones provided. Bracey (1963) had written of the increasing numbers of industrialists becoming aware of the importance of such consultation, in terms of developing a good public image of their businesses. Where educated to the need, there would be

Pressure on the reserves. (*above*) Holiday-makers on the dunes and foreshore of the **Studland Heath NNR** in Dorset. This reserve, leased in 1962, formed part of the South Haven Peninsula at the entrance to Poole Harbour.

(*below*) August Bank Holiday at the north end of the **Braunton Burrows NNR** in north Devon. This large sand-dune system lying along the estuary of the rivers Taw and Torridge was leased in 1964 for its rich flora and fauna.

willing cooperation with amenity societies and interests. It was an obvious point of reference for further discussions.

During his tour of *The Observer* Exhibition held in National Nature Week of May 1963, Prince Philip asked Max Nicholson to organise an early conference of the major national organisations so as to capitalise on the interest aroused. Nicholson turned to Sir Christopher Hinton, Dr Richard Beeching (the Chairman of the British Railways Board) and Lord Robens (the Chairman of the National Coal Board), and invited them to explore the idea with the Nature Conservancy. The three looked at one another, and said there was insufficient time to organise anything that year. Nicholson turned to Boote and asked, 'Could it be done?' Boote thought it prudent to nod his head. Some years previously, Prince Philip had found a two-day Study Conference to be a useful device for securing general discussion of a particular problem, without the need to produce resolutions or recommendations. Those could come later, when issues had been aired and some meeting of minds achieved. Such a conference was held in the remarkably short time of six months, under the aegis of the Conservancy, the Council for Nature, and the Royal Society of Arts, with the Conservancy providing the secretariat and most of the funds for publishing its proceedings. The theme was the 'Countryside in 1970', a date chosen as being certainly in the future but 'near enough to be realistic yet tinged with just a little of the apprehension aroused by George Orwell's "1984" '. Some 220 persons attended from 90 organisations that had an interest in, or impact on, the countryside (Nature Conservancy 1963b, 102–4).

In an Opening Speech, Prince Philip emphasised that conservation was not a polite way of attempting to put the clock back, or to turn the countryside into an open-air natural history museum. In a countryside where almost three-quarters of the land was under intensive cultivation, any attempt to fossilise the landscape would be ridiculous. For the purposes of the Conference, Prince Philip defined 'conservation' in the broadest sense as meaning 'the total management' of rural areas 'for the fair and equal benefit of

Prince Philip addressing the 'Countryside in 1970' conference at the Royal Society of Arts, London, in November 1965.
Seated (left to right): **Lord Strang** (Chairman of the National Parks Commission),
Sir Landsborough Thomson, the Hon. **G.C.H. Chubb** and
Lord Howick.

all groups' who had a direct interest in their use. It meant removing blemishes and creating new beauties and delights for the hard-pressed urban population. It implied that economic and technical progress could still be made, but with the machinery and structures of progress harmonised in scale, outline and design so as to cause less fuss, noise and disturbance. Conservation meant encouraging people to use the countryside intelligently and with understanding – leaving it as they found it (Anon. 1963; PRO, FT 3, 96).

Much of the conference business was conducted in three Working Parties. Whereas the Chairman of the Conservation Working Party, Lord Strang, sought to stress areas of general agreement, the Chairman of British Rail, Richard Beeching, found there was little focus within the almost kaleidoscopic picture that emerged from his Working Party on Organisation. Representing his Research Working Party, Sir Christopher Hinton warned that investigations of the impacts of an increasing population, and of growing industrialisation on the countryside, might be too little, and too late, to have any effect. Michael Dower, in a review for the *Journal of the Royal Society of Arts*, wrote that the very rapid publication of the bulky proceedings had provided 'a first class bit of publicity for the urgent and complex task of protecting and re-shaping the countryside of Britain'. But, however splendid as a 'collective pledge' by people of such diverse interests, there was very little evidence of new ideas (Dower 1964).

There was concern of a different kind in Government. As nominee of the Lord President's Office, Roger Quirk was present at a session of the Research Working Party when Sir Solly Zuckerman was in the chair. Prince Philip joined in and immediately began to ask questions about the control of toxic chemicals. He found it very odd that everything was left to 'a voluntary scheme'. A member of the Ministry's Infestation Control Laboratory, E.E. Turtle, pointed out that a voluntary scheme had been recommended by Zuckerman's Working Party in the 1950s (page 109). In agreeing with Prince Philip as to the inadequacy of trials carried out on new chemicals, Turtle said 'no scientist can predict what would happen' until they were in commercial use. As Prince Philip retorted vigorously, his worst fears were confirmed. Zuckerman justified his Committee's recommendation of a voluntary scheme by saying that it had been 'tipped the wink by the Ministry of Agriculture that no recommendation in favour of compulsory powers would have a chance of being implemented'. If Quirk worried that the discussion had given the Duke 'a pretty poorish impression', Frank Turnbull, the Permanent Secretary of Lord Hailsham's Office, was even more anxious that 'some of this comes pretty close to getting involved in political issues'. Worse still, a further conference was planned (PRO, CAB 124, 2579).

If the first Study Conference had constituted 'a bold experiment', the second represented, in the words of Prince Philip, 'the biggest and most comprehensive "groupthink" ' ever attempted on the subject of the future of the countryside. Some 360 people attended the two-day Conference, held in November 1965. As well as 12 Study Groups having been appointed earlier that year, each to review a topic and make recommendations to the conference, a much larger group drawn from some 90 bodies interested in education had met at Keele university in March. Such preparatory work stemmed from a determination to replace fine words and windy phrases with recommendations that could be acted upon immediately (Anon. 1966; PRO, FT 3, 60 and 68).

Again, reviewers acknowledged the sheer weight of effort invested in the proceedings but, when all the speaking was done, Maurice Ash wondered whether it might only reinforce the status quo. The gathering of all the different interests might only serve notice of the arguments each intended to deploy in the battles ahead (Ash 1966).

But again, much hinged on how Government perceived such gatherings. The Ministry of Housing and Local Government had been the only Department not represented at the first Conference; its Permanent Secretary, Evelyn Sharp, believed it was wrong for officials to engage in public discussion on possible changes to Government policy. As Douglas Haddow, the Secretary of the Scottish Development Department, remarked, he too would be quite happy to keep away altogether from the preparatory groups being convened in readiness for the second Conference. But if all departments did so, and the Conservancy participated, there was a risk of 'the uninhibited view of Nicholson' being taken as the voice of Government. As the Permanent Under-Secretary of the Scottish Office, Sir William Murrie, found, there was little prospect of all departments, let alone the Conservancy, staying away (SRO, DD 12, 2926).

Correspondence revealed a mixture of perceptions as to the utility of the Conferences. The Permanent Secretary of the Ministry of Defence, Arthur Drew, indicated that, beyond sending an observer, the Department had refused to participate in the preparatory Study Group covering military training areas. The Department was not only inhibited by security considerations from discussing openly the number and location of such grounds, but there was 'a real risk that a public confrontation of conflicting interests would lead to a hardening of attitudes'. This would impair 'the reasonably amicable relations' presently enjoyed with the National Parks Commission and 'the more reasonable amenity societies'. The Permanent Secretary of the Ministry of Public Building and

Open Days at the Conservancy's stations became increasingly popular. An Open Day held at **Monks Wood** over a weekend in 1968 caused traffic jams on the A1 and other nearby roads.

Works believed that his Department had much to learn from participation in the Study Group covering the preservation of ancient monuments. His opposite number in Transport hoped that the specialist help of his officials would ensure that the various Study Groups reached sensible conclusions. Far from causing embarrassment, it was right that Departments should be seen to be taking a constructive part in such meetings. The Permanent Secretary of the Ministry of Agriculture, Sir John Winnifrith, had no enthusiasm for 'this propaganda performance' but agreed with Sir William Murrie that 'the balance of advantage' probably lay in participation (CAB 124, 2578–9).

Sir Frank Turnbull believed that officials should participate, so long as they were careful not to venture into argument on the policies they expounded. There was of course a thin line between explanation and defence of a policy but, Turnbull argued, it would surely harm their own image, and that of Government, if civil servants had to remain 'faceless observers without the right to speak except in a completely neutral voice'. Faced with the eight other relevant departments wishing to participate, Evelyn Sharp agreed that her officials should participate. With 'Jericho having fallen' (as Turnbull put it), the Conservancy was informed that its officers were free to take part in discussion, but must 'stand outside any attachment to the conclusions which may be reached' (PRO, CAB 124, 2580).

For the new Ministry of Land and Natural Resources, the conference had a direct and pressing importance. The establishment of the Ministry, following the election of a Labour Government in October 1964, had been taken by many to imply a much more conscious desire on the part of Government to tackle land-use issues on a more holistic basis. To others, the new Ministry was part of a manoeuvre by the Prime Minister, Harold Wilson, to bypass the existing Departments of State in achieving his political ends (Pollitt, 1984). Whatever the purpose, the new Minister, Fred Willey, found himself in a position similar to that of the Minister of Town and Country Planning, some twenty year earlier. He was head of a small new Department, without a seat in Cabinet. Whereas the wartime Ministry of Health had raised little objection to its planning functions being transferred to this new upstart, the Ministry of Housing and Local Government was much less accommodating. Evelyn Sharp had spent three decades of her career in the Ministry and its predecessors. She had become the first woman to be appointed a Permanent Secretary. As the Crossman diaries were later to recount, she was adamant that the statutory planning function must remain in the same department as had direct responsibility for the housing programme. Her success in achieving that object meant that the new Ministry and its minister were reduced to little more than 'a sort of super think-tank'. Although the Ministry survived in name for 26 months, and Harold Wilson never forgave Crossman and his Permanent Secretary for their obstruction, the formal announcement of its demise was made in May 1966 (PRO, PREM 13, 1541).

It would be misleading, however, to dismiss the episode as merely a political aberration. Simply the name of the Ministry had suggested to many a desire on the part of Government to bring some greater competence in the use and management of town and countryside. Such aspirations were fuelled by an increasing frustration with the Ministry of Housing and Local Government, which seemed to be almost exclusively concerned

Frank Fraser Darling at a presentation in 1972, with **Jean Balfour**, Chairman of the Countryside Commission for Scotland. Ecologist and author, Fraser Darling played a pivotal role in deciding that the Nature Conservancy should be a Great Britain body. The Conservancy depended heavily upon him for expert advice on the management of grey seals and red deer in the 1950s. The theme of his BBC *Reith Lectures* for 1969 was 'Wilderness and plenty' (Fraser Darling 1970). As he wrote to Duncan Poore in October 1969, 'The *Reith Lectures* are written, amended and condensed. Achievement never matches enthusiasm or anxiety to do a good job. I have sweated. If I fail I let down so much more than myself' (PRO, FT 22, 3). As an introduction to European Conservation Year, the impact of Fraser Darling's lectures was considerable.

with the regulation building development. Whilst none denied the importance of preserving the green belts, for example, there were now other menacing forces at work. Within Government, it had been left to the Nature Conservancy (and, on a more limited geographical basis, the National Parks Commission) to campaign against the much broader range of impacts that were beginning to transform the character and appearance of the countryside.

If not in a strategic planning sense, it was through his more specific responsibilities that Fred Willey endeavoured to meet some of the great expectations placed on his Ministry. As Minister, he had been given particular responsibility for national parks, common lands, and water resources. In October 1965, he sought the approval of the Cabinet's Home Affairs Committee to proposals for a new Countryside Commission, which would subsume the National Parks Commission and, in addition, encourage the provision or improvement of facilities for the enjoyment of the countryside generally. Exchequer grants would be available to county councils for the establishment of Country Parks, and for such purposes as the removal of eyesores, tree planting, and tree preservation. Willey wrote that, by giving him authority to make such an announcement during his speech to the Second Study Conference the following month, the Government would provide the clearest evidence of its taking the lead. Consent was given and the announcement was made, to considerable effect, at the beginning of the Conference's proceedings.

Further evidence of a growing consciousness of the 'Problems of the countryside' was adduced during a debate initiated by Lord Colville in the House of Lords, in May 1966. In his words, the time had come to implement much of the advice that had been given at the two Study Conferences. In acknowledging the need, the Parliamentary Secretary to the Ministry of Housing and Local Government, Lord Kennet, emphasised that none should be under any illusions as to the enormity of the task. As he remarked in that debate, and again some two years later in promoting the Countryside Bill that was to establish the Countryside Commission for England and Wales

> I do not know what could be a harder thing to plan than the countryside, unless indeed it is the cities whose development makes it so important that we should plan the countryside. We have to think, all at the same time, of next year's harvest, of next year's breeding grounds for the peregrine falcon, of the new towns or districts of towns which we shall need in 1975, of where the water is to come from in 1985, and where the timber is to come from in 2050. Then, with all these, we have to think of next week-end's motorists coming out of the city to enjoy themselves.

The essence of good planning was to ensure that the freedom that went with car ownership was not self-cancelling – that pleasant places should not be ruined simply because they were easier to reach (PD, Lords, 274, 969–5).

It was to assist with that transitional stage, between the recognition of a problem and its resolution, that a third and final Study Conference was planned for 1970. It received powerful impetus in 1966, with the announcement by the Council of Europe that 1970 would be European Conservation Year. The 'Countryside in 1970' organisation would be responsible for initiating a national programme of activities.

EUROPEAN CONSERVATION YEAR 1970

In 1970 Max Nicholson wrote, from an extremely active retirement, how, quite suddenly, the long struggle of a small number of advocates for nature conservation had been overtaken by a broad wave of mass opinion, reacting against the maltreatment and degradation of the environment. Old values, habits of thought and practices were now being challenged. Nicholson's book of that year, *The Environmental Revolution*, was subtitled, *A guide for the new masters of the world*. As an Oxford historian, Nicholson was acutely aware of the fact that revolutions have often overwhelmed their authors, alienating those whom they were meant to benefit. If this 'environmental revolution' was to avoid the shambles of many in the past, an informed and acceptable basis had to be found for deciding where 'we go from here'. An environmental audit was needed (Nicholson 1970).

There was certainly reason to be optimistic that a more strategic view of planning was emerging, both within government and among the wider constituency of industry and the conservation movement. In 1969, Anthony Crosland was appointed to the new post of Secretary of State for Local Government and Regional Planning. He would be the coordinating minister and sole Cabinet representative of the Ministry of Housing and Local Government and the Ministry of Transport. As part of a wider strategy to create super-ministries, proposals for a Department of the Environment (DOE) were further developed by Peter Walker (Crosland's successor) in the Conservative government elected in 1970. A White Paper of October announced that the new Department would also take in the Ministry of Public Building and Works (Draper 1977). Although some awkward boundaries would remain, the DOE, together with the new Department of Trade and Industry and a Central Policy Review Staff (a 'think tank'), seemed to presage a more holistic approach to policy making.

There was also an unprecedented coming-together at the European level. More than twenty countries, from Ireland to Turkey, participated in European Conservation Year (ECY), which opened in February 1970 with a European Conservation Conference at Strasbourg. As well as five princes and ministers from the main participants, there were 350 senior officials, business leaders and representatives of professional and voluntary bodies present. The main achievement was a 'Declaration on the Management of the Natural Environment of Europe', which set out principles to guide the planning and development of Europe's natural resources. Their overriding purpose was to raise environmental awareness and thereby 'to encourage all Europeans to care for, work for, and enjoy a high quality environment'. The Year was marked by over 100,000 events, of which some 10,000 occurred in the UK alone (Boote 1970).

Jon Tinker pronounced in the *New Scientist* of late February that ECY had done far better than many had expected. If politicians were beginning to show signs of wanting to jump onto the conservation bandwagon, the question was now whether environmentalists were ready and capable of steering it. Where were their shopping lists of administrative acts and guidelines to cope with habitat destruction and pollution (Tinker 1970b)? It was possible at one level to point to the Nature Conservancy, which now had a staff of 630 (of whom 288 were scientists) and to the 38 county naturalists' trusts in

The cover of a booklet published by the Standing Committee of the 'Countryside in 1970', as promotion for ECY 1970, depicts a family exploring the countryside around **North Holmwood Church** in Surrey.

In suggesting that individuals, voluntary bodies, churches, landowners and farmers, industry and local authorities play their part in conserving the countryside, the words 'encourage', 'promote', 'stimulate' and 'ensure' were especially prominent.

England and Wales, and to the Scottish Wildlife Trust. There were over 550 trust reserves. The amenity and wildlife wings of the conservation movement were themselves beginning to collaborate through a Council for Environmental Conservation (CoEnCo).

However representative and organisationally sound they might be, such structures would not, in themselves, ensure that ECY had a lasting effect. Powerful personalities were required both to create and to exploit the opportunities offered. The most outstanding in the context of ECY was Bob Boote. As both author and driving force behind the concept of ECY, he had been Chairman of the Council of Europe Organising Committee, and presided over the substantive sessions and discussions of the Conference. A columnist in the *New Scientist* described him as the 'messianic mandarin' (Anon. 1970a); the *New York Times* of 2 September published an article on his 'zealous advocacy of conservation'. In fact, all his contributions to both the '1970' conferences and ECY were undertaken in an unofficial capacity. Yet, in whatever guise he served, they had given him immense experience of trying to put in place a more holistic vision of what was required. Under the pen-name Robert Arvill, Boote wrote a Pelican Original entitled *Man and Environment*. As its name suggested, the book focused on people and their impact on land, air, water and wildlife, and the environment so created. Although there was much damage and destruction to describe, the sub-title of the book, *Crisis and the strategy of choice*, also emphasised the possibilities of re-shaping and creating an environment that fitted the highest aspirations. Published in 1967, by its fourth edition the book had become an Open University Set Book (Arvill 1976).

The Standing Committee of the 'Countryside in 1970' Conferences was responsible for promoting ECY in Britain. It operated from offices in the Conservancy's headquarters in Belgrave Square. Through the good offices of the Chairman of the British Railways

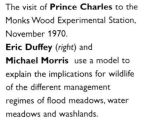

The visit of **Prince Charles** to the Monks Wood Experimental Station, November 1970.
Eric Duffey (*right*) and **Michael Morris** use a model to explain the implications for wildlife of the different management regimes of flood meadows, water meadows and washlands.

Board, Richard Beeching, a meeting had taken place in March 1966, at which the Director of Legal Affairs of the Confederation of British Industry (CBI), Henry J. Gray, emphasised the CBI's keenness to play an active part in the 'Countryside in 1970' Conferences. Such participation would help conservationists to understand the needs of industry more fully (PRO, FT 3, 61–7 and 75–7). As its contribution to ECY, the CBI organised a one-day conference, in September 1970, on the theme of 'Technology and the environment'. As part of a series of presentations and discussions, the Chairman of the Port of London Authority, Lord Simon, characterised the environmental debate as one that was looking for compromise. Even the 'back to nature' school really sought 'nature with mod. cons'. As the pollution control authority for the tidal Thames, the Port of London Authority had found industry generally cooperative where controls were seen to be reasonable and fairly administered. In a concluding address, the Director-General of the CBI, W.O. Campbell-Adamson, called upon industrialists to think much more consciously about the longer-term consequences of their actions. The approach had to be empirical – the solutions would not be the same for all industries or countries. The solutions had to be technically feasible, and the benefits commensurate with the cost of implementing them.

Not only had the CBI further emphasised to Government the seriousness with which business now regarded conservation issues, but the conference itself provided an opportunity for the new Conservative Government to make clear its own concern. In an opening address, the Parliamentary Secretary of the Ministry of Housing and Local Government, Eldon Griffiths, cited the Prime Minister, Edward Heath, in describing the environment as the most vital 'of our social services'. It was 'an area where action counts far more than words'. Eldon Griffiths' responsibilities were for clean air, water and sewerage, noise and related problems. Bills were being introduced to control oil leakages into navigable waters and to end the piecemeal way in which consents were given for reservoir development. Five new industrial processes had been brought under the Alkali Inspectorate. The July summer school of the Conservative Political Centre was on the environment. A paper by Kenneth Mellanby on protecting wildlife was complemented by others given by an urban planning consultant and the Deputy Chairman of Shell Chemicals UK. As Eldon Griffiths wrote, in the foreword to the published proceedings, *Clean and Pleasant Land*, there was both 'a fierce anxiety lest the beautiful world we live in becomes so polluted and refuse-strewn as to be no longer inhabitable', and 'a determination to avoid being carried away by the fashionable flood of pollution-mongering' (Conservative Political Centre 1970).

The Third Study Conference followed in October 1970. It represented the culmination of some four years' preparation by more than 20 expert groups, which Boote and his secretariat had largely formed and serviced. The greatly enhanced status of the conference was reflected in the attendance of over 900 representatives of some 330 organisations. As Lord Howick noted, the speech given by Edward Heath was not only very good, but meant that there was at last 'a personal statement' on conservation from a British Prime Minister. In a letter written afterwards, Heath wrote of 'the enormous value of the Conference in increasing public awareness of environmental needs and, still more importantly, responsibilities'. The more positive stance taken by business and industry was illustrated by Campbell Adamson when introducing discussion on 'Industry and the countryside'. He recalled how the previous seven years had been marked by increasing intolerance of the ugliness and squalor tolerated by previous generations. There was now a greater range of conservation activities in the UK than anywhere else in the world. The environment was seen as significant not only for the quality of human life, but for its very survival. Business recognised that, if it was to recruit the best of young people, companies had to show that they really cared about the environment (Anon. 1970b; PRO, FT 3, 85).

As the Proceedings of the Conference emphasised, the series of three conferences had both responded to, and helped develop, public awareness of environmental issues. Such disasters as the wreck of the oil tanker *Torrey Canyon*, in 1967, and the poisoning of the Rhine in 1969, had instilled a sense of fear of what was happening to the 'world in which we live'. The achievement of the Conferences had been to turn that fear into a positive and constructive force. The First Conference had done more than demonstrate that there were 'two sides' to every question. There was also a willingness on the part of decision-makers to take part in more informed debate. Out of the initiatives of the 1965 Conference had come the Countryside Commission for Scotland, and another for England and Wales. Fresh impetus was given to the drive for a national policy for the reclamation of derelict land and for more cooperation between the land-linked professions. The ECY Secretariat summarised the advances made by the '1970' movement as: enhancing the role and status of the conservation voluntary bodies; increased cooperation between the scientific, professional and technical services concerned with land, air, water and wildlife; readiness of leaders in industry to give their services; and a tremendous upsurge of informed comment in the press, television and radio. That, in turn, had given central and local government confidence to engage more closely and explicitly in environmental issues. The first-ever mention of the environment in a Queen's Speech was made at the opening of Parliament in July 1970.

Where the 'Countryside in 1970' Conferences and the publicity accorded to ECY had significantly advanced public understanding in Britain, the impact made by the Council of Europe meeting had similarly provided a solid base for the World Conference on the Environment, planned for Stockholm in 1972. Both in their message, and in the manner in which the various gatherings were organised, they provided abundant illustration of the way 'everything hinged on persuasion'. In that sense, they could not have been a more fitting way of celebrating the twenty-first anniversary of the Nature Conservancy. A booklet published to mark the event emphasised that the Conservancy was now concerned with much more than the preservation of some arcadian landscape. It had consciously entered 'the broader sphere of conserving the resources of the natural environment for the wise use and long-term benefit of the community' (Nature Conservancy 1970b). It had also become a component part of a larger research council and, therefore, more closely linked with other disciplines in the environmental sciences. The next Chapter focuses on that wider, yet closer, relationship with the scientific community.

CHAPTER SEVEN

THE ENVIRONMENTAL SCIENCES

Whereas Chapter Six explored the role of the Nature Conservancy in bringing about greater understanding and rapport among the various interests whose activities had an impact on the countryside and coast, this Chapter focuses more closely on the fortunes of the Conservancy itself, as it ceased to be a research council in its own right and became part of a larger scientific body.

Such a review might begin with the first parliamentary debate explicitly on the Conservancy, in February 1962. Lord Hailsham had responded positively to the suggestion of instigating such a debate, the obvious pretext being the publication of the Conservancy's *Annual Report* in February 1962. Since Hailsham wanted to wind up the House of Lords' debate, a peer was sought to open it. The Conservancy successfully pressed for Lord Shackleton, on the grounds that he would attract other speakers and deal with the subject in a balanced way. In formally calling attention to the *Report*, and using a brief given him by Nicholson, Shackleton's main purpose was to emphasise the Conservancy's wider relevance. It was much more than the naturalist's counterpart to the National Trust. The Conservancy was concerned with the whole countryside and coast. An amalgam of research and practical management, it was beginning to develop a philosophy of its own that everyone needed to understand (PD, Lords, 237, 959–70 and 976–9).

Following hard on the heels of earlier debates instigated by Lord Shackleton on the impact of pesticides on wildlife, the debate provided further evidence of how the Conservancy was crossing another kind of threshold in terms of the esteem in which it was now held. Pollution was now seen as a threat to both rural and urban life. The powerful rural interests that had previously attacked the Conservancy for its unwarranted interference were also the first to benefit from its endeavours. The side-effects of pesticides struck first and foremost in the game covert and fox earth; they paid little heed to property boundaries. Rather than being always on the 'outside', there was suddenly the prospect of the Conservancy and voluntary conservation bodies becoming part of the most powerful alliance of a political kind. By deliberately setting out to discover and highlight the hazards arising from pesticide use, the Conservancy demonstrated that it had a role to play that transcended its immediate responsibilities for

The Chairman of the Nature Conservancy, **Lord Hurcomb**, and the Warden of the Blean Woods NNR. Although his tenure of the Chairmanship was brief, Lord Hurcomb exerted considerable influence over the Conservancy's affairs, both directly and through the part he played in the House of Lords, as well as in the positions he held in numerous voluntary bodies.

wildlife. Such a shift in perception gave confidence to those in the conservation move-ment who were trying to secure a more holistic approach to the use and management of the countryside. It caused others, however, to wonder whether the Conservancy had both the responsibility and resources required to address the issues on the scale required.

Lord Hailsham's reply to the debate was significant in two ways. Whereas Lord Shackleton might assert 'we have created the minimal requirements in the Nature Conservancy', Hailsham was keen to stress that, although the Conservancy might be the smallest research council, its growth rate was the highest. Its annual Vote had more than doubled since 1955 to £535,000 in 1961–62. And yet Hailsham's instructions to officials, in the course of preparing the speech, betrayed a more fundamental misgiving as to the character and purpose of the Conservancy. Despite the Conservancy's claim to be a scientific body, Hailsham wrote that it was in fact 'a different kind of animal from the other research councils'. Its activities verged on the propagandist. Its literature tended to be glossier and emotional, its *Annual Reports* considerably longer, and its total volume of purely scientific work relatively small. The Conservancy was necessarily concerned with education and public relations. Beyond the reserves, the Conservancy must have on its side the farming community, local authorities, landowners generally, and such bodies as the Wildfowl Trust and rambling societies. It followed therefore that the Conservancy had to organise itself differently from the other councils. Where they had, for the most part, a Fellow of the Royal Society at their head, the Conservancy had a distinguished administrator who had himself come from the Lord President's Office (PRO, CAB 124, 1582; PD, 237, 1008–23).

Reference to the administrative calibre of Nicholson touched a particularly raw nerve. Not the least of his accomplishments had been his part in encouraging two outstanding figures in public life to serve as Chairman. Lord Hurcomb had succeeded Sir Arthur Duncan in March 1961; Lord Howick followed him a year later as Chairman. Hurcomb's last public post had been as founder-Chairman of the British Transport Commission. In retirement he became the most sought-after figurehead of a range of voluntary bodies, including the SPNR and RSPB. He was also founder-President of the Council for Nature. Although a keen ornithologist, his approach was somewhat passive. He kept no record and did not appear to favour any particular group or activity. None, however, fought harder for the welfare and protection of wildlife. Nicholson recalled him as 'a deeply civilised, scholarly, humane man' whose wisdom, sensibility and moderation made him peculiarly suited to the House of Lords. He was ennobled in 1951.

Lord Howick (Sir Evelyn Baring) had been High Commissioner in South Africa until 1951, and then Governor and Commander-in-Chief of Kenya and Chairman of the East Africa High Commission until 1959. Max Nicholson had been much impressed by his concern for wildlife and the introduction of durable game-laws in Kenya. His perception of character and sense of humour, accompanied by a genuine modesty and lack of pomp, often played a key part in winning support at a critical time in negotiation. Although his emotions were those of the naturalist, he quickly grasped what mattered most to the other parties to a dispute. As his biographer remarked, such qualities were put severely to the test as Chairman of the Conservancy (Douglas-Home 1978, 316–18).

And yet such distinguished appointments counted for little when combating the deep-seated animosity and suspicion that resided in parts of government. One of Lord Howick's first acts, on taking office, was to press for the removal of the instruction given by John Boyd-Carpenter that purchase of a reserve had to be approved personally by a Treasury minister (see page 38). The Conservancy now had 108 reserves. With such experience and the frequent need to make quick decisions, it was surely reasonable for it to be given some modest discretion. Not only was consent still required, but Boyd-Carpenter himself returned to the Treasury in July 1962, this time to the Cabinet post of Chief Secretary and Paymaster-General. It was Sir Edward Boyle, as Minister of State with special responsibility for Science, who wrote to Boyd-Carpenter in September 1964, putting forward what he called 'the very moderate proposal that the Conservancy should have delegated authority to purchase land within the limit of £1,000 for any one purchase'. Such denial of delegation amounted to a lack of confidence in the Chairman and members of the Conservancy. Not only did Boyd-Carpenter refuse to budge, but it was clear that Major Morrison continued (albeit less publicly) to exert influence. He had written, in July 1963, that the continued acquisition of reserves amounted to 'nationalising land by the backdoor'. Boyle warned that the matter would have to be considered by the Cabinet's Home Affairs Committee after the pending Election. Such delegation was granted within days of the Labour Government taking office (PRO, CAB 124, 1615).

If that instance of humiliating constraint in the Treasury was eventually removed, the distrust felt by the Scottish Office was less easily dealt with. As part of a general dispersal of government activities from London, it was proposed to transfer the Conservancy's headquarters to Scotland. Although recognising the logic of such a move, with three-quarters of the reserves located there, Nicholson opposed it as premature. For Scotland to realise its potential as a world leader in ecology and conservation, there had to be a 'home market'. Although the Conservancy had ensured that the recommendations of the post-war Committees for nature conservation had been largely implemented (in striking contrast to those for national parks in Scotland), there continued to be serious delay in 'educating young people and public opinion, and in creating an effective support movement in Scotland' (PRO, FT 3, 700). Although encouraged by the expert role accorded to the Conservancy by the Red Deer Commission, the relationship with the new Highlands and Islands Development Board was still to be decided. Such arguments appeared to officials in the Scottish Office as yet another clumsy attempt by the Conservancy to bargain itself into a position where, besides its proper function 'as defending counsel' of a particular interest, it also became 'the arbiter of land use'. Although the Scottish Office did not waver in its recommendation of a transfer to Scotland (SRO, AF 45, 620–1), the opportunity for the Conservancy to become more closely identified with Scotland was soon consigned to the 'ifs and buts' of history, as the question of its fate became subsumed in the larger issue of its status as part of a larger research council.

That more immediate question was addressed by ministers and their officials in an explicitly scientific context, and was in turn informed by the insights and prejudices of the Conservancy's peers in the environmental sciences.

THE NATURAL ENVIRONMENT RESEARCH COUNCIL

The Conservative Party manifesto for the General Election of 1959 had promised to appoint a Cabinet Minister for the purpose of promoting science and technology. That pledge had been met in October by the appointment of Lord Hailsham as Lord Privy Seal and Minister for Science. He immediately asked the Advisory Council for Scientific Policy to review the balance of effort in the civil field of science. It found the situation broadly satisfactory, except in respect of the promotion of research into natural resources. There was no clear, general responsibility for the 'preservation, improvement and proper utilisation of minerals, water, land use or such biological resources as fisheries'. Not only was there inadequate coordination, but those areas falling outside the day-to-day interests of Government departments and local authorities were in danger of being neglected (Lord President of the Council 1960).

If that was the public version of how it all began, the events behind the scenes were considerably less tidy. From the Conservancy's perspective, it had begun with a proposal, in the spring of 1959, that it might take over from the Development Commission responsibility for making grants and therefore coordinating fisheries research (outside the Government's own laboratories). As Nicholson reported to the Advisory Council for Scientific Policy in July, the Conservancy, although not actively seeking that role, was prepared to assume it, if that was the wish of Government after consulting appropriate interests. By that stage, however, a range of other potential improvements to the organisation of science was under close discussion. The Advisory Council decided in

A visit by the Conservancy's Committee for England to the Monks Wood NNR, during a meeting at the Experimental Station in July 1964. **Richard Steele** of the Woodland Research Section points out features, with **A.E. Smith** on his left and **Dudley Stamp** (the Chairman of the Committee) on his right. Steele was Director-General of the NCC between 1980 and 1988.

November, with Lord Todd in the chair, that the time had come

> to consider afresh whether there was a case for one research council to cover research in the general field of our natural resources, including fisheries as one of its interests.

Sir Solly Zuckerman was invited, as Chairman of its Committee on Biology and Allied Sciences, to conduct the review (PRO, FT 22, 17 and 19).

For Nicholson, here was another opportunity to take up questions that engaged their minds so much before, when they were both members of the Lord President's Office. The appointment was also a signal to shift the focus of discussion from simply identifying deficiencies in scientific administration to the much wider question of how such research might be organised in order to raise awareness of its value among potential users. In his view, this would be most effectively done by establishing a new 'umbrella', or 'holding company' type of research council, namely a Natural Resources Research Council, that would both preserve the Conservancy and transform the existing Advisory Committee on Fisheries into a Board with a similarly high degree of autonomy. Zuckerman incorporated the larger part of Nicholson's paper into a series of his own, which were distributed for comment (PRO, FT 22, 16). They described how the sciences dealing with the natural environment of water, air and the earth had recently received much prominence through the International Geophysical Year, whose basic theme was the interdependence of a wide range of sciences. Optimally, the 'environmental sciences' might be placed under an Environmental Sciences Research Council. There was, however, little chance of being able to include the meteorological, oceanographic and geological components. The more realistic course might be to establish a Natural Resources Research Council, covering only the biological and hydrological field (PRO, CAB 132, 197).

The Advisory Council decided, at its meeting of January 1961, that the most practical course was to appoint a Committee to assess the feasibility of Zuckerman's second alternative. Nicholson's was the only dissenting voice. In his view, it would be far cheaper and quicker to adopt a third alternative of establishing a Biological Research Council around the Nature Conservancy. Lord Hailsham, however, favoured the second alternative, which would help to boost those areas of biology of increasing importance whilst redressing the balance of activities in the Conservancy. Not only was the Conservancy over-committed towards conservation, but some of its activities were of doubtful utility. Membership of a larger council would bring it into 'a wider scientific setting' and make the Conservancy more research-minded (PRO, CAB 124, 1819).

As Nicholson was later to remark in a letter to Lord Todd, having first asked the Conservancy to consider taking over responsibility for coordinating fisheries research, and then to work with Zuckerman in developing the concept of a Natural Resources Research Council, the Advisory Council transferred the whole question, in May 1961, to a rather oddly-constituted, small *ad hoc* group (PRO, FT 22, 17). Its Chairman was Sir William Slater, a chemist and Secretary of the Agricultural Research Council. The only member with any real background knowledge of the Conservancy was Zuckerman who, as Chief Scientist to the Ministry of Defence, was rarely able to attend meetings. In his evidence to the Committee, in December 1961, Nicholson said that, like the other three research councils, the Conservancy saw its primary function as that of planning, executing and supporting fundamental and applied research, interpreting and disseminating the results, and promoting relevant educational activities. More than half its budget was spent on research. Although, in the first ten years, priority had naturally been given to reserve acquisition, Nicholson said that the Conservancy had always perceived this as ancillary to the main purpose of research (PRO, CAB 124, 1582).

The only other person to give evidence that related to the Conservancy's field of activity was Professor W.T. Williams of the Botany Department at Southampton University and a member of the Agricultural Research Council. As Slater later remarked, he had 'one of the most creative scientific brains in Great Britain' (PRO, CAB 124, 1819). Although reserves were essential for both research and teaching purposes, Williams protested that nothing like the present number was needed. Apart from their direct costs, a formidable programme of ecological survey and experimentation was required to support their management. Such a diversion of resources meant that to date ecologists had given little attention to raising the agricultural productivity of marginal and unproductive land (PRO, CAB 124, 197).

Slater's Committee formally resolved, at its meeting of July 1962, that it would be quite inappropriate for the Conservancy to be given responsibility for the new Council. Not only was much of the Conservancy's research of the *ad hoc* and superficial kind pursued by naturalists, but its non-research activities would create entirely the wrong balance. Indeed, even as a component body of a much larger Council, the reserves would impose a very heavy and unacceptable burden (PRO, CAB 14, 1573). Slater recommended their being transferred to the National Parks Commission. Whatever the preferred solution, members of the Committee were adamant that the new Council

It was not until the opening-up of the files of the Minister for Science that the prominence of **Roger Quirk** in the development of nature conservation in Britain became clear. Promoted in 1948 as an Under-Secretary responsible for the Gas Division of the Ministry of Fuel and Power, he expressed a wish to continue using his scientific training and was transferred to the Office of the Lord President in 1952. His sudden death at the age of 55, in November 1964, was a grievous blow at a critical juncture in the management of civil science.

should not be placed in the same position as the Conservancy, in the sense of being expected to fulfil two quite disparate functions (PRO, CAB 124, 198).

Although Roger Quirk (the Under-Secretary in Lord Hailsham's Office) also dismissed the idea of the Conservancy as some kind of nucleus or cornerstone of the new Council, he was equally critical of the Committee's recommendations. It was ironical and unfair to accuse the Conservancy of putting too much emphasis on conservation when, only a few years earlier, both Lord Salisbury and Lord Hailsham had criticised it for 'doing too much science'. They had wanted to reduce the number of professors as members of the Nature Conservancy, in order to accommodate more landowners and land agents. The Slater Committee had given far too much credence to the claims of 'one or two critical outside Professors'. The contemptuous references to 'natural history' had been over-played. It was equally misguided of the Committee to recommend that the reserves and advisory functions should be placed under a separate organisation, or 'rolled up with the National Parks Commission'. Not only would the conservation part of the Conservancy be scarcely viable, but the Committee had an entirely misconceived understanding of the National Parks Commission. Unlike that of the United States, it amounted to little more than 'a specialised form of town and country planning machinery'.

Zuckerman again played a critical part. He demanded that the present responsibilities of the Conservancy should be left intact. At a meeting with Slater and Quirk, he spoke of how many sciences had passed through a 'natural history' phase of somewhat unco-ordinated observation. The reserves would be of value to a range of the new Council's activities. The other members of the Committee refused however to change their recommendation. Even in the field of natural history, there was a difference between 'planned, quantitative observation and causal analysis' and 'the quasi-aesthetic study of wild life practised by many naturalists'. Although accepting that two-thirds of the original list of reserves had now been acquired, their management would continue to be 'an onerous and inappropriate task for a research body'. The Medical Research Council was not required to run the hospitals in order to have access to them for clinical research (PRO, CAB 132, 200).

It was at this critical juncture that the Slater Committee and the proceedings of the Advisory Council on Scientific Policy became part of a much larger study. On Lord Hailsham's advice, in April 1962 the Prime Minister, Harold Macmillan, approved the appointment of a committee to assess whether the existing organisational structure of the Government's entire civil-science programme was adequate to the task. The Chairman was to be Sir Burke Trend, a Second Secretary in the Treasury. In the judge-ment of Lord Hailsham's Office, the increasing cost of such scientific activities, and their growing importance to the economy and international affairs, made a closer rela-tionship between Government and the scientific community inevitable (PRO, CAB 124, 1813).

Lord Todd was a member of the Trend Committee and Chairman of the Advisory Council on Scientific Policy; Professor C.H. Waddington, an embryologist, was a mem-ber of those bodies and of the Slater Committee. Both were lobbied as to the future of the Nature Conservancy. Waddington wrote that, following discussions with Zuckerman and Nicholson, he had been persuaded that the entire Conservancy might be accommodated in a new research council, provided steps were taken to prevent the conservation aspect from attaining a dominant position. In February 1963 Nicholson wrote to Todd, warning that support for a 'federal' Natural Resources Research Council would be undermined, unless the recommendation of the Slater Committee to divide the Conservancy were overturned. There was absolutely nothing to be gained from destroying all that had been achieved so laboriously since 1949. In the light of public reaction to *Silent Spring*, any attempt to divide the Conservancy would be interpreted by naturalists and a wide band of public opinion as evidence of chemists and agriculturalists taking steps to dismantle a body that had, in Nicholson's words, 'proven inconveniently good at its job' (PRO, FT 22, 16–17).

Todd informed the Trend Committee, in April 1963, that the Slater Committee had supported the concept of a new Natural Resources Research Council with responsibility for research on fisheries, hydrology, land use, ecology and oceanography. A majority of members had recommended that only the scientific research work of the Conservancy should be transferred. Todd added, however, that, after careful consideration, the Advisory Council believed

> there were stronger arguments for the dissenting view, expressed by Sir Solly Zuckerman, that the responsibility for the Reserves need not impose an undue burden on the new Council provided adequate arrangements were made for the delegation of management.

The Council had therefore concluded that it would be both 'unnecessary and undesirable to separate the reserves from the scientific research responsibilities at present exercised by the Conservancy' (Lord President of the Council 1963; PRO, CAB 124, 1814 and 132, 167).

The report of the Trend Committee was published in October 1963. It recommended that the Lord President, as Minister for Science, should play a more positive role both in the coordination of scientific effort and the supply of scientific manpower. He should therefore have responsibility for the universities and higher education generally (Prime Minister 1963). Hailsham pressed Macmillan for a rapid Government response. The 'long-expected Science offensive' of the Leader of the Labour Party, Harold Wilson, had begun. The Royal Society supported greater powers of scientific direction (PRO, CAB 124, 1815). It was announced in April 1964 that the functions of the Minister for Education and Minister for Science would be combined within a newly-created post of Secretary of State for Education and Science, with Lord Hailsham appointed to that position. Rather than the research councils continuing to submit separate estimates to the Treasury, he would negotiate and decide their proportional allocations.

Whilst the Trend Committee had upheld the principle of semi-independent research councils, it put forward a series of proposals for major restructuring. Lord Hailsham agreed that the Department of Scientific and Industrial Research (DSIR) should be dissolved and a Science Research Council be created to discharge its responsibilities for university research and post-graduate studentships. A Natural Resources Research Council should be established on the lines of the Slater model. It should include the whole of the

Nature Conservancy, together with the Geological Survey and grant-awarding functions of the Development Commission in respect of fisheries research (PRO, CAB 124, 1815). Members of the Nature Conservancy, meeting in the same month, welcomed the general line of the Trend report, and particularly its rejection of the 'objectionable proposals' of the Slater Committee. Two members, Major Morrison and Lord Porchester, attached considerable importance to preserving the identity, name and existing functions of the Conservancy, as well as extending its terms of reference to include game preservation and regulation of toxic chemicals. Links with the voluntary bodies must be preserved. Another member, Frank Fraser Darling, warned of the disastrous consequences if 'the reserves of knowledge' acquired by the Conservancy became dissipated. Provided such concerns were met and some access to ministers was preserved, the Conservancy had no objection to the interposition of a Natural Resources Research Council (PRO, FT 22, 106).

In a statement on the Trend report, made to the House of Commons in February 1964, the Prime Minister affirmed the intention to form a Natural Resources Research Council (PD, Commons, 688, 1339–45). However, the controversy continued. Academic oceanographers fiercely opposed having their subject field included within the new Council. If the Conservancy feared its distinctive identity being lost through forced association with other sciences, oceanography and the other earth sciences were equally adamant that they should not become part of an inward-looking ecological or biological body, run by Max Nicholson (PRO, CAB 124, 1819).

As the newly appointed Permanent Under-Secretary for Education and Science, it fell to Sir Maurice Dean to implement the recommendations of the Trend report. At a meeting with Barton Worthington and the Conservancy's Administrative Secretary, Hilary Cooper, in March 1964 (Nicholson being abroad), Dean spoke of expecting the forthcoming inter-departmental discussions to be 'somewhat of a bear garden'. Worthington attributed much of the hostility towards the Natural Resources Research Council to the fact that the Trend report had treated it as 'a kind of ragbag'. A considerably more positive approach was needed (PRO, FT 22, 18). The points were taken up vigorously by Roger Quirk, who similarly advised that the only chance of securing the necessary confidence was to promote the new Council as strongly as possible from the earth-sciences aspect. It must be seen to include everything from the ionosphere to the underlying geological formations (PRO, CAB 124, 1815). In inter-departmental discussions, Dean strongly emphasised that the Natural Resources Research Council was intended to be much more than an aggregate of its various parts. It would break new ground by achieving what had never been done systematically before, namely 'the study of man in his environment'. It would be outward-looking, and embrace all the physical, biological and other relevant sciences. As well as breadth, it would have 'depth in being responsible for basic research as well as, for example, the nature reserves' (PRO, CAB 124, 1820).

The residual anxieties can be discerned in the debate over the title of what Nicholson at one time called the 'Nameless Research Council'. The Royal Society disliked the name 'Natural Resources Research Council', which suggested a bias towards ecology and conservation. Quintin Hogg (previously Lord Hailsham) thought it meant 'such things as steel and coal'. Dean welcomed the Royal Society's advocacy of 'Earth Sciences Research

Council' in making even more explicit the importance of geology and oceanography in the new council. Nicholson protested that it would appear to exclude the biological sciences. As he complained to Roy Clapham, who had been present at the Royal Society discussions, it was more than a question of semantics. It was a further example of physicists 'trying to hog the picture'. Clapham's response was to argue that the name 'earth sciences' was a small price to pay for reassuring the geological and oceanographic sciences. The new research council needed them, if it was to attain a minimal level of annual expenditure of some £5 to £10 million, and therefore viability alongside the other councils. Whereas Conservancy officers would have preferred to retain the original title, 'Environmental Research Council' was their second choice. Bob Boote suggested adding 'Natural' to make it clear that towns and cities were left out. Nicholson again sought the good offices of Zuckerman, but it was Sir Graham Sutton, the Director of the Meteorological Office, who brought matters to a resolution. In discussion with Dean and Zuckerman, in July 1964, Nicholson reported that Sutton also disliked 'Earth Sciences', which appeared to exclude studies of the atmosphere. On the premise that 'Natural' should be retained in the title, Sutton believed that the best course would be to adopt the title 'Natural Environment Research Council'. As Dean conceded, it aroused the least resistance (PRO, CAB 124, 1615 and 1815–16 and 1820, and FT 22, 18).

The way was now clear for the Secretary of State to announce in July, that the Council was to be formed, the word 'environment' being substituted for 'resources' in its name in order to emphasise its wide-ranging terms of reference (PD, Commons, 699, 285–9). A Science and Technology Bill was introduced within two months of the new Labour Government's taking office. It transferred *inter alia* the statutory powers of the Conservancy to the Natural Environment Research Council. It was announced, during the Bill's unopposed passage, that Sir Graham Sutton had been appointed founder-Chairman. In correspondence with Lord Strang (the Chairman of the National Parks Commission), Nicholson wrote that discussions with Sutton had encouraged him to believe that the changes in status and functions for the Conservancy would be minimal. Much would, however, depend on the way business was handled by both sides (PRO, FT 22, 107).

The Natural Environment Research Council was required, by its Royal Charter, to cover the fields of geology, meteorology, seismology, geomagnetism, hydrology, oceanography, forestry, nature conservation, fisheries, and marine and freshwater biology. The Treasury Solicitor had rejected the proposal that the Conservancy might retain its Charter. The solution was to place an obligation on the Council to appoint

> a committee called the Nature Conservancy for carrying out those activities of the Council that are concerned with the establishment and management of nature reserves ... and with the provision of advice and the dissemination of knowledge concerning nature conservation and for carrying out and supporting such research as the Conservancy consider appropriate having regard to those activities.

The Conservancy objected that, even as a Charter Committee, it would lose the sense of identity and continuity so important in dealing with landowners and the public generally. Further compromise was found in the realisation that the Council might have more

The cover of a booklet published in 1969 on *The miners' track*. This visitors' guide described what might be seen from nine stations along the track, as marked by a centre-piece map. One of a series of booklets, the cover typically bore the NERC seal, adapted for use by the Nature Conservancy.

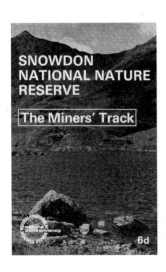

than one corporate seal. Thus, the Conservancy might operate under a seal that included the words 'Nature Conservancy'. In acting as expert advisor, the Treasury Solicitor's Office warned, however, of the danger of blurring the Conservancy's status to the point where it appeared to have a separate existence (PRO, CAB 124, 1920 and 1843).

THE NATURE CONSERVATION REVIEW

As a component part of NERC, the Conservancy was no longer required to submit an annual report. Instead, it published in 1968 what was intended to be the first of a biennial series of *Progress Reports*, together with a *Handbook* of its reserves. As well as amplifying what could only be summarised in the NERC *Annual Reports*, such richly-illustrated booklets became even more essential in emphasising the role of the Conservancy as official guardian and trustee of nature conservation (Nature Conservancy 1968a and b). Since public perception was largely shaped by a few dramatic incidents, it was important for those events to be seen in the context of the more normal activities and preoccupations of the conservation movement. In a chapter entitled 'Working with others', the *Progress Report* outlined the many contacts established with government, and with the professional and voluntary bodies, for the most part 'behind the scenes'. An increasing number of leaflets was published on conservation topics and individual reserves. There were open-days at the research stations. Exhibitions were organised at the Chelsea Flower Show, agricultural shows, and other large public events (PRO, FT 3, 2).

The mid-1960s marked a fresh beginning for the Conservancy, not only for its incorporation into a larger research council, but also for the retirement of Max Nicholson in March 1966, and John Berry a year later (who was succeeded by his Conservation Officer, Joe Eggeling). Barton Worthington had left in 1965 to become Scientific Director of the International Biological Programme. Now part of a larger research council, it was seen as inevitable that the next Director should be a scientist. Duncan Poore was appointed.

The last meeting of the Nature Conservancy attended by **Max Nicholson**, 1965.
Left to right: **Professor C.F.A. Pantin, Lord Strang, John Berry, Sir Charles Connell, Lt-Col. C.M. Floyd, Professor L. Dudley Stamp, E.M. Nicholson** (Director-General), **Lord Howick** (Chairman), **R.E. Boote, R.J.H. Beverton** (Secretary, NERC), **Martin Holdgate, Professor J.A. Kitching, Professor J.A. Steers, Professor A.R. Clapham, Professor P.W. Richards, G.V. Jacks.**

He had left the Conservancy in 1956 to become consultant ecologist for Hunting Technical Services and, three years later, Professor of Botany in the University of Malaya, at Kuala Lumpur. Back in the Conservancy, he was supported by two Deputy-Directors, Bob Boote covering the field of conservation and management and Martin W. Holdgate (the Senior Biologist of the British Antarctic Survey) as head of the Research Branch. The *Progress Report* emphasised that division of responsibility did not imply a separation of the two functions. On the contrary, such reinforcement recognised that 'the closest possible integration of scientific work with management' was essential for the health and strength of the organisation.

As the Report explained, the Conservation Branch was largely responsible for the acquisition and management of the reserves, and for wider advisory work. The Conservation Officers for England, Scotland and Wales operated respectively through six regional offices in England, three in Scotland, and two in Wales. The regional officers, deputy and assistant regional officers, and warden-naturalists were perceived as essentially 'administrative scientists'. The chief warden and reserve wardens undertook the day-to-day management of the reserves and other local duties. The Senior Land Agent and his staff had offices in London, Shrewsbury and Edinburgh. The Research Branch operated from seven sites. The Bangor Research Station was opened in 1960, with Elfyn Hughes as Director. As the *Progress Report* emphasised, the research called for close coordination between botanists, zoologists, soil scientists and many other specialists. Besides the eight specialist sections and Biological Records Centre, interdisciplinary sections covered eight major habitats: research on mountains and moorlands was focused on Banchory; woodlands on Merlewood; and agricultural land and lowland grasslands on Monks Wood. Furzebrook was the centre for lowland heath research; its responsibility for coastal research was transferred to the new research station at Colney, near Norwich, formally opened in July 1969. Wetlands and hill grasslands were covered by the research units at Edinburgh and Bangor respectively.

How might cross-links between the two Branches be strengthened without disrupting the management responsibilities of conservation officers and station directors? Whilst regional staff might be appointed as 'corresponding members' to the appropriate habitat research section, such terminology hardly conveyed the parity of esteem required for constructive partnership. The further step was taken of establishing Habitat Teams, comprising members of the relevant habitat section, those regional staff with a personal or geographical interest in the particular habitat, and representatives of such specialist sections as biometrics and geology. A memorandum drafted by Duncan Poore in December 1967 proposed that each team should meet at least annually, under the chairmanship of the head of the habitat section. It would review the entire spectrum of the Conservancy's activities, identify what was required, distil what had been learnt, and ultimately disseminate such knowledge and understanding through a series of conservation manuals (PRO, FT 3, 433).

The initial meetings served to highlight the differences in aspiration and preoccupation. The challenge was to turn that greater self-knowledge to positive advantage in capitalising on the unique array of expertise and experience represented by the two Branches. Wide circulation was given to remarks made by Martin Holdgate at the

At the Nature Conservancy party, December 1972.
Duncan Poore, the Director of the Nature Conservancy between 1966 and 1973 (*right*), with **Bob Boote**, Deputy Director (Conservation and Management). **Martin Holdgate** (*centre*) was Deputy Director (Research) from 1965 to 1970.

inaugural meeting of the Lowland Grassland Habitat Team which met under the chairmanship of Eric Duffey in April 1969. Never before had so large a proportion of staff been given the chance to participate in discussions that covered 'the whole inter-linked system of scientific issues'. Here was an opportunity to encompass, in one discourse, reserve management, the dissemination of advice, and formulation of research needs. An obvious priority was to update 'the national map of conservation value'. Another was to predict more precisely the response of wildlife species and populations to manipulative practices, through monitoring rates of change where sites were undergoing known forms of management. Close study of the competitive relationships both within and between species populations was also required. How might a community be maintained? What determined the rate and direction of change? How might species react to such external factors as climate, nutrients and grazing?

None pretended that the perfect bonding between the two branches of the Conservancy had been found. As the new Director for Scotland (and former Conservation Officer), John Morton Boyd, wrote in January 1970, the Habitat Teams were the first permanent functional link, 'knitting the Conservancy into one single, indivisible unit'. They were, however, still too focused on the research dimension. Whilst they had obvious value as 'an embodiment of Conservancy experience', Poore believed they were too large to make or enact policy. Beyond the annual meeting and occasional major symposia, there should be smaller habitat liaison groups, where there could be greater parity of representation and a more tightly focused agenda. Where Boote sought a more streamlined structure, the newly-appointed Director of the Merlewood Research Station, John N.R. Jeffers (formerly Head Statistician of the Forestry Commission) pressed for the leaders of the individual Habitat Teams to be given a measure of executive responsibility. Kenneth Mellanby, at Monks Wood, was also worried that another series of committees would be formed, which could discuss but had no 'teeth'. In his view the solution was to let the Teams evolve of their own accord. Where there was enthusiasm, they would flourish; otherwise they should be allowed to fade away.

Paradoxically, such organisational matters took second place to an initiative that so clearly depended on the closest rapport between the two Branches. As a stock-taking exercise of the nation's 'natural heritage', the *Nature Conservation Review* became the Conservancy's most ambitious venture by far. Its planning, execution and realisation were likely to give the clearest indication as to whether something considerably more radical than the loosely structured Habitat Teams was required.

The *Review* began in a comparatively modest way in 1965, when Bob Boote initiated reviews covering almost all aspects of the Conservancy's administration, management and financial functions. An 'Acquisition and Management Review' would, for example, provide valuable briefing for the incoming Director in deciding the overall targets, criteria and procedures for securing more NNRs. The need for such a review had been pressed by the Chief Land Agent, Jamie V. Johnstone, as early as May 1963. On the one hand, potential reserves had to be 'snapped up' whenever opportunity arose or when their survival was threatened. On the other hand, the resources of the Conservation Branch were already overstretched. Although owners were usually willing to agree to terms, much time and hard bargaining were required. Thereafter far too many reserves were left largely to look after themselves (PRO, FT 3, 698). The Playfair Committee had expressed considerable misgivings some ten years earlier. Reference to the optimal number of reserves, in discussions leading up to the establishment of NERC, had given ample notice of the tough battles ahead. This time they would involve scientists from other disciplines as well as politicians.

Both of the Conservancy's Branches stood to gain from an Acquisition and Management Review. The inaugural meeting of the Conservation Officers, Land Agents and Administration (COLA) Group, in October 1965, put a high priority on completing the *Review* (PRO, FT 3, 699). The Research Branch not only supported the acquisition of further reserves, but believed that it had an essential role in achieving this. Whilst expert ecologists and local naturalist had been extraordinarily diligent in promoting the claims of individual sites and localities, Martin Holdgate believed that such a subjective approach could no longer suffice. If the reserve series was to be truly representative of the major British ecosystems and their variants, a considerably more rigorous and comprehensive approach was needed. In developing and applying it, a mass of data would be collected that would be of inestimable value to both researcher and manager (PRO, FT 3, 454).

A situation rapidly developed where it seemed that the Acquisition and Management Review had not only been hijacked, but transformed into what became known as the *Reserves Review*. Far from easing the difficulties of the Conservation Branch, its execution seemed only to add to them. As Joe Eggeling warned, in April 1966, the central purpose would be lost if the *Review* was allowed to become too scientific. Even if there were gaps in the series, and a few NNRs might not be entirely of the highest standard, a sense of proportion was required. The Conservancy surely had sufficient confidence in itself to say that most of the relevant information for identifying deficiencies in the series was already to hand (PRO, FT 3, 698). Duncan Poore was not convinced. Evidence was at that time being prepared for the hearings of the Lords' and Common's Select Committees on the Bill to construct the Cow Green reservoir in Upper Teesdale (see page XX). By publishing a strategic plan for the use of the water resources of England and Wales, the recently-established Water Resources Board had secured for itself a strong position in determining priorities over other aspects of land use. In the wake of the highly-publicised clash over Teesdale, a Water Use Study Group was instituted in March 1967, comprising the Chairmen, directors and senior officers of the Water Resources Board and the Conservancy, which would meet twice yearly. Through an exchange of information and views, it was hoped that future differences might be settled without resort to a public inquiry (PRO, FT 3 349). In Poore's view, such developments made a wide-ranging and rigorous *Reserves Review* all the more essential.

Once initiated, the *Review* rapidly acquired a momentum of its own. It was seen as an outstanding opportunity to demonstrate how the two Branches might work together. As Duncan Poore emphasised, it would indicate that the Conservancy was just as capable as the other component bodies of NERC of mounting a large-scale project. It would be of such magnitude and public relevance as to be acknowledged as a major initiative of NERC itself.

The collaborative intent of the *Reserves Review* was emphasised by Holdgate's being placed in overall charge, with the Conservation Officer (England), J.F. Derek Frazer, as coordinator and Derek Ratcliffe as scientific assessor. As Poore wrote, in April 1966, an initial assessment by regional officers would be followed by a more 'scientific' survey from a national perspective. To Ratcliffe, it was 'an admirable opportunity' for 'killing two birds with one stone'. Its immediate purpose of identifying and filling gaps in the reserve series could only be met by carrying out a national inventory of the entire wildlife and habitat resource. Account had to be taken of not only existing and proposed reserves, but every site of potential conservation value in Britain. For Ratcliffe, it was an exercise that should have been done long ago (PRO, FT 3, 418). Although conservation and regional officers might be sceptical as to whether it was possible, and station heads made 'disgruntled noises' about the disruption to research programmes, there could be no weakening of resolve once NERC had been informed. As the Secretary of Council, Ray J.H. Beverton remarked, in November 1967, it would at last be possible to demonstrate both to NERC Council and the Council for Scientific Policy that reserves were being acquired or extended as part of a closely-defined and agreed programme (PRO, FT 3, 415).

In launching the *Review* in October 1967, Poore emphasised that administrative and professional factors must play a large part in deciding the eventual choice of reserves, but the immediate goal was one of scientific evaluation. This meant devising a classificatory system on which site appraisal could be based. Since nothing appropriate existed, Ratcliffe developed one based (as Holdgate put it) on 'the more traditional subjective British ecological approach'. It followed the principal divisions of woodland, lowland grass-heath, coastland, wetland and uplands, with subdivisions based on life-forms and physiognomy, as well as edaphic conditions. Ratcliffe later wrote how a number of criteria came to be adopted 'by general agreement and established practice'. As well as the size or extent of the site, these criteria were the diversity, 'naturalness', rarity, fragility, and typicalness or representativeness of the wildlife.

Whilst the fullest use must be made of existing information and opinions, Ratcliffe was adamant that the *Review* should be more than 'a desk study'. There had to be a concerted effort to survey the less well known areas and habitats. Following a broad survey by regional staff of semi-natural vegetation and interesting sites, the list and details of the more 'elite' sites would be passed by Ratcliffe to habitat survey groups, drawn from the relevant research sections for further examination from a national perspective. The final assessment would be made by Ratcliffe himself (PRO, FT 3, 414).

A five-point scale of grading was devised. Grade 1 sites would be of NNR status. Those which were 'the European headquarters for the particular community, species or feature' were later distinguished as Grade 1 'starred' sites. Grade 2 included the 'second string' sites of similar or slightly lower status. Grades 3 and 4 were sites of first- or second-rate regional importance respectively, and those in Grade 5 had some conservation value, perhaps for teaching. A range of difficulties was encountered. An area of Callunetum of virtually identical floristic composition might be highly rated in one part of the country but dismissed as too common in others. There was a need to reconcile the different approaches to classification adopted by ecologists for different habitats. Much greater emphasis was, for example, placed on physiographical factors when classifying coastal habitats (PRO, FT 3, 419).

Even more fundamentally, the late 1960s was a time of increasing debate about the optimal approach to classificatory systems of every kind. As leader of the Woodland Habitat Team, John Jeffers wrote in October 1969 that, unless fundamental changes were made to the current drafts of the woodlands part of the *Review*, he would have to dissociate his Team from the approach adopted and interpretation placed on its findings. Holdgate indicated that, whilst the views of the individual habitat teams would be closely noted, Ratcliffe had the authority to override such advice where he felt there was an extremely strong case. His final 'staff' assessment would be 'screened' by the Conservancy's Scientific Policy Committee. However fundamental the objections of a particular team, no exception could be made to the philosophy and procedure followed over the previous two years. Nor would it be wise for any team to dissociate itself from any hypothetical series of judgements. The more appropriate tactic, Holdgate wrote, was to indicate that the treatment of the particular habitat was regarded as preliminary and liable to further interpretation as knowledge and understanding grew. To a degree, that was the position for all parts of the *Review* (PRO, FT 3, 418).

Although the *Review* was urgently needed as an instrument of policy, it was agreed the first priority was to publish a scientific appraisal. But, as Ratcliffe remarked of his first draft of the introductory section to the habitat and site descriptions, administrative and policy considerations were bound to have some bearing on scientific judgement. Whilst they might be concealed, it was far better to give a complete and honest account of all the factors considered in making the final selection of Grades 1 and 2 sites. Not only would this remove the embarrassment of having to admit their existence at a later date, but the Review would be that much more valuable as a guide to conservationists 'newer to the game' in other countries. Holdgate agreed that a complete rationale should be published. Besides explaining more fully what was meant by the criterion of 'fragility', a further four criteria were defined: the extent to which the history of the site was documented; geographical relationship to sites of high ecological value; potential for improvement through appropriate management; and intrinsic appeal. The last acknowledged 'the awkward philosophical point' of human bias towards particular organisms (Ratcliffe 1977b, 6–10).

Although generally referred to as the *Reserves Review*, instruction was given that it should be described at all times as the *Nature Conservation Review*. The utmost care had to be taken to avoid the kind of fracas that had occurred over the list of proposed national nature reserves that had given rise to the Playfair Committee. It was reasoned that if sites were described merely as illustrations of ecosystems found more generally by scientists in Britain, there should be no grounds for objection (PRO, FT 3, 417). It was in any case, as the Chief Land Agent, Jamie Johnstone, warned in February 1970, quite unrealistic to think that even a large proportion of the 419 Grade 1 sites could be acquired. Together with the 314 Grade 2 sites, they covered about 4 per cent of Great Britain. Only 19 per cent of the Grade 1 sites were NNRs. Nor was large-scale acquisition necessary, since voluntary bodies, local and central government, and landowners and

The *Nature Conservation Review* offered unprecedented opportunity for ecologists of the Nature Conservancy to assess the wildlife of the countryside.

(*top*) The suction apparatus made for rapid sampling of the invertebrate life of sites. Very heavy to use, it gave rise to much speculation among onlookers as to its real purpose, especially when used in fields of cows!

(*above*) A ten pointer being used for quadrat recording of the density of plants.

(*right*) **Derek Wells** of the Lowland Grassland Research Section at Monks Wood, with **Mike Horwood** of South Region, in the field.

occupiers generally, should all be encouraged to play their part in ensuring that such areas were managed along ecological lines. About one-third of the 72 coastal sites already received some protection from being part of one of the 34 Heritage Coasts designated by the Countryside Commission and local authorities in England and Wales (PRO, FT 3, 455–6).

But even if the overriding policy objective was to promote a more favourable climate for considering how individual areas might be safeguarded, there remained the insistent demand from NERC Council and the Council for Scientific Policy for specific figures as to the likely number and cost of the eventual NNR series. A series of average costs was calculated, with no allowance made for development value. Where lowland grasslands might be valued at £250 per acre and woodlands at £80 per acre, the uplands could be as low as £10 per acre. If account were taken of the total acreage of each habitat in Grade 1, the overall average cost was £40 per acre. To date, it had been necessary to purchase 27 per cent of the total NNR area. If that pattern continued, some 120,000 acres might have to be purchased; on a 20-year programme, this would require financial provision of £250,000 per annum. The annual running costs of reserve management (estimated for 1970–71) were about £2,300 per reserve (PRO, FT 3, 458 and 460).

As Jon Tinker remarked in the *New Scientist*, it took eight times longer to complete the *Review* than the Domesday Survey of 1086. The original Mark I was ready in April 1970. As well as checking and updating entries, the Treasury had to be assured that publication would not lead to demands for the purchase of all the sites included (Tinker 1976). It was eventually Mark VII that was published in July 1977, sub-titled: *The selection of biological sites of national importance to nature conservation in Britain*. The first volume set out the rationale and criteria for site selection. The second was made up of site descriptions (Ratcliffe 1977b). It was by far the most comprehensive evaluation of the distribution of scientifically-important sites ever attempted for any country in the world. The *Annual Report* of that year recounted

> we cannot expect all of these to become National Nature Reserves, but after wide consultations with Government Departments and Agencies, local authorities, voluntary bodies and organisations representing owners and occupiers of land, we shall be putting forward a range of proposals for safeguarding these sites by a variety of means (Nature Conservancy Council 1977a, 2).

Not only had the original goal of drawing up a considerably more rigorous basis for discussion and negotiation been achieved, but the two volumes received 'very favourable comment in the press', including a centre-page article in *The Times* of 21 July 1977 (Nature Conservancy Council 1978, 2). But, as the foreword to the published *Review* implied, much had happened in the meantime. As the signatures of both the Secretary of State for the Environment and the Secretary of State for Education and Science indicated, the responsibility for capitalising on the achievement had passed, in both the managerial and scientific sense, to other bodies (PRO, FT 3, 459). The following Sections of the Chapter will relate how such fundamental changes of organisation had come about.

ENVIRONMENTAL PROTECTION

NERC had become the point of reference for all the Conservancy's activities. The fourth NERC *Annual Report* emphasised that the obvious difficulties of bringing together previously-unrelated establishments should not be allowed to obscure the far-sighted wisdom of giving greater unity and prominence to the environmental sciences. It had been a bold experiment that had put Britain ahead of the world (Natural Environment Research Council 1969, 8). It would, however, not only take time for old loyalties to give way to new, but the Trend report had done nothing to allay anxieties as to whether the nation was getting good value from its investment in science. Searching questions continued to be asked as to whether there were better ways of allocating priorities (Wilkie 1991).

In the short term, both NERC and its component bodies could count their blessings. There was not only an historically-remarkable growth in the Government's science budget, but the proportion spent on the environmental sciences rose. As the House of Commons' Select Committee on Science and Technology found, in its scrutiny of NERC, they had been treated relatively generously. Although the lion's share (46 per cent) went to the Science Research Council, the NERC proportion was as high as 17.7 per cent of the £92.3 million awarded to the research councils in 1967–68. It was as large a slice of the science 'cake' as individually received by the Agricultural and Medical Research Councils. Within NERC, the earth sciences accounted for 32.9 per cent of expenditure, the marine sciences 24.3 per cent, and the terrestrial and freshwater sciences 16.9 per cent. The budget of the Nature Conservancy had risen by 51 per cent to £1.5 million (Parliamentary Papers, 1968–69).

The stature of the NERC, even within its allotted area of environmental concern, could not be taken for granted. At times, it seemed all too likely that the Government, having assembled NERC, would start to unravel it. The warning signs were there. In a statement to the House of Commons in October 1969, the Prime Minister, Harold Wilson, announced wide-ranging responsibilities for the new Secretary of State for Local Government and Regional Planning (Anthony Crosland), including an urgent review of all aspects of pollution (PD, Commons, 788, 33). Notice was given, two months later, of a standing Royal Commission on Environmental Pollution. In the Prime Minister's words, it would 'act as a watchdog'. The same announcement described how Crosland had set up a Central Scientific Unit on Environmental Pollution (PD, Commons, 793, 638–45). Martin Holdgate became head of the Unit in April 1970. In May 1970, a White Paper was published with the title, *The protection of the environment: the fight against pollution* (Secretary of State for Local Government 1970).

As an institute-rich council, much would depend on NERC's ability to capitalise on the

Newborough Warren.
Ynys Llanddwyn NNR was designated, from 1955 onwards, as one of the largest and biologically richest expanses of sand dunes in western Britain and the finest of its type in Wales. All stages of plant colonisation and succession from beach zone to fixed dune grassland were well represented.

distinctive strengths of its component bodies, both in a scientific and administrative sense. In terms of networking with relevant Government departments and professional and voluntary bodies, the Conservancy was unique in having such a well-developed regional presence. Such public utility was perhaps most obviously put to the test by the escalating pressures on the coastal resource. The Dungeness Inquiry, and the prospect of further nuclear power stations and other major developments, caused the Conservancy urgently to assess whether it had the relevant information readily to hand. Four exploratory meetings were held with interested organisations to assess both the coastal resources and the priorities for their protection. It was found that roughly 10–15 per cent of the coastline fell within an existing National Park or Area of Outstanding Natural Beauty. Some 2 per cent was encompassed within the 22 NNRs that abutted the coastline. The National Trust held a further 4.5 per cent, of which half was in Devon and Cornwall and the rest mainly in Pembrokeshire and Norfolk (Nature Conservancy 1960, 44–7). The Nature Conservancy later claimed that it was during the course of these meetings that the germ of the idea emerged (and was vigorously encouraged) that the National Trust should mount a campaign to raise monies for the purchase and protection of the more attractive and vulnerable lengths of coastline. Enterprise Neptune was launched in May 1965.

The Ministry of Housing and Local Government (which had sent a technical observer to the latter two meetings) issued in September 1963 a Circular, *Coastal preservation and development*, to local planning authorities with coastal boundaries. Although it was originally drafted from an amenity and recreational perspective, input from the Conservancy ensured that reference was made to the importance of protecting the scientific interest from being unnecessarily damaged (PRO, FT 3, 564). On being asked to undertake an intensive study of land-use planning along the whole coastline, the National Parks Commission sought the Conservancy's assistance. The Conservancy wrote one of the two volumes that made up the 'Special Study' on *Coastal preservation and development*, submitted to ministers in 1969. The Conservancy's volume emphasised the need for a more holistic view of the coast, for research on its capacity to withstand the increasing pressures of human activity and, thirdly, for raising public awareness as to the improvements required in its management. The Conservancy particularly commended planning policies which extended to a greater depth inland, which concentrated or zoned development so as to minimise pressures on the remaining lengths of unspoilt coast, and which diverted from the coast development that could as easily, or more appropriately, be accommodated inland (Countryside Commission 1969).

Inevitably, perhaps, the Conservancy was most closely judged by its handling of major pollution incidents. As with its increasing involvement in pesticides research, here was a further opportunity to demonstrate that, in devising ways of protecting wildlife, the Conservancy was also safeguarding its economic and social value. Almost all holiday-makers at the seaside had experienced oil on their feet or clothes at some time. They had probably come across the remains of oiled seabirds. The efforts of the International Convention for the Prevention of Pollution of the Sea by Oil, and the introduction of the 'load on top' system for tankers, had done much to reduce routine pollution by oil tankers and other vessels at sea. Accidental spillages were now the more serious threat. There was heavy loss of birdlife in September 1966 when a mishap caused oil from the tanker *Seestern* to escape into the Medway estuary near the Isle of Grain refinery. Nothing, however, prepared the politicians and public alike for the television pictures of oil-drenched birds and beaches, some six months later, and the desperate attempts of the Royal Air Force to ignite the oil left in the stricken vessel.

The Liberian-registered oil tanker *Torrey Canyon* ran aground between the Isles of Scilly and Land's End on the morning of 18 March 1967. Its cargo of 117,000 tons of Kuwait crude oil was bound for the BP refinery at Milford Haven in Pembrokeshire. As a Royal Navy helicopter confirmed, 2 hours later, large quantities of oil had already begun to leak into the sea. The Parliamentary Under-Secretary for the Navy flew to Plymouth the next day to coordinate both the Government response to attempts by a Dutch salvage vessel to refloat the tanker and efforts to break up and disperse the oil slicks at sea. Naval vessels were soon joined by chartered boats in spraying detergent onto the oil. Stocks were rushed to all Cornish coastal authorities. A battalion of soldiers prepared to assist when the oil came ashore (Gill et al. 1967).

The condition of the tanker had so deteriorated that, on 21 March, the Prime Minister, Harold Wilson, contacted Sir Solly Zuckerman, now the Chief Scientific Advisor to the Government. Zuckerman wrote later

> from the moment I was asked to concern myself with the problem of the *Torrey Canyon* I focused my attention entirely on the problem of trying to reduce the threat of coastal pollution (PRO, PREM 13, 1460).

Within a day, Zuckerman had recruited an expert group from the Scientific Civil Service that, further enlarged, became the Cabinet Committee of Scientists on the 'Scientific and technological aspects of the Torrey Canyon disaster'. Zuckerman instructed it to prepare advice as to what action should be taken to meet 'the worst possible hypothesis'.

Politically, the priority for the Government was to defend itself from charges that it had been slow to react. Although the Cabinet had affirmed, at its meeting on 23 March, that everything must be done to combat the threat of pollution, it was not until the tanker broke her back three days later, and all hope of salvage was finally abandoned, that approval was given for bombing missions designed to burn as much oil as possible, before it left the tanker. The bombs had to be timed so as to detonate after they had entered the oil compartments, but before going through the bottom of the hull. At Harold Wilson's instigation, a White Paper was hurriedly drafted and published on 4 April, describing how the first oil came ashore on 25 March, the same day as the Minister of Housing and Local Government left for Cornwall to assure local authorities they would receive grant aid of up to 75 per cent of the cost for cleaning-up operations. Three junior ministers were to help coordinate the response from Plymouth, Portsmouth and Folkestone (Secretary of State 1967). In a Commons' statement that day, Wilson further emphasised that everything was being done, for example, to protect the Cornish tourist industry, which had an estimated value of over £100 million per annum (PD, Commons, 744, 38–54).

Although appalled by what was happening to the coast and wildlife of Cornwall, the Conservancy also realised that the disaster presented an outstanding opportunity to demonstrate by practical example its unique, yet relevant, qualities. Invited by Zuckerman to join his expert Committee, it was Duncan Poore's responsibility to co-ordinate the measures required to protect both wildlife and conservation sites. The immediate priority was for the Conservancy and fisheries scientists of the Ministry of Agriculture (MAFF) to draw up a list of key sites requiring protection. Agreed over the phone, the list of 26 areas, many of them estuaries, was sent to the Home Office on 30 March. Bob Boote had instructed all staff in the affected or threatened regions to be deployed on the emergency. The regional offices were to act as both intelligence centres and clearing houses for information passing between the Ministerial Centres, local authorities and voluntary conservation bodies. The Regional Officer for South-west England, W.O. (Bill) Copland, established a temporary office at the Plymouth Marine Laboratory of the Marine Biological Association (MBA), a grant-aided body of NERC. Besides being close to the Ministerial Centre, it assured close rapport with the MBA and MAFF scientists, who had similarly taken accommodation there. Besides his own and additional staff drafted to the region, Copland was closely supported by Derek Ranwell, the head of the Coastal Ecology Section, in providing the specialist guidance required in assessing the ecological implications of the measures being taken against the oil (PRO, FT 22, 113).

A priority for the Conservancy's coordinative role was to apportion responsibility. A meeting of the relevant organisations on 29 March decided that, while the Conservancy and RSPB should have overall direction, the RSPCA, working with the RSPB and local voluntary organisations, would physically collect the oiled birds and establish cleansing and rehabilitation centres. The Cornwall Naturalists' Trust had already begun coastal patrols and opened centres. The total bird casualties was eventually estimated at over 25,000. Of nearly 8,000 birds brought to the rehabilitation centres, mostly guillemots and razorbills, only 450 survived the first month of the wreck, and considerably fewer were eventually returned to the sea. The Conservancy's own priority was to identify and recommend ways of preventing or minimising the damage to Sites of Special Scientific Interest (SSSIs) and other important areas, including those managed as nature reserves by the voluntary bodies. Whilst the immediate concern was the Cornish coastline, contingency plans were laid for the entire coast from the Thames Estuary to South Wales. A supplementary list of 70 sites of conservation importance was distributed to Ministerial Centres and local authorities on 5 April. Regional staff and members of the Coastal Ecology Section made numerous tours on foot and by boat and helicopter, detailing the extent and severity of pollution.

The Home Secretary, Roy Jenkins, in moving a Commons debate of 10 April (PD, Commons, 49, 758–821), spoke of how the disaster had been unique in both scale and the circumstances that had brought it about. By the end of April, 140 miles of the Cornish coast, between Trevose Head, Land's End and the Lizard, had been contaminated. Some 40 holiday-beaches were seriously affected. It could, however, have been much worse. Only two top-priority conservation sites, West Lizard and Penhale Sands, were polluted, and then only moderately. The only major estuary to be significantly damaged was that of the River Hayle, which included the sanctuary managed by the Cornwall Bird Watching and Preservation Society. Seventeen second-priority sites were affected,

The *Torrey Canyon* wreck.
Fire officers spraying detergent onto
the oil, with a protective boom in the
background, in **Porthleven Harbour,
Cornwall**.

the foreshore of twelve of them being contaminated fairly heavily. As Copland emphasised, the statistics gave something of a false picture because most of the Cornish SSSIs
had been scheduled either for geological or geomorphological interest, or for the rich
cliff and cliff-top vegetation. It ought to be considered whether the schedules for this
and other lengths of coastline should now be urgently reviewed to include examples of
the rich marine life of the shore and inter-tidal waters that had previously been taken
so much for granted.

The Conservancy emerged from those frantic days with mixed feelings. It had met its
immediate political and humanitarian goal. Harold Wilson minuted his gratitude to the
'services, local authorities, scientists, conservancy and animal folk' (PRO, PREM 13,
1461). The Secretary of State for Education and Science wrote to Duncan Poore in June,
formally conveying the Government's appreciation. And yet there remained a feeling
within the Conservancy that wildlife could have been better protected, if its advice had
been more closely heeded. Where the first concern of the Cabinet's *Torrey Canyon*
Committee had been to ask farmers for the loan of their crop-sprayers, the priority soon

changed to one of requesting heavy earth-moving equipment to remove the oiled sand bodily from the beaches. As the Committee recognised, at its fourth meeting of 27 March, the main value of detergents was that of reassuring public opinion that something was being done. In the meantime, however, supplies had become so plentiful, and pressure from the media and public opinion so intense, that there was no holding back the authorities in their use of detergents. When one of the Conservancy's staff asked an American colonel and his men not to use detergent on a particularly vulnerable section of coast, he was told, 'I've got the goddam stuff to use, and I'm going to use it.' In fact the situation deteriorated further as even the more remote, rocky sections were sprayed so as to prevent 're-contamination' of cleansed beaches. An appeal by the Conservancy on 7 April emphasised the need to avoid spraying nature reserves, SSSIs and other areas important for their wildlife.

Although conceding something had to be 'seen to be done' on such well-known holiday-beaches as Sennen Cove, Derek Ranwell wrote how, even here, detergents might hinder the main purpose of the cleansing operation. By enabling the oil to mix with water rather than float on top, detergents frequently helped it to sink into the sands, only to reappear on later high tides (or when holiday-makers dug it out). Ranwell spent five days in late April touring the Brittany coast. Although contamination had been generally heavier and more continuous than on the Cornish coast, Ranwell expected recovery and re-colonisation to be much more rapid. Detergents had hardly been used. Drawing on observations of earlier oil spillages in Milford Haven, he believed there would be much greater potential for marine life to metabolise and remove the oil, albeit slowly, by natural processes (PRO, FT 22, 115).

The Zuckerman Committee emphasised, in a report published later in the year that

> practically every issue on which decisions for action had to be taken during the period of crisis was at least partly of a scientific or technical nature (Cabinet Office 1967).

It was therefore important that a team of scientists was similarly appointed at the earliest point in a future crisis. The Committee acknowledged that the greatest criticisms of the authorities in the recent emergency had been the harm caused to marine life by the their excessive use of detergents on the beaches. Ways had to be found of combining the maximum effectiveness of emulsifiers with minimum toxicity and persistence. For the Conservancy, the more pressing issue was to ensure that 'considered advice based on exact knowledge' was implemented by those physically carrying out the cleansing operations. Copland believed the ecological advice would have been more readily taken up if the Government had acted in an executive capacity, rather than simply as an adviser and facilitator to local government. As Copland wrote, in early May

> what we cannot understand is why supplies of detergent continue to be issued when it is becoming widely known that the consensus of scientific opinion is completely against their use.

Even native Cornishmen deplored their use. Only the Chamber of Commerce and hotel-industry lobby continued to press for them (PRO, FT 22, 114).

The immediate priority was to respond to the requirements and opportunities afforded by Circulars sent by the Ministry of Housing and Local Government and the Scottish and Welsh Offices to their respective local authorities, in July 1968, offering guidance in dealing with future oil spillages. They emphasised the need to consult the local District Inspector of Fisheries and the Regional Officer of the Nature Conservancy. A meeting of representatives of MAFF, the Marine Biological Association and the Conservancy, convened by Duncan Poore in November 1968, agreed the format of the maps to be provided for the relevant authorities, identifying for the entire coastline the key areas for protection. Whilst those maps should obviously carry warnings against the use of detergents, the parties to the meeting were extremely reluctant to set out more positive prescriptions as to the treatments to be followed. Apart from taking account of such factors as seasonal conditions, there was a real danger of the local authorities regarding such advice as being complete in itself. There had to be the closest liaison both before and throughout an oiling incident (PRO, FT 3, 663 and FT 22, 116–7).

Further opportunity to demonstrate the ability of NERC and its component bodies to monitor and respond to pollution incidents was afforded by the Irish seabird 'wreck' of the autumn of 1969. Where oil pollution was strikingly visual, the only evidence that something had gone badly wrong in parts of the Irish Sea was the discovery of exceptional numbers of bird carcases. Within a few days, NERC headquarters had brought together scientists from its own institutes (and most obviously the Conservancy), universities, Departmental laboratories, and the voluntary bodies to assess the cause and extent of the losses to bird life. But if there was encouragement of an organisational kind, there was frustration at the failure to establish the cause of the seabird 'wreck'. A report published later by NERC speculated from post-mortem examinations that the presence of polychlorinated biphenyls (PCBs), an industrial by-product, might have added to the stress already imposed on the birds by storms, moulting and starvation (Holdgate 1971). Further examination at Monks Wood caused the Conservancy to suspect the PCBs had been implicated even more directly in the deaths (Sheail 1985, 212–21).

A NERC Council meeting of January 1970 identified three complementary lines of research needed before any kind of early-warning system of pollution could be provided. First, there had to be long-term and systematic studies of the ecology and dynamics of natural systems in order to identify, measure and explain any significant changes. Second, experiments were required to investigate the effects of specific pollutants, or combinations of pollutants, on the physiology, biochemistry and behaviour of individual organisms or populations. Third, research was needed on the persistence and degradation of the pollutants in the physical environment and the tissues of organisms, and on the ways in which they might be transmitted or dispersed (Sheail 1992). Whilst the Conservancy was fully supportive of such priorities being placed on its research, there was increasing concern that such imperatives, and guidance as to their purpose and application, were increasingly arising not from the first-hand expertise and experience of the Conservancy committees, but from higher and wider counsels in which the Conservancy was only one of many parties. That tension and its eventual resolution are the subject of the concluding Sections of this Chapter.

THE 'CHARTER' COMMITTEE

A priority for the new Council had been to create a main committee structure based on the component bodies. Committees were formed to cover hydrology, geology and geophysics, oceanography and fisheries, and forestry and woodland research. The Nature Conservancy Committee, however, was special. The NERC Charter required not only its appointment at the first meeting of Council, in June 1965, but even specified the names of the founder-members.

To onlookers from outside, and indeed for most of the Conservancy's staff, it was business as usual. Except for the loss of its grant-awarding committee, the Conservancy's committee structure was unchanged. There were Committees for England, Scotland and Wales, as well as a Scientific Policy Committee. There was continued achievement to report. The number of NNRs rose from 113 in 1965 to 130 by 1971, covering 270,000 acres (109,000 hectares). There was considerable expansion of research facilities, and wide acknowledgement of the Conservancy's advisory and educational functions. But if there was praise, there remained misgivings on the part of NERC as to the appropriateness of the Conservancy's more explicitly conservation-orientated activities. The Conservancy was accustomed to the often ill-informed criticisms of members of parliament, ministers and their officials. For the most part, these were seen as an inevitable consequence of being a public-sector body. It was the interposition of NERC and, therefore, scientists from other subject areas, that caused particular resentment.

Matters were not helped by a series of controversies regarding the advice that the Conservancy might give on questions of public policy, and the manner in which it might be given. The most obvious was the controversy over proposals to impound the upper River Tees for the supply of water to the industrial north-east of England. There were in effect two schemes, the one pre-dating and the other post-dating incorporation within NERC. The first began with a letter from six professors of botany and a number of other leading botanists to *The Times*, on 13 February 1957. It warned of the damage to wild plant-life if a reservoir were built on the upper Tees. Although probably premature, Nicholson also expressed 'horror' at the proposal, lest the Conservancy's silence might later be taken as acquiescence. As well as warning the local planning authority that the Conservancy would object, Nicholson took the precaution of informing Roger Quirk who, in turn, sought to discover more from the Ministry of Housing and Local Government. He warned that the Conservancy was bound to oppose the inundation of an area of such unique importance for its geology and rare plants. Although a Private Bill was drafted, it was clear by November 1957 that the prospect of opposition from both the Conservancy and National Parks Commission had been one of the factors that caused the scheme to be dropped. As Nicholson recalled, in correspondence with the Parliamentary Secretary for Science, Denzil Freeth, in February 1961, that particular battle had been won in the sense that a reservoir was constructed at an alternative site, at Balder Head on the Lune (PRO, CAB 124, 1603).

The Conservancy found its freedom to oppose such schemes considerably more restricted when, in 1965, the Tees Valley and Cleveland Water Board made a further attempt to resolve what was perceived to be a pending water-supply crisis. It sought consent for the construction of a dam at Cauldron Snout in Upper Teesdale. The Cow Green reservoir (as it was called) would flood 770 acres (300 hectares), of which 18 acres (6 hectares) were in the Moor House NNR and another 95 acres (38 hectares) within the proposed extension of another Reserve. The remaining area had already been scheduled as a Site of Special Scientific Interest. Whilst acknowledging the Conservancy's deep concern, the Chairman of NERC, the distinguished meteorologist Sir Graham Sutton, emphasised, at the Council meeting of January 1966, that the Conservancy's evidence to the Parliamentary Select Committees should deal only with the damage to the scientific interest. In as much as the Bill also dealt with 'matters of national concern quite outside the scientific competence and responsibilities of Council', the Conservancy should say nothing that might be construed as opposition to the Bill.

Although the immediate concern was the Bill, the attitude of NERC Council to the Conservancy left considerable bitterness. Both the Conservancy and voluntary nature-conservation bodies were appalled that its terms of reference should be interpreted so narrowly. A Teesdale Defence Committee, comprising the Botanical Society of the British Isles, the British Ecological Society, the Linnean Society, and three County Naturalists' Trusts petitioned against the Bill. They had assumed the automatic and uncompromising support of the Conservancy. Martin Holdgate gave evidence on behalf of the Conservancy to both the Lords' and Commons' Select Committees. He explained how, whilst no rare species would be rendered extinct, the truncation of the remarkable variety of ground conditions would make it much harder for ecologists to study the

An exhibit illustrating careers in the Nature Conservancy, created for an Open Day in the late 1960s.

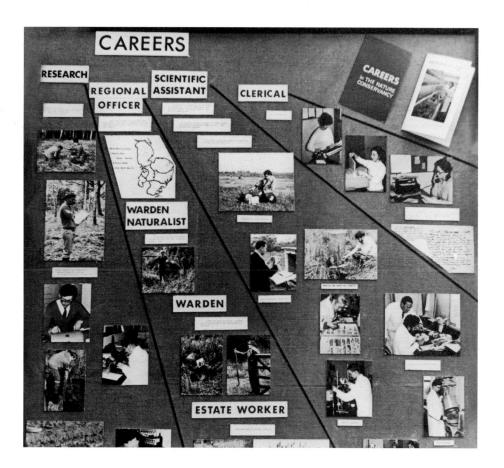

preferences and tolerances of such species. In as much as both the promoters and the Select Committees broadly accepted the scientific importance of the area, the fundamental point at issue was whether the irreplaceable but unmeasurable scientific interest, or the major and measurable economic needs of the region, should prevail. The Bill to construct the reservoir was given the Royal Assent in March 1967 (Gregory 1971).

An indication of the resentment felt by some members of the Nature Conservancy Committee was provided by a letter written by the Chairman of the Committee for England, Major Ralph Verney, to the House of Commons Select Committee on Science and Technology, whose scrutiny of NERC was published in July 1969. It was written even before the Committee had started to take evidence. It complained of the 'entirely negative effect of the absorption of the Conservancy into NERC'. According to Verney, it had achieved nothing worthwhile in terms of financial control, integration of research, or effectiveness in conservation. In his evidence to the Committee, Lord Howick took a different view, describing how NERC, and particularly its Secretary, had 'done us very well for money'. Bearing in mind that, even if run by the Archangel Gabriel, there would always be a danger of its becoming 'a slightly cumbersome or slow machinery', he believed NERC was very well managed (Parliamentary Papers 1968–69).

In determining whether the Conservancy should remain in NERC, the Select Committee believed that the most important consideration was whether it was essential for conservation and research to work hand in hand. From a conservation perspective, Ralph Verney argued that 'we should be better on our own or in some other grouping'. All other witnesses were adamant that the links between conservation and research should be preserved. Members of the Committee agreed with Lord Howick that the rewards of remaining in NERC outweighed those of any departure. It was doubtful whether perfection could ever be attained.

As had been recognised in the years prior to the formation of NERC, it was not simply a question of de-coupling the nature reserves from the research functions. There had to be an assurance that the Conservation Branch could continue to develop what Bob Boote called the 'catalyst' function in terms of determining the future management of the countryside. As was emphasised in the Foreword to the *Report on Broadland*, published by the Conservancy in 1965, the countryside was undergoing immense change, in both the physical and social sense, particularly in respect of the leisure habits and mobility of the population. How might consideration be more effectively given to deciding the 'most efficient long-term use' of rural resources (Nature Conservancy 1965)? In the case of Broadland, and perhaps more generally, the Conservancy believed its role was not one of issuing detailed plans. Rather, the Conservancy's mission was one of helping to establish the facts of the situation, and of presenting them in a balanced and objective way, intelligible to the layman. The Broads Survey had provided a model of the way facts might be considered and agreed, other people's problems recognised, divergencies exposed, and a climate of opinion created in which the various conclusions could be welded into an authoritative set of policy objectives.

Whilst acknowledging the value for such initiatives, there were increasing misgivings on the part of NERC Council and its officers. One was the apparently limitless scope and demand for this kind of catalytic work. Another was the political use to which the find-

Bruce Forman was successively the Nature Conservancy's Regional Officer for East Anglia, Conservation Officer for England, and the NCC's Director of the England headquarters at Banbury.
The publicity given to nature conservation by European Conservation Year led to many more calls for advice. On the desk, there are copies of the triennial Monks Wood report, the paperback version of Kenneth Mellanby's *Pesticides and Pollution*, and the Conservancy's third monograph, *Wildfowl in Great Britain* (Atkinson-Willes 1963).

ings might be put. Although Council agreed in late 1965 that the Conservancy should continue to act on a caretaker basis, the Ministry of Land and Natural Resources was pressed to take over the function as quickly as possible. The decline in the growth rate of the Government's Science Budget made NERC even keener to shed responsibilities that distracted its components' bodies from what Council members perceived to be their central purpose, namely that of research. On the other hand, the Conservancy became increasingly reluctant to divest itself of functions that it had worked so hard to develop. Unconsciously echoing John Berry, some years earlier, Duncan Poore wrote in October 1967 of the way modern thought in nature conservation encompassed far more than the selection and safeguarding of individual sites. It extended to a concern for the use and management of the entire land surface, air, water and wildlife. Nature conservation, and the research that supported it, had to be regarded as a continuum with the work of planners, agriculturalists and others concerned with the countryside.

If the Broads Survey had been a 'notable success', Langstone Harbour in Hampshire was an example of how, by allowing the catalyst function to go by default, the concept of multiple resource use might be entirely lost. Langstone Harbour was one of the larger tidal inlets to the east of Portsmouth in south Hampshire, comprising some 5,000 acres (2,000 hectares) of water and mud flat. As a navigable waterway, it was administered by the Langstone Harbour Board. The sheltered waters were ideally suited for sailing and cruising, fishing and water-skiing, while the marshes were popular with wildfowlers. The Conservancy had designated one area as a proposed National Nature Reserve for its wildfowl interest. The adjacent land, particularly Hayling Island, was well suited for holiday use and the associated permanent and temporary development of holiday camps, chalets and caravans, each with its separate demand for car parks, hardstandings, and access to the water. Competing with the scientific and recreational interests was the demand for land for residential and industrial development. Over the previous 15 years, the population of Havant and the Waterlooville Urban District had trebled. The Portsmouth City Development Committee had put forward a scheme to create island units to accommodate 150,000 people, each unit being connected to the mainland by elevated causeways.

At the instigation of the Conservancy, an inter-departmental meeting was convened, in February 1966, to discuss the future of Langstone Harbour. It revealed an extraordinary degree of fragmentation. In a recital of their respective responsibilities, the Ministry of Land and Natural Resources described its concern as that of the overall planning of the country's land and mineral resources, and in developing methodologies applicable to the solution of those strategic problems. Statutory planning powers, however, resided in the Ministry of Housing and Local Government and the local planning authorities, of which two had responsibility for parts of the Harbour. The Ministry of Agriculture was concerned to protect adjacent farmland. The Board of Trade explained that its interest, and that of the Harbour Board and its Advisory Committee, was confined to the harbour and possible dangers to navigation. The Conservancy reiterated its belief that a long-term plan should be considered for the entire Harbour area, based on a full assessment of all demands. From 'a proper appreciation of its total capacity to sustain these demands', a plan for the multiple use of the Harbour should be drawn up. The meeting concluded, however, that no action should be taken until a consultant's report on the Portsmouth and Southampton area, commissioned by the Ministry of Housing and Local Government, was completed. As the Conservancy was later to protest, nothing was done even when that report had been published. Although an official of the Ministry of Land and Natural Resources agreed that somebody should grasp the nettle, there was no possibility of the Ministry or its successor doing so. The Conservancy abandoned negotiations for the proposed National Nature Reserve.

It was not until March 1968 that the ministers agreed in principle that the Conservancy's responsibility for catalyst functions should be formally transferred to the Countryside Commissions. As Poore pointed out, this represented two years of lost opportunity. Worse still, there was little evidence of their being willing, or able, to make up the lost ground. Discussions with the Ministry of Housing and Local Government, in June 1968, revealed that there was to be no regional structure nor senior post in the Countryside Commission for England and Wales to cover those functions. In forecasting trouble ahead, the Secretary of NERC, Ray Beverton, believed the Ministry had 'sorely underestimated the magnitude of the task'. As Poore remarked, a gap remained that 'must someday concern someone involved with the machinery of Government' (PRO, FT 8, 41).

None of this helped Council to resolve what a meeting of September 1969 perceived as the two principal challenges. How could the demands for increased research-funding be met at a time of diminishing resources? How could NERC respond to the increasing need for research that cut across the conventional boundaries of disciplines? Council appointed a Working Party in October to review its committee structure. Lord Howick and other Chairmen of the standing committees were members. Its report found that, far from being a strength, the standing committees remained a source of weakness in developing a more corporate spirit. The outlook of the committees, and none more so than the Nature Conservancy Committee, had remained insular and competitive. As the workload increased and required further delegation, the sense of remoteness between Council and its component bodies became ever more striking. There was a need to simplify the infrastructure of Council, to sharpen the responsibilities of its Secretary, NERC headquarters and the directors, and to streamline reporting procedures (Sheail 1992).

The Working Party's main proposal was to replace the existing committees with five Preparatory Groups: three covering the Earth Sciences, Terrestrial Life Sciences, and Marine Sciences while the remaining two would deal with Antarctic research and university support. Such Groups would deal with the detail of Council business, with only significant policy issues referred to Council itself. Although Council accepted the recommendations in May 1970, there was vigorous opposition from some members of the Nature Conservancy Committee. Harry Godwin protested that the Preparatory Group for the Terrestrial Life Sciences would either sideline the Nature Conservancy Committee or interfere in the most damaging way with its relationship to Council. Such an interpretation was strenuously denied by the Chairman of Council, Vero Wynne-Edwards, who was himself a distinguished animal ecologist. As he explained, the Preparatory Groups were not intervening committees, but a part of Council itself.

Anthony Crosland with the Chairman of the National Coal Board, **Alf Robens** on his left, and **Duncan Sandys** and **Bob Boote** on his right.
The Civic Trust conference held at Stoke on Trent in April 1970, took as its theme 'Derelict land'.

Through the Groups, members of Council would have far greater opportunity to probe issues in depth and consult directors in informal discussion.

Besides its own misgivings, NERC was conscious of anxieties within Whitehall itself as to the appropriateness of Conservancy personnel being so intimately involved in the '1970' conferences and European Conservation Year. Paradoxically, such tension increased as the success of those ventures became clearer. Beverton emphasised on several occasions that both NERC and the Conservancy must hold aloof from the policy aspects. First Nicholson, and then Boote, emphasised that their close participation was in an entirely personal capacity. It was Lord Howick's habit to drop into offices for an informal chat and, on one occasion in the late 1960s, he did so to satisfy himself that such involvement by Boote, and the small secretariat of Conservancy personnel supporting him in such activities, was neither detracting from their other duties nor implying any formal commitment on the part of the Conservancy. Fully satisfied, he continued to offer every encouragement.

There was further indication of the sensitivity of Government departments, following a Civic Trust conference at Stoke-on-Trent in April 1970 on the restoration of derelict land. The '1970' Standing Committee had decided that one of its members, F.C. Baker of the National Coal Board, should give a paper. He was, however, taken ill, and Boote was the only person available to take his place. As always, he began by emphasising that he was speaking on behalf of the Standing Committee. There was nevertheless official complaint as to the content of the paper. Following some months of correspondence between Departments and NERC, which included reference to ministers, Bob Boote and those in the Conservancy who had supported him concluded that enough was enough. Their withdrawal in early 1971 effectively meant the end of the '1970' movement.

As Poore wrote later, the Nature Conservancy Committee came increasingly to believe that it could only operate an effective conservation policy by leaving NERC. There were three principal areas of dissatisfaction. Areas of scientific activity such as physiography and meteorology were scaled down, with a view to withdrawing them, where NERC believed they were more appropriate to another component body. Secondly, the Conservancy's Scientific Policy Committee was increasingly side-lined; it was the scientists on NERC Council who ultimately determined whether the *Nature Conservation Review* went ahead, and its findings were published. Thirdly, and most seriously, was the failure to make the case for funding conservation activities on a different basis from research priorities. The funding of reserve acquisition and management, and of the advisory services, had to compete with the massively expensive projects of the geological and oceanographic sciences. Perhaps most fundamentally of all, advocacy had become almost impossible. As Poore observed, the Agricultural Research Council and Medical Research Council might enthusiastically promote good farming and medicine in their respective research programmes, but an environmental enthusiasm was seen as 'unscientific' (Poore 1987).

A year after the Preparatory Group system was introduced, nine members of the Nature Conservancy Committee and Scientific Policy Committee wrote, in April 1971, to the Secretary of State for Education and Science, Margaret Thatcher, pressing for the Conservancy to be given its former independent status. There was no need for the superimposition of NERC, a body that was never intended to have the needs of nature conservation foremost in its mind. Margaret Thatcher declined to consider the views expressed until they had been considered by both the Nature Conservancy Committee and NERC Council. A special meeting of the former was held in late July 1971, with Lord Howick in the chair. Wynne-Edwards was also present. He emphasised that any appraisal should take account of a 'tapering' growth-rate for spending on civil science. If the Conservancy were to leave NERC, the Department of the Environment was likely to take over the reserves and advisory functions, leaving the research element within a research council. He then left the meeting. His sentiments were supported by two members of the Conservancy Committee, one warning that the prospect of independence was illusory and the other claiming that it would be financial suicide (PRO, FT 5, 62; Sheail 1992).

Of those who had signed the memorandum addressed to Margaret Thatcher, Godwin spoke of the inherent incompatibility of the two bodies, and Verney of how NERC had never 'appreciated the importance of public relations'. As Sir Charles Connell remarked, the Conservancy had to speak out with a singleness of purpose, in a way that NERC had never done. The Secretary of the Society for the Promotion of Nature Reserves, Ted Smith, believed close cooperation with the voluntary conservation bodies was far more important than any closeness with other NERC bodies. As Godwin observed, the loyal support of those bodies had been an important factor in enabling the Conservancy to develop so powerfully. From the Chair, Howick warned that there could be no going back to the pre-1965 situation. It was a choice of NERC or absorption into a Government department. The latter would mean even greater dictation of policy from above. Not only would the status of the Conservancy further diminish, but there was every likelihood of the research function remaining within NERC. The meeting passed a resolution, by 11 votes to 3, in support of what had become known as the 'Godwin'

Ray Beverton, founder-Secretary of NERC. Previously Deputy-Director of the Fisheries Laboratory at Lowestoft, he had established an international reputation for research on the dynamics of fish populations and their ecological basis, pioneering the scientific basis for fisheries management.

memorandum sent to Margaret Thatcher. It called for a review, at the highest level in Government, of the status and location of the Conservancy (PRO, FT 5, 62).

At a meeting of NERC Council in September 1971, Lord Howick advised Council to recommend to Margaret Thatcher that the proposition be rejected. The meeting of the Conservancy Committee had been so highly charged that most of those present had made no attempt to listen to reasonable argument. The strong feelings did not go deep in the Conservancy's staff. Although one Council member, Sir Edward Bullard, believed the situation was irretrievable, other members of Council believed every effort should be made to keep the Conservancy in NERC. A way had to be found to cool the dispute. It was at this point that the Secretary of Council, Ray Beverton, claimed that the arrangement was constitutionally flawed and could no longer be tolerated. Whereas the Science and Technology Act had been quite explicit in saying that 'the activities of the Nature Conservancy... shall be taken over by the NERC', the provision made in the Charter for a Nature Conservancy Committee had encouraged its members to believe that they were somehow organisationally separate. It had caused the Conservancy to behave not so much as a scientific body, but as one concerned with land-use policy.

In a brief historical review, Beverton recalled how the overriding purpose of the Conservancy had been to give scientific advice. Despite having responsibility for a series of National Nature Reserves, it had never been intended to exercise a 'protectionist' role. However, because no part of Government had been interested in receiving and implementing its advice (the Ministry of Housing and Local Government was most unsympathetic), the Conservancy had been obliged to stray from its Charter functions. According to Beverton, the Treasury had hoped that, through its incorporation into NERC, more control might be exerted over its activities. The Conservancy had, however, become so closely involved in the 'Countryside in 1970' activities that such detachment had to be postponed. European Conservation Year had, however, come and gone. It was now time for NERC to straighten out the tangles. The minutes of the Council meeting record how, in the course of further discussion, there was substantial, but not unanimous, agreement that the Conservancy was an uncomfortable partner for NERC, but that there was no alternative to its remaining a component body.

The Chairman of Council accordingly wrote to Margaret Thatcher, in October 1971, expressing regret that the Nature Conservancy Committee should wish to become independent. It was Council's firm opinion that NERC must remain responsible for basic and strategic research in terrestrial ecology and biology. Although conservation policy and practice must be firmly based on scientific advice of the highest quality, Council was far less convinced that research and conservation activities must remain integral parts of the same executive body. His Council accordingly recommended an enquiry to examine the issues. If its recommendation was to retain the Conservancy as a component body, Council would wish to change its formal relationship, so as to permit greater integration of policy and function within the rest of NERC's activities (PRO, FT 5, 62).

At a meeting with the Chairman and Secretary, Margaret Thatcher indicated that she had no intention of granting the Nature Conservancy independent status under the Department of Education and Science. It was doubtful whether any other Department would do so. She welcomed the idea of a 'factual' enquiry into the relationship of the

The Chairman of the Nature Conservancy from 1962 onwards and founder-member of the NERC Council, **Lord Howick**, visiting the Farne Islands in 1961.
Staff recalled his many visits to reserves and research stations for the infectious enthusiasm he conveyed in his questions and comments on their work.

Conservancy with NERC. At its next meeting, Council appointed a Committee under the chairmanship of C.E Lucas, comprising for the most part members who were 'as disinterested as possible, whilst providing the right combination of experience to conduct an effective enquiry'. Its report identified two reasons why the Conservancy should remain. First, NERC would always require expertise in terrestrial ecology. Even if it could be 'rebuilt' following the loss of the whole Conservancy, the Treasury would never consent to such wasteful duplication. Secondly, the Committee had been greatly impressed by the strongly-held view of the overwhelming majority of Conservancy staff that conservation and research should remain inseparable. In the Committee's judgement, the urge to return to the pre-1965 position was largely confined to members of the Nature Conservancy Committee and the Director. The middle and other senior ranks made little complaint.

Fundamentally, the question came down to clarifying the Conservancy's aims. The Lucas Committee conceded that it was difficult for the Conservancy to fulfil the aspirations of all those who looked to it for guidance and encouragement. So much of the conservation ethic was subjective, and even emotional. It was, nevertheless, quite inappropriate for the Conservancy Committee to act as a public pressure group within a research council, which must necessarily draw its strength from 'the dispassionate approach associated with science'. The Lucas Committee therefore believed it was high time for the Conservancy to focus its attention on the scientific issues arising from land-use change generally. Such guidance was urgently required in assessing the consequences of changes in farming and intense urbanisation. Entry into the Common Market might bring further changes on a broad canvas.

The key figures had emerged as Lord Howick and the Secretary of Council, Ray Beverton. Whilst not opposing the Committee's recommendation that NERC's Charter should be amended to achieve better integration, Howick emphasised to Council the continued need to safeguard the Conservancy's unique executive role. The Conservancy had not behaved as a pressure group, as the Lucas Committee contended. Rather, it had acted as the 'public voice in the conservation movement'. The need for such a link between that movement and the Government was as strong as ever. Lord Howick believed that much could be achieved by a change of personnel on the Conservancy Committee. Beverton disagreed. If it were legally possible, the solution might be for the Conservation Branch to be given more autonomy, and for the Research Branch to become a new institute on essentially the same footing as other NERC institutes. Separated from the cut-and-thrust of the necessarily crusading spirit required for promoting nature conservation, it would at last have the scientific integrity required of a research council. Lord Howick indicated that he could not 'possibly support any solution that involved splitting the Conservancy to any serious degree'. The differences of emphasis were so great that, at its meeting of January 1972, Council asked Margaret Thatcher for more time to consider the recommendations of the Lucas Committee.

'THE SPLIT'

At the time of writing this book, Cabinet and Departmental papers were not available for the years after 1967. There are nevertheless strong indications that, even without such obvious acrimony, the Nature Conservancy, would have undergone major surgery. Its all-encompassing responsibility for undertaking and using the results of research in pursuit of its executive and advisory functions ran counter to the way Government had come to believe research and development should be organised in the public sector. The introduction of the so-called 'Rothschild customer/contractor principle' gave ministers a ready-made solution to the impasse that had developed in the relationship between the Conservancy and NERC.

The year, 1970, that should have represented a crowning achievement for the Conservancy marked the start of its demise. As part of a review of all Government departments, designed to ensure that responsibility and accountability were clearly defined at all levels, Lord Rothschild, as Head of the Central Policy Review staff (popularly known as the 'Think Tank'), undertook a personal review of 'Government research and development'. His report was published in November 1971 under the title: 'A framework for Government research and development'. It was essentially a Green (Consultative) Paper. The only 'White' part was a two-page 'Memorandum' indicating that the Government welcomed and endorsed Lord Rothschild's recommendation that Government research and development should be undertaken on the customer/contractor principle. As a contractor, NERC was particularly affected. Whereas Council had anticipated an allocation of £15.3 million from the Department of Education and Science for the year 1972–73, Rothschild recommended that it should receive only £7.7 million. The shortfall of £7.6 million would be made up by payments for research commissioned by customer-Departments, namely £4 million from the Department of the Environment (and Scottish Development Department), £3.2 million from the Department of Trade and Industry, and £400,000 from the Ministry of Agriculture. Lord Rothschild recommended that the Conservancy should remain within NERC, but be principally financed by the Department of the Environment and Scottish Development Department (Lord Privy Seal 1971).

The publication of the Rothschild report gave the Nature Conservancy Committee the opportunity publicly to make known its wish to leave NERC. Advantage was also taken of an enquiry by the Commons' Select Committee on Science and Technology as to the implications of the Green Paper. Speaking on behalf of the Conservancy Committee, Duncan Poore argued strongly for the Conservancy's being given statutory independence under the most appropriate minister. Most of the research should remain within the Conservancy. Perhaps a third might be commissioned from a NERC ecological institute. The Chairman of NERC assured the Select Committee that his Council, Lord Howick, and most of the Conservancy's staff wanted the conservation and research elements to remain in NERC (Parliamentary Papers 1971–72).

Others weighed into the argument. Jon Tinker, in the *New Scientist*, wrote that this was not simply another boundary squabble. It was a question of whether there should be an independent, professional authority capable of giving ecological advice on the long-term use of land and natural resources. It was about preserving the Conservancy's peculiar genius for developing the unique relationship between research and practical management, for which it had acquired a world-wide reputation. The Director of the RSPB, Peter Conder, described the further down-grading of the Conservancy as a 'horrifying prospect'. Tinker suspected that the outcome would be for the Conservancy to end up in the Department of the Environment. There, its status and character might well be decided by the obvious desire of the Secretary of State, Peter Walker, to make 'a big splash' at the forthcoming United Nations' conference on the environment in Stockholm. He could hardly destroy the UK Government's capability in nature conservation and expect to wield great influence with other nations as the world's first plenipotentiary environment minister (Tinker 1972).

Despite the considerable comment received on the Rothschild report, and outright hostility in some quarters, the Government saw little need to give ground. The White Paper, *Framework for Government research and development*, published in July 1972, reaffirmed the Government's intention to apply the customer/contractor approach to all its applied research and development (Lord Privy Seal 1972). Any changes between the Green and White Paper were of tone and detail. Scientists were no longer described as being subservient to policy makers in Government departments. The relationship was to be one of 'partnership'. No one was under any illusion. Some 47 per cent of the research of NERC's institutes (excluding the British Antarctic Survey) would thenceforth have to be funded by Government departments (Sheail 1992).

If much of this had been predictable, the shock came in the announcement as to the

(*above*) **John Thompson** (standing) was appointed warden-naturalist to the Reserves of Woodwalton Fen, Holme Fen, Monks Wood and Castor Hanglands, based at the Monks Wood Experimental Station in 1960, He moved to Attingham Park in 1964, as an Assistant Regional Officer for the West Midlands, becoming its Regional Officer in 1966, a post he held for 24 years.

(*right*) **John Marriott** had been managing the wood for many years when the Monks Wood NNR was acquired in 1953-4. A representative ash-oak woodland of the Oxford Clay soils, it was a classic locality for rare insects, the most famous being the black hairstreak butterfly.

future of the Nature Conservancy. Both the White Paper, and a joint note by the Department of the Environment and the Department of Education and Science, described how half the Conservancy's effort went into the reserves and advisory responsibilities. Most of its research was related to wider NERC programmes. The Government believed that such duality of purpose had 'caused stresses difficult to resolve within the present framework'. If the original purposes of setting up the Nature Conservancy in 1949 and a Research Council for the environmental sciences in 1965 were to be fulfilled, a fresh start had to be made. A simple reversion to the pre-1965 position would be inappropriate. NERC would not be able to meet its Charter responsibilities for fundamental research in terrestrial ecology. Such a step would also overlook the coordinative role of the Department of the Environment. The reserve and advisory functions should be financed by the environmental, rather than the science, budget. The Government had therefore concluded that the Secretary of State for the Environment (in consultation with the Secretaries of State for Scotland and Wales) should have ultimate responsibility for the conservation functions of the Nature Conservancy, and that NERC should continue to meet its Charter responsibilities for fundamental ecological research.

The White Paper gave notice that a Bill would be introduced to abolish the Nature Conservancy Committee, and to establish a new Nature Conservancy Council (NCC) as an independent statutory body. It would receive grant-in-aid to discharge the present responsibilities of the Conservation Branch for the reserves and advisory functions (about £1.1 million on 1971–72 figures) and for commissioning applied research (about £300,000). The monies would be transferred from NERC to form part of the environment budget of the Department of the Environment. The laboratories and staff of the Research Branch, with a balance of £700,000, would remain with NERC.

Although the decision to 'split' the Conservancy might not be welcomed, the Minister for Local Government and Development remarked, during the debate on the Bill, that most agreed that the marriage of 'the conservancy girl' had not been happy. Put bluntly, a bill of 'divorcement' was needed (PD, Commons, 859, 457). A fresh stimulus was required for research in terrestrial ecology, as well as recognition of the essential part wildlife conservation must play in broader environmental policies. As Peter Walker told the Nature Conservancy Committee in July 1972, ministers were determined to prove that separation would present no barrier to communication. His Permanent Secretary, Sir David Serpell, emphasised that, as an independent body, the NCC would be given 'a loose rein'. Regarding the component parts of the Conservancy, the most contentious decision was that of leaving the Monks Wood Experimental Station, and particularly the Biological Records Centre, within NERC.

Where before it had been the Conservancy's other responsibilities that excited controversy, now it was its successor's capacity to do research that gave rise to the greatest misgivings. At a meeting of NERC Council in July 1972, Lord Howick expressed concern that the draft Nature Conservancy Council Bill included powers 'to encourage, support and commission research and to carry out or promote such other investigations as may be necessary'. Whilst the NCC should have powers to carry out factual surveys for the purpose of assessing sites, any more would jeopardise 'the vitally important interrelationship with NERC'. For the preparatory Committee of the NCC, the main business of its meeting of April 1973 was whether to support an amendment to the Bill, tabled by Lord Cranbrook, which went considerably further. It placed a duty on the NCC to undertake research. Lord Howick had died following a walking accident. Ted Smith took the chair, and warned that there was bound to be controversy if the amendment was supported. NERC had already warned of both the confusion and wastage that would occur if such duplication of responsibility was permitted. Both 'sides' were relieved to learn that the Government had agreed with Lord Cranbrook a compromise amendment, which appeared to limit the NCC's powers of research to those of commissioning or supporting research undertaken by others, and of carrying out studies directly required for resolving conservation problems at the local and regional levels.

The vesting day for the NCC was 1 November 1973. Shortly following his retirement, Sir David Serpell had been invited to become the NCC's first Chairman. As he asserted from the chair at a preliminary meeting of Council, it was time to provide positive leadership and clear guidance on policy. The NCC would achieve that goal through its good relationship with the Department of the Environment and an ability, on the part of Council, to reach corporate decisions. Within NERC, Council accepted the recommendation, at its meeting in February 1973, that the stations of the former Research Branch should constitute the larger part of a new Institute of Terrestrial Ecology (ITE).

CHAPTER EIGHT

THE WIDER COUNTRYSIDE

No one was entirely happy with the outcome of the 'Split'. The surgery could have been handled better. So much would depend on goodwill in turning what none had really wanted into a success. Certainly, there were inherited strengths. When he was appointed, John Berry had literally been the Nature Conservancy in Scotland. There was only himself and his wife to clean the newly-acquired but filthy premises of Hope Terrace, which were formally opened by the Under-Secretary of State in May 1950. Now, there were some 65 staff at the Edinburgh headquarters and three regional offices. Scotland had 41 NNRs, occupying 78,728 hectares (194,546 acres). There were altogether 140 reserves in Britain, covering 114,514 hectares (282,976 acres), of which 41 were held on the basis of a Nature Reserve Agreement, 39 by lease, 28 were owned, and the remainder acquired by a combination of tenure. The total staff complement of NCC exceeded 450, distributed between the Great Britain headquarters, three territorial offices, and the regions.

The strengths brought to the senior posts of the new bodies were equally important. If the appointment of Sir David Serpell as Chairman meant the new Council would be well versed in the ways of Government, many believed it was also the most explicit indication that the successor-body to the Conservancy would be kept on a very tight leash. The founder-Director was Bob Boote. A columnist in the *New Scientist*, in February 1970, had written of the paradox where no one had greater experience in the administration of conservation planning, yet none could see where his further career might take him. Norman Moore was appointed to the specially-created post of Chief Advisory Officer. It was perhaps the appointment of Derek Ratcliffe as the NCC Chief Scientist that had the most far-reaching implications. He had been appointed Deputy-Director (Research) of the Conservancy in March 1970. He might therefore have been expected to become the founder-Director of ITE. A long period of uncertainty was brought to an end with the announcement that Martin Holdgate would 'return' in April 1974, with John Jeffers as his Deputy-Director. Jeffers became Director of ITE two years later, following the termination of Holdgate's secondment from the Department of the Environment.

A priority for both the NCC and ITE was to highlight and delimit their respective responsibilities. At a meeting with the NCC Council, in May 1974, the Minister for Planning and Local Government in the new Labour Government, John Silkin, saw its

NCC Council members with regional officers and other senior staff, April 1974.
Front row, left to right: **J. McCarthy, Dr D.A. Bassett, Jean Balfour, Sir Christopher Serpell** (Chairman), **A.E. Smith, H.A. Maxwell and R.E. Boote**, who retired as Director-General in March 1980. Boote's contribution to nature conservation was internationally recognised by the award of the Van Tienhoven Prize in that year.

role as that of providing overall leadership in nature conservation matters. In an introductory letter to ITE staff, Martin Holdgate recalled his appointment in the spring of 1970 as Head of the Central Unit for Environmental Pollution, first in the Cabinet Office and then the Department of the Environment. His Unit had acted as the focus of the UK contribution to the United Nations' Conference on the Environment at Stockholm in 1972. From such a vantage point, Holdgate had become even more conscious of the way that decisions were frequently taken without the underpinning knowledge. His ambition was to develop ITE as 'the natural place to which those needing scientific guidance on ecological matters can turn'.

If a natural complementarity between the interests of the two bodies emerged, it was mediated through the enabling mechanism of the Rothschild customer/contractor principle. Where 60 per cent of ITE's budget was derived from the NERC Science Budget, the remainder had to be obtained through applied research undertaken for 'customer' departments, and most obviously the NCC. Some 60 per cent of the NCC's requirement was for survey work in the broadest sense. Experience soon revealed what many had foreseen. Much of the work was so integral to the executive needs of the NCC that it was simply not amenable to the necessarily formal customer/contractor relationship. Appointed Chairman of the NCC in May 1977, Professor Fred G.T. Holliday approved the Chief Scientist's Team being brought up to its full complement, in order to increase the volume of possible in-house research. Some 20 scientific and supporting staff were appointed to field units, based on headquarters in England, Scotland and Wales. Such support was financed by reducing by one-third, over a three-year period, the amount of money previously spent on commissions with ITE.

By the time the appointments were made, scarcely any pretence of a special relationship remained. The NCC had been thrown into acute financial crisis, following the curtailment in public expenditure and a particularly drastic cut in the budget of the Department of the Environment. In Holliday's words, the year 1979 was one of 'stringency and crisis'. By 1979, the NCC's commissions with the ITE had fallen by over 50 per cent (in real terms) of their original value. That trend, together with instances of the NCC's placing large commissions in the university and private sectors (as, for example, a National Vegetation Survey), caused the ITE to diversify its funding, and therefore its research base, even more consciously. It also accelerated the shift in attitude required of the research base by the 'Split'. Although it would undertake conservation research where commissioned or required by NERC's Charter responsibilities for giving environmental advice, it was not for ITE staff to advocate particular policies for conservation. It would be for the NCC or, for that matter, any other customer of ITE's research, to provide 'an overlay of value judgements' as to what the factually-orientated studies of ITE had found.

Since a principal object of the *Nature Conservation Review* had been to encourage the close working of the Conservation and Research Branches, its publication was the most obviously outstanding business of the Conservancy. The prefatory statement by ministers indicated that, although neither the Government nor landowners were committed to any course of action on particular sites, the Review would be a valuable aid to planners and managers in reaching decisions about the future use of land (Ratcliffe 1977b, xi). Fine words, but what further role did scientists wish to play? Both the NCC and ITE saw merit in the Royal Society of London convening a meeting to discuss its scientific findings. The meeting took place in June 1976, with Bob Boote delivering the final remarks. It all seemed a far cry from the bitter acrimony that had marked the last years of the Conservancy. Whether stung by the perception that the research element of the Conservancy had been undervalued, or the realisation that the scientific community could no longer take such research monies for granted, conservation research had acquired a new-found respectability.

In a preface to the volume of papers presented at the Royal Society meeting, Roy Clapham noted how the term 'nature conservation' had come increasingly to mean 'the development and wiser use of material natural resources'. A scientific understanding was clearly needed in order to maintain renewable resources at the highest possible level, both in terms of basic biological principles and of the special requirements of those plants and animals that provide utilisable crops. But in recognising the importance of that goal at a time of increasing pressure on resources, contributors to the conference also emphasised the continuing need for nature reserves on general scientific, educational and amenity grounds. If much of this was reaffirmation of what had been said and written some 20 years previously, there was now supportive evidence, most topically in the considerable use made of reserves for fundamental studies of functional or natural ecosystems as part of the UK's contribution to the International Biological Programme. Reserves might also protect species of potential value for scientific investigation. They were a source of genetic material. They offered obvious opportunity to monitor the environmental changes brought about by pollution. There was, similarly, a scientific dimension to reserve management, whether the intention was to maintain a system or create perhaps a more diversified habitat or one richer in species (Smith et al. 1977).

Derek Ratcliffe received one of the earliest Nature Conservancy post-graduate awards. He joined the Conservancy to survey and classify Highland Vegetation with Donald McVean. His national peregrine survey of 1960–61 revealed a marked and unprecedented decline in the British population. As well as providing the scientific direction of the Nature Conservation Review, he became Deputy Director (Research) of the Nature Conservancy. Following the 'Split' he was appointed Chief Scientist of the NCC, a post he held until his retirement in 1989.

If the conference at the Royal Society acknowledged in the most public way the legitimacy and significance of conservation research, it also sought a more explicit understanding of the relationship between scientific inquiry and conservation management. As Ratcliffe (1977a) recalled, the Huxley Committee and the Nature Conservancy had placed great emphasis on the importance of the 'circular relationship between nature conservation and science' – they existed to serve one another. Such terms as 'scientific interest' and 'scientific importance' were freely used. They were incorporated into the language of legislation. Whilst this inevitably led to their use in correspondence with ministers and negotiation with NERC, the term 'scientific' caused confusion. In some quarters, it suggested that the Conservancy was woolly, if not pretentious, in its thinking. As Ratcliffe emphasised, where the word 'scientific' carried a strong implication of objectivity, nature conservation was underlain with layers of value judgement. Its priorities were to be measured in terms of human values. It represented a consensus, or more usually a compromise, as to what was desirable or important about the state of nature over an extremely wide field of interest.

As Ratcliffe (1977a) observed, nature conservation was invariably presented as a rearguard action against the inexorable advance of overwhelmingly superior forces. Every effort was bent towards minimising the otherwise inevitable losses in national diversity of both species and habitats. That had been the purpose of the *Nature Conservation Review* and its adoption of criteria such as size of area or populations, diversity, naturalness, rarity and fragility. As Ratcliffe had earlier emphasised in that context, each took close account of the irreplaceability or chances of survival of the site, as well as its intrinsic merits. It meant the *Review* had highlighted the exceptional rather than the typical. Failure to grasp that point had caused some scientists to claim that such surveys were insufficiently objective in terms of orthodox sampling theory. Nature conservation was not, however, concerned with neutral or objective phenomena. A scale of values had already been imposed. That was not to deny that methodological rigour was important. As Ratcliffe emphasised, it was rather a case of such scientists recognising the need to choose the methods appropriate to the objectives and limitations of the data and their collection. It was equally important that conservationists did not pretend to be more scientific than they could ever be. Nature conservation was an activity that sought to integrate a wide range of needs and viewpoints, of which science could only be one aspect.

'GUARDIANS OF THE COUNTRYSIDE'

If the conservation movement did little to conceal its disparate nature, the pre-eminence of the Country Landowners' Association (CLA) and NFU (and the equivalent Scottish bodies) may give a somewhat false impression of a unity of outlook and resources amongst the membership of those bodies. The Conservancy found an immense variety of attitude in its dealings with landowners and farmers.

Perhaps the earliest and most striking impression of the contrasting cultures of land ownership within Great Britain were the differences in outlook between the Scottish uplands and the remainder of the country (Smout 1991). The proportionately much larger area of Scottish upland covered by Nature Reserve Agreements reflected not only the terrain, but what John Morton Boyd later described as a quite different climate of opinion. He attributed this to the success of the land-owning interests in preventing the establishment of national parks in Scotland, and of their consequent willingness to co-operate with the Conservancy on terms that were scarcely ever unfavourable to themselves, but which also complemented the goodwill shown towards the National Trust for Scotland in respect of historic and cultural conservation. Landowning interests were well represented by the Secretary of State's appointees, as members of the Nature Conservancy and its Scottish Committee. The man-in-the-street saw both the Conservancy and National Trust as lairds' organisations. At the operational level, the landowning background of John Berry and the Senior Land Agent, John Arbuthnott, who succeeded to the Viscountcy in 1966, greatly helped the Conservancy in its dealings with the Scottish Landowners' Federation. An eminent forester, naturalist and sportsmen, Joe Eggeling brought immense diplomacy and down-to-earth good sense. Within that framework of trust, it was the task of the regional officers, Morton Boyd, Nancy Gordon, Tom Huxley and Grant Roger, to make the Nature Reserve Agreements work through survey and management plans.

Within the remainder of the United Kingdom, the story was dominated by a different kind of rapport, in which the Conservancy was notably excluded. The close links between land-owning and farming interests and post-war Governments have been held up as a model of corporatist relationships. The alliance of interests was so strong that conservation and recreational interests had the greatest difficulty penetrating, let alone influencing, the policy-making process (Winter 1995). Such exclusion was of little concern, however, when interests seemed to be so obviously in accord with those of conservation. Even in wartime, the County Agricultural Executive Committees thought it scarcely 'profitable to cultivate the areas now proposed as National Nature Reserves'. Both the wartime Scott Committee and John Dower's seminal report on national parks had assumed that there was a natural affinity between farming and the protection of amenity and wildlife.

Far from being some pious hope on the part of conservation, the Ministry of Agriculture defined the purpose of modern farming as increasing the diversity of use of the countryside. Given the nature of the climate and soils of the British Isles, wartime inquiries concluded that the only way of ensuring healthy crops and livestock was by making the fullest use of modern science and mechanisation in introducing 'systems of mixed farming with a proper balance between arable and grass, crops and livestock'. This implied a cultivated area of some 12 million acres (5 million hectares), compared with as little as 9 million acres (3.6 million hectares) before the war. The overriding goal should be not self-sufficiency nor, indeed, increasing the area under such cash crops as sugar beet, but rather of keeping 'the plough going on as much land as possible'. The Scottish system of alternative husbandry, or ley farming as popularised by Sir George Stapledon, should be extended further, as part of a rotational system that kept the land clean and well supplied with nutrients (PRO, MAF 53, 162).

The requirements of post-war reconstruction were rapidly put in place. Exchequer

Lullington Heath NNR in **Sussex** was leased, in 1956, as one of the largest areas of unploughed chalk-heath remaining on the South Downs. The great botanical interest of this reserve arose from the fact that shallow-rooted plants requiring acid soil (such as ling and bell heather) were mingled with deeper-rooted ones, needing a limy soil.

support was provided for both public and private forestry, under a series of Forestry Acts beginning in 1945. A 'bargain' was similarly struck with the farming industry. Under the Agriculture Acts, ministers were required, when setting agricultural price-support levels, to consult 'such bodies of persons who appear to them to represent the interests of producers in the agricultural industry'. In effect, the Ministry (and the Scottish Secretary), and the NFU and its Scottish equivalent, were expected to maintain close contact at all levels over the many issues, large and small, that arose in the development and implementation of policy. In return for such a partnership, the wartime powers of the County Agricultural Executive Committees were extended into peacetime, so as to ensure that adequate standards of farming were met. More positively, every farmer was encouraged and helped to emulate the best by the National Agricultural Advisory Service, founded in 1944 for the purpose of 'giving free of charge technical advice and instruction, whether practice or scientific, on agricultural matters'. It was one of five services subsumed in 1971 into an Agricultural Development Advisory Service (ADAS).

Not only did the amenity and nature conservation movements appear as the unconscious beneficiaries of such raised standards of husbandry, but the Ministry of Agriculture responded to appeals by Tansley and Nicholson in circulating a memorandum in early 1948, calling upon those directing the food production campaign to cooperate in protecting sites of scientific value (PRO, MAF 141, 195). In a letter of February 1949, Nicholson wrote that, whilst farmland was an integral part of national parks, its wildlife had already been so reduced as to be invariably excluded from nature reserves. The only exceptions might be the extensive areas of low-quality grazing that acted as an adjunct to neighbouring farms; wetland areas of perhaps high potential value, if

Fyfield Down NNR, Wiltshire, in April 1991.
This is one of the finest remaining tracts of unreclaimed high chalkland in England and of considerable archaeological interest. The threat to the sarsen stones (the large blocks of sandstone) on part of the site, posed by agricultural reclamation, led the Nature Conservancy to contemplate using its powers of compulsory acquisition .

drained, for farming; and the occasional fields of just-cultivable land adjacent to many heathlands. Nicholson wrote that the Huxley Committee had made such modest demands for land that he hoped the Ministry of Agriculture would raise no objection to its designation as nature reserves. A Deputy-Secretary in the Ministry, George Dunnett, saw no insurmountable difficulty (PRO, FT 3, 100).

Such confidence seemed well-placed until the mid-1950s, when the Government's 'agricultural productivity programme' appeared to falter. Although the numbers of livestock continued to increase, tillage decreased. A further loss of 600,000 acres (243,000 hectares) in 1951 threatened a serious shortfall in animal feedstuffs. An emergency measure was introduced, whereby a grant of £5 per acre was to be paid for ploughing up grassland. There followed an enabling Bill in April 1951, which empowered the Government, on an annual basis, to set the level and type of grants. Within a fortnight of the Bill's gaining the Royal Assent, parliament approved a scheme whereby Part I grants of £5 per acre were to be paid for ploughing up grasslands of 3 years or more. Part II grants of £10 per acre would help to meet the 'abnormal' costs of bringing into cultivation land that had been under grass since before the war. In a Commons' debate, Anthony Hurd, a Conservative backbencher and the *Times* agricultural correspondent, welcomed the way assistance was to be given to both upland and lowland farmers. He expected several thousand acres of downland in Wiltshire to be ploughed (PD, Commons, 505, 947–55; Sheail 1997b).

No habitat type was under greater threat than chalk grassland. Where historically there had been no conflict, in as much as a measure of grazing was needed to preserve the wildlife interest, pasture improvement now meant ploughing and re-seeding (Nature

Conservancy 1957, 64). It was such an instance that caused the Conservancy to consider for the first time using its compulsory powers under the National Parks and Access to the Countryside Act. Fyfield Down in Wiltshire had been identified by the Huxley Committee as a Geological Monument. It included the largest assemblage of sarsen stones in Britain. It was therefore to preserve both these and the associated chalk grasslands that a Nature Reserve Agreement was successfully negotiated for 610 acres (245 hectares) of the downland in January 1955. The remaining 130 acres (52 hectares) were owned by English Farms Ltd. The Chairman, Anthony Hurd, rejected an Agreement but offered to consider purchase. By the time Treasury consent and a District Valuer's price of £3,350 had been obtained, the offer was withdrawn. The company had acquired a new Managing Director with an unlimited enthusiasm for reclamation (PRO, CAB 124, 2649).

Disappointment quickly turned to alarm at news that the company intended to employ the army to blow up the stones, preliminary to reclaiming the land. The Ministry of Works indicated that, because the stones were scattered naturally as opposed to being standing features, they were ineligible for protection as Ancient Monuments. Hurd insisted that the company could go no further than preserving 'a considerable acreage' of 40 acres in 'its natural unimproved state'. He wrote 'we are not philanthropists', but 'a farming company with shareholders', and that it seemed a reasonable compromise between food production and nature conservation. In as much as Hurd was 'a prominent Government supporter', Roger Quirk thought it prudent to warn Lord Salisbury. He wrote

> it seems extraordinary that in this day and age, a prominent MP should be light-heartedly embarking on an act of vandalism hardly less serious than that of the 17th century destroyers of Avebury.

It was learned, almost the same day, that troops had blown up a first set of stones. Although Nicholson found, on a visit to the site, that these stones were away from the main site, he took the unprecedented step of applying for consent to invoke compulsory purchase, both to prevent further destruction and as an indication of 'the special enormity of the case'. In further trying to secure a voluntary sale, the Conservancy needed to know whether ministers would sanction compulsion, as a last-resort power.

In the event, ministers were spared the decision. Salisbury wrote, in a letter to Hurd, that he had much sympathy with those who were doing their utmost to raise food production and extend the area of farmland. But he also warned how such destruction of features 'so closely identified with the origins of our civilisation' would seriously shock geologists and antiquarians alike. As President of the Society of Antiquities, Sir Mortimer Wheeler wrote of his Society's concern at the threat to such 'an integral part of the visual history of our countryside'. The Parliamentary Under-Secretary of State for War, Fitzroy Maclean, wrote to Lord Salisbury, regretting that, due to its recent return from Korea, the unit of the Royal Engineers responsible for blowing up the stones had overlooked the need for permission from their headquarters before carrying out such a 'training' mission.

It was against this background that Lord Hurcomb and Nicholson had a very amicable meeting with Hurd and his Company's Managing Director, who now seemed to have second doubts as to the wisdom of large-scale reclamation, particularly following the withdrawal of the army. The Conservancy's *Annual Report* described how an informal agreement was drawn up for the area abutting the NNR, owned by English Farms Ltd, whereby the company undertook to preserve its scientific value and grant access for survey and experimentation (Nature Conservancy 1956, 34).

A clash of interest might arise, either directly from farming operations or from the preliminary works required to make such investment worthwhile. The most desperate need on many properties was to improve drainage. Whilst individual farmers might accomplish much, only a river board or internal drainage board was likely to have the administrative and financial resources required for larger schemes. In as much as such boards were invariably made up of the most progressive personalities in the drainage and farming industries, they were even more likely to pursue such large-scale improvements with a single-mindedness of purpose. The Conservancy signalled its increasing concern in a memorandum to the Secretary of State, Quintin Hogg, in January 1964. Not only were such schemes, which required considerable sums of public money, of doubtful economic justification but, Nicholson protested, there had been little willingness to meet, or even listen to, the Conservancy's objections (PRO, CAB 124, 1612 and FT 3, 348).

The immediate reason for complaint was a threat to the proposed National Nature Reserve of Borth Bog, in Cardiganshire. Of immense scientific and educational importance, the sequences of pollen in the peat profiles provided a record of climate and sea-level changes over the last 6,000 years. More than ten universities used it for undergraduate teaching. As Nicholson recounted, a Lincolnshire farming syndicate had begun buying land with the intention of reclaiming as much of the Bog as possible. With great difficulty, the Conservation Officer for Wales, Elfyn Hughes, had negotiated 'a compromise standstill arrangement' whereby, of the area originally proposed for a NNR of 12,340 acres (5,000 hectares), some 380 acres (150 hectares) would be left undamaged. Whilst the purpose of the Gwynedd River Board, acting as the Internal Drainage Authority, was ostensibly to improve that greater area, the Conservancy believed that the effect would be to destroy the scientific value of the whole. As Quintin Hogg insisted, in a letter to the Minister of Agriculture, Christopher Soames, the Board's Chairman should at least be made to discuss the matter with the Chairman of the Conservancy's Committee for Wales. Even if compromise was not possible, there should at least be an agreed statement of the irreconcilable differences. The most recent communication from the Clerk of the Board had been 'a monument of clod-hopping bad manners'. Soames agreed that the 'wretched business' should be sorted out locally. A Deputy-Secretary of the Ministry, G. Peter Humphreys-Davies, organised a meeting attended by six members of the Board (the chairman was on holiday in the Bahamas), seven from the Conservancy, and at least twelve representatives of the Ministry. The Board's representatives agreed to put before the whole Board the Conservancy's counter-proposal, which would preserve the central area of the Bog, known as 'The Lung'.

Whilst urging the Board to accept the alternative scheme, Humphreys-Davies privately warned the Conservancy that the only certain way of protecting the Bog was to acquire it as a NNR. Urgent consultations were held with the Charity Commissioners as to how this might be achieved. The regional officer, Peter Walters-Davies, was required to look up the Inclosure Award of 1847 to try and establish ownership. Not only had the land been made over to hundreds of different people but, whilst many were found, there was no assurance that all had been identified. The Treasury Solicitor confirmed that there was no practical alternative to using the Conservancy's powers of compulsory purchase. Frank Turnbull assured the Secretary of State for Wales (whose approval was required) that this represented no change in Government policy. Walters-Davies was required to erect a notice in the centre of the Bog, announcing the terms of the Order. He nearly ran his car off the road the next day, when he saw somebody reading it! The first meeting of NERC Council, in June 1965, formally approved the first invocation of such powers.

Whilst the Conservancy had largely met its purpose at both Fyfield Down and Borth Bog, the necessity to take the ultimate step of reference to the minister highlighted the weakness of the Conservancy's position, even when it came to protecting what were, by definition, the most precious examples of wildlife in the country. For all the self-assertiveness of the Conservancy, no one was under any illusion as to where power really resided. The situation at Fyfield Down had been saved by the fact that the Ministry of Agriculture did not oppose the designation of a nature reserve provided that a large stock of sheep and cattle was maintained. As Humphreys-Davies made clear, the Minister had no statutory right to dictate terms to the drainage authorities over Borth Bog. Although he was in that instance prepared to use his good offices, it was ultimately for the Conservancy to look to its own powers, whether of an advisory or executive kind.

SITES OF SPECIAL SCIENTIFIC INTEREST

If the Conservancy's powers to protect reserves from land improvement were deficient, the analogy of David to Goliath seemed even more apposite when it came to protecting the wider countryside. Goliath was not only a production department offering grant-aid on an unprecedented scale, but it was resolutely opposed to any move to bring agricultural usage under statutory planning control. Even describing the Conservancy as David exaggerated its strength. The sling was essentially empty. Not only did the Conservancy have a minuscule budget compared with the Ministry, but the Lord President had publicly forsworn the use of compulsory purchase except in the most exceptional circumstances. The Conservancy was left with nothing but the advisory powers conferred by the National Parks and Access to the Countryside Act. As events were to show, even these proved inapplicable when they were most required to defend wildlife from irreversible destruction.

The Huxley Committee had recognised that NNRs could not, by themselves, safeguard the natural heritage. It accordingly identified a further 35 'scientific areas' within the national-park areas proposed by the National Parks Committee (see page 22). Three corresponded with the full extent of the Lakes, Peak and Broads park-areas. Each was characterised by a mixture of farmland, villages, and even small towns, with large sweeps of semi-natural and natural countryside. The Ritchie Committee proposed 22 'nature conservation areas' and one special conservation area – an area of 468,180 acres (190,000 hectares) of north-west Scotland – each to be protected by 'the wise application of planning control'. And finally, the Huxley Committee identified a further and most minor category, the 'Site of Special Scientific Interest', which included the many small sites of importance scattered throughout the country. They too would require little positive protection beyond some consideration in any comprehensive planning scheme (Minister of Town and Country Planning 1947b).

Ministers accepted that there should be National Nature Reserves, as well as National Parks and what became Areas of Outstanding Natural Beauty, but they believed a fourth category of 'Areas of Outstanding Scientific Importance' would be too confusing. Whilst this was a setback, Diver and Nicholson were not unduly disturbed. The local planning authorities, agricultural executive committees, and the Forestry Commission might still closely consult the Conservancy through 'administrative arrangement'. Besides defining the boundaries of such areas, the Conservancy might prepare management plans that warned of the kinds of development or land-use change that would damage that scientific interest. The main concern of Diver and Nicholson was not whether the Conservancy would be listened to, but whether the advice would be given in the first place. The obvious course was for the National Parks and Access to the Countryside Bill to make it a statutory duty. Nicholson claimed later that, almost overnight, he drew up a clause whereby the Conservancy was required to notify local planning authorities of the existence of those 'Areas of Special Scientific Interest' that were not currently held and managed as NNRs. Those authorities were required to consult the Conservancy before granting a statutory planning consent for building and other forms of 'development'. The compromise and the rapidity and scale of change in the use of the countryside soon caused the Sites of Special Scientific Interest (popularly known as SSSIs) to assume a significance never intended (Sheail 1993).

However humble their beginnings, the SSSI series became 'an invaluable adjunct to the network of NNRs' through what Ratcliffe (1977a) called 'its corporate influence on the statutory planning process'. Although many were destroyed or seriously damaged, more were probably saved or had their harm mitigated. The SSSI's principal deficiency was that scheduling affected only the use, and not the management, of the Site. In as much as changes in the agricultural or silvicultural management of land were exempt from planning control, they were not affected by scheduling. Even so, Diver felt confident that the Conservancy's guidance would be followed, if given in 'the right way'. From the assurances offered by the Agricultural Departments, it seemed they would be both able and willing to provide adequate protection.

This assumption was severely jolted in March 1954, when the West Suffolk Agricultural Executive Committee, acting as agents for the Ministry of Agriculture, approved a grant of £10 per acre towards the cost of ploughing up 152 acres (61 hectares)of heathlands. Only then did the Ministry's headquarters learn that 50 acres (20 hectares) fell within the proposed Cavenham Heath NNR. The Ministry described it as an 'unfortunate oversight'. Nicholson wrote that so much of the Breckland had already been lost that the incident had to be treated as 'a test case'; grant aid should be rejected wherever it might affect a proposed NNR or SSSI. At a meeting with the Permanent Secretary to the Ministry, Sir Alan Hitchman, Nicholson explained how rarely conservation needs would clash with those of farming. Perhaps no more than 10,000 acres (4,000 hectares) of downland, marsh and heath were at issue. But these areas of semi-natural countryside were the most irreplaceable from a scientific point of view. Their value stemmed from having been left undisturbed for hundreds, if not thousands, of years. Only recently had a combination of greater capital investment in food production and new forms of machinery made their cultivation possible. The scientific interest could be destroyed within hours. It was on these sites that agriculture policy had to take explicit account of other objects of Government policy (PRO, MAF 141, 175).

Nicholson spoke of the mounting concern of informed opinion that, unless the greatest restraint was shown, irreparable damage would be done for a trifling increase in agricultural output. Some farmers seemed wilfully ignorant of the value of SSSIs as living museums and open-air laboratories. Their missionary fervour was so strong, and their resources so considerable, that little would be achieved without a clear lead from the Minister. Without that, there was risk not only of the Conservancy's wasting its resources in preparatory moves to acquire reserves or schedule SSSIs, but of much wider criticism of public money being used both to protect and destroy the scientific interest of the same areas of land. Whilst expressing sympathy, Hitchman went no further than to agree the desirability of the Minister's issuing a circular to farmers at some suitable opportunity. In December 1954, each Provincial Land Commissioner was asked to ensure that, when a County Committee believed there was a case for approving a grant that affected an SSSI, the Conservancy's regional officer should be informed. Where there was dispute, the case should be referred to their respective headquarters (Sheail 1997b).

If Nicholson believed 'a most dangerous chink' in the Conservancy's 'armour' had been revealed (PRO, FT 3, 101), Ministry officials also took stock of the situation. Their Legal Branch advised that, whilst the Minister could use discretion when requiring that agricultural criteria be met, the Act said nothing about his withholding grants for non-agricultural reasons. Officials concluded that the only non-agricultural grounds for disqualifying an application must be where ploughing would constitute a criminal offence. It would otherwise be for an aggrieved party to take civil remedy. Since the ploughing-up of land and other changes in agricultural land-use did not constitute 'development' under the Town and Country Planning Act, an SSSI must continue to attract grant aid. The effect would otherwise be to punish a farmer for carrying out what remained a legal activity (PRO, MAF 141, 175).

The significance of that ruling was demonstrated in April 1963, when a Lincolnshire farmer applied for a Part II grant towards ploughing up the SSSI of Waddingham Common. At a site meeting arranged by the Ministry's Regional Controller, the farmer offered to leave an acre unploughed. Representatives of the Conservancy and Lincolnshire Naturalists' Trust insisted that at least 5 acres were needed to preserve the unique assemblage of plants found in the small peat-bog overlying limestone. With no prospect of any compromise and the ploughing season about to begin, the Ministry believed it had no alternative but to confirm the land was eligible for a grant. The entire site was ploughed in December (PRO, FT 3, 108 and MAF 141, 176).

Goodwill had deteriorated to the extent that a Joint Working Party of the Ministry and the Conservancy found it impossible to agree even a common statement of their respective positions. Conservancy representatives refused to sign any declaration of there being no inherent conflict between farming and conservation unless the Agriculture Departments also affirmed that there was no longer a need to maximise food production. Otherwise there was nothing to stop modern farming from obliterating the scientific interest. In Wiltshire, for example, 15 of the 27 downland SSSIs had already been ploughed up. As Nicholson emphasised in December 1963, the Conservancy did not seek a veto on grant-aid, simply an assurance that, if the scientific arguments were strong enough, no grant would be given. Without that, there would inevitably be a clash and strong criticism in parliament and the country (PRO, FT 3, 84). The Ministry's response was in two parts. In a written reply to a Parliamentary Question from the local Member of Parliament, Marcus Kimball, regarding the loss of Waddingham Common, the Parliamentary Secretary reaffirmed that there was no provision in the various ploughing-grant schemes for disqualifying SSSIs (PD, Commons, 687, 73). Privately, the Conservancy was urged to do more in obtaining the cooperation of owners and occupiers through moral persuasion. Farmers should be offered suitable annual payments for agreeing to use and mange the land in a manner agreed by the Conservancy (PRO, MAF 141, 173).

There was cause for reflection in both the Conservancy and the Ministry. The Conservancy had to play its full part. There was much to commend a dedication scheme of the kind employed by the Forestry Commission but, in doing so, there was a risk of leaving unchallenged the immorality of the 'relatively unquestioning, unsupervised, unrestricted subsidizing of hopelessly uneconomic agricultural projects'. Far from leaving farmers and landowners to manage their land as they saw fit, it was high time the Ministry broadened its propaganda of the 'wise land-use' type to encompass the idea of trusteeship (PRO, FT 3, 108). Within the Ministry, the head of the Land Use and Smallholdings Division wrote, in January 1964, that farming operations had been exempted from planning control partly on the assumption that any changes made to the agricultural use and management of land need be only temporary. Ploughed land could always be grassed down again. Whilst this was true to a certain degree, the Conservancy was fully justified in arguing that modern ploughing might destroy the indigenous flora and fauna as comprehensively as any development subject to statutory planning control. In similarly reviewing the options open to the Ministry, the head of the Grassland/Crop Improvement Division suggested, in a paper of February 1964, that the Ministry might withhold an improvement grant, except where approved by the local planning authority after due consideration of the scientific interest. This would virtually 'insulate' the Ministry from further controversy. As anticipated, such a 'certification' procedure was roundly condemned by other senior officials as 'sadly misguided'. However modestly at first, farming and forestry would be drawn inexorably into the ambit of statutory planning control (PRO, MAF 141, 176).

Again, it needed some extraneous force to stimulate further inter-agency discussion.

Marcus Kimball promoted a Private Member's Bill, in June 1964, that required owners and occupiers to give six months' notice of any potentially damaging operation affecting an SSSI, the idea being to give the Conservancy the chance to dissuade them. The Agriculture Departments would withhold any grant for that period. Although acknowledging that the Conservancy was entirely dependent on the goodwill of owners and occupiers for the protection of SSSIs, the Agriculture Departments protested that such regulation would be premature, in as much as no one had any idea as to the eventual number of SSSIs. There were already over 1,700. Their potential for disruption to farm businesses and profit was considerable. In a short discussion, the Parliamentary Under-Secretary for Education and Science informed the Cabinet's Legislation Committee that, whilst the Conservancy supported the principle of the Bill, it rejected such reliance on restriction and compulsion. Without scope for more 'positive conservation measures', the Bill would provide little protection for the SSSIs once the six months had expired. It was agreed that ministers of the relevant departments should explain to Kimball that, even if there were parliamentary time, the Bill could not be allowed to proceed in its present form. Inter-departmental discussions would be held to 'establish the lines of legislation that would be acceptable to the Government'. As an official of the Scottish Office complained, ministers seemed unaware of the considerable discussion that had already taken place on the subject. As it was, a meeting convened a month later by the Department of Education and Science simply remitted the search for a solution back to the Conservancy (SRO, DD 12, 2841 and PRO, FT 3, 108, 379 and 381).

Whilst Kimball's Bill had caused the issue to be discussed by Cabinet Committee, the Conservancy had lost any residual goodwill on the part of the Ministry. Even its existing, extremely modest, powers came under increasingly hostile scrutiny. The 'hectoring and intransigent line' that naturalists were perceived to have taken over Waddingham Common caused Peter Humphreys-Davies to enquire how the Conservancy had been permitted to make its own rules about what constituted an SSSI. The Conservancy was not even required to consult the owner or obtain the approval of a minister. It could schedule the whole of Wales in a night. None could gainsay it (PRO, MAF 141, 176).

For senior officers in the Conservancy, such as Bob Boote, it was time to change tack. It was quite unrealistic to imagine an absolute ban being imposed on the agricultural development of SSSIs. Not only did the Conservancy lack the resources to meet the claims for compensation, but such a 'blanket' approach was unnecessary. Roughly half of the 2,000 SSSIs so far scheduled were geological. Many of the remainder were free from threat. As archaeologists had found in respect of their statutory safeguards for ancient monuments, the Conservancy would continue to depend on the sympathy and understanding of owners and occupiers. The worst way of attracting that support was to enact legislation that restricted their freedom in the interests of conservation. A scheme was required that positively encouraged farmers to contact the Conservancy and thereby give notice of a potential threat. The Conservancy should have the power to enter into management agreements for Sites, chosen on the basis of their vulnerability and high scientific interest (PRO, FT 3, 108, 379 and 695).

For the most part, the Ministry of Agriculture sidestepped the detail of argument by simply insisting that it was for the Conservancy to secure any further legislation required to safeguard SSSIs. The difficulty for the Conservancy was that, whereas Agriculture and Town and Country Planning Bills were promoted relatively frequently, an opportunity to amend the National Parks and Access to the Countryside Act of 1949 did not arise until the late 1960s. News that the Ministry of Housing and Local Government was exploring the possibility of such legislation caused members of the Nature Conservancy, in July 1960, to resolve that 'substantial' changes in agricultural and forestry use of SSSIs should be brought under planning control (PRO, FT 3, 379; SRO, DD 12, 2841). Not only was this bound to be slow and costly, but discussions with the NFU on 'a strictly informal and "without commitment" basis' suggested an alternative course. By the mid-1960s, there had emerged from such dialogue the notion of conservation-management payments awarded, perhaps, on the 50 finest SSSIs that were most vulnerable to agricultural operations. As Boote insisted, they would not be regarded as compensation payments, but rather in acknowledgement of the contribution the farmer was making to the protection of such sites. Far from there being any compulsory element, the whole scheme would be based on winning the sympathy, understanding and close cooperation of the landowner and farmer.

The Conservancy applied for a clause in the forthcoming Countryside Bill that enabled financial incentives to be given for the preservation and appropriate management of SSSIs. The offer would be conditional on improvement grants being withheld. Not only would it be wasteful, but the Conservancy could not possibly compete with the scales of grant aid available from the Agriculture Departments (PRO, FT 3, 108 and 179–80).

It was extremely unlikely that the Ministry of Housing and Local Government would proceed with the clause if it was opposed by the Ministry of Agriculture. As a letter from the Ministry made clear, in May 1967, it saw no difficulty in owners and occupiers entering into voluntary agreements with the Conservancy for selected SSSIs. It remained opposed, however, to any provision that enabled, or required, the Minister to withhold grants on non-agricultural grounds. If the Conservancy had predicted that part of the response, it was astonished to learn of a further objection – that the proposed amendment would undermine 'the whole discretionary basis' on which the system of agricultural grants operated. The Ministry's letter expressed puzzlement that the Conservancy should think that the Agriculture Departments were bound to approve every proposal that met agricultural criteria. The legal position was not nearly so rigid. Admittedly, lawyers had their doubts, but the Ministry believed a grant could be refused where a breach of management agreement might otherwise occur. The correspondent therefore recommended that a Ministerial statement should be made during the passage of the Countryside Bill, indicating that the Agriculture Departments would scrutinise grant applications to ensure that no damage was caused. Since the agreements were entirely voluntary, the denial of an improvement grant could hardly be represented as a hardship. Although the most modest of concessions, Boote confirmed that it was a proposal the Conservancy could 'not seriously resist' (PRO, FT 3, 380).

The embodiment of such powers in the Countryside Bill, which received the Royal Assent in July 1968, and the undertaking given by the Minister, effectively scotched further consideration of bringing SSSIs under planning control until experience had been gained with the management agreements. Even that seemed an elusive goal. As well as insisting that the cost of such agreements should be met from the Conservancy's existing budget, the Treasury sought assurances that only modest sums were involved. On the premise that SSSIs were less important than NNRs, Boote indicated that their cost should not exceed the cost of Nature Reserve Agreements, which had historically ranged from one shilling to £1 per acre. The Treasury took this to imply a ceiling of £1 per acre for all SSSI agreements. Particularly at a time of inflation, it was hardly surprising that negotiations proved abortive. The scientific interest of further sites was destroyed. Besides the frustration expressed by Conservancy members and voluntary conservation bodies, Lord Craigton, the chairman of the parliamentary all-party Conservation Committee, wrote to Margaret Thatcher, in June 1972, seeking to discover whether the failure to complete a single agreement arose from the Conservancy's being starved of funds or from the ponderous procedures which it was required to follow. It was not until September 1973 that the Treasury indicated that the limit of £1 per acre would be waived where overall expenditure was less than £4,000 per annum. With that modest measure of flexibility, the Conservancy was able to complete its first six agreements (PRO, FT 3, 381–2; Sheail 1997b).

'NEW AGRICULTURAL LANDSCAPES'

Whereas the main thrust of executive responsibility in the previous quarter-century had been the acquisition of reserves and development of appropriate techniques for managing them, the first policy statement of the Nature Conservancy Council (NCC), November 1974, put far greater emphasis on its advisory functions. With increasing evidence that nature reserves alone could never ensure a place for wildlife in an increasingly hostile environment, the NCC became one of numerous official, professional and voluntary bodies that sought a more robust, yet flexible, means of accommodating the competing interests in the countryside.

It was both the extent and rapidity of 'modernisation' that caused farming to replace urban development as the greatest perceived threat to the appearance, wildlife and recreational value of the countryside. Although it contributed only about 2.5 per cent of the UK gross domestic product in 1976 (roughly the equivalent of that of the electrical engineering industry), farming was the foremost rural industry. The White Paper, *Food from our own resources*, published in April 1975, expected the average annual growth rate of 2.5 per cent that had existed since 1950 to continue. Whilst conceding that there was pressure for greater control over agricultural pollution and the destruction of the 'traditional' appearance of the countryside, the Government believed that projected increases could be reconciled with a commitment to proper safeguards for the environment (Secretaries of State for Northern Ireland et al. 1975).

A far less sanguine view was taken by the Countryside Commission. A series of studies had been commissioned since 1972 under the title, *New agricultural landscapes*. Undertaken by two consultants, Richard Westmacott and Tom Worthington, they had revealed, in the words of the Commission's Chairman, 'fresh and deeply disturbing facts about the nature and scale of changes taking place'. Over 10,000 miles of hedgerow were being removed each year. More than half the hedges in parts of the Eastern Counties had been lost in the 25 years up to 1972. Up to 90 per cent of field-boundary trees had been lost from the Eastern Counties over the previous quarter-century. Although Dutch Elm disease had taken a heavy toll, most had been deliberately removed as part of the enlargement of fields required to accommodate modern cereal-farming machinery. On average, only one sapling had been planted for every 2.3 mature trees felled (Countryside Commission 1974).

The CPRE's reaction indicated that the voluntary movement was becoming considerably more active. Rather than a hurried and somewhat superficial response, a small but broadly-based Working Party was appointed. Its Secretary was Marian Shoard. In introducing its 14,000-word report, *Landscape – the need for a public voice*, the Director of the CPRE Christopher Hall wrote that the countryside was 'too precious a possession to be left any longer to untrammelled individual decisions'. A means had to be found of giving the public a larger voice in deciding its future. Landowners and farmers should be required to inform the local planning authority of their intention to remove, say, a hedge or stone wall, or to plough up downland or open heath. On the premise that no farmer should suffer financial loss from having to retain 'uneconomic' landscape features, the report pressed for a package of tax reliefs and other forms of inducement to meet the costs of preservation. Only if all else failed should the local authority have last-resort preservation powers (Council for the Protection of Rural England 1975).

Wetlands were particularly vulnerable to destruction. The area affected each year by grant-aided drainage schemes rose four-fold to 100,000 hectares (250,000 acres) during the 1970s (Baldock et al. 1990). Besides the general view of the Ministry of Agriculture that a further one-fifth of farmland in England and Wales required drainage (Trafford 1978), Purseglove (1989) wrote that land drainage continued to be 'the Vatican of the water industry: a state within a state'. This was despite the further major step taken towards integrated catchment-management under the Water Act of 1973. Whereas the ten regional water authorities, covering England and Wales, were generally responsible to the Environment Secretary, land drainage remained largely in the hands of uniquely separate regional land-drainage committees, whose chairmen were appointed by the Minister of Agriculture. The committees were for the most part dominated by farmers, who typically served as chairmen of the relevant IDBs which, in turn, generally comprised those farming the larger and more progressive holdings.

It was against this background of apparent autonomy that the application of the Southern Water Authority for grant aid towards a pumped-drainage scheme, in July 1977, became a *cause célèbre*. The Amberley Wild Brooks was an area of 365 hectares (900 acres) of pastureland within the floodplain of the River Arun in West Sussex. Of the total cost of £339,000, the Authority sought to recoup £245,000 under the Land Drainage Act of 1976. So great was the outcry that the Minister of Agriculture acceded to representations from the county council and the NCC that a public inquiry should be convened. It was held in March 1978. An even greater precedent was set by the Minister's acceptance of the Inspector's recommendation that grant aid should be withheld. A press notice described how the Inspector, a member of the Planning Inspectorate of the Department of the Environment, had found the probable agricultural benefit of the proposed scheme in relation to its cost to be questionable. It could not compensate for the losses that would occur to the flora and fauna (including wildfowl) or to 'the uniquely valuable peat deposit on the site' (Public Local Inquiry 1978). As a principal witness to the inquiry, the Chief Advisory Officer of the NCC, Norman Moore, warned, 'if conservation is not paramount in this case, no site can be considered safe'. Conservation bodies were wary of welcoming 'a false spring', both in terms of the site itself and wetlands more generally. Although the abandonment of the pumped-drainage scheme meant that pastures and plant life of the ditches were likely to survive, the extension of gravity drainage would continue to reduce the extent of winter flooding. The attractiveness of the grasslands for over-wintering birds would diminish (Purseglove 1989, 233).

Another wetland area of major controversy was the Ribble estuary, which the Nature Conservation Review had identified as a Grade 1 site of international importance for its wildfowl and wading birds. The NCC Council learned, at its meeting of May 1978, that some 1,000 hectares (2,400 acres) of saltmarsh and 1,200 hectares (3,000 acres) of tidal flats were being offered for sale by tender. As leader of a consortium, the RSPB pledged £200,000 towards the purchase cost; the World Wildlife Fund offered £50,000. Bob Boote advised Council that the case was so urgent as to justify the NCC's applying to the Treasury for a special grant to meet the £300,000 shortfall in making up the tender. The site was, however, sold to developers intent on embanking and draining the area for intensive agricultural use. When such works were completed, the developers estimated the land would be worth some £6 million.

The signing of the contract for the purchase of the **Ribble NNR** in March 1979.
The NCC's Chief Land Agent, **Jamie Johnstone**, pointing, the Director-General, **Bob Boote**, about to sign, with **Nettie Bonner** and **Derek Langslow** behind him.

Denis Howell, the Minister of State in the Department of the Environment, had been kept fully informed and supported the NCC's continued attempt to acquire the area as a NNR. Following a breakdown in the already-protracted negotiations, the Council saw no alternative but to institute proceedings for compulsory purchase. Faced with this, the new owners agreed reluctantly to sell the whole site at the District Valuer's valuation of £1,725,000. Contracts were exchanged in March 1979. Whilst relieved at the outcome, the conservation movement was deeply concerned. Had so much Exchequer and political support been used that none was left for other sites that were either immediately threatened or the subject of an unrepeatable opportunity to safeguard them (Nature Conservancy Council 1980, 3)?

Any last stand for the protection of amenity and public access was likely to be fought in the national parks. Ever since the early 1960s, the Exmoor Society (a branch of the CPRE) had campaigned against the further ploughing of moorland in the Exmoor National Park by farmers who, it was estimated, derived over half their income from land-improvement grants. The levels of payment available under management agreements negotiated with National Park Authority were far too low to persuade farmers to forego both the improvement grants and consequent higher productivity from the land. Not only had 650 acres (260 hectares) of moorland already been destroyed, but there was evidence of similar losses occurring in other national parks and the country as a whole (MacEwen and MacEwen 1982, 173). In April 1977, the Secretary of State for the Environment appointed Lord Porchester to study the problem. As well as confirming the figures for moorland loss, he recommended that the National Park Authority should be empowered to make moorland conservation orders. In addition to a once-and-for-all capital payment to reflect the reduction in land value, the farmer might receive conservation grants as a positive incentive to carry out the type of management desired by the park authority (Department of the Environment, 1977).

The principal object of a Countryside Bill, introduced by the Labour Government in late 1978, was to empower ministers to designate specific areas of open moor or heath, and the National Park Authorities to make Moorland Conservation Orders to protect them from the damaging effects of ploughing or other forms of agricultural improvement. A local Member, Edward du Cann, attacked the Bill for the 'unprecedented system of legal controls' it sought to impose on 'the farmer's traditional freedom to pursue his farming policies in accordance with his circumstances'. The solution was for sufficient money to be found to enable the National Park Authority to offer enough compensation to make it possible for farmers to enter into management agreements (PD, Commons, 961, 1283–92). Although the Bill had completed its Committee Stage when the Labour Government fell in April 1979, the Conservative Whips refused to allow the remaining stages to be passed 'on the nod'. There was no longer bipartisan support for countryside legislation.

As Harvey and Whitby (1988) later remarked, the decade of the 1970s had seen much agitation as to the environmental effects of intensive farming methods, but the policy establishment was still not prepared to give ground. Such episodes as the Porchester inquiry and loss of the Bill were as if 'warm-up rounds' for the major debate surrounding the Wildlife and Countryside Bill of the next Administration.

THE COUNTRYSIDE REVIEW COMMITTEE

Whilst many professed to be shocked at what was perceived to be the minimalist approach taken by the Wildlife and Countryside Bill, enacted by the incoming Conservative Government, the 1970s were significant for much more than highly-publicised conflict. It had also been a time for more 'considered' debate as to the concept and practice of 'multiple land-use'. Evidence of the search for a broader yet more flexible approach to accommodating the otherwise competitive user-interests emerged, perhaps most clearly, through the publication from the mid-1970s onwards of a series of Discussion Papers by a Countryside Review Committee.

Whereas the earlier advisory reports to Ministers had been written from outside the Government service, the NCC received notice in November 1973 that the Secretary of State for the Environment had approved the appointment of a Countryside Review Committee (CRC) made up of officials from relevant Government departments and agencies. Bob Boote attended its principal meetings. Its task would be to review the state of the countryside and the pressures upon it, the effects of Government policy, and thirdly

> to advise whether, given such objectives as the need to maintain agricultural production, there was scope for reconciliation, where there was conflict with the conservation of the countryside, the enhancement of its natural beauty, and its enjoyment by the public.

It was in effect to act as an 'academic seminar', designed to stimulate and 'fuel' debate on countryside issues with a background of facts and options.

In an introductory Discussion Paper, *The countryside – problems and policies*, published in August 1976, the Minister for Planning and Local Government, John Silkin, emphasised that rural problems were considerably more complex than was commonly supposed. The Committee saw its role as that of breaking new ground within Government. Although the concept of a 'total' approach was increasingly familiar in urban studies, the Discussion Paper represented its first major application to the countryside. In a series of Topic Papers on *Leisure and the countryside* and *Rural communities* (July 1977), *Food production in the countryside* (April 1978), and finally *Conservation and the countryside heritage* (September 1979), the Committee's purpose was to study each topic in a wider context. In a small island like Britain, there would always be potential for conflict between what the Committee described as the nation's commitment to economic growth and the conservation of the countryside itself. The solution could not be found in establishing a single-use system. The multi-use principle had to apply even where land had been designated for a specific purpose (Countryside Review Committee 1976).

Whereas most public controversy in the 1950s and 1960s had centred on large-scale building proposals such as an oil refinery or electricity station, in its third Topic Paper the CRC described how farming had become 'the principal destroyer' of the countryside (Countryside Review Committee 1978). As the NCC had pointed out, in its publication *Nature Conservation and Agriculture*, the reason was simple. The new agricultural habitats failed to provide the basic requirements of most species. If the countryside were to consist solely of arable crops, grass leys, chemically-treated ditches, and a few trees and bushes for visual amenity, some 60 per cent of butterfly species and 80 per cent of bird species would disappear (Nature Conservancy Council 1977b). As Norman Moore emphasised, at a meeting of the CRC in June 1977, whilst the NCC welcomed such conservation exercises as the establishment of 'new' sites in gravel pits and around reservoirs, they did not touch the real problem, in so far as most habitats and species were concerned (PRO, FT 8, 24).

The CRC sought balance in emphatically rejecting the view that conservation was a luxury and that farming should always be given overriding priority. Whilst the industry was rightly concerned not to be hamstrung by regulation, the Committee insisted that it had responsibilities to society that went far beyond food production. By the same token, the CRC rejected any major extension of statutory planning to include farming and forestry operations. Such controls would be cumbersome, costly and unconstructive. They would be even more likely to institutionalise conflict − they would be divisive. Since 'any new policy must have the broad support of the farming community', the same resources would be far better spent developing a 'voluntary and flexible policy, based on advice, encouragement, education and financial inducements'.

The Committee found encouraging evidence that the industry was already becoming closely involved in positive conservation measures. The NFU and CLA had jointly published a guide in November 1977, entitled *Caring for the Countryside*, which gave practical advice as to how members might combine food production with conservation (National Farmers' Union 1977). Their confidence had been boosted by the setting up of a Farming and Wildlife Advisory Group, an initiative in which the Nature Conservancy had played a principal part. Although Norman Moore, first at Monks Wood, and later as Chief Adviser to the NCC, had done as much as anyone to expose the damaging effects of modern farming, he remained convinced that farmers' cooperation was essential for conservation. He had been one of a small group of farmers and conservationists to take part in an exercise, in July 1969, to discover what was practical by way of conservation, given different farming scenarios, on a specific farm. The holding, owned by the *Farmers Weekly*, was near Tring in Hertfordshire, but participants were accommodated at the nearby Silsoe College (Barber 1970). In order to retain the obvious rapport established during what became known as 'the Silsoe exercise', a Farming and Wildlife Group (FWAG) was formed and a part-time adviser appointed to organise further Silsoe-type exercises. As local FWAGs were developed, they became, in Moore's words, 'a cooperative agency for promoting such things as coppicing woodland, hedgerow and grassland management, and digging ponds'. An experiment in Gloucestershire and Somerset, financed by the local Naturalists' Trusts, the Countryside Commission and the NCC, highlighted how many more farmers would seek advice if a paid full-time adviser were appointed to each county. A Farming and Wildlife Trust was formed as a charitable trust to finance such advisers. By the mid-1980s, there were 62 county FWAGs with over 30 full-time advisers (Moore 1987, 104–8).

The Minister of Agriculture had asked his own Advisory Council for Agriculture and Horticulture, in May 1977, to review ways in which economic production might be reconciled with other national objectives, in 'the light of public interest in recreation and access and in conservation and amenity'. Under the chairmanship of Sir Nigel Strutt, the Council's report of May 1978 warned that 'only imaginative action, and adequate resources of manpower and money' could avert further conflict. Through its long and close working relationship with farmers, ADAS was uniquely placed to demonstrate how appropriate management on the ground might simultaneously protect conservation interests without reducing farm incomes (Advisory Council for Agriculture and Horticulture 1978). The CRC similarly believed it should be as easy to obtain advice on conservation as that on raising food output. ADAS officers should be empowered to give general advice on agricultural improvement and problems affecting conservation and recreation, the availability of all forms of grant aid and, perhaps most importantly, when and where farmers should seek specialist advice.

The last CRC Topic Paper, of September 1979, focused on the part the conservation movement might play in bringing about a better balance

> between the interests of the agricultural community and the nation as a whole, both
> as consumers of food and participants or observers in the countryside.

Beyond detailed prescriptions as to how the CRC thought national parks and nature reserves might be designated and administered, it believed the most essential prerequisite for a more holistic approach to the countryside was a willingness on the part of Government to draw up clearly-defined policies and to provide the resources to implement them. Whilst Section 11 of the Countryside Act of 1968 enjoined ministers, Government departments and public bodies to 'have regard to the desirability of conserving the natural beauty and amenity of the countryside', the Committee believed there was considerable public scepticism as to how far this obligation was heeded. Not only was there a lack of transparency in policy making but, as the CRC pointed out, the low level of public expenditure hardly suggested that conservation measures were taken seriously. Beyond an increase in Exchequer support, the CRC believed that more thought should be given to raising funds from private sources. In the same way as the arts and world of sport had benefited from private patronage, so public enthusiasm should be more directly tapped for conservation purposes (Countryside Review Committee 1979).

The CRC might seem to have been only one of many bodies to be ignored or simply forgotten with the change in Government in 1979. In fact, such an anonymous group of officials required no public acknowledgement of its labours. The Topic Papers were intended as no more than an early and rudimentary form of public consultation. Their historical value is to be found in the insight they provide as to the line of argument officials were likely to develop in the course of drafting the Wildlife and Countryside Bill.

THE WILDLIFE AND COUNTRYSIDE ACT

The promotion of the Wildlife and Countryside Bill has invariably been portrayed as a time of high drama. Stress is laid on some 200 hours of debate and over 2,000 amendments tabled before the Bill received the Royal Assent in October 1981 (Adams 1986). Much of the discussion, both inside and outside parliament, centred on the need to safeguard wildlife habitat. A senior official in the House of Commons was quoted as saying he had never known a major Bill, put forward by a Government with a substantial majority, being so materially altered (Dalyell, 1981). Cox et al. (1986) saw such vigorous and public opposition as evidence of growing resentment on the part of the voluntary conservation bodies to the long-standing and 'close symbiotic relationship' of the farming industry with Government. The assault also revealed the striking differences in the way the two interest-groups organised themselves. Whereas the landed interests continued to present themselves as a united front with the Ministry of Agriculture, Cox and Lowe (1983) characterised conservationists as falling into three camps: the NCC was bound to be cautious and prudent in its utterances; most voluntary bodies wanted 'cooperation plus safeguards', namely a fall-back position where voluntary arrangements failed; a third and much smaller group took up a 'rejectionist' position, demanding the imposition of planning controls.

Behind the public rhetoric, the limited documentation currently available suggests that the origins of the Bill were somewhat prosaic. They arose from the kind of briefing given to any new Government on taking office. With the election of the Conservative Government on 2 May 1979, the new Secretary of State for the Environment, Michael Heseltine, was told by his officials that legislation would be required to implement the EEC Birds Directive and ratify the Council of Europe Convention on Wildlife and Natural Habitats. He intimated that, as a 'passionate' nature conservationist, he wanted reference in the Queen's Speech to the Government's intention to introduce a comprehensive Wildlife Bill. Guidance was sought from the NCC as to what else might be included. Besides further controls over the introduction of non-native animals, there was agreement that the Bill might sweep into one measure the provisions of the Protection of Birds Acts, the Conservation of Wild Creatures and Wild Plants Act 1975, and the Endangered Species (Import and Export) Act 1976 (PRO, FT 9, 34).

Both DOE and NCC officials acknowledged that there was little point in undertaking such a major administrative exercise unless there were adequate measures to safeguard the habitats on which the individual groups and species depended. At a time when the NCC estimated that some 4 per cent of SSSIs were destroyed or damaged annually, the Secretary of State could hardly give such an assurance. The most widespread and serious threat arose from changes in agricultural and silvicultural usage. Since these activities were exempt from statutory planning control, the NCC had no certain means of anticipating their occurrence. Even where it had sufficient warning to attempt negotiation, and even threaten compulsory purchase, there was nothing to stop an unsympathetic owner from destroying the nature-conservation value of the site before proceedings could be completed. Officials were acutely conscious that the threat to the Ribble estuary had only become known, and the site subsequently saved for the nation, because the owner needed to build an embankment and had, therefore, to give notice of the intention to reclaim the marshes. The height of the projected wall brought it within the ambit of statutory planning control.

Although no reference was made to a Bill in the Queen's Speech, it was announced in

June that one would be introduced during that Session 'to strengthen the protection afforded to wildlife and their habitat, and to embrace our international obligations' (PD, Lords, 400, 1102). Not only did the Secretary of State continue to take a personal interest, but an official wrote that the whole question had 'been brought sharply into focus in recent weeks by the restriction in growth of the NCC finances'. Far from being able to pursue a systematic programme of acquisition, there was doubt as to whether the NCC could even intervene to save a single key-site or take advantage of its availability for purchase. Whilst acquisition must always be dependent on the competing claims for Exchequer monies, a Bill ought publicly to demonstrate that the Secretary of State would always be in a position to assess the merits of a key site (PRO, FT 9, 34).

Following approval by the Cabinet's Home Affairs Committee of the principle of a Bill, six consultation papers were issued by the DOE. One of the most contentious papers covered the 'Conservation of habitats'. It described how designated sites might be chosen, either for their role in meeting international obligations, or to ensure the survival of species otherwise imperilled, or thirdly to enable the Secretary of State to intervene where it was deemed to be 'in the national interest'. Where made, a Nature Conservation Designation Order would require the owner or occupier to give the NCC perhaps six months' notice of such damaging operations as the ploughing of an old meadow or drainage of a marsh. The NCC would use 'the breathing space' to negotiate, where necessary, either a management agreement or voluntary purchase. It might apply for a compulsory purchase order as a last resort (PRO, FT 9, 34).

All had cause for concern. Officials of the DOE were disappointed by the apparent failure of the conservation bodies to recognise that a far-reaching principle had been conceded by ministers, namely that there were instances where changes in the management of land required statutory regulation. Whilst designating only a hundred sites within the first few years might seem trivial, the precedent at least would be established. Although there was no guarantee even for these sites, it would be impossible, in terms of practical politics, for ministers to deny protection where they themselves had caused a site to be designated (PRO, FT 9, 36).

For the 23 bodies that made up the Wildlife Link Committee of the Council for Environmental Conservation (CoEnCo), none of this was sufficient to compensate for the disruptive effect such designation would have on the wider SSSI system. As a meeting of September 1979 warned, special treatment of a small number of SSSIs – the super-SSSIs – would undermine the standing of the remainder. Although originally intended as a check on building development, the SSSI system had come to assume a much wider role in indicating that every Site should be protected for its contribution to the wider countryside. Not only had DOE officials anticipated the demand that all 3,000 'biological' SSSIs should be eligible for designation, but they had rejected it on the grounds that parliament would never agree to so large an area being set aside, albeit temporarily.

The Council of the NCC acknowledged the logic of the voluntary bodies' argument but, at a meeting in January 1980, strongly opposed any move to extend prior notification (an integral part of designation) to all SSSIs. A recent survey had shown that most SSSIs were destroyed or damaged not through lack of notification, but because of a lack of the resources required to take effective action. More fundamentally, Council hoped that, by limiting the Bill to modest, yet useful, measures, the NCC would remain in 'a good position to orchestrate the proper evolution of the SSSI system'. Any extension of prior notification to all Sites would lead to 'an unacceptable polarisation of landed interests'. There would inevitably be a demand from those interests for a curtailment of the Council's discretion in scheduling such Sites (PRO, FT 9, 35).

From the discussions that had already taken place over designation of elite sites, it was clear that the autonomy of the NCC in the scheduling process was again threatened. Whilst Council particularly applauded the firm statement in the Consultation Paper as to the Government's duty to conserve the wildlife resource and the implication, therefore, that monies would be found for that purpose, Council was extremely concerned by the suggestion that such designations should be made by the Secretary of State. Rather than introducing another tier into the process by which sites were identified and registered, Council believed the NCC should have the responsibility for designating such sites from the existing schedule of SSSIs. The Government response was twofold. At a meeting with Council members in November 1979, DOE officials said that, whilst the Secretary of State believed the SSSI system was a good one, within its limits, ministers believed it was politically impossible to impose further restraints on the use and management of SSSIs as long as scheduling remained entirely in the hands of the NCC. There must be 'the imprint of central Government' even on the much smaller number of designated sites. Michael Heseltine expressed it differently, in a letter to the Chairman of Council. Whilst affirming that any choice would be made from a list of key sites drawn up by the NCC, there were 'sound reasons' why the Secretary of State should make the designations. It was the most effective way of demonstrating the importance which the Government attached to the protection of such sites. Since designation implied a commitment, ministers must be in a position to review all relevant factors. Occasions might arise where an Order was perfectly justified in wildlife terms, but not in the overall national context. It was for Government to decide the balance of priorities (PRO, FT 9, 36).

As an officer of the NCC reasoned, Council had three broad options. One was to mount an independent campaign of the most public kind, and another to join forces with the voluntary bodies. Whilst both would ensure the NCC was seen to be taking action, there were weighty arguments against both. Not only did the NCC (unlike the voluntary bodies) have an official channel of communication with the DOE but, since the Secretary of State was sponsoring the Bill, there was every reason to foster, rather than jeopardise, that link. Association with an obstructive parliamentary campaign, or even close identification with the manoeuvres of the voluntary bodies, would quickly lose Departmental sympathy. It would also confirm prejudice among those who regarded the NCC as just another pressure group. A third and more positive approach was for the NCC to support the voluntary case wherever possible, but to do so as an adjunct to its official role as statutory adviser to the Department. The NCC had to be perceived as 'talking scientific sense', infused with a degree of political awareness of what was practicable in a Government Bill at that juncture in time (PRO, FT 9, 35).

Pressures on the parliamentary timetable prevented a Bill from being introduced to

Natural limestone 'pavement' on **Hutton Roof Crags, Cumbria**, a Grade 1 site identified in the *Nature Conservation Review*.
Pavements such as this are important both for their rich flora and for their geological and physiographic features. They have been increasingly threatened by removal of surface stones, especially for rockeries.

the first House, the Lords, until November 1980. Expressing sentiment of the kind used by the Countryside Review Committee, Government spokesmen emphasised the innovativeness of the Bill in avoiding any inbuilt bias towards farming or other interests. It was drafted so as to favour no particular group. Michael Heseltine himself asserted, in moving the second reading in April 1981, that it sought in no way 'to create a Maginot Line'. The aim was to strike 'a balance between the often conflicting and deeply held views of people whose motivations and sincerity are not in question, although they line up on opposite sides of many arguments' (PD, 6th series, 3, 524–608).

Developments during the period following the postponement of the Bill had caused the NCC to shift its ground significantly. At a meeting of Council members with Heseltine in March 1980, the Chairman, Fred Holliday, said that attitudes to nature conservation were becoming more demanding. Whilst continuing to seek a balanced view, the time might come when Council was forced to adopt 'a more single-minded approach'. The Secretary of State appeared to welcome a more assertive stance. In describing the NCC as 'an informed and articulate pressure group', Heseltine said that it must be for Council to decide what was best for nature conservation. It was for himself 'to determine the balance of advantage between conservation and other interests'. Whilst acknowledging the widespread anxiety regarding the future of land, he believed many large landowners would be prepared to manage their land at less than the maximum economic advantage in order to protect areas for nature-conservation purposes (PRO, FT 9, 37).

Whereas Heseltine's remarks encouraged the NCC to discuss strategy and tactics more openly with the voluntary bodies, developments within the farming industry offered pretext for assessing how far the Secretary of State's optimism as to the attitude of landed interests might be borne out. The new Chairman of the NCC, Sir Ralph Verney, had taken the Chair at a meeting of the NCC with the Wildlife Link Committee a day before his own Council meeting, some four days before the second-reading debate in the Lords in November 1980. As Verney wrote to Heseltine, whilst the NCC continued to support the central role of Designation Orders, Council believed that their whole context had changed. As part of the Rayner Scrutiny of the efficiency of Government departments, Agriculture Ministers had announced, in early 1980, proposals for streamlining the administration of their capital-grant schemes. The NCC expressed alarm at the basic supposition that farmers would no longer have to apply for prior approval for carrying out work upon which they intended to claim grant. Ministry personnel would no longer be in a position to forewarn the NCC of planned works affecting SSSIs. Ministers agreed to an administrative arrangement, under the new scheme approved by parliament in August, requiring farmers to give the NCC three months' notice where they intended to make such a claim affecting an SSSI. A precedent for prior notification of SSSIs had been set. Its overriding purpose was to give all parties the chance to explore the merits of management agreements (PRO, FT 9, 41–2).

As Verney insisted, the concessions should not be all one way. Throughout his long involvement with the Conservancy and now the NCC, Ralph Verney claimed that his aim had been to demonstrate how a prosperous agriculture and thriving forest industry were the best guarantors of conservation. Himself a landowner, he had been President of the CLA between 1961 and 1963, Vice President of the European Confederation of Agriculture from 1965 to 1971, and a founder-member of the Timber Growers' Organisation. He was accordingly extremely well placed to recognise the potential of a compromise embedded in amendments moved by Lords Buxton and Craigton, whereby the NCC would notify owners of the existence of an SSSI on their property, giving details of the activities that would damage that interest, on the basis that owners would

Chairman of the NCC, **Sir Ralph Verney**, **Lord Arbuthnott** (Deputy Chairman), and the Senior Stalker, **Geordie Sturton**, and Stalker, **Louis Macrae**, at Kinloch Castle, Isle of Rhum, in October 1980. As the Master of Arbuthnott, the Deputy Chairman was the Nature Conservancy's Land Agent in Scotland.

have the reciprocal duty of informing the NCC before carrying out such operations. The CLA and the NFU intimated, in informal discussion, that they would not oppose such a reciprocal arrangement provided that it was seen to be required by Government.

Verney accordingly wrote to ministers in February 1981, expressing considerable concern that, despite obvious support at the Lords' Committee Stage for the reciprocal duty, the Government had readily adopted the further duties being imposed on the NCC, but had rejected the reciprocal arrangement. As Verney protested, what was the point of the NCC going to the considerable trouble and expense of notifying every SSSI owner, if there was still no certain way of discovering whether damage was likely to occur? The Minister of Agriculture, Peter Walker, was unmoved, telling Verney, at a meeting in mid-February, that he much preferred to rely upon voluntary action and cooperation wherever possible. Not only did he refuse to create what he called 'a new series of bureaucratic processes to bolster the conservation movement', but he dismissed out-of-hand notions that perhaps 2 per cent of the £176 millions of grant-aid awarded annually for agricultural improvement might be used for conservation measures. According to Walker, the agricultural industry was already in a depressed state and needed all the money that could be raised by way of capital grants (PRO, FT 9, 42).

The NCC's insistence on providing 'teeth' for any improved 'early warning system' appeared to be amply supported by events taking place during the actual passage of the Bill. Between December 1980 and the following February, all but 30 hectares (74 acres) of a heathland of 134 hectares (330 acres) at Horton Common, in Dorset, were roto-vated for conversion to improved grassland. Attempts by the NCC and voluntary bodies to conclude a management agreement or voluntary sale had failed. An article published in the *New Scientist* of 22 January 1981, by David Goode, the Assistant Chief Scientist, indicated that, of a sample of 20 counties, some 10 per cent of SSSIs had been destroyed or damaged in 1980, with the most dramatic returns of 32 per cent and 17 per cent from Dorset and Northamptonshire respectively (Goode 1981). A NCC press notice issued before the Lords' Committee Stage claimed that such losses were not the work of a few 'maverick' farmers, but the consequence of economic pressures forcing land users to maximise income. This proved that the Bill did not go far enough; the NCC might have a statutory duty to protect such sites, but it remained powerless to prevent their destruc-tion. Effective action was needed, if such 'a massive decline in the quality and extent of wildlife habitat' was to be reduced (PRO, FT 9, 42).

Michael Heseltine wrote, in a letter to Peter Walker in February 1981, of 'an awkward situation' arising in regard to the Bill which, taken as a whole, remained 'an important and constructive measure'. Unless some concessions were made to conservation interests before the Report Stage was reached, there was not only a risk of defeat on the habitat clause but, more seriously, a risk of filibustering tactics on the part of the Opposition cre-ating difficulties for the legislative programme in the Commons. By accepting the sec-ond half of the reciprocal package, the Bill would not only go to the Commons much improved but with general goodwill. Heseltine found it difficult to understand why the difficulty had not already been resolved. A landowner claiming capital grant was already obliged to consult the NCC. Those who claimed to be concerned about conservation (and most undoubtedly were) required no prompting. Even the less conservation-minded could hardly claim that a delay of, say, two months was 'a very onerous imposition'. True, it might lead to a Designation Order, but if the SSSI was of such outstanding importance as to warrant an Order, it was hardly possible for 'a conservation minded Government' to go to the extreme lengths of preserving the right to destroy it without warning or consultation (PRO, FT 9, 46).

In the event, two amendments were moved on the Lords' Report Stage in March 1981. A Government amendment envisaged a code of conduct which owners of SSSIs would be encouraged to follow. In protesting that all previous codes had been broken, the NCC warned that the continued lack of faith would only create more antagonism. NCC Council therefore supported an All-Party amendment which, as an extension of the voluntary code, would require reciprocal notification. Whereas the Government amendment was approved without opposition, the succeeding All-Party one was defeated by 109 to 100 votes. In correspondence, the Parliamentary Under-Secretary for Wales, Michael Roberts, wrote that, whilst the strength of feeling among conservationists was well known, the Government had also to take account of the agricultural community

> with their knowledge of, and aptitude for, the land and nature – many of whom in
> any case are not unsympathetic to the cause of conservationists

The Government had to consider not only the cost implications but the manner in which the All-Party amendment would have imposed obligations without those affected having recourse to appeal. The Director-General of the NCC, Richard Steele, wrote of his considerable disappointment at the outcome. The closeness of the vote, however, had left none in doubt as to the gathering strength of conservationists. The onus was on the farming and landed organisations to make the voluntary code work. The NCC would monitor the outcome closely, so as to alert Government to any deficiencies (PRO, FT 9, 46).

In moving the Second Reading in the Commons, Heseltine insisted that

> In our view, the cause of conservation is done no good by using compulsion as the
> primary means of making landowners and farmers manage their land for the gen-
> eral benefit of our heritage (PD, Commons, 6th series 3, 531)

The Bill was, however, pushing perilously close to the end of the parliamentary session, and the Labour Opposition threatened to talk it out, rather than allow it to be passed unamended (Cox and Lowe 1983; Adams 1986, 103). Concessions included enabling powers to establish marine nature reserves, the protection of limestone pavements and, most crucially for habitat protection, a statutory requirement that owners and occupiers wanting to carry out potentially-damaging operations on an SSSI must first notify the NCC. Instead of acting as the front-line defence for a small number of Sites, Designation Orders became what the NCC and the wider conservation movement had always wanted, a back-up power in cases where it had proved impossible to find a voluntary means of protecting an SSSI. Whilst the package simply put the existing procedures for scheduling SSSIs on a statutory basis, the NCC was also required to notify (or, rather, re-notify) owners and occupiers of existing SSSIs on their properties, their nature-conservation interest, and the nature of any activities that might cause damage. The

NCC was assured, during the passage of the Bill, that it would be given the resources needed to complete this massive administrative task (PRO, FT 9, 48).

However widely the terms of the Bill had been drawn, none could lose sight of the controversy over Exmoor. At the Report Stage in the Lords, Lord Sandford had moved an amendment that widened the scope of the Farm Capital Grant scheme, so as to enable Agriculture Ministers to make grants to conserve national parks and 'such other areas as may be specified'. Where an improvement grant was opposed by a national park authority, it would be determined jointly by Ministers. As Sandford emphasised, the effect would be to give the industry the same level of grant aid, but there would be 'a slight readjustment' in the way it was spent. Whilst everything possible would be done to encourage rather than harass them, hill farmers must realise that the hills had a value beyond 'so many kilograms of sheepmeat'. In developing the rural economy, a balance had to be struck between the price of lambs at market and the 'spiritual refreshment' of millions of people visiting national parks. The amendment was welcomed by the House for the way in which it recognised how grant aid to farmers might be used to help resolve conflict (PD, Lords, 418, 480–9).

The NCC Council gave 'a very firm welcome' to any device that encouraged farmers to give more than lip-service to conservation. Whilst the amending clause was extended to include SSSIs, further controversy was caused by a Government amendment in June, which required the cost of compensation to be met not by the agricultural budget, but by the conservation bodies. If, after consulting the Environment Secretary, the Minister of Agriculture decided that an application should be refused, the national park authority or the NCC (in respect of an SSSI) would be required to offer, and meet the cost of, a management agreement within guidelines laid down by Ministers (PD, 1980–81, Commons Standing Committee D, Wildlife and Countryside Bill, 509–27, and Lords, 424, 513–17). The Director of the CPRE, Robin Grove-White, protested in *The Times* of 6 October 1981 that the further amendment gave 'legal expression to the surprising notion that a farmer has a right to grant aid from the tax-payer'. If denied a grant, albeit in the wider public interest, it was assumed that 'he must be compensated for the resulting, entirely hypothetical "losses" '. Perhaps even more worryingly, such compensation was to be paid not by the Ministry 'whose relentless promotion of new farming methods through the grant system' had caused such conflict, but by conservation agencies, whose meagre budgets could not possibly permit them to object to 'the many controversial (and even mischievous) grant proposals that will arise'.

A later Lords' amendment to reject the formula, tabled by the two Conservative peers, Lords Buxton and Onslow, and supported by all the major conservation bodies, failed by only 59 to 57 votes. A letter from the NCC was not only heavily exploited by the Government, but may have been critical to the finely-balanced outcome. It welcomed the amendment, in as much as it removed the uncertainty that had previously bedevilled negotiations with farmers. It placed a firm commitment on the Government to provide the necessary funding (PD, Lords, 424, 498–518). As an officer of the NCC later explained, the Government had either to find the money, or come up with 'a better arrangement to safeguard threatened sites' (Cox and Lowe 1983, 69).

CHAPTER NINE

ARRESTING THE 'ENGINE OF DESTRUCTION'

The Statement of policies, published by the NCC in 1974, began with the advisory role, so as to emphasise its importance. Besides exhibitions, it was the era of the leaflet, the priority being to reach the users and managers of the countryside and schools. As well as more effective use of television, Council acknowledged the importance of 'farming and countryside' seminars and closer collaboration with Agricultural College advisers and research centres.

A range of strategies was used to raise public awareness. At the suggestion of Philip Oswald, the Head of Publicity, the author of several best-selling books on the country-side, Richard Mabey, was invited to write one for the NCC. It would explore the way the traditional countryside had formed a vital part of cultural history, and the lessons that could be learnt from this experience to develop an imaginative rural land-use policy – a land ethic for the future. With the title, *The Common Ground. A place for nature in Britain's future?*, it was published by Hutchinson for the NCC in May 1980 (Mabey 1980).

In the educational sector, Mike Henchman, whose first assignments were for the 'Countryside in 1970' conferences, recalled later the partnerships that were formed with

The NCC mobile exhibition unit, 1975.

individual companies. Perhaps the most outstanding was that with the makers of the breakfast cereal, Weetabix. A series of cardboard habitat models was designed by his Section to help schools with their nature-study lessons. In making them, children would have something practical to do, while learning about the wildlife to be found within the different habitats. Through parents reading the back of the cereal packets, and collecting and sending away the tops for a model, it was reckoned that some 36 million people were introduced to the NCC and its work.

Whilst the number of bodies concerned with planning greatly increased, the NCC's *Statement of policies* continued to give first priority to both central and local government. Much effort was expended on Structure and Local Plans, both in exerting influence over specific development proposals and formulating more general policies and measures in respect of the countryside, coast and (increasingly) the town and city. The Public Inquiry into the location of an oil refinery at Nigg Point in the Cromarty Firth was the first instance of a clash with the Highland Regional Authority. As the Regional Officer for North-west Scotland, Peter Tilbrook, recalled, the Authority won the case, but the Secretary of State overturned the verdict. The refinery was never built, but the opprobrium remained – jobs were so important and there seemed to be so much countryside in that part of Scotland. Rawdon Goodier, the Regional Officer for East Scotland, was seconded as a Specialist Advisory Officer, working with the Chief Planning Officer, in the Scottish Development Department. As he later recalled, the National Planning Guidelines of 1976 required local planning authorities to consult the Secretary of State where they proposed to disregard advice given them by the NCC in respect of any site in the *Nature Conservation Review*. It considerably sharpened awareness of the role of the NCC among such authorities.

Rapport had to be established not only with interest groups that had the formidable capacity to wreak havoc, but with other conservation bodies. Bill Copland (now the Conservancy's Interpretative Officer at headquarters) regarded a one-day seminar held at Monks Wood, in October 1969, as a turning point in relations with the National Trust. In a series of presentations, the Chief Land Agent for the Trust, Ivan Hills, observed how the Trust's special position and ability to hold land inalienably meant it could practice long-term management. Whilst it might be conservative in outlook, it recognised the need to keep pace with the rapid changes taking place in land use. Its dilemma was how to hold the balance between competing interests. In illustrating their affinity of interests, Duncan Poore spoke of how much nature conservationists could learn from the Trust as to the economics of land management and handling of visitors. More specifically, the National Trust was seen as having a significant role in protecting areas identified by the *Nature Conservation Review*.

So much was expected of the relationship with the county naturalists' trusts that relations were bound to be difficult at times. An informal 'tour of the horizon', in December 1960, had made it clear that the trusts had no intention of becoming 'pensioners or agents of the Conservancy'. Nor was it in the interests of the Conservancy that they should become so. As Max Nicholson wrote, in support of an early application for a grant from such grant-awarding bodies as the Pilgrim Trust, naturalists' trusts might not only act as an invaluable 'watchdog' in making representations to public inquiries, the press,

Illustrations of reserve management from the first *Annual Report* of the NCC.
(*above*) A specially-designed machine was used to pump mud from the dykes of the **Bure Marshes NNR** in the Norfolk Broads, in an attempt to restore suitable conditions for the once-rich aquatic life.

(*right*) Scrub on **Lullington Heath NNR** being cleared with a mechanical swipe to encourage the spread of heathland flora and fauna, which would then be maintained by grazing.

and members of parliament, but as a spur and stimulant to local authorities and bodies such as the Conservancy itself. Where Barton Worthington cautioned regional officers not to appear patronising, Bob Boote wrote, in November 1962, that 'we must not drag our feet' in fully developing a partnership wherever there were 'enthusiastic and competent officers and appropriate tasks to devolve' (PRO, FT 22, 57).

An obvious instance of collaboration between the Conservancy and voluntary bodies was in making surveys of SSSIs, maintaining contact with their owners and occupiers, and alerting the Conservancy to any threat. A Liaison Committee was formed in June 1964. An obvious difficulty was that of obtaining a similar level and quality of response from each trust. Whereas the Cambridgeshire and Lincolnshire Trusts rapidly assembled files of information on their SSSIs, the Norfolk Trust claimed to be too preoccupied with its reserves. Perhaps more importantly, SSSIs were being damaged and destroyed on such a scale that, far from devolving responsibility, the Conservancy and its successor were themselves expected to carry out the necessary surveillance and protective measures. Nor was it always practical for trusts to be given a prominent role, even in survey work. Martin Holdgate wrote that the *Nature Conservation Review* was 'not the type of exercise for local amateurs once it got beyond "the grass roots" stage' (PRO, FT 3, 416).

In the event, it was not so much the material support given by the voluntary bodies, but their pressure on the political process, that proved so valuable to the NCC, particularly as the advocacy of the trust movement and RSPB came to be reinforced by the more radical bodies of the 1970s and, most obviously, Friends of the Earth. Although not the chief reason for 1981 becoming known as 'the year when wildlife came to Westminster', the voluntary bodies caused that visit to be especially memorable for its 'long and often heated debate in both Houses of Parliament' (Nature Conservancy

Council1982). For their part, the nature conservation bodies benefited considerably from pump-priming grants and loans made from 1974 onwards under the Nature Conservancy Council Act. Almost three-quarters of the grant aid disbursed by the NCC went to the trusts in 1980–81. As well as continued support for its Beached Bird Survey, the RSPB received grant aid for management work on its reserves of Minsmere in Suffolk and Ynys-hir in Dyfed (Nature Conservancy Council 1981, 66).

With the considerably greater demands imposed by the 1981 Act, and intense pressure from the Secretary of State to reduce staff numbers, it was especially timely for the *Annual Report* of 1980-81 to be emphasising both the scale and range of the NCC's responsibilities. Far from diminishing, its long-standing obligation for site safeguard had evolved into three distinct mechanisms. Under powers conferred by the Countryside Act of 1968, 70 management agreements had been drawn up, and financial contributions were made towards safeguarding the wildlife interest of some 2,500 hectares (6,200 acres). Of the more long-standing duties, over 80,000 hectares (197,000 acres) were held on the basis of Nature Reserve Agreements, many of which expired in the 1980s and required renegotiation. They would be substantially more expensive to renew. And lastly, nearly 52,000 hectares (128,500 acres) had been purchased or leased as NNRs, increasingly on the basis of special grants and loans from the Department of the Environment.

The difficulties faced by the NCC in acquiring Grade 1 sites, even where owners were keen to dispose of them, were graphically illustrated by the eventual purchase of Scotland Lodge Farm, in Wiltshire. It included the Grade 1 site of Parsonage Down, one of the most important areas of chalk downland in Britain, where some parts still had a diversity of as many as 40 species per square metre. For over half a century, a traditional pattern of cattle and sheep grazing on this land had retained the wide range of grasses and flowering plants once widespread over large areas of South Wessex. The owner had died and, under the terms of his will, the NCC was given an option to buy the freehold of the 408-hectare (1000-acre) farm at the extremely advantageous price of £500,000, compared with a District Valuer's valuation of £1.59 million. NCC Council resolved, in November 1974, to proceed with negotiation, subject to special funds being made available by the Department of the Environment. Whilst the creation of a 'con-servation farm' would be an exciting venture, in May 1975 Council members concluded that this would not only attract criticism but divert resources from more conventional conservation tasks. The areas of least conservation value should therefore be sold. The NCC's finances had become so parlous by the late 1970s that the question arose as to whether it would even be possible to pursue a break-even policy, whereby sufficient land could be sold to reimburse the Treasury and yet all the Grade 1 downland be retained. On the understanding that such a balance would be achieved, the Secretary of State for the Environment approved application for a supplementary grant in January 1980. The outstanding deficit of £68,000 after the sale of the land was met by the disposal of livestock.

The Regional Officer for the South-west of England, Peter B. Nicholson, wrote that the commonly-used term, 'site safeguard', hardly did justice to 'the strong Regional culture' that had developed within the NCC. For many staff, the fight to prevent the loss of wildlife became a passionate life's work, bordering almost on a religion. That commitment had begun perhaps as a childhood interest in natural history. It was further developed in the sixth form and college, as the science of ecology was learnt and the underlying ethics of the environmental movement became better known. On graduating, such persons became part of a culture where, in the words of Duncan Poore,

> we must insist that in the present vulnerable and already battered state of this small
> planet, it is no longer acceptable for decisions vitally affecting its future to be taken
> by managers, engineers, chemists, banks, economists and others who literally do not
> know what they are doing and have not even a vestige of training or experience con-
> cerning what they take out of the environment and what they spew back into it.

As Peter Nicholson observed, few other parts of the Civil or Public Service enjoyed such a sense of mission. Nancy Gordon had worked at the Malham Tarn Field Centre before becoming Regional Officer for the North-east and Central Scotland in 1960. Without much idea of what the work would entail, she was attracted by the marvellous countryside and the contact with people. One day it was a meeting with crofters, and the next perhaps with the laird. Chris Bradenoch was out-posted within two years of his appointment as Assistant Regional Officer for the Scottish Borders in 1973. Rather than arriving in a smart suit, from a remote office, he experienced at first hand the benefits of being seen going about an everyday job, visiting the local shops, and joining, say, the parent-teachers' association.

Inevitably, perhaps, such commitment to a particular reserve, locality and region engendered an independence of mind and suspicion of guidelines imposed from 'above' or 'outside'. An obvious topic of mutual interest, but frequently little agreement, was the optimal form of reserve-management plans. Appointed as a reserve warden in 1961, Ray Collier later recalled an acceleration in the preparation of such plans following the

Winterton Dunes NNR, Norfolk, acquired by a Nature Reserve Agreement in 1956, is the largest mainland dune system on the East Anglian coast. Endeavours to establish the sand-holding marram grass here represented some of earliest attempts at habitat restoration on reserves in Lowland England.

PLEASE KEEP OFF NEWLY PLANTED MARRAMS

Acquisition and Management Review of the mid-1960s. Seconded to the Lincolnshire Trust in 1971, he became one of a small group who suggested a more standard format for trust reserves. The model drawn up for the purpose was largely ignored. Although the NCC grasped the nettle once again in the mid-1970s, it did so by commissioning those running the MSc Conservation Course at University College London to devise a handbook for the preparation of such plans. This was both praised and damned for its comprehensiveness. The drafting of a management plan for the Rannoch Moor NNR led to a NCC working party being convened in 1981. As Collier recalled, the breakthrough was made by concentrating on the crux of the plan – the final part that set out the programme of management work required. Such a reductionist approach also made it possible for the NCC to insist, for the first time, that such guidelines must be followed. So great was the demand from the voluntary bodies for copies that an abridged version was produced.

Wherever the balance was struck between standardisation and flexibility, much of the local autonomy that characterised the Conservancy and early years of the NCC was removed, as the combination of heightened public awareness and mounting pressures on the countryside called for greater investment of resources and, therefore, accountability as to how they were deployed. The greater uniformity and rigour as represented by the *Nature Conservation Review* was extended to the scheduling of SSSIs, using criteria developed largely by Norman Moore, as Chief Advisory Officer. The Wildlife and Countryside Act had, in any case, made SSSIs part of what Peter Nicholson called 'a serious legal process'. Beyond the immediate need for a completely new survey and assessment of existing SSSIs, the consultation mechanism rapidly became 'a daunting hurdle that gave rise to much aggravation and stress on all sides'. Whilst on the one hand legal deadlines were imposed, the increasing centralisation of approval mechanisms meant delays and much re-examination of the evidence. Such report-writing and liaison at all levels were, however, inevitable where the end result might be a public inquiry or even High Court action. Even where things went well, any pronouncement as to the science or conservation aspects of a Site became increasingly challenged by a growing legion of professional consultants and planners.

Sandy Kerr was not alone in perceiving the Wildlife and Countryside Act as both reflecting, and further stimulating, a marked change in the rapport between farming and forestry, and conservation as the third force in the countryside. After five years at the Monks Wood Experimental Station, he had become Deputy Regional Officer in South Scotland. As he recalled, there was still a feeling that, with so much wildlife around, there was little need for pitched battles. Something equally good might be found down the road. The losses might be sad and, at times, infuriating, but for Kerr it was not until the 1980s that the job took on 'fairly horrid' aspects. So much of the wildlife of the countryside had been lost that conservationists no longer had room to manoeuvre. It was not so much that landowners and occupiers resented being told not to do something; they simply hated taking instruction from a piece of legislation.

Tealham and Tadham Moor, Somerset, February 1979. The *Second Report* of the NCC included a chapter on 'Nature conservation and agriculture', which described how the principal interest for nature conservation on farmland in the lowlands and more fertile uplands was not in the cropped areas themselves, but in the small uncropped portions and those few pastures, downs and meadows which still retained the diversity of flora and fauna encouraged by past systems of agricultural management

THE BATTLE GROUND OF NATURE

More than usually, it was the Act itself that appeared to be on trial. Both sides acknowledged that the manner in which the Wildlife and Countryside Act was interpreted and implemented within its first few years would determine the level of restriction that might ultimately be required.

Almost immediately, the worst fears of conservationists seemed to be confirmed. The owner of 150 acres (60 hectares) of wet grassland within the Walland Marshes SSSI of Kent gave notice of its drainage and cultivation. Besides an unusual saltmarsh flora, the Site supported breeding populations of snipe, garganey, bearded tit and, rarest of all, black-tailed godwit. The Department of the Environment refused the NCC's application for additional funds to secure a management agreement. The Council dared not commit resources that might later be required for more pressing cases. The land was consequently de-scheduled, and the Site ploughed (Purseglove 1989, 242–4). The Director of the RSPB, Ian Prestt, protested, in a letter to *The Times* of 21 March 1982, that the NCC 'must object loudly when any site is at risk, whether or not it has the money to pay compensation'. Only then would the public and parliament realise that 'the real cause of the destruction of our wildlife heritage' was the Government's failure to provide the cash required.

Wetland areas remained a crucial battleground for nature conservationists, and one of increasing importance for those concerned with landscape and outdoor recreation. A consultation paper published by a NCC Working Party made up of representatives of the Ministry of Agriculture, Wessex Water Authority, Somerset County Council and voluntary conservation bodies, together with the NCC, had been the first to warn, in 1977, of the growing threat to the wildlife of the Somerset Levels and Moors, from both agricultural improvement and peat extraction. It broke new ground by developing the concept of 'key areas', where conservation should be given priority even over farmland (Working Party 1977). In deciding the size and 'viability' of such areas, all parties acknowledged that it would never be enough to acquire and designate a few scattered meadows as nature reserves. Their value would be severely prejudiced by what happened on adjacent land. The drainage system was so integrated that the value of each Moor and Level far exceeded the sum of the individual drainage-compartments. That too had been the conclusion of the chairmen of the local Internal Drainage Boards (IDBs) in putting forward proposals for a series of comprehensive pumped-drainage schemes, following a visit to the Lincolnshire Fens. By such means, all the pasture land might be turned over to abundant crops of wheat, potatoes and sugar beet. The proposals included a £1-million scheme for upgrading the pumping station and improvement to the main drain of West Sedgemoor. After considerable discussion, local farmers rejected it on the grounds of cost, both in terms of higher drainage rates and such immediate outgoings as fencing (Purseglove 1989, 244–58).

None regarded the reprieve as anything more than temporary. A national campaign was mounted against such schemes, wherever they might occur in the Somerset Levels and Moors. The RSPB began buying land on West Sedgemoor. As a single hydrological and ecological unit, it supported flocks of 25,000 lapwing, as well as between one-third and one-quarter of the entire region's population of snipe, curlew and redshank. Together with the Somerset Trust for Nature Conservation, the RSPB threatened to take legal action if the whole of West Sedgemoor was not scheduled as an SSSI. The NCC sent every owner formal notice of its intention to schedule the Moor, together with a list of the farming activities that would constitute 'potentially damaging operations'. The entire Moor was scheduled in November 1982. The President of the NFU voiced 'extreme dismay'. The Somerset Members of Parliament, Edward Du Cann and John Peyton, called upon the Environment Secretary to intervene. In their words, NCC Chairman, Sir Ralph Verney, had clearly been 'quite unable to keep his zealots and minions in any kind of effective check'.

Government ministers became even more directly embroiled following the appointment of Tom King, the Member for the nearby constituency of Bridgwater, as Secretary of State for the Environment. His decision not to appoint Verney to a second term of office as Chairman of the NCC was regarded, not least by Verney himself, as dismissal. Verney's effigy, and those of the Regional Officers of the NCC and RSPB, were burnt by angry farmers before television cameras in February 1983. West Sedgemoor had, nevertheless, been scheduled and, as the *Guardian* noted, a day later on 23 February 1983, farmers risked fines of up to £1,000, and a further £100 per day, where they waged, as threatened, a campaign of civil disobedience. In addressing a highly-charged private meeting on West Sedgemoor in March, King also emphasised that 'we are right in the front line of battle to preserve the voluntary approach to conservation'. Besides giving assurance that compensation would be paid for any loss of capital value, which went beyond the provisions of the 1981 Act (Baldock et al. 1990), King announced that one of the Ministry's specialist staff would be seconded to the NCC to help negotiate the necessary management agreements. All parties could claim some measure of success. Through their challenge to the scheduling of the SSSI, farmers had secured *ad hoc* concessions and assurances. By 1990, there were nevertheless ten SSSIs, along with the NNR of Shapwick Heath, covering 6,900 hectares (over 17,000 acres) of the Somerset Levels and Moors.

It was the preservation of landscape amenity, rather than wildlife, that caused the Halvergate Marshes of the Norfolk Broads to become the most hotly contested area in the early 1980s. The chief protagonists were the Countryside Commission and the Broads Authority, a body appointed in 1978 'to conserve and enhance the natural beauty and amenity' of Broadland. As Purseglove observed, the Authority was careful not to depend on such subjective criteria as 'natural beauty'. The wide, open spaces would remain, even if the marshes were drained and ploughed. The Authority emphasised instead how ploughing would transform the character of the marshland. It would no longer be dominated by 'rough texture, vegetated dykes, field gates, grazing animals and birds' (Purseglove 1989, 266–78).

With the workability of voluntary management agreements still in question, it was the turn of the Halvergate Marshes to acquire symbolic value. A leader in *The Times* of 17 March 1984 described them as 'the Flanders of the great war between farming interests and the objectives of nature conservation'. Considerable publicity was given to the fact that more than a thousand acres (400 hectares) had already been ploughed in the two years since the 1981 Act, including some 870 acres (350 hectares) without notice being given to the Broads Authority. Even where there was prospect of saving some of the remaining 5,000 acres (2,000 hectares) by agreement, Lords Buxton and Onslow warned, in a letter to *The Times* of 18 February 1984, that taxpayers would have to meet the estimated annual (index-linked) cost of £1 million. It was not as if the majority of the hundred farmers stood to gain. Over half owned livestock-holdings of less than 25 acres (10 hectares) each; their income was likely to decline as the pasture deteriorated through the drainage improvements demanded by the few large farmers bent on large-scale cultivation. The higher drainage rates would make it even more difficult for stockholders to remain in farming.

The Lower Bure IDB sought to bring matters to a head by claiming that, rather than simply replacing the worn-out pumps, it would be considerably more cost effective to embark on a three-part scheme, costing £2.33 million. The Countryside Commission demanded that a public inquiry should be held before any decision on grant aid was announced. The IDB responded by claiming that, if a grant was refused, it would finance the scheme entirely from its own resources. Some 18 months later, the *New*

Scientist carried a report that the Ministry of Agriculture had made concessions in a successful attempt to dissuade the Department of the Environment from holding a public inquiry (Anon. 1982). It announced in November 1982 that grant aid would not be given for increasing the capacity of the pumps for the Seven Mile/Berney schemes. There remained, however, the question of the cost of compensation payments for not ploughing up the pastures. One-third of the budget of the Broads Authority was already absorbed by such payments. Ministers agreed, in March 1984, to look for alternative financing, on the condition that farmers agreed to suspend operations. There was sufficient assurance for the Minister of State for the Environment, William Waldegrave, to inform parliament on 4 April that 'Halvergate is safe for a year.' The Department was in consultation with the Ministry of Agriculture 'to see whether we can ensure its long-term security, which is of great importance' (PD, Commons, 57, 954).

Once again, a threat to a specific site forced the pace of public policy-making. A farmer dissatisfied with the promised level of compensation engaged a contractor to clear his ditches as a preparatory move to ploughing the grassland. Friends of the Earth mounted a well publicised demonstration. In the same month, June 1984, negotiations broke down with another farmer, about to plough up marshes in the Yare valley. The Prime Minister, Margaret Thatcher, insisted that Ministers should take the exceptional step of issuing a Planning Direction under Article 4 of the General Development Order and thereby secure a stay of execution. During a visit to Halvergate in the autumn, the Secretary of State for the Environment, Patrick Jenkin, said that further ploughing of the marshes would represent 'a major tragedy and a failure for conservation'.

As Purseglove (1989, 269) remarked, with so much publicity and even the Prime Minister being forced to intervene, something had to be done. In May 1985, a Broads Grazing Marshes Conservation Scheme was introduced, based on the alternative and more positive approach long canvassed by the Countryside Commission. Instead of compensation paid for profits forgone (as enshrined in the 1981 Act) farmers would receive subsidies for voluntarily continuing with traditional stock-grazing methods. Prescriptions were laid down as to stocking rates; a limit of 240 units of nitrogen per hectare was set; and only one crop a year of hay or silage was permitted. The Treasury consented to the Ministry and the Countryside Commission, jointly, paying up to £123.55 per hectare over a three-year experimental period. Although this was an emergency measure, the fact that almost 90 per cent of farmers entered the Scheme meant that the 'boot was on the other foot'. As Purseglove explained, even if only one farmer ploughed, he would be perceived as having denied the whole farming community the benefits of joining the Scheme. Some 5,000 hectares were protected at a cost of £1.7 million in public money.

Despite such clashes over particular areas of countryside, and well-publicised claims that the Act represented 'a dead end' (MacEwen and MacEwen 1982), most farmers met the Government's expectations. The NCC rarely had to extend the period of notification, or threaten an application to the Minister for a Nature Conservation Order, to prevent a potentially damaging operation being carried out. None of this, however, prevented mounting public concern over what was happening to the countryside. As Baldock and Lowe (1996) remarked, the comparative absence of controls on agricultural land-use became even more glaring as the industry boasted that it was transforming the use and character of the countryside. The extraordinary impact of Marion Shoard's book, *The Theft of the Countryside*, published in 1980, reflected both her skills as a polemicist (Shoard 1980) and the crossing of a threshold in public perception of the large-scale changes caused by modern farming practices.

Public awareness had been raised by both the passage of the Wildlife and Countryside Bill and the controversy as to whether it was working. The NCC had, at long last, begun to publish quantitative data that covered the whole country. A summary outline, under the title, *Nature Conservation in Great Britain*, described how agricultural intensification had damaged or destroyed the wildlife interest of 97 per cent of lowland neutral grasslands since the war. Some 80 per cent of the sheepwalks of chalk and Jurassic limestone country had been significantly damaged, largely by conversion to arable or improved grassland. Half of the lowland fens, valleys, and basin mires had been lost or damaged through drainage operations, reclamation for agriculture and chemical enrichment of drainage water. Afforestation, new reservoirs, reclamation of abandoned mineral workings, and establishment of amenity woodlands had done little to compensate for such catastrophic losses of existing habitat (Nature Conservancy Council, 1984).

Less than three years after its enactment, the Wildlife and Countryside Act was scrutinised by the Commons' Environment Committee. It considered 120 written submissions, held seven evidence sessions, and made a visit to the Swale SSSI in the Isle of Sheppey. Apart from its report of January 1985, the inquiry was highly significant for the evidence given by William Waldegrave, on behalf of the Department of the Environment (Parliamentary Papers, 1984–85). The Government's response to the Committee's findings, published as a White Paper in the names of the Secretary of State for the Environment, the Secretary of State for Wales, and the Minister of Agriculture, welcomed its firm support of the Government's conscious attempt to strike a balance between the various user interests through 'a process of voluntary co-operation, backed by the selective use of more rigorous measures' (Secretaries of State for the Environment, Wales et al. 1985).

Among witnesses before the Environment Committee, only Friends of the Earth (FoE) continued to press for the extension of town and country planning to cover major farming operations. FoE argued that such planning constraints were not only the most effective means of protecting the countryside, but they would be cheaper than reliance on management agreements. They would give people a voice in decisions on their local environment. Whilst not discounting some role, Waldegrave spoke in his evidence of being absolutely sure that

> the wholesale detailed management of the countryside as if it were the built environment, through the planning system, would be both impracticable and probably, in the end, disastrous.

Whereas it was both possible and legitimate to use such powers to stop a speculator from pulling down a fine Georgian house, a quite different principle would be involved in preventing a farmer from responding to market forces in the course of his business. The NCC's estimate of 'a top figure of £15 million' for management agreements indicated it would be 'quite an expensive policy', but not impossibly so compared with 'some of the other resource-allocation questions facing Government'. The Environment Committee agreed that far more could be achieved by

> the farming community being convinced by and willingly espousing the conserva-
> tion cause rather than by their being placed in a position of looking for ways of cir-
> cumventing resented restrictions and bureaucratic red-tape.

The Act had preserved a necessary degree of flexibility. Instead of imposing perma-nent statutory controls, it had allowed for temporary restrictions while management agreements were negotiated. Ultimately, however, if the farmer was determined to develop the land regardless of the damage caused and level of compensation offered, it was the essence of the voluntary approach that he should be free to do so. It was the only way 'to develop good will towards conservation in the farming community and a stable system of consent and common purpose in the long term'.

The Environment Committee believed its task was not to repair failure, but to capi-talise on the opportunities arising from the Act. Even where such bodies as the CPRE remained sceptical as to whether a voluntary approach would suffice, there was almost universal acknowledgement of 'a climate of change in the farming world'. The Environment Committee was greatly impressed by the remark of the Chairman of the Countryside Commission, Sir Derek Barber, that 'once you get farmers hooked on con-servation there is a tendency for them to be hooked for life'. According to ADAS, many were already pursuing practical measures, quite often at no cost to the public purse.

The Environment Committee believed that the Department of the Environment (DOE) had been right to concentrate on protecting the heartlands, the 'core landscape which has historic, or habitat or wildlife interest'. It would have been completely wrong to have attempted to extend the powers of the Act so as to manage the whole country-side with the sort of detail followed in the national parks. Besides being a waste of resources, William Waldegrave had claimed in his evidence that 'the engine of destruc-tion' could be turned off much more effectively by achieving a better balance of agri-cultural and other land-use incentives. There was need to 'go a little further back into the grant-giving structure'. As the Committee observed, the 'novel and generous basis for financial compensation' could not conceal 'the character defect' of management agree-ments. Negotiations arose from a farmer threatening a Site, and the NCC's response by way of 'imposing restrictions' and identifying potentially damaging operations. Success depended on agreeing the sum required to cover the income otherwise obtained from land improvement, including that generated by capital grants and price-support mechanisms. It would otherwise be very unfair, as Waldegrave acknowledged, 'to put the particular farmer who happens to be in a conservation area at a disadvantage because of that reason', when compared with an adjacent farmer free of such constraint and there-fore eligible for grant aid.

To the Environment Committee, the onus was on the Ministry of Agriculture to find better ways of accommodating conservation objectives. There was an obvious need for food. The Ministry was not 'a nature-devouring monster', but there was an illogicality in its offering financial inducements for something which another part of Government (the DOE and related bodies) had then to pay to prevent happening. 'The whole jigsaw' would fall into place if such grant aid was redirected towards conservation objectives. Management agreements would become promotional, rather than simply preventative, mechanisms. Rather than being compensated for doing nothing, farmers would be further encouraged to embark on positive conservation.

Whereas every party, including the CLA and NFU, recognised the need for 'a serious change in direction', the Committee accused the Ministry's policymakers of dragging their feet when they should have been leading. In his evidence to the Committee, the Parliamentary Under-Secretary for the Ministry of Agriculture, Lord Belstead, emphasised that the needs of conservation had been accommodated, wherever possible, in the promotion of an efficient agricultural industry. The Ministry had established an Environmental Co-ordinating Unit in July 1984. It supported the Farming and Wildlife Advisory Group. Whilst acknowledging the requirement placed on ADAS to develop an even closer relationship with conservation, Lord Belstead also emphasised the paramount importance of ADAS officers retaining the confidence of individual farmers.

In the conclusion to its report, the Environment Committee described the 1981 Act as being universally regarded as 'a major step in protecting environmentally sensitive areas of the countryside'. There were, however, still anxieties as to the adequacies of the voluntary approach. As at Halvergate, there continued to be 'disturbing crises'. But even when further adjustments had been made to the legislative and administrative aspects, the Committee warned that the wider agricultural structure would continue to fuel what Waldegrave had famously referred to as the 'engine of destruction'. Responsibility for the consequences of that structure rested not with farmers, but with Government. The DOE had played its part, but unfortunately the same could not be said of the Ministry. Its stock answer was to say that the Ministry had no powers to pay grants wholly for conservation purposes. The Committee asked, why not? The Crown was one and indivisible. Without fundamental change, conservation would 'continue to be set in weak opposition to the forces of intensive and paradoxically, frequently unwanted, production', rather than as an integral part of good husbandry. In the Committee's words, 'The Ministry must reappraise its attitudes.'

THE AGRICULTURE ACT 1986

The Wildlife and Countryside Act had done little to allay conflict between the competing interests of the countryside. The present Section looks more closely at the stance of both the NCC and Agriculture Departments in seeking a more positive outcome.

Insight into the respective positions of those within the environmental sector is provided by the record of a second visit paid by Michael Heseltine to the NCC Council in November 1981, a month after the enactment of the Wildlife and Countryside Bill. Ostensibly, it was an opportunity for the Chairman, Sir Ralph Verney, to congratulate him on the measure. Put bluntly, the NCC had been on the way out and the Act had given it hope, at least in terms of developing a new partnership with landowners, farmers, foresters and the organisations that represented them. The visit was also an opportunity to raise the awareness of the Secretary of State as to the need for substantially more resources. As Verney reminded him, both the CLA and NFU had hammered home the point that there had to be sufficient staff to ensure the increased personal contact upon which the SSSI provisions depended. There must be firm assurance of funding for the mandatory management agreements where agricultural or forestry grants were refused on nature-conservation grounds.

Although the Act appeared to have brought the various parties together, at least in their demand for more resources for rural protection, the Secretary of State left none in doubt as to his hostility to the notion of more Exchequer monies being made available. Indeed, positions could not have been further apart. The NCC's priority was to take full advantage of the re-notification of some 4,000 SSSIs covering 1.3 million hectares (3.2 million acres), owned and managed by perhaps as many as 30,000 people. It was an obvious opportunity to retrieve a situation where some 14 per cent of posts had to be left unfilled. The ratio of regional staff was as low as one to 691,000 acres (an area the size of Gloucestershire). Although much might be achieved by taking on temporary staff and contract labour, Verney emphasised that the longer-term reciprocal arrangements for notification would require a 7 per cent increase in staff over three years. Heseltine protested that such demands contradicted the NCC's overriding priority to make internal economies and seek greater commercial sponsorship. If the NCC reduced its staff from the current level of 530 to 200 it would be able to make considerably more effective use of the remainder of its budget. Council members retorted that, whilst the NCC had received a grant of £15,000 from Shell UK for publicising the new Act, companies generally supported only those projects with public appeal. Only central Government could finance the hard core of scientific and professional work.

The Secretary of State demanded a reduction not only of expenditure, but executive action of any kind. The Council's powers to enter into management agreements were discretionary. 'A low key approach' should be adopted until it became clearer whether the present budget was adequate for the new legislation. Any intimation that the Government would provide additional resources for site conservation would only result in the NCC being regarded as 'a soft touch'. The figures for habitat losses were in any case exaggerated. Few SSSIs were under any kind of threat. Although 'prairie farming' as pursued by the large City institutions with the help of grant aid posed a threat, it was for the NCC to take the issue of SSSIs up with them.

Turning to the other demands made by the Act, Council members emphasised that the number of species requiring statutory protection, excluding birds, had risen from 29 to well over a hundred. The establishment of marine reserves and the drafting of associated bye-laws were entirely new responsibilities. A comprehensive survey of the marine resource should be mounted, along lines similar to those of the *Nature Conservation Review* and the ongoing Geological *Conservation Review*. Heseltine insisted that parliament had envisaged only a few marine reserves. Not only was their choice self-evident, but there would be little opposition to those designations. The NCC would have to wait until opposition to the more controversial areas had subsided, before proceeding further. It should not undertake even modest surveys until it was proven that universities and voluntary bodies could not undertake them. Council members protested that it was impossible to draw up any kind of strategy without comprehensive, up-to-date information.

From the chair, Verney readily agreed that nature conservation was a shared responsibility, and that Britain was fortunate in having the strongest and most effective voluntary nature-conservation bodies in the world. Although willing to enter into a positive, cooperative relationship, such voluntary bodies were not prepared to accept responsibilities imposed by statute on the NCC. Far from helping the Government to make savings in that direction, they expected the NCC to be sufficiently viable and effective to provide the leadership required in developing their voluntary effort, most obviously through pump-priming in the form of grant aid. For every pound the NCC could offer, the voluntary bodies were able, and willing, to find two or more. Heseltine's response was to warn the NCC against harnessing itself too closely with the voluntary sector. Some organisations had a high political profile and could readily alienate landowners. The priority for the NCC should be to seek the advice and help of the CLA and the NFU in establishing a good working relationship with the farming community.

There was a very different atmosphere, exactly two years later in November 1983, at celebrations to mark the NCC's tenth anniversary. William Waldegrave spoke of the dramatic widening and deepening of interest in nature conservation during those ten years, amid growing awareness of the grave threats facing Britain's wildlife. The NCC had pursued its statutory duty to advise Government 'with great commitment and vigour under a succession of distinguished Chairmen' (Nature Conservancy Council 1984, 1). Sir William Wilkinson had become Chairman in the previous May. His distinguished business career had always been marked by a fascination with natural history, archaeology and much else. His disciplined, yet optimistic, hand as Honorary Treasurer had been crucial in the development of the RSPB through a period when both its membership and reserves holdings had considerably increased. His approach was encapsulated by an interview, given shortly after announcement of his appointment. In his view, it was not for the NCC to compromise, nor to act as a broker between farming and conservation. However much one might sympathise with the farming community and the financial pressures it laboured under, the job of the NCC was to protect SSSIs. Although the appointment as Chairman was part-time, Sir William Wilkinson resigned his directorship of the Merchant Bank, Kleinwort Benson, in order to give more time to it (Potts 1996).

A greater rapport began to develop within the conservation sector. Sir William Wilkinson later recalled the good relationships with the successive Secretaries of State for the Environment, Patrick Jenkin and Kenneth Baker. It had been largely through the personal efforts of William Waldegrave that Britain's first Marine Nature Reserve had been declared around Lundy Island in November 1986. Amending legislation came into effect in August 1985, which closed loopholes in the Wildlife and Countryside Act that had allowed an SSSI to be damaged or destroyed during the period of notice and formal notification, without fear of penalty. Twenty-one Sites were affected before the oversight was removed by a Private Member's Bill, which received Government assistance. The Act also met the wishes of the Commons' Environment Committee by extending the duties of the Forestry Commission, under the Forestry Act 1967, so as to require a reasonable balance to be struck between its primary duties and conservation.

The response of the White Paper to the report of the Commons' Environment Committee had essentially been a holding-statement. The further conflict over such areas as the Somerset Levels and Norfolk Broads had placed even greater pressure on the Government to provide material support for conservation. More fundamentally, there was need, in an institutional sense, to remove the deep divisions so clearly evident. The stresses were revealed not only in the unusually direct responses made by William Waldegrave, but in the frustration shown by landowning and farming interests. Exposed to the criticisms of environmentalists perhaps more than any other interest groups, the CLA and the NFU had both responded to, and actively pursued, opportunities to enter into public discussion with conservation groups. It was the only way of demonstrating what could be achieved through voluntary cooperation and the goodwill of farmers (Cox et al. 1986, 193).

Evidence of growing self-confidence on the conservation side had to be seen in the context of changing perceptions of the agricultural sector. As Potter (1998) wrote, it was more than a question of mild concern turning to public anger over what was happening to the countryside. It was the speed with which criticisms that had formerly been directed at individual landowners and farmers were increasingly aimed at farm policies and the institutions of Government itself. Time was not on the side of Government. Even the White Paper of 1985 was concerned lest there should be a return to polarised positions, just as 'a new consensus' seemed to be emerging among 'responsible environmentalists and farmers'. Waldegrave spoke of how, rather than simply blaming the industry for the damage caused by farm modernisation, the priority was to decide fresh policies. In his words, 'What I think we are now saying is that the process has gone far enough, perhaps a bit too far.' There was need for another policy alongside, and to some extent superseding, the policy for ever-increasing agricultural output.

Tactically, too, the Government was under pressure. Although it had successfully used the spirit of 'voluntarism' to fend off the imposition of statutory planning over agricultural operations, the greater involvement of ADAS meant that the conservation movement now had even more reason to concern itself with the instruments of agricultural policy. Conservationists were accordingly quick to intervene in the debates on the Agriculture Bill of 1986, which proposed the introduction of a charging policy for advice given by ADAS staff to farmers. The NCC protested that this would destroy the liaison which officers were just beginning to develop between the industry and conservation movement. Ministers agreed that an exception to the charging policy should be made, where advice was given on the conservation of natural beauty and wildlife, and 'any other agricultural activity or other enterprise or benefit to the rural economy' (PD, Commons, 87, 614–23). In effect, Agriculture Ministers were empowered for the first time to use public monies for a range of non-agricultural activities in any part of the countryside (Howarth and Rodgers, 1992).

Such raised political consciousness might appear to be 'a triumph for the steady attrition by the environmental lobby'. Perhaps politicians had begun to notice that the membership of the several dozen bodies that comprised the conservation movement had more

An illustration of the strained relations at the **Westhay Moor SSSI** in Somerset in March 1989, in the form of a notice to the NCC and STNC (Somerset Trust for Nature Conservation).

than doubled in the 1980s to over 3 million (Whitby and Lowe 1994, 6). Here was perhaps the kind of reward to be expected, when the conservation movement shook off 'the political instincts of a hedgehog', which 'was prickly but prone to curl up in front of lorries' (Purseglove 1989, 223–4). But whilst conservationists might feel emboldened, the dominance of the agricultural industry over rural affairs also appeared to be weakening. As the food surpluses achieved under the European Common Agricultural Policy (CAP) grew ever larger, the policy of supporting the primacy of food production through public subsidies was perceived as an even more legitimate target for challenge, not only from conservationists but economists (Whitby 1996).

The Commons' Environment Committee was not alone in pressing Agriculture Ministers to exert their negotiating strength in Brussels. An earlier Lords' Committee on the European Community had accused the Ministry of being altogether too negative in its approach to the drafting of a revised Regulation for improving farm structures. The draft was still 'too closely production-orientated, despite its gestures in other directions' (Parliamentary Papers 1983–84). In replying to the Committee's criticisms, Lord Belstead insisted that the Government could not act in isolation from the rest of Europe. He nevertheless undertook to press for powers that would 'enable us in environmentally sensitive areas to encourage farming practices which are consonant with conservation' (PD, Lords, 455, 88–93).

A senior official later wrote of the look of incredulity as he and the Minister, Michael Jopling, explained to their counterparts in Brussels the concept of making payments to farmers to farm below the maximum (Smith 1989). Explanations of the experiment under way in the Halvergate Marshes were typically met with incomprehension and apathy. Member States and the Commission asserted that it would be legally impossible to accommodate conservation requirements within the amended regulations covering agricultural structures. The perseverance of Ministers and their officials nevertheless paid off. Much of the UK draft text became the basis of Article 19 of EC Regulation 979/85, which permitted Member States to make payments to farmers for the provision of 'public goods'. Regulation 1760/87 allowed an element of EC funding.

Amid all the chaos that followed what Gilg (1992) described as the 'incremental knee-jerk responses' to the plight of the CAP, the Agriculture Act 1986 represented, in his words, 'a laudable attempt to impose some order'. The symbolic importance of the National Parks and Access to the Countryside Act 1949 had far outweighed the individual powers actually awarded in helping to establish a third force in the countryside. The Agriculture Act 1986 similarly came to assume a powerful symbolic importance. Despite the enhanced role assumed by Agriculture Ministers under the Wildlife and Countryside Act 1981, their outlook hardly appeared to have changed since the Countryside Commission complained, in its *Annual Report* of 1979, that

> over the years we have regularly had cause to regret a lack of regard for conservation and recreation in Ministry policy and practice: we have tended to make more progress dealing with the private farming and landowning organisations directly (Countryside Commission 1980).

Despite opposing such a clause under the Wildlife and Countryside Act and its Amending Act of 1985, Agriculture Ministers accepted only a year later in the Agriculture Bill a statutory duty 'to achieve a reasonable balance between the promotion and maintenance of a stable and efficient agricultural industry', the economic and social interests of rural areas, conservation and enhancement of amenity, wildlife and historic interest, and promotion of the public enjoyment of the countryside.

As Baldock and Lowe (1996) wrote, the commitment to environmental concerns stemmed not so much from a newly-found deep conviction for conservation, but rather from recognition that a major shift in agricultural strategy was called for. An 'inward-looking and defensive' stance would no longer guarantee the self-preservation of the Agriculture Departments and the farming community. It might have stood them in good stead over many years by protecting their autonomy in administering agricultural policy and allowing farmers and rural landowners to decide for themselves how to use agricultural land. But something more was required to withstand the critical comment of the 1980s and the Thatcherite pressures to commercialise, privatise and reduce the Departments' advisory and grant-giving role. If the Agriculture Act of 1947 marked the apotheosis of corporate planning, that of 1986 reflected Government determination to advance the pace of deregulation. The growing political clamour for environmental improvement offered the best chance of retaining a role for the Department. Having identified the opportunity, no time was lost in adopting a considerably more positive and promotional stance.

It was not so much a case of surrendering autonomy as one of giving further statutory recognition of the support required by farmers to accomplish what they themselves chose to do by way of conservation. Where existing designations for countryside protection were the responsibility of the environment sector of Government, the

Agriculture Act empowered Agriculture Ministers, with the consent of the Treasury, to identify and administer the Environmentally Sensitive Areas (ESAs). Whereas existing designations drew distinctions between the amenity, recreational, wildlife and historic value of features in the countryside, ESAs treated them together as a unified whole, under the all-encompassing concept of 'national environmental significance'. Each ESA was to represent a discrete and coherent unit of environmental interest. The Minister was empowered to make voluntary agreements, specifying management practices and rates of payment in fulfilment of those prescriptions.

Fears that it might be little more than tokenism seemed to be refuted when first half, and then the full twelve, ESAs shortlisted by the conservation agencies in England and Wales were designated in 1987, with first two and then three further Areas in Scotland. They became the first and largest agri-environmental scheme in the UK. They were a role model for other schemes based on a contract entered into voluntarily, with flat-rate payments in return for compliance with management prescriptions and guidelines, and regular payment reviews. Whatever their precise form, they enabled farmers to secure revenue from an alternative 'crop' whilst doing 'their bit for the environment' (Clark 1997).

And yet, however bold the precedents set, Agriculture Ministers could represent them to the industry as simply a further example of the incrementalism that had distinguished the relationship of Government with the industry since the war. Rather than negotiating compensation for forgone profit under management agreements with the Department of the Environment, as required by the 1981 Act, the ESA scheme followed the considerably more familiar course of entirely voluntary agreements, based on predetermined levels of payment and administered by ADAS officers. Although it meant a further class of desig-nated areas, Baldock et al. (1990, 156–7) wrote that this was a small price for Agriculture Ministers and the industry to pay for regaining the initiative in the continuing debate over the future management of the countryside. From what had begun as a fundamental attack on the agricultural-policy community, Whitby and Lowe (1994, 20) went so far as to assert that conservation pressure groups had not only been repulsed, but defeated. They had again been marginalised in the wider management of the countryside.

FORESTRY AND THE SCOTTISH DIMENSION

One commentator wrote that it was possible to discern, from his seven *Annual Reports*, Sir William Wilkinson's initial optimism turning first to frustration, and then disap-pointment. Ironically, the European Year of the Environment of 1987–88 was seen as a turning point. Following the General Election William Waldegrave moved to another part of Government. At official level, the departure of Martin Holdgate for the post of Director-General of the International Union for Nature Conservation (IUCN) was a grievous blow. As Chief Scientist at the Department of Environment, he had been a well-informed and much respected ally of conservation. The pattern of appointing Directors from the relevant disciplines of the NCC was broken in 1985, when John

Morton Boyd retired and it was announced that John Francis was to be seconded from the Scottish Office as the new Director of the NCC in Scotland. His background was in nuclear physics, the development of the Scottish oil industry, and policy making on health, housing and transport matters. Timothy R. Hornsby succeeded Richard Steele as Director-General of the NCC itself in July 1988. An Under-Secretary, he had previously been Director of Rural Affairs in the Department of the Environment.

If the three cardinal points of establishment of the Nature Conservancy had been the integral role of management and research, the reserve series, and its being a UK body, the first had been lost with the 'Split' in 1973 and the other two appeared to be increasingly threatened. Council took the opportunity of a meeting with the Secretary of State, Nicholas Ridley, in February 1988 to inform him of a review that was being made of existing reserves and how a further 60 sites might be given better protection. Ridley pressed for the review to be extended to investigate whether the management, and indeed ownership, of some of the existing reserves might be transferred to private owners. In August, he wrote that no further reserves should be declared until future policy was agreed with Government. Such designations might otherwise have to be reversed, if it was decided that fewer reserves were needed in 'the changed climate of the 1990s'. Rather than rushing forth in protest at the 'imbalance' caused by such an arbitrary freeze, the NCC believed the more prudent course was one of waiting, so as to ensure that any battles fought were on a ground, and at a time, of the Council's choosing.

As Sir William Wilkinson remarked, in presenting the NCC's last *Annual Report* in November 1990, it was the Wildlife and Countryside Act that had determined the role – and indeed the fate – of the NCC. The task of renotification had been completed and more than 2,000 management agreements negotiated, but the status of an SSSI still did not convey absolute protection. As he emphasised, the Act only offered a framework for consultation. It was flawed in the sense that it created an essentially adversarial relationship where, even if there was goodwill on both sides, two years or more might be required to reach an agreement. Worse still, much of the frustration and acrimony associated with the Act and farming was also experienced in respect to forestry. 'The uncontrolled expansion of afforestation' had become the 'single largest area of concern.'

Having played a significant part in raising public awareness of the consequences of modern farming and begun to achieve some success in improving the conservation prospects for existing broadleaf woodlands, the NCC turned an increasing proportion of its attention in the 1980s to forestry, particularly in the uplands. As a policy document of June 1986, entitled *Nature conservation and forestry in Britain*, observed, much had been written over the previous ten years about the need for further afforestation, but there had been no adequate statement as to its bearing on nature conservation (Nature Conservancy Council 1986).

Timber was the only principal crop not in surplus. Although productive woodlands (including half in private ownership) now covered 2 million hectares, or nearly 10 per cent of the UK space, they still met only 12 per cent of domestic needs. The main aim of Government forestry policy was to encourage further expansion of commercial softwood planting, principally through the Forestry Grant scheme introduced in October 1981 and (for amenity species) by a Broadleaved Woodland Grant scheme of October

1985. The scale of Exchequer support, together with rapidly developing technologies for establishing plantations in hitherto inhospitable terrain, made afforestation in the uplands an increasingly attractive financial investment.

The scope for damage to wildlife had been highlighted by proposals for one of the wildest and most remote parts of upland Wales, the Berwyn Mountains (Lowe et al. 1986, 209–29). Following the completion of an extensive survey by the RSPB in September 1977, the Welsh office of the NCC agreed that nine areas were 'vital if viable populations of upland birds are to be maintained in upland Wales', and therefore worthy of being scheduled as SSSIs. But, as the NCC *Annual Report* observed, 'the problems of notifying this amount of land would be quite considerable' (Nature Conservancy Council 1979, 63). It therefore commissioned, in consultation with the Welsh Office Agricultural Department and the Forestry Commission, a study by the former Chief Surveyor for ADAS, R.G.A. Lofthouse, who was already acting as a part-time specialist adviser to the NCC on agriculture (Nature Conservancy Council 1980, 20). His report of November 1979 identified three broad zones where afforestation, agricultural improvement or nature conservation should be given priority. The baseline data and what Lofthouse called guidelines (not recommendations) were welcomed by the Under-Secretary of State for Wales, in a debate on the report in June 1980. It represented 'a most valuable fresh approach'. With goodwill from all sides, it could be turned into 'an exciting new strategy model'.

Far from such a strategy emerging, there was even greater evidence of what Lofthouse described as the unequal relationship between the three parties. The Economic Forestry Group announced, in early 1979, that it intended to acquire and afforest the Llanbrynmair Moors, which was one of the areas identified by the RSPB for its wildlife value. The NCC first opposed and then withdrew its objection to afforestation. Not only did it lack the resources to purchase, but the Moors were not included in Lofthouse's large area zoned for nature conservation. To the RSPB, such vacillation was a further instance of

The Berwyn Mountains, Clwyd, in September 1981, showing a mixture of blanket bog (top left), improved pasture (top right) and conifer plantation (top centre).

the vigour and determination with which forestry interests pursue their objectives and the relative weakness and uncertainty of the NCC attempts to defend important ornithological sites (Prestt 1980).

A later NCC *Annual Report* described how 'a long-term management programme for integrated land-use' was being developed with owners in the Berwyn Mountains (Nature Conservancy Council 1982, 26–7). But perhaps the most important lesson for the conservation movement was the need to secure and retain the initiative. Whatever the ultimate outcome, it was a sign of weakness to be always responding to the demands and criticisms made by others.

Consciously drawing on such lessons, Sir William Wilkinson launched, at a press conference in July 1987, a tightly-written report entitled *Birds, Bogs and Forestry. The peatlands of Caithness and Sutherland* (Ratcliffe and Oswald 1987). His purpose was not to attack forestry 'properly located and carried out', but rather to draw media, and therefore public, attention to the risk posed by afforestation to 'a unique national asset', namely the peatlands of Caithness and Sutherland (Wilkinson 1987). This actively-growing blanket bog was the largest in the world. There was no larger primeval ecosystem in the UK. The pools and surface patterning (the 'flows') supported a specialised range of mosses and vascular plants. They accommodated some 66 per cent of the breeding populations of greenshank, 35 per cent of dunlin, and 17 per cent of golden plover in the European Community. Afforestation already affected some 15 per cent of the Flow Country, which once covered some 401,000 hectares. Only eight of the 41 hydrological systems remained free of some form of planting. Most of the planting had occurred since the 1981 Act. If continued, it would represent 'the most massive loss of important wildlife habitat in Britain since the second world war'.

The NCC called upon the Government to declare a moratorium on further planting, so as to give all the relevant parties time to identify the solutions most appropriate for local people and the protection of 'this unique piece of our national and indeed the world's heritage'. Whilst forestry was held out as a valuable source of employment, so too were the traditional occupations of crofting and outdoor sporting activities. Not only had they played a key part in protecting the Flow Country area but they too were threatened by such large-scale afforestation. Since it was the total extent, continuity and diversity that made the Flow Country so unique, the NCC rejected the normally 'balanced' and sensible solutions of designating NNRs and scheduling SSSIs. The only feasible course was to declare a Heritage Area, where further planting would be stopped and active support given to the development of more traditional activities.

An alleged reluctance on the part of the Scottish headquarters of the NCC to host the launch of the report at the suggested venue of Inverness meant it was held in London. This made it even easier for the Scottish press to present it as an attempt by an English QUANGO to ban forestry and thereby destroy the hopes of a further 2,000 jobs in Scotland. It was not so much the venue that so outraged the Highland Regional Council. Nor indeed was it Wilkinson's dismissal of the usual forms of compromise by his assertion that 'there are occasions when "absolutes" must prevail'. It was the realisation that, this time, roles were reversed. Through careful preparation and media manipulation, it was the NCC that had seized the high ground. Wilkinson (1987) spoke at the press conference of how those who had blown up the Parthenon were rightly reviled. Now, 'the masterpieces of God and nature' had similarly to be cherished, whether in the tropical rainforests or in Britain. It might be claimed that much damage had been wrought before there was relevant legislation or a conservation movement. A further excuse was that large-scale afforestation in the Flow Country continued to be legal. Wilkinson claimed, however, that with the publication of the findings of the RSPB and NCC surveys, 'the picture and the issues were clear'. No longer could anyone plead ignorance. Any further losses would be deliberate.

Critics challenged the scientific validity of *Birds, Bogs and Forestry*. The Highland Regional Council convened a working party to examine land-use options. The NCC published a more substantive account of its Peatland Survey of Northern Scotland in March 1988 (Ratcliffe and Oswald 1988). Although it substantially confirmed the warnings in the earlier report, the Secretary of State had already rejected calls for a moratorium on further afforestation. Instead, the compromise was adopted of agreeing that there was a case for protecting half the peatland area. The NCC was invited to proceed with scheduling that half as an SSSI. This much of the Flow Country was 'saved', but the effect on the NCC had been mortal.

As Chairman, Sir William Wilkinson expressed his concern at the charge that the NCC appeared arrogant in its attitude towards the regions (Potts 1996). Although the Treasury Solicitor advised that the Council's powers to delegate the greater part of its responsibilities for Scotland and Wales were severely circumscribed, Council had continued to explore that end. Indeed, plans were about to be presented to the Secretary of State when Nicholas Ridley himself announced, in July 1989, the most fundamental restructuring of the conservation movement since the 1949 Act. The current 'organisational arrangements' had proved both 'inefficient and insensitive' to the needs of the different parts of the UK. The solution was to 'split' the NCC into separate bodies for England Scotland and Wales (PD, Commons, 156, 484–5).

The announcement gave rise to immense speculation as to the factors that had caused it. Mackay (1995, 103–5) believed that the root cause was Ridley's alarm at the anticipated costs of management agreements for the Flow Country. It had prompted him to suggest, in the autumn of 1987, that Scotland might be hived off. Scotland should shoulder its own costs. The Scottish Secretary, Malcolm Rifkin, was also aware of the political advantages of having full responsibility for nature conservation. In January 1988, the Scottish Development Department had submitted a paper to Scottish Ministers, outlining how the Scottish part of the NCC might be detached and merged with the Countryside Commission for Scotland. Not only did the Welsh Secretary, Peter Walker, press to follow suit, but the small size of the Welsh component of the NCC made it even more expedient that it should be combined with the Welsh office of the Countryside Commission. The prospect of a unified country agency for Wales made the case for Scotland even more persuasive. Demanding to be brought into the discussions, Wilkinson was informed in June 1989 of the proposed split. An appeal to the Prime Minister was to no avail, and the announcement was made in a written answer to an arranged Parliamentary Question (Reynolds and Sheate 1992).

The decision to merge both the Scottish and Welsh agencies had the effect of blunting opposition to the break-up of the NCC. Whilst deep concern was expressed in all quarters as to whether such surgery was simply a device for reducing Government expenditure, none could voice the same root-and-branch opposition to closer integration

The last Chairman of the NCC, **Sir William Wilkinson.**

of countryside and nature conservation in Scotland and Wales. Indeed, Ridley incurred considerable unpopularity in some quarters for his steadfast refusal to instigate a similar merger in England, arguing that the administrative costs would be substantially greater. The Cabinet having reputedly examined the question three times, the proposals to establish what became English Nature, the Countryside Council for Wales, and Scottish Natural Heritage were enacted by the Environmental Protection Act and, shortly afterwards, the Natural Heritage (Scotland) Act of 1991.

Particular concern was expressed as to the void left at the Great-Britain level. The new Secretary of State for the Environment, Chris Patten, announced, on the day the Environmental Protection Bill was published, that a Joint Coordinating Committee would be appointed to give advice to the Government on nature-conservation issues with a UK or international dimension. It would seek to establish common standards for designation, research, monitoring and data analysis. It soon became clear that ministers were having the greatest difficulty in conferring powers on the Joint Committee without appearing to undermine autonomy of the three country agencies. It therefore suited Government that the House of Lords' Science and Technology Committee should instigate an inquiry into another cause of anxiety, namely what was perceived as a further weakening of the 'science' base. Given the NCC's difficulties in securing staff and funds for the Chief Scientist's Directorate, it seemed highly unlikely that the Treasury would find the resources three times over for the 'scientific' underpinning required by the individual agencies. In evidence to the Lords' Committee, the NERC was one of a number of bodies pressing for a UK-wide centre, which would formulate the strategic views of the three agencies for research, specialist support and databases. The proposed Joint Committee was the obvious vehicle for achieving that degree of coordination (Parliamentary Papers 1989–90)

The conservation and scientific communities generally welcomed the report of the Lords' Committee, in March 1990, and its 'positive and workable strategy' (within the constraints prescribed by Government). By establishing a Joint Nature Conservation Committee, with an explicitly scientific responsibility, the Government was able to concede the establishment of a more powerful body than previously conceived, and yet continue to uphold the administrative autonomy of the agencies. For critics in the wider countryside movement, it was a further example of the 'scientific' argument hijacking the debate. The welcome accorded to the Government's response to the Lords' Committee, published on the eve of the Second Reading of the Bill in the House of Lords in May 1990, had the political effect of deflecting attention from the Government's continued refusal to integrate the English agency with the Countryside Commission (for England). Merging the different interests in England, or on the joint committee, would have created a 'green' lobby powerful enough to upset the political balance which the Government had struggled hard to achieve with Scotland and Wales (Nature Conservancy Council 1989; PD, Commons, 212, 777–84).

CHAPTER TEN

THE HISTORICAL
PERSPECTIVE

The focus of the book has been deliberately inward-looking at the British record of official involvement in nature conservation. The Nature Conservancy owed its origins to a small number of naturalists and ecologists. It would be misleading to suggest that there was, at that time, a large and popular movement to protect the natural heritage. Nor was there any greater enthusiasm for conservation at the international level. Even the handful of pioneers promoting nature conservation in Britain urged restraint when it came to initiatives overseas. As Max Nicholson wrote in August 1948, from the perspective of the Lord President's Office, the priority was to set 'our own house in order in this country and the Colonies' (PRO, CAB 124, 1063).

The British hand was, however, forced by the Swiss and then the Americans. There was some forewarning of the impatience of the Swiss League for the Protection of Nature, during a tour of the Swiss National Park and nature reserves which Julian Huxley arranged for members of his Committee in June 1946 (Minister of Town and Country Planning 1947b, 8–9). Whilst impressed by what they saw, Nicholson (1970) recalled their surprise at finding themselves part of 'a miniature impromptu international conference'. Quite unprepared, they could do nothing but reserve the British position on the proposals put forward for a new international organisation. Not only did the League appear to be taking advantage of the straitened circumstances of the remainder of Europe, but even greater resentment was felt at its apparent disregard for the pre-war International Office for the Protection of Nature in Brussels. Although a conference at Brunnen went ahead, pressure from the relevant British voluntary bodies led the British embassy to make overtures that persuaded the Swiss government to withhold official recognition. Twenty-four countries were represented. With much difficulty, the British delegation managed to limit discussion to 'constructive preparatory work', on the understanding that a further conference would be held within a year (PRO, CAB 124, 1062).

Whilst Julian Huxley, in his capacity as Director-General of UNESCO, took up the challenge enthusiastically, organising with the French government a conference at Fontainebleau for the autumn of 1948, the British position remained defensive. The grandiose ideas of the Swiss League showed little heed of the dangers of establishing inter-governmental bodies in a rapidly worsening 'Cold War' climate. As Europe took its first faltering steps towards post-war recovery, any initiative had to be confined to those few urgent issues which depended on collaboration at the international level. Such instances might include cross-boundary interests, the High Seas, and Antarctica. In a brief to representatives of the British voluntary bodies at the Fontainebleau meeting, Nicholson wrote that the immediate priority was to 'get our own organisation into shape and not dissipate our efforts in too many directions'. It was only through developing the expertise and experience, as exemplified by the deliberations of the Huxley Committee, that Britain would be able to make a worthwhile and distinctive contribution to international discussions. Where some delegations continued to place excessive reliance on legal enactments, the insights gained from preparing the Huxley Committee's report emphasised the overriding importance of education and public information (PRO, CAB 124, 1063).

The relatively large delegation from Britain, led by H.G. Maurice of the Zoological Society of London, played a key part in securing the establishment of the International Union for the Preservation of Nature (IUPN). Through Nicholson's good offices, the Foreign Office had extensively re-drafted the constitution, which offered membership to both national and international bodies, both official and non-governmental. The Swiss nomination of Basle for the international office was rejected in favour of accommodation provided by the Belgian government in the Natural History Museum in Brussels, where considerable expertise and experience were readily available on such issues as marine conservation, bird protection and the pressing problems of wildlife preservation in Africa and other colonial territories. A British Coordinating Committee was established (PRO, CAB 124, 1064–5).

Where Nicholson pressed for a breathing space, 'the small and motley band of naturalists and professional biologists' continued to receive notice of meetings. Somewhat grudgingly, Britain was represented at most of them. Not only was there nothing else but, by the time of the Salzburg Assembly of October 1953, the IUPN was beginning to provide 'a useful channel for the exchange of technical information on a variety of problems' of real importance (PRO, FT 22, 2 and 8). Progress was sufficiently encouraging for Lord Hurcomb (a Vice-President) and Nicholson to raise the possibility of the Nature Conservancy and SPNR jointly organising a General Assembly and Technical Meeting in Edinburgh. John Berry developed such 'coat-hangers' as 'the rehabilitation of biologically devastated land', as a means of attracting participation from a range of bodies (PRO, CAB 124, 1599). The prospect of such a meeting provided obvious pretext for Nicholson to advocate that, after eight years of probation, the IUPN had become sufficiently effective and useful for the Government to give it official recognition. Where Lord Salisbury, as Lord President of the Council, was 'not much impressed by the claims of this body', Sir Edward Playfair at the Treasury acknowledged the value of having the Conservancy, the British Museum (Natural History) and a wide variety of non-governmental bodies taking part in the Union's affairs. A Government subscription of £1,200 per annum was trivial. The Chancellor of the Exchequer, Peter Thorneycroft, nevertheless ruled that it would be too embarrassing for Britain to join IUPN officially, at a time when every effort was being made to reduce commitments to other inter-

Members of the IUCN Commission for Education, North-west Europe Section, with the Regional Officer, **Eric Duffey** (on the right), at the **Hickling Broad NNR, Norfolk,** in April 1961. The visit was made during a regional conference held at the Conservancy's headquarters in London. A final resolution called upon UNESCO to hold an enquiry into the place that conservation should occupy at all levels of education.

A less formal moment at the inaugural meeting of the World Wildlife Fund, held at the Royal Society of Arts in September 1961.
Left to right: **Peter Scott, Lord Hurcomb** (Chairman of the Nature Conservancy), **Sir Julian Huxley** and **Professor Jean G. Baer**, President of the World Wildlife Fund.

national organisations such as UNESCO. Compromise was found in the Nature Conservancy's making a larger contribution from its own budget (PRO, FT 22, 8–9).

As President of the Technical Meeting of IUCN, held in Edinburgh in June 1956, Nicholson emphasised that

> we are now getting through the period of propaganda, of sentiment and of generalisation, and we are getting down to hard problems (Nicholson 1956).

The Union was certainly acquiring stature, and taking on fresh challenges. At American insistence, it was renamed the International Union for the Conservation of Nature and Natural Resources (IUCN). Its headquarters were transferred from Brussels to Lausanne in Switzerland in 1961, so as to distance itself symbolically from its earlier colonial associations. Little would be accomplished without funds and publicity. A series of articles by Sir Julian Huxley in *The Observer* brought the dangers threatening African wildlife to public attention. With the encouragement of Peter Scott (who had succeeded Lord Hurcomb as a Vice-President) and Guy Mountfort, a leading international ornithologist and businessman, Max Nicholson drafted an outline scheme for an organisation that quickly became known as the World Wildlife Fund, with the giant panda as its symbol. The consent of Prince Philip to be its President, and Prince Bernhard of the Netherlands as its first Patron, ensured that the new organisation had worldwide contacts among key figures in international and national conservation (Nicholson 1970, 226–7).

The IUCN Assembly at Warsaw in July 1960 was remarkable for the presence of a large number of professional zoologists and wildlife managers who had either responsibility for, or exceptional knowledge of, managing large herbivores, which was the main theme of the meeting. Nicholson pressed Huxley, who was then touring Africa, to collect the names of politicians, administrators and other powerful figures in the newly-independent countries of Africa, especially those who were known to be sympathetic to conservation. Nicholson later wrote that, despite warnings from 'high authority' that it would be a waste of time, a Symposium on 'The Conservation of Nature and Natural Resources in Modern African States' was held at Arusha, in Tanganyika in September 1961. As well as the familiar band of international and expatriate conservationists, approximately 50 leading African scientists, game wardens and politicians attended (PRO, FT 22, 2–3).

A formal request from the Colonial Office in 1957 that the Nature Conservancy should provide information and assistance proved of mutual value, both in further developing, and in some cases establishing, careers that encompassed research overseas. Advice was immediately sought on the establishment of a research unit on wild fauna in Kenya, and on a proposal from the Tanganyikan government to reduce the area of the Serengeti National Park. William Pearsall undertook a survey of the Park ostensibly for the Fauna Preservation Society. Not only was Pearsall, as Chairman of the Scientific Policy Committee, able to keep the Conservancy fully informed of progress, but formal comment was made on drafts of the eventual White Paper, incorporating revised proposals aligned much more closely to ecological principles (Nature Conservancy 1957, 27).

Within Britain, staff became involved in an increasingly intricate web of international networks. According to the Conservancy's last *Annual Report*, Barton Worthington was a Vice-President of IUCN and therefore attended meetings of its Executive Board. The Director of the Merlewood Research Station, J.B. Cragg, was Vice-Chairman of its principal scientific advisory body, the Commission on Ecology. Norman Moore was Secretary of its committee concerned with the ecological effects of chemical controls (Nature Conservancy 1964). Such links provided opportunities to gain insight into overseas' experience and to draw attention to British achievement. The first European Conference on Wildfowl Conservation, held at St Andrews in October 1963, was an obvious occasion to publicise the Conservancy's newly-published monograph, *Wildfowl in Great Britain*, largely compiled from surveys undertaken by the Wildfowl Trust with grant aid from the Conservancy (Atkinson-Willes 1963).

For many of the Conservancy's scientists, their first experience of participation in international research was through the British component of the International Biological Programme (IBP), which began in 1964 as a world-wide study of biological productivity and human welfare. The Royal Society acted as the coordinating body in the United Kingdom. The Conservancy was well represented on its IBP Committees. Contributions were made to three of the Programme's Sections, the largest being to that covering the 'Productivity of terrestrial communities.' Major projects were undertaken: at Meathop Wood, near Merlewood, on decomposer processes; at Moor House on the productivity of upland peat moors; and at Snowdonia on the productivity of mountain grasslands. As its Scientific Director, Barton Worthington, wrote later, the ten-year Programme played a major part in causing ecology to emerge from a descriptive to an experimental and, indeed, predictive science (Worthington 1983, 160–77).

'THIS COMMON INHERITANCE'

If the positive and dynamic qualities of nature conservation helped naturalists and ecologists to catch the political imagination in the 1940s, another pair of ordinary words, sustainable development, came to signify the crossing of another threshold in the 1980s. Where Julian Huxley was generally credited with importing the usage of the word 'conservation' from North America, the concept of 'sustainable development' arose from a series of African-based conferences in the 1960s, in which the science of ecology again played a significant role (Riordan 1988).

The Eighth General Assembly of IUCN, held in Nairobi in 1963, was the first world conference of its size to be held in East Africa. Delegates recognised that the only chance wildlife had of competing with other forms of land use was through being regarded as a renewable resource. As a sustainable attraction for tourism it represented a valuable source of income. By the IUCN assembly of 1973, conservation was defined as

> the management of air, water, soil, minerals and living systems, including man, so as to achieve the highest sustainable quality of life.

The Assembly of 1978 further emphasised the importance of relating conservation issues to the wider socio-economic context. The most crucial stage in building confidence between governments and the environmental movement (as it now self-consciously called itself) came, however, with the publication of the *World Conservation Strategy*, in 1980, by the IUCN and World Wildlife Fund, under the aegis of the United Nations' Environment Programme (UNEP). Never before had the finite nature of the world's resources been so succinctly explained. On the one hand it demanded a new kind of stewardship, based on 'development without destruction'. On the other hand, it also gave notice that conservationists had abandoned some of their more unrealistic notions. By infusing ecological principles into economic development, the gulf between the anti-growth groups and advocates of development-at-all costs could be bridged. Sustainable utilisation had become the language of mediation.

Staff of the Nature Conservancy and the NCC were engaged in international liaison, both through attendance at meetings of representative bodies and in more personal initiatives overseas. **Norman Moore** (*left*), **Alfred Dunbarin Butcher** and **John L. George** represented the IUCN's Committee on the Ecological Effects of Chemical Controls, at the IUCN Technical Meeting in Delhi, India, in November 1969. Moore was the Secretary of the specialist Committee.

A UK response, *Conservation and Development Programme*, was published in the summer of 1983 by the Council for Environmental Conservation (CoEnCo), the Royal Society of Arts, and the World Wildlife Fund UK, together with the NCC and two Countryside Commissions (Johnson 1983). A Government response was called for. That came in a booklet, *Conservation and Development*, published by the Department of the Environment in May 1986. The Secretary of State, Kenneth Baker, wrote in a foreword that the *World Conservation Strategy* had challenged governments 'to involve the whole community in achieving economic growth based on sustaining our renewable resources'. The booklet was confident that such exacting standards for environmental protection could be met, where there was cooperation backed by a selective use of mandatory measures. Describing the Wildlife and Countryside Act as 'the lynch-pin of policies' in the UK, the book recounted that over 240 management agreements had been made, involving capital costs of £715,000 and annual payments of over £350,000. The NCC's grant-in-aid had been increased from £7.9 million in 1979–80 to £32.1 million in 1986–87 (Department of the Environment 1986).

The United Nations had appointed a World Commission on Environment and Development as an independent body in 1983, under the chairmanship of the Norwegian Prime Minister, Gro Harlem Brundtland. Its report of April 1987, *Our Common Future*, not only provided powerful advocacy of the concept of sustainable development, but demanded more rigorous definition as to how that goal might be met (World Commission on Environment and Development 1987). A further response from the UK Government, in July 1988, welcomed the report for the way it brought together and analysed for the first time in coherent fashion the strands of economic growth and conservation of natural resources (Department of the Environment 1988). The more immediately significant impact on British politics was the public declaration by the Prime Minister, Margaret Thatcher, that 'no generation has a freehold on the earth'. She continued, 'all we have is a life tenancy – with a full repairing lease'. Although spoken at her Party's annual conference in October 1988, when ministers traditionally escape the leash of their officials, the implications of that 'elegant metaphor' were tremendous. As Cairncross (1991) pointed out, only governments could ultimately set the terms of such a 'full repairing lease'.

The UN Conference on Environment and Development, held in Rio in June 1992, succeeded in taking the debate across a further threshold of political perception. It was attended by the leading statesmen of almost every country. The Earth Summit and signing of a Biodiversity Convention were treated with a seriousness previously reserved for Summit Conferences on disarmament and the plight of the world economy. As a topic where the UK claimed much expertise and experience, it was a chance to display leadership on the world stage. As an exemplar to others, the UK was among the first to publish, in January 1994, Action Plans for Biodiversity and Sustainable Development (Secretaries of State et al. 1994a and b). It was the first to publish, in December 1995, costed targets and action plans for an initial tranche of key habitats and threatened, or endangered, species (UK Biodiversity Steering Group 1995). In a foreword to the Government's response of May 1996, the Prime Minister re-emphasised the Government's commitment to remaining 'among the leading countries of the world in nature conservation and among the first to turn our international treaty commitments into positive action at home' (Secretary of State for the Environment et al. 1996).

The wider, global context gave further political point to the consciously holistic approach being adopted in the domestic governance of town and countryside. The names of the Secretary of State for the Environment, the Secretaries of State for Scotland and Wales, and the Minister of Agriculture (together with a further 7 ministers), appeared on the title page of 'Britain's first comprehensive White Paper on the Environment', *This Common Inheritance*, in 1990. It represented the most explicit acknowledgement by Government of the extent to which anxieties as to the use and management of the natural environment excited public concern. Although generally perceived as the brainchild of the new Environment Secretary, Chris Patten, the White Paper was prefaced by a letter from the Prime Minister, as if to emphasise over and above any notion of collective responsibility that all Government departments were expected to contribute actively to its implementation. As well as setting out a vision for the 1990s, the report made 350 commitments and proposals for action. There would be an environmental expert on relevant Government committees and bodies, each Department would develop an environmental housekeeping strategy (Secretaries of State et al. 1990).

The 'First year report' of 1991 was distinguished by being signed by a further four ministers, including that of the Chancellor of the Exchequer. There was a further letter from the Prime Minister, now John Major, as if to indicate there had been no tailing off in Government interest (Secretaries of State et al. 1991). By the third annual report, of May 1994, a foreword by the Environment Secretary, John Gummer, was sufficient. It emphasised that sustainable development must be the touchstone of Government policy (Secretaries of State et al. 1994c). His further foreword to the fourth report, of March 1995, spoke of sustainable development already raising 'our sights from the workbench to the world we hope to leave to our children and later generations' (Secretaries of State et al. 1995).

Given the acrimony over the Wildlife and Countryside Act, it was clear that little would be achieved by way of meeting urban, national and even international demands, without close cognisance of the aspirations and circumstances of those who actually lived and worked in the countryside. John Gummer announced, in October 1994, his intention to publish a White Paper focused explicitly on the English countryside. The press announcement described how, from his current and previous post as Minister of Agriculture, he had become convinced of the need for a more holistic view, both in terms of generating wealth and protecting the rural environment. Although an obvious way of demonstrating the Government's commitment to 'sustainable development', some commentators also discerned a more immediate political concern. A leader-writer in *Country Life* saw clear evidence of the Liberal Democrats usurping the Conservatives as the natural party of the countryside. Not only was it home to 12 million people, but the countryside itself was the focus of such powerful bodies as the National Trust and RSPB (Anon. 1994).

Whereas previous enquiries into the countryside had been undertaken by outside expert opinion, civil servants, or through publications of individual Government departments, the Environment Secretary intended to proceed straight to a policy statement. It was all the more reason why the Minister of Agriculture should want to join the exercise at its earliest point. A further precedent was established, whereby it was agreed that the two ministers would jointly present the White Paper to parliament. It was published with the title, *Rural England. A nation committed to a living countryside*, in October 1995 (Secretary of State for the Environment and Minister of Agriculture 1995). At the obligatory press conference, John Gummer emphasised the Government's determination 'not to allow the countryside to be turned into a museum'. The overall purpose of the White Paper was to help to identify ways in which rural England could remain 'a living working place', without harming the environment.

Although the White Paper was impressive for its comprehensive inventory of rural problems, there were none of the calls for strong executive action by which the virility of previous reviews had been judged. In making a virtue of rejecting new controls and regulations, it steered a careful course between the strident advocacy of environmental groups and the demands of the landowning and farming lobbies for a dramatic easing of planning controls as the key to enabling them to turn their land over to alternative economic uses. As the White Paper made clear, any expectation of assertive policies and large-scale expenditure was misplaced. The future health of rural England did not rest primarily in the hands of government, whether central or local, or their respective agencies. As in centuries past, the countryside continued to be the product of a myriad of human actions. Rural life had to be perceived through the eyes of those who lived in the countryside, rather than from some administrative viewpoint in Whitehall. Such a sense of diversity of interest was reinforced at a national scale by the appearance of a separate White Paper, *Rural Scotland*, in December 1995, and another for Wales in the following year, published by their respective Secretaries of State (Scottish Office 1995; Welsh Office 1996).

In words reminiscent of many previous reviews, the White Papers asserted that their purpose was to set the scene for wider debate. The question was no longer whether there was a place for nature conservation, or even for a third force besides farming and forestry, in the countryside. The economy, health, housing and education, or the environment were no longer to be looked at in isolation. Much more positively, the question was how to give prominence to each within a society 'where a decent quality of life' should be available to everyone in each part of the country. As the Deputy Prime Minister in the new Labour Government, John Prescott, emphasised in a consultation paper for a review of the UK Strategy for Sustainable Development, the needs of society should not be met at the expense of future generations. Scarce and valuable natural resources must be conserved (Department of the Environment, Transport and the Regions 1998). Where once the presumption would have been to pass such an agenda to a central authority, Government in the 1990s had set an example of humility by leaving it to rural interests and those dependent on them to decide what was best. Such consultation might occur through the Government Panel on Sustainable Development (a UK Round Table of some 25 organisations) and such groups as the UK Strategy for Biodiversity, with the Chief Executive of English Nature, Derek Langslow, as Chairman. But ultimately of much greater importance was the increased awareness and opinions formed through local groups, as represented by Local Agenda 21 and such initiatives as 'Going for Green' and 'Forward Scotland'.

Every conservation body reappraised its position. On the one hand, Government had come to recognise the importance of nature conservation in both the widest sense of Gaia and as a natural resource, and more specifically in relation to individual species and habitats. On the other hand, it perceived its role on all economic, social and environmental issues to be that of an enabler of self-help. The *Annual Reports* of the official conservation agencies emphasised their change in culture, new ways of working, and organisational change, with more emphasis on cost-effective outcomes. It was more than just an attempt to distinguish themselves from the previous NCC. Each body sought to make itself more relevant to the new 'working environment'. English Nature's strategy document, *Beyond 2000*, remarked that scientists had played so large a part in establishing statutory nature conservation. Some 50 years later, much of the drive and personal commitment came from emotional and ethical concerns. A priority for the conservation agencies was not so much to act as executive agencies in applying scientific information, but rather to ensure that this knowledge and understanding became part of the public understanding of the values, risk assessments and judgements that must ultimately underpin conservation policy (English Nature 1997a).

Reflecting the approach of Government itself, conservation agencies saw their role as one of providing the structural framework and material support for an increasingly informed and educated public. One such innovation was the map of the Natural Areas of England, as defined by their characteristic wildlife, geology, soils, land use and culture. Within such a readily-intelligible framework, partnerships could be formed to meet the targets set by the UK Biodiversity Action Plan. English Nature's *Annual Report* for 1997 described how, through the face-to-face discussions required by the new Site Management Statements, a more positive attitude was already evident in managing the 4,000 SSSIs. Of the 185 English NNRs, some 36 were now managed in partnership with Approved Bodies, as defined under the Wildlife and Countryside Act. Such partners included local authorities, industry, wildlife trusts and other conservation organisations (English Nature 1997b).

There was nothing particularly novel about English Nature's claim, in its strategy document, that

> our particular strength is the capacity to link the local practice of nature conservation, through land and water management, with national policy advice.

That had always been a reason for establishing nature reserves, giving expert advice and undertaking relevant research. Such increasing emphasis, however, on forms of partnership where the role of Government agencies was increasingly that of facilitating what others might materially achieve, raised fundamental questions as to the size and shape of those bodies in their next half century. The appearance of the Environment White Papers and nomination of 'green' ministers in every Department in the early 1990s might have presaged a more assertive role for the successor bodies of the Conservancy and the NCC. By the end of the decade, such state-sponsored partnerships seemed to affirm even greater primacy for landed interests. Those interests had, however, also become more diversified by what Dwyer and Hodge (1996) identified as the increasing role of CARTS, namely the 'Conservation, Amenity and Recreation Trusts'. As responsibility for individual NNRs passed from the official conservation bodies, the prominence of the National Trust, the RSPB and the wildlife trusts became accordingly greater.

Two scenarios may be painted. One may show the first 50 years since the founding of the Nature Conservancy as a springboard for greater State involvement in the use and management of the countryside. The other scenario may show the first-hand involvement of the Conservancy and its successors as a model of what, in the course of time, private bodies and individuals might come to emulate and surpass, as they are required to reclaim responsibility for the direct and practical management of the 'jewels in the rural crown' in the next half century. If that seems a throwback to the situation confronted by Rothschild and the SPNR before the First World War, as they drew up lists of areas 'worthy of protection', a fundamental difference might be discerned. There might be a greater preparedness on the part of the State and its agencies to offer encouragement through grant aid and expert advice, and by acting as the proxy customer in commissioning the research required. Particularly through information technology, there might be unprecedented opportunity for those living in both town and countryside to become 'stakeholders' in the ownership and management of what Tansley, some 50 years previously, called *Britain's Green Mantle*.

THE INSIDE STORY

History is written for two reasons. It may arise from curiosity as to what life was like in the past. Alternatively, the past may be studied as a way of understanding how the present has come about. This book has sought to fulfil both purposes as they relate to nature conservation in Britain. It has focused deliberately on the pioneering efforts of Britain's first official nature-conservation body, the Nature Conservancy. In the words of its *Progress Report* of 1968, 'No other country had an organisation with such comprehensive responsibilities for nature conservation' (Nature Conservancy 1968a). This book has traced how the Conservancy came to acquire such powers to hold reserves, to give advice and to undertake research. It has illustrated the manner in which such responsibilities were exercised and adapted to meet the particular requirements of species and habitats, within the opportunities and constraints of the administrative process and political circumstances of the time. The 'Countryside in 1970' conferences, and incorporation within NERC, are obvious points of reference in recounting the Conservancy's final years. That first quarter-century, when Government shouldered at least some of the burdens of nature conservation, is related to the 1990s by reference to the activities of the NCC and such obvious staging points as the Wildlife and Countryside Act 1981 and IUCN initiatives.

There are at least two ways of writing history. The most commonplace is to make the fullest use of hindsight in writing what are essentially critiques of the perceptions and activities of the past. Even before the millennium is out, a cluster of books has considerably advanced understanding of the making of the modern British countryside. Winter (1995) adopted an 'unashamedly historical' perspective in his study of *Rural Politics*, as they revolve around agriculture, forestry and the environment. In their volume, *Rural Change and Planning*, Cherry and Rodgers (1996) set out to explain how the countryside has been transformed since 1914. David Evans' volume on the history of nature conservation begins with the earliest of coffee-house social clubs, but most attention is given to the present-day conservation bodies with a membership counted in millions (Evans 1997). Stephen Bocking's book, *Ecologists and Environmental Politics*, acknowledges that the two are commonly seen as inseparable. From an international perspective, it illustrates how such a relationship evolved (Bocking 1997). A distinguishing feature of all these books has been their heavy reliance on both hindsight and published sources. Their interpretations of the past have been drawn largely from the books, reports and journals that conveyed what their authors of years past wanted to communicate and implant in the minds of their readers. Such published sources are immensely valuable historically, and must suffice where nothing else is available. Their story is, however, very incomplete. It may give a false impression of what it really felt like to be developing and implementing policies for the countryside at that point in time.

Although historical writing can never be entirely free of hindsight, the present book consciously attempts to reconstruct the period of the Nature Conservancy as it literally appeared to those caught up in its activities at the time. Like the decision makers of today, they did not have the benefit of hindsight in discovering how things would turn out. To achieve the necessary degree of intimacy with the past, the historian requires access not only to published sources but, even more obviously, to the private, if not personal, communications of the self-same authors. Besides the published annual reports of those public, business, professional or voluntary bodies, there is need to delve more deeply into the generally confidential files of the time that dealt with policy or established precedents.

An early intimation of the potential of such post-war archives was given by the series of Environmental Planning volumes published by the Stationery Office, covering such topics as national parks and new towns for the period up to 1969. The announcement that such histories had been commissioned by the Cabinet Office coincided with the Government decision of that year to reduce the period of closure on official papers from 50 to 30 years. Now, some 30 years later, historians can explore for themselves the relevant archives in piecing together what Cullingworth (1975) called 'the inside story'. As well as learning more about why policies came to be accepted or rejected in the glare of publicity, it is possible, and perhaps as important, to discover what policies were considered and cast aside entirely behind 'closed doors'. In undertaking such investigative work, Cullingworth emphasised (and this book further illustrates) the importance of not having exaggerated expectations. The opening up of Cabinet proceedings or, for that matter, the files of the Conservancy and NCC, rarely reveals entirely unexpected situations. Rather, their principal value is that of gaining greater understanding of how and why initiatives and events were taken, and how their outcome was perceived.

Whilst Cullingworth warned of mountains of paper to go through, there is still little

Max Nicholson, Director-General of the Nature Conservancy between 1952 and 1966, the first recipient of the Gold Medal of the IUCN at the Union's Annual Assembly in Nairobi, September 1963.

prospect of a definitive history being written. There may be obvious starting-points in searching the indexes of the Public Record Office or other repositories, but the historian can never be sure everything of relevance has been seen. Even if all the relevant papers were found, they might withhold as much as they reveal. In the same way as Cabinet minutes hardly extend beyond the conclusions reached, so committee minutes of such bodies as the Conservancy may give little sense of discussion and the manner in which decisions were reached. The key contributors to files may have been too busy, or saw little need, to make copious notes of what was so well-known to themselves. Where disagreement generates considerable paperwork, consensus frequently leaves little. It becomes all the more important to seek out every possible source of information, whether a hurried minute, a carefully crafted application to the Treasury, or an exchange of information on a topic of common concern, being handled separately by the English (and Welsh) and the Scottish Departments. But even where fuller explanations can be found, it is doubtful whether they are complete or entirely objective. Their overriding purpose was to secure or, at least, smooth the path for fresh policies or their implementation. The archival data available to the historian today were by design an integral part of the decision-making process.

An obvious course is to supplement the published and manuscript record with personal recollections. Max Nicholson, Barton Worthington and Norman Moore have put much of theirs into print, the former writing of how he had been privileged to share 'the thoughts and advice' of many of the most gifted leaders of the conservation and environmental movements. He was thereby 'able to recall what they had in mind, and the events which they shaped' (Nicholson 1987). The geographer, L. Dudley Stamp, made considerable use of the insights and material obtained as a member – and briefly Chairman – of the Conservancy's England Committee, in writing his book, *Nature Conservation in Britain* (Stamp 1969). The present book has drawn on many reminiscences and reflections, and particularly those assembled by the NCC in respect of its Thin Green Line project. Although frequently able to corroborate, modify, correct or extend the detail obtained from other sources, such oral evidence also has inherent limitations. Whilst such evidence may serve as a warning to the historian not to believe everything recorded in the files, there may also be instances where personal memories have been edited or re-worked, so as to correspond more closely with the past as the witness would prefer to recall it.

Far from simplifying matters, Cullingworth (1975) warned that the greater knowledge that comes with probing 'under the surface' is likely to make the task of explanation even more complicated. There is seldom 'a logical path from the identification of problems, through studies of alternative ways to meeting them, to neat solutions in legislative and administrative action'. Whilst such a concern to interpret aright the 'administrative rigmarole' might seem tedious in the extreme for those searching for what they anticipate to be the cut-and-thrust of 'conservation in action', it is only by working through such complex detail that better understanding is gained of the tensions that invariably exist between what individual conservationists passionately believe to be necessary and the brokerage that is required of any agency in receipt of public monies or, for that matter, membership subscriptions.

CONSERVATION IN PRACTICE

There is another sense in which the historian's work is never done. Fresh questions are constantly asked of the past. Even the most well-worked periods are reworked for context on contemporary issues. It is not simply that questions have continued to be asked about the longer-term consequences of the Second World War but, as early as the 1970s, they were couched in terms of 'What went wrong?' In exploring the economic and social dimensions, Marwick (1982) described a gloom that descended upon 'the man-made islands' of Britain in the 1970s. There was increasing consciousness of the implications of money-making technologies and their accompanying spoliation and pollution. A number of fluent and imaginative environmentalists stampeded themselves and many others into 'an orgy of pessimism' (Nicholson 1987). Nor was such despondency confined to Britain. The term 'environmental history' was popularised in America to describe such urgent questioning of how and why degradation had come about (Worster 1988). One of the first to respond from a British perspective was Max Nicholson. If there was much to regret, Nicholson (1987) found grounds for optimism in a history of the environmental movement itself, which 'the harbingers of gloom and doom' had acknowledged but already written off.

Such questioning of the post-war years has given added purpose to exploration of the role of ideas. If Ralf Dahrendorf's definition of an idea — that it is a notion of 'where we go from where we are' — is adopted, such scenarios of change have clearly been important both for their impact on the outlook of a whole generation and, at a more tactical level, in facilitating what was already in progress (Seldon 1996, 263). On both counts, the ideas associated with Tansley, Elton and their wartime generation of ecologists were significant. Duncan Poore wrote, in the early 1980s, that ecology was unlikely to produce its penicillin, lasers and silicon chips. Its contribution to knowledge had been of a philosophical rather than a technical kind. Its impact was therefore less dramatic, but ultimately perhaps more significant. As well as trying to arrest and repair the physical damage of millennia, ecologists sought to break the human habits of the past, when ignorance and greed had taken such a heavy toll of natural resources (Poore 1982).

If those who obtained a Conservancy research studentship were among the first to apply such ideas in ecology, their number was considerably enhanced by the many who graduated from the MSc Conservation Course at University College London. A distillation of the emerging expertise and experience was published by leaders of that course under the title, *Conservation in Practice* (Warren and Goldsmith 1974). As the Conservancy's *Progress Report* of 1968 made clear, the need to turn ecological theory into practice became ever more pressing and wide-ranging in the attempt to understand and manage a rapidly changing world. Where early ecologists had been able to take for granted a reasonable profusion of wild animals and plants, the economics of farming and forestry had caused 'drastic changes in the balance of living organisms'. People had become so mobile in their leisure time that no part of Britain was too remote. Increasing numbers were attracted to the very same areas that were especially important for their wildlife, namely the coasts, heaths and mountains (Nature Conservancy 1968a).

In assessing the role of ideas in post-war Britain, Seldon (1996) claimed, in an avowedly deterministic model, that ideas could only flourish where they were perceived to be benign or positive, where the circumstances for their propagation were favourable, and where they received powerful advocacy. In that sense, the period of post-war recovery might have seemed the worst possible time to press for the preservation of amenity, wildlife, and the recreational potential of the countryside. Robins and Jones (1997) have written, however, that it may not be too fanciful to discern the forging of 'a species of social contract between citizen and government'. At no time had government and people been so united by common purpose and expectation. But if there was unprecedented support for what might be called 'popular socialism', Government knew it had to deserve such trust and confidence. From the draft proposals prepared by Fryer and Nicholson, Herbert Morrison recognised the value of the Conservancy in helping to protect the Government from charges of its mis-using the land and natural resources.

If with hindsight the Conservancy and nature-conservation movement appear to have developed inexorably, contemporary files convey a very different picture. Indeed, as Jones and Robins (1997) commented, British society 'changed beyond what any sane person in the immediate post-war years could have ever envisaged'. Whilst the sustained expansion of the west European economies brought physical upheaval, with massive environmental problems, it also brought a degree of affluence that, from the somewhat puritanical perspectives of 1945, would have seemed excessive. Besides shorter working hours, increased disposable income opened up mass markets for motor cars and television. There was both the opportunity and the means to discover for oneself the scale of habitat destruction and of 'invisible, all-pervasive and insidious' pollution that arose not only from nuclear fall-out but from such 'peaceful' activities as the chemical revolution in farming. At last, there seemed to be wide and popular support for the mission of the Nature Conservancy – and indeed the National Parks Commission. Of the British adult population, approximately one person in ten had joined an environmental group by the 1980s. With an estimated 2.5 to 3 million supporters, the environmental movement was larger than any political party or trade union. Simply by virtue of its size and growth, it qualified as a major social phenomenon (Lowe and Goyder 1983).

There was a political price to pay for appearing so successful. As Ratcliffe (1977a) recalled, some 150 NNRs were established. Many research papers had been written, based on the use of 'outdoor laboratories' such as the Moor House and Rhum NNRs. In the advisory field, the Conservancy achieved notable success in raising public awareness of the side-effects of pesticide use. It had encouraged, and had itself immeasurably benefited from, the growth of the voluntary movement. In meeting such goals, the Conservancy helped to foster the view that nature conservation was too important to be left to its protagonists. It should be incorporated into the larger strategies being developed for 'the machinery of government'. By the early 1960s, it had become the received wisdom of the scientific community, as reinforced by the Minister for Science, that a more broadly-based research council was needed. The Conservancy accordingly became part of the NERC. However persuasive the arguments for a body that encompassed both conservation management and the research to meet its needs, such concentration of responsibilities ran counter to the philosophy of the Rothschild 'customer/contractor' principle. Thus, the new NCC was expected to commission its research needs.

As Duncan Poore remarked of 'the Split' of the Conservancy's responsibilities, 'the British Government has a fatal proclivity to tinker with its most imaginative institutions'. It tended to weaken those very qualities that had caused them to be so admired in other parts of the world (Poore 1987). Still the uncertainties remained. Only three years after the NCC was formed, there were reports of Departmental representatives on the Countryside Review Committee trying to secure reappraisal of the Council's role. The Chairman of the NCC, Sir David Serpell, protested that 'a besetting weakness of this country is the belief that changes in machinery are tantamount to improvements in policy' (PRO, FT 8, 24). If that further review was thwarted, controversies as to the future use of parts of the countryside reached such a point in the 1980s as to make further restructuring unavoidable. Plans for a large measure of devolution within the NCC were thwarted by more radical measures. Ministers concluded that conservation issues had become so demanding of political consideration and resources that they should be handled on a territorial, as opposed to a Great-Britain, basis.

As Seldon's model emphasises, the fulfilment of ideas owed much not only to the force of circumstances but the array of interest groups affected. Perhaps none was more affected, in terms of the early development of the conservation movement, than the scientific community itself. In her presidential address to the American Association of the Advancement of Science, in February 1997, Jane Lubchenco spoke of how scientists were privileged to be able to indulge their passions for science. With that privilege went the responsibility of providing something useful for society (Lubchenco 1997). In that sense, the present book can be seen as a case study of how a handful of British ecologists some fifty years ago sought to indulge their own passions for field survey and experimentation by providing a service to those generally concerned with the use and management of the countryside. In terms of both research and training, the Conservancy sought to provide the knowledge, understanding and predictive powers its committee members and officers adjudged society to need. If an interest group is bound together by common aims, there can also be bitter dissension as to how they are achieved. The documentary evidence affords some insight into the acrimony within the scientific community at the time of the formation of NERC and later demise of the Conservancy, and within and between the conservation bodies during the debates on the Wildlife and Countryside Bill.

If at times the conservation movement seemed fragmented, the unity of landed and farming interests might appear more apparent than real (Smith 1992). At one level, the protests of John Morrison and other influential figures on the back-benches of parliament in the 1950s, regarding what they represented as 'land nationalisation by the back-door', gave voice to the resentment felt by any interest group whose entitlements and freedoms appear to be challenged. Much of the opposition from the agrochemical industry and its sponsoring department, the Ministry of Agriculture, arose from the Conservancy and conservation bodies being perceived as a rival for the public 'ear' in determining how the countryside might be used. And yet behind the facade of unity, there were those, for example within the horticultural industry, who, in the confidential discussions of the NFU and the Ministry, expressed anxieties similar to those of conservationists regarding the unregulated use of pesticides. Even such critics as John Morrison became protective of the Conservancy's research function in the 1960s, when they recognised its value in alerting the owner of the fox-earth, game preserve and wildfowl shoot to the dangers arising from the persistent pesticides increasingly used by the 'progressive' farmer.

The political scientist has written much as to the role of policy and issue networks in linking such interest groups with the core executive of Government or, more particularly, with the component parts of Government departments. If such networks brought together those whose ambitions for a particular policy on that occasion coincided, they might equally marginalise those with different priorities (Marsh and Rhodes 1992). In describing such functional relationships, comparatively little importance has been accorded to the power of personalities. At least for the Nature Conservancy and its period of existence, 'the inside story' would indicate that individuals could play a major part in deciding how networks might be manipulated in pursuit of the minor affairs of government.

For most of the post-war period, nature conservation was regarded as a worthy, but comparatively minor, concern of government. Even Herbert Morrison made no mention of it in his autobiography (Morrison 1960). Yet ministers did not only exert considerable influence over the pace and direction of its affairs but, in doing so, they might also have revealed more of their own attitude towards politics and administration. The decision of Rab Butler to override the advice of Boyd-Carpenter, citing his reading of Trevelyan's *History*, may say much for the importance of personality within 'the core executive'. Was it personal interest, or concern as to his standing as a politician and minister, that caused Lord Hailsham to expend so much intellectual and emotional energy on his most minor of research councils? When he was Chairman of the Conservative Party, Lord Hailsham was critical of the emphasis the Conservancy placed on its research activities. He showed equal intolerance of its land-holding responsibilities when more overtly Minister for Science.

As intended, those who counselled and sought to carry out the wishes of ministers were 'shadowy figures'. The 'inside story' of the Nature Conservancy provides abundant illustration of the importance of such insider 'experts' as Solly Zuckerman. In a reference to the Prime Minister's telephone call asking for help over the *Torrey Canyon*, Zuckerman wrote in his day journal that it seemed to have more to do with morale than anything else (University of East Anglia, Zuckerman archives). A large measure of confidence-building can be discerned in the interventions made by Sir Edward Playfair over Lord Salisbury's 'storm in a teacup', and in Roger Quirk's endeavours to remove misapprehensions on the part of Lord Hailsham as to the Conservancy's purpose and activities. The networking of civil servants themselves was heavily dependent on confidence. If the Permanent Secretary of the Treasury, Sir Edward Bridges, might write darkly of having had 'some experience of how these people [the Nature Conservancy] go about their business' (PRO, T 223, 292), it was the long-standing respect which other officials felt towards Max Nicholson that caused them to be protective of the Conservancy's interests. As a senior official, Roger Quirk was exceptional in having a scientific training. Whilst it helped him to comprehend the needs of scientists, it also made him more aware of their predicament in communicating with ministers and his colleagues. As he once remarked to Norman Moore, the Conservancy faced the hardest task among research councils. Whilst none pretended to know anything about, say, nuclear physics, ministers (and particularly Conservative Lord Presidents of the Council) regarded themselves as already expert on anything of importance affecting the ways of the countryside and its wildlife.

Occupying the ill-defined ground between Government departments and interest groups (Mackay 1995), such bodies as the Conservancy might be unusually dependent upon, and therefore give considerable licence to, powerful personalities. If the Chairman had an obvious figure-head role, that of other members was less clear. Mabey (1991) recalled the NCC Council as functioning like a cabinet, with no precisely defined responsibilities or majority votes allowed. 'The inside story' suggests that individual members could exert considerable influence. Perhaps more importantly, it was intended that they should 'educate' themselves and pass on that knowledge and understanding within their respective 'networks'. A member of the Nature Conservancy Committee, and then NCC Council, Hew Watt, recalled how

> The Conservancy did me good. I was no different to most farmers when I was appointed ... I found myself changing, taking a broader view.

Whatever the purpose of 'lay' committees in the system of 'checks and balances' on executive power, posts of responsibility, whether held in the public or voluntary sector, became little more than reference points for the more powerful personalities in developing larger agendas amid a bewildering array of networking. Donoughue and Jones (1973) described Max Nicholson as 'a man of mercurial intelligence, firing ideas like a catherine wheel'. At times he appeared almost larger than life. Sir Frank Turnbull described him as 'a natural propagandist' (PRO, CAB 124, 1819). But, as Nicholson recalled in another context, such assertiveness was essential if the Conservancy's ideals were to prevail whilst always having to play the weaker hand in discussions with the other research councils or, say, the Ministry of Agriculture. How else might the Conservancy appear to have the self-confidence worthy of national recognition, when the conservation movement at that time was so comparatively weak? When confronted earlier with opposition to afforestation, the Forestry Commission had pressed on, believing its benefits would become self-evident as the plantations grew and demonstrated their worth. The Nature Conservancy was similarly assertive in its reserve-acquisition and other programmes. Their value would become even more evident, as the wildlife of the countryside became generally impoverished.

Whatever their particular responsibilities, every participant in 'the inside story' was united by one thing: the volume and variety of issues that had to be considered, and some response made, within the day or week. In focusing on particular issues, and therefore on the files that contain their documentation, there is danger of exaggerating their importance whilst overlooking much else that occupied the minds of the self-same decision makers. A fuller and more balanced impression of the interlocking pattern of concerns – of the intricacies of such personal and institutional networking – will only begin to emerge as 'the inside story' of other key practitioners in conservation begin to appear (Lamb 1996).

Bob Boote, in a paper to the Royal Society in 1976, spoke of how, for him, nature conservation had always been the indicator, or litmus paper, of human impact on the natural environment. It was at the sharp end. Concern for wildlife and its habitat was 'for many people their conscience about the quality of our one biosphere and a recognition of their obligation to posterity' (Boote 1976). The present book has explored only one period and the official part of that expression of conscience. If it encourages others to search out and study the archives of the more recent period (as they become available) and of the other participants in the 'making' of the modern British environment, the book will have begun to meet its purpose.

REFERENCES

Adams, W. M. 1986. *Nature's Place. Conservation Sites and Countryside Change*. London, Allen & Unwin.

Advisory Committee on Poisonous Substances used in Agriculture and Food Storage, 1964. *Review of the Persistent Organochlorine Pesticides*. London, HMSO.

Advisory Committee on Pesticides and other Toxic Substances, 1969. *Further Review of Certain Persistent Organochlorine Pesticides Used in Great Britain*. London, HMSO.

Advisory Council for Agriculture and Horticulture in England and Wales, 1978. *Agriculture and the Countryside*. London, HMSO.

Allen, D. E. 1976. *The Naturalist in Britain: a Social History*. London, Allen Lane.

Anonymous 1923. Obituary: The Hon. N.C. Rothschild. *Nature* **112**, 697.

Anonymous 1944a. Ecological principles involved in the practice of forestry. *Journal of Ecology* **32**, 83–115.

Anonymous 1944b. Nature conservation and nature reserves. *Journal of Ecology* **32**, 45–82.

Anonymous 1946. Nature conservation in England. *Nature* **157**, 277–80.

Anonymous 1961a. Notes and views. *Nature* **190**, 488–9.

Anonymous 1961b. Industrialization and the countryside. *Journal of the Royal Society of Arts* **109**, 652.

Anonymous 1963. *The Countryside in 1970*. London, HMSO.

Anonymous 1966. *The Countryside in 1970. Second Conference*. London, Council for Nature.

Anonymous 1969. DDT – uneasy compromise. *New Scientist* **44**, 626.

Anonymous 1970a. Messianic mandarin. *New Scientist* **45** (687), 274.

Anonymous 1970b. *Countryside in 1970. Third Conference*. London, Council for Nature.

Anonymous 1982. Marshes saved as Whitehall brawls. *New Scientist* **96** (1332), 406.

Anonymous 1994. Mr Ashdown puts mud on his boot. *Country Life* **188** (10), 63.

Arvill, R. 1976. *Man and Environment*. Harmondsworth, Penguin.

Ash, M. 1966. Notes on books. *Journal of the Royal Society of Arts* **114**, 701–2.

Astor, Lord & Rowntree, B. Seebohm 1935. *The Agricultural Dilemma*. London, King, 62–3.

Astor, Lord & Rowntree, B. Seebohm 1938. *British Agriculture*. London, Longmans Green, v–xiv.

Atkinson–Willes, G. L. (ed.) 1963. *Wildfowl in Great Britain*. London, HMSO.

Axell, H. 1978. Geoffrey Dent. *Birds* **7**, 10.

Baldock, D., Cox, G., Lowe, P. & Winter, M. 1990. Environmentally Sensitive Areas: incrementalism or reform? *Journal of Rural Studies* **6**, 143–62.

Baldock, D. & Lowe, P. 1996. The development of European agri–environmental policy. In *The European Environment and CAP Reform. Policies and Prospects for Conservation* (ed. M. Whitby), pp 2–25. Wallingford, CAB International.

Barber, D. (ed.) 1970. *Farming and Wildlife: a Study in Compromise*. Sandy, RSPB.

Blackwood, J.W. & Tubbs, C.R. 1970. A quantitative survey of chalk grassland in England. *Biological Conservation* **3**, 1–5.

Bocking, S. 1997. *Ecologists and Environmental Politics. A History of Contemporary Ecology*. Yale University Press 38–62.

Boote, R.E. 1970. The Dawes Memorial Lecture. *Environmental Health* **78**, 415–20.

Boote, R.E. 1976. Concluding Remarks. In *Scientific Aspects of Nature Conservation in Great Britain* (ed J.E. Smith et al.), pp 101–3. London, Royal Society.

Boyd Carpenter, J. 1980. *Way of Life*. London, Sidgwick & Jackson.

Bracey, H.E. 1963. *Industry and the Countryside*. London, Faber.

Cabinet Office 1967. *Torrey Canyon*. London, HMSO.

Cairncross, F. 1991. *Costing the Earth*. London, Economist Books, pp 15–16.

Cameron, E.A. 1997. The Scottish Highlands as a special policy area. *Rural History* **8**, 195–216.

Cannadine, D. 1995. The first hundred years. In *The National Trust* (ed. H. Newby), pp 11–31. London, National Trust.

Carson, R. 1963. *Silent Spring*. London, Hamish Hamilton.

Cherry, G.E. 1975. *Environmental Planning. Volume II. National Parks and Recreation in the Countryside*. London, HMSO.

Cherry, G.E. 1982. *The Politics of Town Planning*. London, Longman, pp 29–30.

Cherry, G.E. & Rodgers, A. 1996. *Rural Change and Planning. England and Wales in the Twentieth Century*. London, Spon.

Clapham, R. 1980. Edward James Salisbury. *Biographical Memoirs of Fellows of the Royal Society* **17**, 511–40.

Clark, A. 1997. Impact of Environmentally Sensitive Areas on farm businesses. In *Grassland Management in Environmentally Sensitive Areas* (ed. R.D. Sheldrick), pp 188–200. Reading, British Grassland Society Occasional Symposium 32.

Colville, J. 1981. *The Churchillians*. London, Weidenfeld & Nicolson, pp 176–8.

Conservative Political Centre 1970. *Clean and Pleasant Land*. London, Conservative Political Centre.

Conway, V.M. 1957. Lines of development in ecology. *Proceedings of the Chemical Society*, 246–50.

Council for the Protection of Rural England 1975. *Landscape – the Need for a Public Voice*. London, CPRE.

Countryside Commission 1969. *Nature Conservation. Special Study Reports – Volume Two, containing the report of the Nature Conservancy*. London, HMSO.

Countryside Commission 1974. *New Agricultural Landscapes*. London, HMSO, CC 76.

Countryside Commission 1980. *Twelfth Report 1978–79*. London, HMSO, 2.

Countryside Review Committee 1976. *The Countryside: Problems and Policies. A Discussion Paper*. London, HMSO.

Countryside Review Committee 1978. *Food Production in the Countryside. A Discussion Paper*. London, HMSO.

Countryside Review Committee 1979. *Conservation and the Countryside Heritage. A Discussion Paper*. London, HMSO.

Cox, G. & Lowe, P. 1983. A battle not the war: the politics of the Wildlife and Countryside Act. In *The Countryside Planning Year Book. Volume 4* (ed. A. Gilg), pp 48–76. Norwich, Geobooks.

Cox, G., Lowe, P. & Winter, M. 1986. *Agriculture: People and Policies*. London, Allen & Unwin.

Cramp, S. & Conder, P.J. 1961. *The Deaths of Birds and Mammals*. London, Royal Society for the Protection of Birds.

Cramp, S. & Conder, P.J. & Ash, J.S. 1962. *Deaths of Birds and Mammals from Toxic Chemicals*. London, Royal Society for the Protection of Birds.

Crump, W.B. 1913. Two nature reserves. *Country Life* **33**, 678–9.

Cullingworth, J.B. 1975. *Environmental Planning. Volume 1. Reconstruction and Land use Planning 1939–1947*. London, HMSO.

Dalyell, T. 1981. Wildlife and political muscle. *New Scientist* **91** (1263), 243.

Department of Education and Science 1966. *Report of the Land Use Study Group. Forestry, Agriculture and the Multiple Use of Rural Land.* London, HMSO.

Department of the Environment 1977. *A Study of Exmoor. Report of Lord Porchester.* London, HMSO.

Department of the Environment 1986. *Conservation and Development: the British Approach. The United Kingdom's Response to the World Conservation Strategy.* London, HMSO.

Department of the Environment 1988. *Our Common Future. A perspective by the United Kingdom.* London, HMSO.

Department of the Environment, Transport and the Regions *1998. Opportunities for Change.* London, DETR.

Donoughue, B. & Jones, G.W. 1973. *Herbert Morrison: Portrait of a Politician.* London, Weidenfeld & Nicolson.

Douglas–Home, C. 1978. *Evelyn Baring. The Last Proconsul.* London, Collins, pp 316–19.

Dower, M. 1964. Notes on books. *Journal of the Royal Society of Arts* **112**, 619–20.

Dower, M. 1965. *The Fourth Wave. The Challenge of Leisure.* London, Civic Trust.

Draper, P. 1977. *Creation of the DOE: a study of the merger of three departments to form the Department of the Environment.* London, HMSO, Civil Service Studies, 4.

Duffey, E. 1971. The management of Woodwalton Fen: a multidisciplinary approach. In *The Scientific Management of Animal and Plant Communities for Conservation* (eds E. Duffey & A. Watt), pp 581–98. Oxford, Blackwell Scientific.

Duffey, E. 1974. *Nature Reserves and Wildlife.* London, Heinemann Educational.

Duffey, E. & Morris, M.G. (eds) 1965. *The Conservation of Invertebrates.* London, Monks Wood Experimental Station, Symposium 1.

Duffey, E., Morris, M.G., Sheail, J., Ward, L.K., Wells, D.A. & Wells, T.C.E. 1974. *Grassland Ecology and Wildlife Management.* London, Chapman & Hall.

Dunlap, T.R. 1981. *DDT: Scientists, Citizens and Public Policy.* Princeton University Press.

Dwyer, J. & Hodge, I. 1996. *Countryside in Trust.* Chichester, John Wiley.

Edelsten, H. McD. 1950–1. John Claud Fortescue Fryer. *Obituary Notices of Fellows of the Royal Society* **7**, 95–106.

Edlin, H.L. 1952. *The Changing Wild Life of Britain.* London, Batsford.

Eggeling, W.J. 1960. *The Isle of May: a Scottish Nature Reserve.* Edinburgh, Oliver & Boyd.

English Nature 1997a. *Beyond 2000. English Nature's Strategy for Improving England's Wildlife and Natural Features.* Peterborough, English Nature.

English Nature 1997b. *Sixth Report.* Peterborough, English Nature.

Evans, D. 1997. *A History of Nature Conservation in Britain.* London, Routledge, second edition.

Financial Secretary to the Treasury 1931. *Report of the National Park Committee.* Cmd 3851. London, HMSO.

Fitter, R. 1990. The view ahead from 1945. *Ecos* **11**, 7–11.

Forestry Commission 1943. *Post-war Forestry.* Cmd 6447. London, HMSO.

Fraser Darling, F. 1970. *Wilderness and Plenty. The Reith Lectures 1969.* London, British Broadcasting Corporation.

Gaskell, E. 1848. *Mary Barton. A Tale of Manchester Life* (reprinted Harmondsworth, Penguin, 1970), p 75.

George, M. 1992. *The Land Use, Ecology and Conservation of Broadland.* Chichester, Packard.

Gilg, A. 1992. Policy options for the British countryside. In *Contemporary Rural Systems in Transition. Volume 1. Agriculture and Environment* (eds I.R. Bowler, C.R. Bryant & M.D. Nellis), pp 206–18. Wallingford, CAB International.

Gill, C., Booker, F. & Soper, T. 1967. *The Wreck of the Torrey Canyon.* Newton Abbot, David & Charles.

Godwin, H. 1977. Sir Arthur Tansley: the man and the subject. *Journal of Ecology* **65**, 1–26.

Goode, D. 1981. The threat to wildlife habitat. *New Scientist* **89** (1237), 219–23.

Gregory, R. 1971. *The Price of Amenity. Five Studies in Conservation and Government.* London, Macmillan, pp 306–17.

Hailsham, Lord 1975. *The Door Wherein I Went.* London, Collins, pp 180–6.

Hampshire County Council, Countryside Commission, Nature Conservancy *et al.* 1968. *East Hampshire Area of Outstanding Natural Beauty.* Winchester, Hampshire County Council.

Harding, P.T. & Sheail, J. 1992. The Biological Records Centre: a pioneer in data gathering and retrieval. In *Biological Recording of Changes in British Wildlife* (ed. P.T. Harding), pp 5–19. London, HMSO, Institute of Terrestrial Ecology Symposium 26.

Harrison, J.F.C. 1961. *Learning and Living, 1790–1960. A study in the history of English adult education movement.* London, Routledge & Kegan Paul.

Harvey, D. & Whitby, M. 1988. Issues and policies. In *Land-use and the European Environment* (eds M. Whitby & J. Ollerenshaw), pp 155–9. London, Belhaven Press.

Hinton, C. & Holford, W. 1959. *Preserving Amenities.* London, Central Electricity Generating Board.

Holdgate, M.W. (ed.) 1971. *The Seabird Wreck in the Irish Sea.* London, NERC.

Home Secretary 1951. *Report on the Committee on Cruelty to Wild Animals.* London, HMSO, Cmd 8266.

Howarth, W. & Rodgers, C.P. (eds) 1992. *Agriculture, Conservation and Land Use. Law and policy issues in rural areas.* Cardiff, University of Wales Press.

Huxley, J. 1973. *Memories II.* London, Allen & Unwin.

International Union for the Conservation of Nature 1980. *World Conservation Strategy: Living resource conservation for sustainable development.* Gland, IUCN.

Johnson, B. 1983. *The Conservation and Development Programme for the UK: a response to the World Conservation Strategy.* London, Kogan Page.

Jones, B. & Robins, L. 1997. Conclusion. In *Half a Century of British Politics* (eds L. Robins & B. Jones), pp 236–7. Manchester University Press.

Lamb, R. 1996. *Promising the Earth.* London, Routledge.

Lewis, G. 1997. *Lord Hailsham. A Life.* London, Jonathan Cape.

Lord President of the Council 1957. *Forestry, Agriculture and Marginal Land. A report by the Natural Resources (Technical) Committee.* London, HMSO.

Lord President of the Council 1960. *Annual Report of the Advisory Council on Scientific Policy 1959–60.* London, HMSO, Cmnd 1167.

Lord President of the Council 1963. *Annual Report of the Advisory Council on Scientific Policy 1962–63.* London, HMSO, Cmnd 2163.

Lord Privy Seal 1971. *A Framework for Government Research and Development.* Cmnd 4814. London, HMSO.

Lord Privy Seal 1972. *Framework for Government Research and Development.* Cmnd 5046. London, HMSO.

Lowe, P., Cox, G., MacEwen, M., Riordan, T. O' & Winter, M. 1986. *Countryside Conflicts. The politics of farming, forestry and conservation.* Aldershot, Gower.

Lowe, P. & Goyder, J. 1983. *Environmental Groups in Politics.* London, Allen & Unwin.

Lubchenco, J. 1998. Entering the century of the environment. *Science* **279**, 491–7.

Mabey, R. 1980. *The Common Ground.* London, Hutchinson.

Mabey, R. 1991. Goodbye to the NCC. *The Countryman* **96** (1), 79–85.

MacEwen, A. & MacEwen, M. 1982. *National Parks: Conservation or Cosmetics.* London, Allen & Unwin.

Mackay, D. 1995. *Scotland's Rural Land Use Agencies.* Aberdeen, Scottish Cultural Press.

Macklin, D. 1991. Still fighting after all these years. *Conservation Now*, February–March, 23–5.

McIntosh, R.P. 1985. *The Background of Ecology. Concept and theory*. Cambridge, Cambridge University Press.

McVean, D.N. & Ratcliffe, D.A. 1962. *Plant Communities of the Scottish Highlands*. London, HMSO.

Marren, P. 1995. *The New Naturalists*. London, Collins.

Marsh, D. & Rhodes, R.A.W. (ed.) 1992. *Policy Networks in British Government*. Oxford, Clarendon Press.

Marwick, A. 1982. *British Society Since 1945*. Harmondsworth, Allen Lane, pp 188–204.

Mellanby, K. 1967. *Pesticides and Pollution*. London, Collins.

Mellanby, K. 1992. *The DDT Story*. Farnham, British Crop Protection Council.

Merrett, P. (ed.) 1971. *Captain Cyril Diver. A Memoir*. Wareham, Nature Conservancy.

Minister of Town and Country Planning 1945. *National Parks in England and Wales*. Cmd 6628. London, HMSO.

Minister of Town and Country Planning 1947a. *Report of the National Parks Committee*. Cmd 7121. London, HMSO.

Minister of Town and Country Planning 1947b. *Conservation of Nature in England and Wales*. Cmd 7122. London, HMSO.

Minister of Transport 1958. *Report of the Committee of Inquiry into Inland Waterways*. Cmnd 486. London, HMSO.

Minister of Works and Planning 1942. *Report of the Committee on Land Utilisation in Rural Areas*. Cmd 6378. London, HMSO.

Moore, N.W. 1962. The heaths of Dorset and their conservation. *Journal of Ecology* **50**, 369–91.

Moore, N.W. 1966. An assessment of the discussions of the Symposium on Pesticides in the Environment and their Effects on Wildlife. *Journal of Applied Ecology, supplement 3*, 291–5.

Moore, N.W. 1987. *The Bird of Time. The science and politics of nature conservation*. Cambridge, Cambridge University Press.

Moore, N.W. & Ratcliffe, D.A. 1962. Chlorinated hydrocarbon residues in the egg of a peregrine falcon from Perthshire. *Bird Study* **9**, 242–4.

Morris, M.G. 1969. Populations of invertebrate animals and the management of chalk grassland in Britain. *Biological Conservation* **1**, 225–31.

Morrison, H. 1954. *Government and Parliament: a survey from the inside*. London, Oxford University Press, pp 39 & 329–32.

Morrison, H. 1960. *Herbert Morrison*. London, Odhams Press.

Morton Boyd, J. 1986. *Fraser Darling's Islands*. Edinburgh University Press.

Morton Boyd, J. 1994. Dr Joe Eggeling. *The Scotsman*, 12 February.

National Farmers' Union and Country Landowners' Association 1977. *Caring for the Countryside*. London, NFU and CLA.

Natural Environment Research Council 1969. *Annual Report*. London, HMSO.

Nature Conservancy 1954. *Report*. London, HMSO.

Nature Conservancy 1956. *Report*. London, HMSO.

Nature Conservancy 1957. *Report.*. London, HMSO.

Nature Conservancy 1958. *Report.*. London, HMSO.

Nature Conservancy 1959. *The First Ten Years*. London, Nature Conservancy.

Nature Conservancy 1960. *Report.*. London, HMSO.

Nature Conservancy 1963a. *Grey Seals and Fisheries*. London, HMSO.

Nature Conservancy 1963b. *Report.*. London, HMSO.

Nature Conservancy 1964. *Report.*. London, HMSO.

Nature Conservancy 1965. *Report on Broadland*. London, Nature Conservancy.

Nature Conservancy 1968a. *Progress 1964–68*. London, Nature Conservancy.

Nature Conservancy 1968b. *Handbook 1968*. London, HMSO.

Nature Conservancy 1970a. *Nature Conservancy Research in Scotland*. Edinburgh, Nature Conservancy.

Nature Conservancy 1970b. *Twenty-one Years of Conservation*. London, Nature Conservancy.

Nature Conservancy Council 1977a. *Third Report*. London, NCC.

Nature Conservancy Council 1977b. *Nature Conservation and Agriculture*. London, NCC.

Nature Conservancy Council 1978. *Fourth Report*. London, NCC.

Nature Conservancy Council 1979. *Fifth Report*. London, NCC.

Nature Conservancy Council 1980. *Fifth Report*. London, HMSO.

Nature Conservancy Council 1981. *Sixth Report*. London, NCC.

Nature Conservancy Council 1982. *Seventh Report*. London, HMSO.

Nature Conservancy Council 1984. *Nature Conservation in Great Britain*. Peterborough, NCC.

Nature Conservancy Council 1986. *Nature Conservation and Afforestation in Britain*. Peterborough, NCC.

Nature Conservancy Council 1989. *Fifteenth Report*. Peterborough, NCC.

Nicholson, E.M. 1956. Nature conservation and the management of natural areas. In *Proceedings and Papers of the Sixth Technical Meeting of the International Union for the Conservation of Nature*, 8–27. London, Society for the Promotion of Nature Reserves.

Nicholson, E.M. 1957. *Britain's Nature Reserves*. London, Country Life.

Nicholson, M. 1970. *The Environmental Revolution*. London, Hodder & Stoughton.

Nicholson, M. 1974. Foreword. In *Conservation in Practice* (eds A. Warren & F.B. Goldsmith), pp v–ix. London, John Wiley.

Nicholson, M. 1977. Review. *New Scientist* **75** (1061), 176–7.

Nicholson, M. 1987. *The New Environmental Age*. Cambridge, Cambridge University Press.

Nicolson, L.F. 1986. *The Mystery of Crichel Down*. Oxford, Clarendon Press.

Oliver, F.W. 1914. Nature reserves. *Journal of Ecology* **2**, 55–6.

Oliver, F.W. (ed.) 1917. *The Exploitation of Plants*. London, Dent.

Oliver, F.W. 1928. Nature reserves. *Transactions of the Norfolk and Norwich Naturalists' Society* **12**, 317–22.

Ovington, J.D. 1956. Scientific research and nature reserve management. In *Proceedings and Papers of the Sixth Technical Meeting of the International Union for the Preservation of Nature*, pp 48–50. London, Society for the Promotion of Nature Reserves.

Parliamentary Papers, 1957–58, volume 5. *Seventh Report from the Select Committee on Estimates. Nature Conservancy*.

Parliamentary Papers 1968–69. *Select Committee on Science and Technology. Third report. Natural Environment Research Council*.

Parliamentary Papers 1971–72. *Select Committee on Science and Technology. First Report. Research and development*.

Parliamentary Papers 1983–84. *Select Committee on the European Community*.

Parliamentary Papers 1984–85. *Commons Committee on the Environment. First report. Operation and Effectiveness of Part II of the Wildlife and Countryside Act 1981*.

Parliamentary Papers 1989–90. *Lords Select Committee on Science and Technology, Second Report, Nature Conservancy Council*.

Pearsall, W.H. 1964. The development of ecology in Britain. *Journal of Ecology* **52** (Supplement), 1–12.

Perring, F.H. & Walters, S.M. (eds) 1962. *Atlas of the British Flora*. London, Nelson.

Pigott, D. 1988. Obituary. *Journal of Ecology* **76**, 288–91.

Pollitt, C. 1984. *Manipulating the Machine. Changing the pattern of ministerial departments, 1960–83. London,* Allen & Unwin.

Poore, M.E.D. 1956. The ecology of Woodwalton Fen. *Journal of Ecology* **44**, 455–92.

Poore, M.E.D. 1982. Ecology and conservation – a practitioner's view. *New Phytologist* **90**, 405–17.

Poore, M.E.D. 1987. Changing attitudes in nature conservation: the Nature Conservancy and Nature Conservancy Council. In *Changing attitudes to nature conservation* (eds R.J. Berry & F.H. Perring), pp 179–87. London, Linnean Society of London.

Potter, C. 1998. *Against the Grain. Agri-environmental Reform in the United States and the European Union.* Wallingford, CAB International, 1.

Potts, G.R. 1996. Obituary. *Ibis* **138**, 795–6.

Prestt, I. 1980. Comment. *Birds* **8** (1), 6–7.

Prime Minister 1963. *Committee of Enquiry into the Organization of Civil Science.* London, HMSO, Cmnd 2660.

Public Local Inquiry 1978. *Proposal by the Southern Water Authority for Drainage of Amberley Wild Brooks.* Unpublished Inspector's report and evidence.

Purseglove, J. 1989. *Taming the Flood. A History and Natural History of Rivers and Wetlands.* Oxford, Oxford University Press.

Ranlett, J. 1983. 'Checking nature's desecration': late-Victorian environmental organization. *Victorian Studies* **26**, 197–222.

Ratcliffe, D.A. 1958. Broken eggs in peregrine eyries. *British Birds* **51**, 23–6.

Ratcliffe, D.A. 1977a. Nature conservation: aims, methods and achievements. In *Scientific Aspects of Nature Conservation in Great Britain* (ed. J.E. Smith et al.), pp 11–30. London, Royal Society.

Ratcliffe, D.A. 1977b. *A Nature Conservation Review. The selection of biological sites of national importance for nature conservation in Britain.* Cambridge, Cambridge University Press.

Ratcliffe, D.A. 1980. *The Peregrine Falcon.* Calton, Poyser.

Ratcliffe, D.A. & Oswald, P.H. (eds) 1987. *Birds, Bogs and Forestry. The Peatlands of Caithness and Sutherland.* Peterborough, Nature Conservancy Council.

Ratcliffe, D.A. & Oswald, P.H. (eds) 1988. *The Flow Country. The Peatlands of Caithness and Sutherland.* Peterborough, Nature Conservancy Council.

Reith, J.S.W. 1949. *Into the Wind.* London, Hodder & Stoughton, 403–47.

Reynolds, F & Sheate, W.R. 1992. Reorganization of the conservation agencies. In *Agriculture, Conservation and Land Use. Law and Policy Issues in Rural Areas* (eds W. Howarth & C.P. Rodgers), pp 73–89. Cardiff, University of Wales.

Riordan, T. O' 1988. The politics of sustainability. In *Sustainable Environmental Management* (ed. R.K. Turner), pp 29–50. London, Belhaven.

Ritchie, J. 1920. *The Influence of Man on the Animal Life of Scotland.* Cambridge, Cambridge University Press.

Robins, L. & Jones, B. (eds) 1997. *Half a Century of British Politics.* Manchester, Manchester University Press.

Rothschild, M. & Marren, P. 1997. *Rothschild's Reserves. Time and Fragile Nature.* Colchester, Harley Books.

Royal Commission on the Distribution of the Industrial Population 1940. *Report.* Cmd 6153. London, HMSO.

Schulte Fischedick, K. 1995. *Practice and Pluralism: a socio-historical analysis of early vegetation science, 1900–1950.* Amsterdam University.

Scottish Office 1995. *Rural Scotland. People, Prosperity and Partnership.* Cm 3014. Edinburgh, HMSO.

Secretaries of State et al. 1990. *This Common Inheritance.* Cm 1200. London, HMSO.

Secretaries of State et al. 1991. *This Common Inheritance. The First Year Report.* Cm 1655. London, HMSO.

Secretaries of State et al. 1994a. *Biodiversity. The UK Action Plan.* Cm 2428. London, HMSO.

Secretaries of State et al. 1994b. *Sustainable Development. The UK Strategy.* Cm 2426. London, HMSO.

Secretaries of State et al. 1994c. *This Common Inheritance. The Third Year Report.* Cm 2549. London, HMSO.

Secretaries of State et al. 1995. *This Common Inheritance. UK Annual Report 1995.* Cm 2822. London, HMSO.

Secretaries of State for the Environment and Wales, and Minister of Agriculture 1985. *Operation and Effectiveness of Part II of the Wildlife and Countryside Act 1981. The Government's reply to the First Report of the Environment Committee.* Cmnd 9522. London, HMSO.

Secretaries of State for Northern Ireland, Scotland and Wales, and Minister of Agriculture 1975. *Food From Our Own Resources.* Cmnd 6020. London, HMSO.

Secretary of State for Local Government and Regional Planning 1970. *The Protection of the Environment. The Fight Against Pollution.* Cmnd 4373. London, HMSO.

Secretary of State for the Environment and Minister of Agriculture 1995. *Rural England. A Nation Committed to a Living Countryside.* Cm 3016. London, HMSO.

Secretary of State for the Environment et al. 1995. *Government Response to the UK Steering Group Report on Biodiversity.* Cm 3260. London, HMSO.

Secretary of State for the Environment and Minister of Agriculture 1996. *Rural England 1996.* Cm 3444. London, HMSO.

Secretary of State for the Home Department 1967. *The Torrey Canyon.* Cmnd 3246. London, HMSO.

Secretary of State for Scotland 1947. *National Parks and the Conservation of Nature in Scotland.* Cmd 7235. Edinburgh, HMSO.

Secretary of State for Scotland 1949. *Nature Reserves in Scotland: Final Report.* Cmd 7814. Edinburgh, HMSO.

Secretary of State for Scotland 1954. *Report of the Committee on Close Seasons for Deer in Scotland.* Edinburgh, HMSO, Cmd 9273.

Seldon, A. 1996. Ideas are not enough. In *The Ideas that Shaped Post-war Britain* (eds D. Marquand & A. Seldon), pp 257–89. London, Fontana.

Sheail, J. 1976. *Nature in Trust. A History of Nature Conservation in Britain.* Glasgow, Blackie.

Sheail, J. 1977. The impact of recreation on the coast: the Lindsey County Council (Sandhills) Act, 1932. *Landscape Planning* **4**, 53–72.

Sheail, J. 1981a. Wild plants and the perception of land-use change in Britain. *Biological Conservation* **24**, 129–46.

Sheail, J. 1981b. *Rural Conservation in Inter-war Britain.* Oxford, Clarendon Press.

Sheail, J. 1985. *Pesticides and Nature Conservation. The British Experience, 1950–1975.* Oxford, Clarendon Press.

Sheail, J. 1987. *Seventy-five Years in Ecology. The British Ecological Society.* Oxford, Blackwell Scientific.

Sheail, J. 1989. Applied ecology and the search for institutional support. *Environmental Review* **13**, 64–79.

Sheail, J. 1991a. The regulation of pesticide use: an historical perspective. In *Innovation and Environmental Risk* (eds L. Roberts & A. Weale), pp 38–46. London, Belhaven.

Sheail, J. 1991b. *Power in trust. The Environmental History of the Central Electricity Generating Board.* Oxford, Clarendon Press.

Sheail, J. 1992. *Natural Environment Research Council: a history.* Swindon, Natural Environment Research Council.

Sheail, J. 1993. The management of wildlife and amenity – a UK post-war perspective. *Contemporary Record* **7**, 44–65.

Sheail, J. 1995a. John Dower, national parks, and town and country planning in Britain. *Planning Perspectives* **10**, 1–16.

Sheail, J. 1995b. War and the development of nature conservation in Britain. *Journal of Environmental Management* **44**, 267–83.

Sheail, J. 1995c. The ecologist and environmental history – a British perspective. *Journal of Biogeography* **22**, 953–66.

Sheail, J. 1996a. From aspiration to implementation – the establishment of the first National Nature Reserves in Britain. *Landscape Research* **21**, 37–54.

Sheail, J. 1996b. Sustaining the countryside: a Welsh post-war perspective. *Rural History* **7**, 69–85.

Sheail, J. 1997a. Scott revisited: post-war agriculture, planning and the British countryside. *Journal of Rural Studies* **13**, 387–98.

Sheail, J. 1997b. 'Guardianship' and the 'rural workshop' – the first quarter century of UK experience in nature conservation. *Journal of Environmental Management* **50**, 429–43.

Sheail, J. & Wells, T.C.E. 1983. The fenlands of Huntingdonshire: a case study in catastrophic change. In *Mires, Swamp, Bog, Fen and Moor. B. Regional Studies* (ed. A.J.P. Gore), pp 375–93. Amsterdam, Elsevier Scientific.

Shoard, M. 1980. *The Theft of the Countryside*. Aldershot, Temple Smith.

Smith, A.E. 1987. The Nature Conservation Trust movement. In *Changing Attitudes to Nature Conservation* (eds R.J. Berry & F.H. Perring), pp 189–96. London, Linnean Society of London.

Smith, E.G. 1989. Environmentally Sensitive Areas: a successful UK initiative. *Journal of the Royal Agricultural Society of England* **150**, 30–43.

Smith, J.E., Clapham, A.R. & Ratcliffe, D.A. (eds) 1977. *Scientific Aspects of Nature Conservation in Great Britain*. London, Royal Society.

Smith, K. 1996. *Conflict over Convoys*. Cambridge, Cambridge University Press.

Smith, M.J. 1992. The agricultural policy community: maintaining a closed relationship. In *Policy Networks in British Government* (eds D. Marsh & R.A.W. Rhodes), pp 27–50. Oxford, Clarendon Press.

Smith, W.G. 1903. Botanical survey for local naturalists' societies. *Naturalist, Hull*, 5–13.

Smout, T.C. 1991. The Highlands and the roots of green consciousness, 1750–1990. *Proceedings of the British Academy* **76**, 237–63.

Stamp, D. 1969. *Nature Conservation in Britain*. London, Collins.

Stuart, C. 1975. *The Reith Diaries*, pp 266–87. London, Collins.

Tansley, A.G. 1904. The problems of ecology. *New Phytologist* **3**, 191–200.

Tansley, A.G. 1911. *Types of British Vegetation*. Cambridge, Cambridge University Press.

Tansley, A.G. 1914. Presidential address. *Journal of Ecology* **2**, 194–203.

Tansley, A.G. 1939a. British ecology during the past quarter century. *Journal of Ecology* **27**, 513–30.

Tansley, A.G. 1939b. *The British Islands and their Vegetation*. Cambridge, Cambridge University Press.

Tansley, 1942. *The Values of Science to Humanity*. London, Allen & Unwin.

Tansley, A.G. 1945. *Our Heritage of Wild Nature*. Cambridge, Cambridge University Press.

Tansley, A.G. 1949. *Britain's Green Mantle*. London, Allen & Unwin.

Thomas, A.S. 1960. Changes in vegetation since the advent of myxomatosis. *Journal of Ecology* **48**, 287–306.

Thomas, A.S. 1963. Further changes in vegetation since the advent of myxomatosis. *Journal of Ecology* **51**, 151–83.

Thomas, K. 1983. *Man and the Natural World. Changing Attitudes in England 1500–1800*. London, Allen Lane.

Tinker, J. 1970a. Pesticides – time for firm decisions. *New Scientist* **45**, 15–7.

Tinker, J. 1970b. ECY: steering the bandwagon. *New Scientist* **45**, 250–5.

Tinker, J. 1972. Nature Conservancy on a knife edge. *New Scientist* **53** (778), 68–70.

Tinker, J. 1976. Comment: Wildlife Domesday never comes. *New Scientist* **70** (996), 114.

Trafford, B. 1978. Recent progress in field drainage. *Journal of the Royal Agricultural Society of England* **139**, 139–40.

Trevelyan, G.M. 1929. *Must England's Beauty Perish?* London, Faber & Gwyer.

UK Biodiversity Steering Group 1995. *Meeting the Rio Challenge*. London, HMSO.

Warren, A. & Goldsmith, F.B. (eds) 1974. *Conservation in Practice*. London, Wiley.

Wells, T.C.E. (ed.) 1965a. *Grazing Experiments and the Use of Grazing as a Conservation Tool*. London, Monks Wood Experimental Station Symposium 2.

Wells, T.C.E. 1965b. Chalk grassland nature reserves and their management problems. *Handbook of the Society for the Promotion of Nature Reserves*, 1–9.

Wells, T.C.E., Sheail, J., Ball, D.F. & Ward, L.K. 1976. Ecological studies on the Porton Ranges: relationships between vegetation, soils and land-use history. *Journal of Ecology* **64**, 589–626.

Welsh Office 1996. *The Working Countryside for Wales*. Cm 3180. Cardiff, HMSO.

Whitby, M. 1996. The United Kingdom. In *The European Environment and CAP Reform. Policies and Prospects for Conservation* (ed. M. Whitby), pp 186–205. Wallingford, CAB International.

Whitby, M. & Lowe, P. 1994. The political and economic roots of environmental policy in agriculture. In *Incentives for Countryside Management. The case of Environmentally Sensitive Areas* (ed. M. Whitby), 1–24. Wallingford, CAB International.

Wigglesworth, V.B. 1945. DDT and the balance of nature. *Atlantic Monthly* **176**, 107–13.

Wilkie, T. 1991. *British Science and Politics Since 1945*. Oxford, Blackwell.

Wilkinson, W. 1987. *Address by the Chairman of the Nature Conservancy Council at the launch of 'Birds, bogs and forestry'*. Peterborough, NCC unpublished manuscript.

Williams, O.B., Wells, T.C.E. & Wells, D.A. 1974. Grazing management of Woodwalton Fen: seasonal changes in the diet of cattle and rabbit. *Journal of Applied Ecology* **11**, 499–516.

Winter, M. 1995. *Rural Politics*. London, Routledge.

Working Party 1977. *The Somerset Wetlands Project. A consultation paper*. Taunton, Nature Conservancy Council, South West Region.

Working Party on Precautionary Measures against Toxic Chemicals used in Agriculture 1953. *Toxic Chemicals in Agriculture: Residues in Food*. London, HMSO.

Working Party on Precautionary Measures against Toxic Chemicals used in Agriculture 1955. *Toxic Chemicals in Agriculture: Risks to Wild Life*. London, HMSO.

World Commission on Environment and Development 1987. *Our Common Future*. Oxford, Oxford University Press.

Worster, D. 1988. Doing environmental history. In *The Ends of the Earth. Perspectives on Modern Environmental History* (ed. D. Worster), pp 289–307. Cambridge, Cambridge University Press.

Worthington, E.B. 1983. *The Ecological Century. A Personal Appraisal*. Oxford, Clarendon Press.

INDEX